Walcheren to Waterloo

Walcheren to Waterloo

The British Army in the Low Countries during the French Revolutionary and Napoleonic Wars 1793–1815

Andrew Limm

Pen & Sword
MILITARY

First published in Great Britain in 2018 by
Pen & Sword Military
an imprint of
Pen & Sword Books Ltd
47 Church Street
Barnsley
South Yorkshire
S70 2AS

Copyright (c) Andrew Limm 2018

ISBN 978-1-47387-468-8

Typeset in 11/13 point MinionPro

Printed and bound by TJ International

Pen & Sword Books Ltd incorporates the imprints of Pen & Sword Archaeology, Atlas, Aviation, Battleground, Discovery, Family History, History, Maritime, Military, Naval, Politics, Railways, Select, Social History, Transport, True Crime, and Claymore Press, Frontline Books, Leo Cooper, Praetorian Press, Remember When, Seaforth Publishing and Wharncliffe.

For a complete list of Pen & Sword titles please contact
PEN & SWORD BOOKS LIMITED
47 Church Street, Barnsley, South Yorkshire, S70 2AS, England
E-mail: enquiries@pen-and-sword.co.uk
Website: www.pen-and-sword.co.uk

Contents

Acknowledgements

This book is dedicated to my wife Reena whose love and support has been instrumental in the completion of this study.

I would like to thank my parents, Peter and Catharine, for their encouragement and guidance.

My thanks must also go to Professor Michael Snape, Professor Jeremy Black, Professor Bruce Collins, Professor Gary Sheffield, Dr Daniel Whittingham, Dr Armin Grünbacher and Dr Huw Davies for their valuable insights during my research.

Finally, I would like to thank the editorial team at Pen & Sword for their efforts in seeing the book through to publication.

Andrew Limm, May 2018

Abbreviations

AG   Adjutant General
AHR   *American Historical Review*
BCMH   British Commission for Military History
BMJ   *British Medical Journal*
C-in-C Commander-in-Chief
EHR   *English Historical Review*
EJIR   *European Journal of International Relations*
HJ   *The Historical Journal*
HLQ   *Huntington Library Quarterly*
IHR   *International History Review*
JBS   *Quarterly Journal of British Studies*
JCH   *Journal of Contemporary History*
JMH   *Journal of Modern History*
JMHS   *Journal of Military History Society*
JSAHR   *Journal of the Society for Army Historical Research*
JSS   *Journal of Strategic Studies*
MPH   War Office Maps and Plans extracted to flat storage
PP   Parliamentary Papers
RUSI   *Royal United Service Institute Journal*
QMG   Quartermaster General
WMQ   *William and Mary Quarterly*

Maps

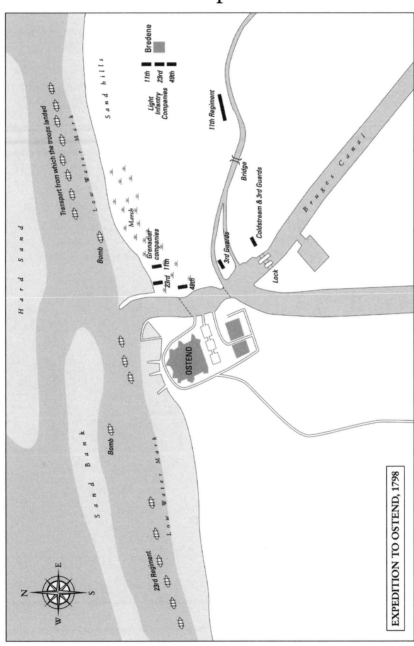

Light Infantry Companies: 11th, 23rd, 49th

Bredene

11th Regiment

Bridge

Coldstream & 3rd Guards

3rd Guards

Lock

Bruges Canal

OSTEND

Grenadier companies

Marsh

1fth

23rd

48th

Bomb

Low Water Mark

Sand hills

Hard Sand

Transport from which the troops landed

Sand Bank

Bomb

Low Water Mark

23rd Regiment

N / E / S / W

EXPEDITION TO OSTEND, 1798

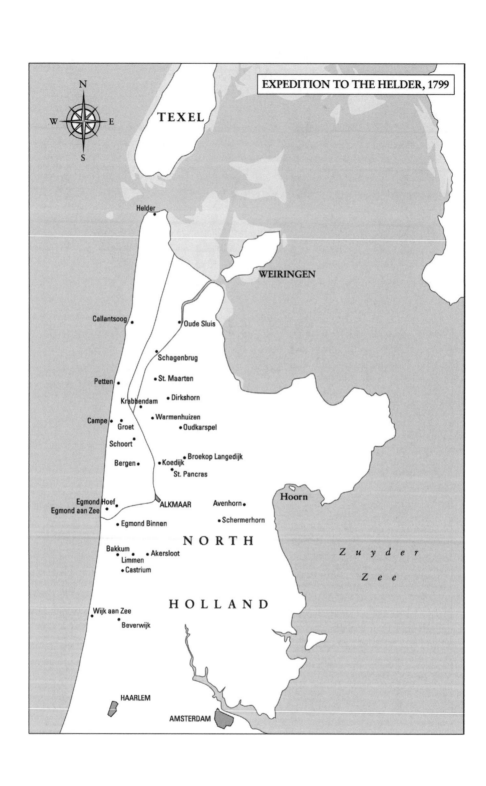

EXPEDITION TO THE HELDER, 1799

N
W E
S

TEXEL

Helder

WEIRINGEN

Callantsoog
Oude Sluis

Schagenbrug

Petten
St. Maarten

Dirkshorn
Krabbendam

Campe
Warmenhuizen
Groet
Oudkarspel

Schoort

Broekop Langedijk
Bergen
Koedijk
St. Pancras

Egmond Hoef
Egmond aan Zee
ALKMAAR
Avenhorn
Hoorn

Egmond Binnen
Schermerhorn

NORTH

Bakkum
Akersloot
Limmen
Zuyder
Castrium

Zee

HOLLAND

Wijk aan Zee
Beverwijk

HAARLEM

AMSTERDAM

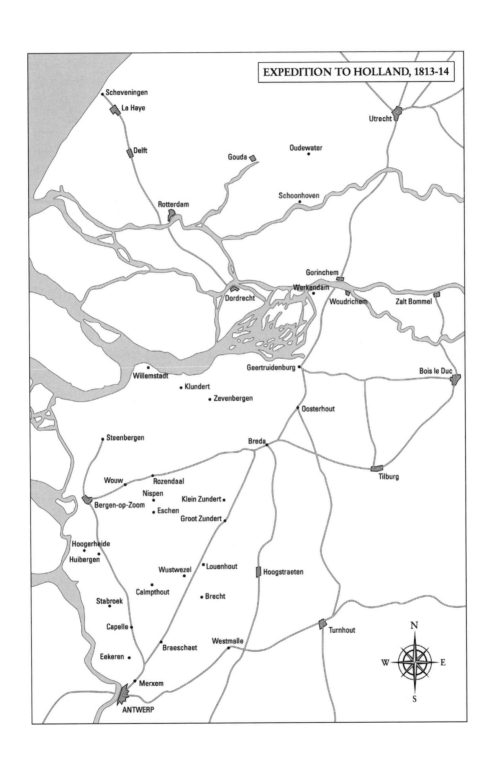

EXPEDITION TO HOLLAND, 1813-14

Scheveningen
La Haye
Utrecht
Delft
Oudewater
Gouda
Schoonhoven
Rotterdam
Gorinchem
Werkendam
Dordrecht
Woudrichem
Zalt Bommel
Geertruidenburg
Bois le Duc
Willemstadt
Klundert
Zevenbergen
Oosterhout
Steenbergen
Breda
Tilburg
Wouw
Rozendaal
Nispen
Klein Zundert
Bergen-op-Zoom
Eschen
Groot Zundert
Hoogerheide
Huibergen
Wustwezel
Louenhout
Hoogstraeten
Calmpthout
Brecht
Stabroek
Capelle
Turnhout
Braeschaet
Westmalle
Eekeren
Merxem
ANTWERP

N
W   E
S

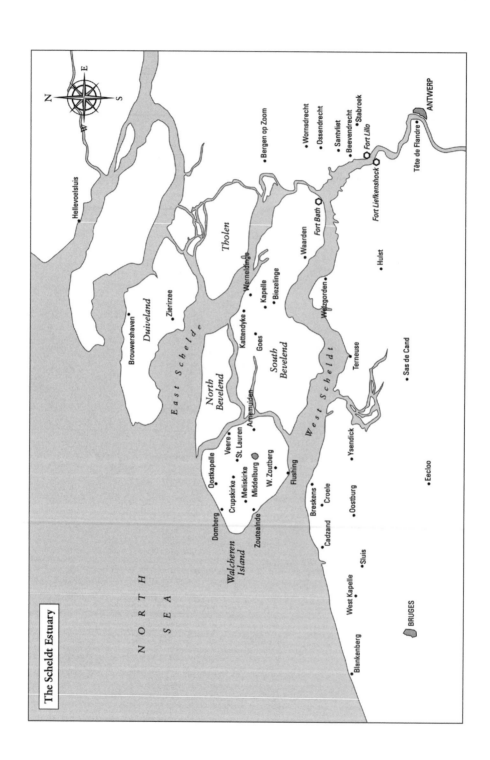

The Scheldt Estuary

Introduction

This study evaluates the performance of the British army in the French Revolutionary and Napoleonic wars with specific reference to four of its campaigns in the Low Countries between 1793 and 1814. In doing so it provides a critique of the current view that, following the reforms of the Duke of York (1795–1809), the British army was transformed into a well-led and efficient fighting force. The campaigns studied are York's expedition to Flanders in 1793; the Anglo-Russian expedition to Holland in 1799; the expedition to the island of Walcheren in 1809; and Sir Thomas Graham's expedition to Bergen-Op-Zoom in 1813–14.

During the period 1793 to 1815 the protection of the Low Countries from France was the overriding objective of British foreign policy. This originated from the British fear of an invasion being launched from the Low Countries by an aggressive foreign power – as had happened in 1688.[1] It led the British to intervene increasingly in the affairs of the Dutch and to the British-inspired creation of the United Kingdom of the Netherlands in 1814.[2] The Low Countries played a dual role in British strategic thinking. On the one hand, the region was viewed as a staging area for a French invasion of the British Isles, whilst on the other it was seen as a potential springboard for British intervention in Europe.[3]

Throughout the eighteenth century the British had committed their military forces to safeguard their interests in the Low Countries and protect the region from French aggression; a prime example being the Duke of Marlborough's campaigns in the Low Counties in 1705–8.[4] During the French Revolutionary and Napoleonic Wars British strategists maintained this approach and instigated a number of significant British military interventions in the Low Countries. Indeed, the British government entered the war of the First Coalition in 1793 to safeguard their interests in the Dutch and Belgian lowlands.[5]

Naval considerations were also important and the British were fixated with the need to ensure a hostile power did not achieve dominance over the ports of Ostend, Flushing and Antwerp on the Flanders and Dutch coasts.[6] Invasion by France was the most important challenge to Britain during this period.

If a French army had landed on the Kent or Suffolk coastline Britain's very survival as an independent nation would have been under threat. At the same time, however, a successful British intervention in the Low Countries, with Allied support, had the potential to threaten the foundations of French power in Northern Europe and the French frontier.

Between 1793 and 1814 six major British expeditions were sent to the Low Countries but, despite high expectations of military success, each ended in disaster. Moreover, despite the fact that historians have agreed that the Low Countries were vital to British interests, none has sought to undertake a comparative study of these campaigns or to provide an explanation for the poor British military record during these years. This book sets out to redress this imbalance, provide a new evaluation of British strategic thinking regarding the Low Countries, and re-evaluate the fighting qualities of the British army in the French Revolutionary and Napoleonic Wars with reference to its performance in the Low Countries between 1793 and 1815.

Historiography

The British army in the French Revolutionary and Napoleonic Wars has always been a popular topic for historians. However, as Michael Howard has pointed out, wider changes in the nature of military history have altered how historians have written about the British army.[7] Gone are the days when to write about military history was to devote one's time solely to the study of battles and the creation of heroic national myths. This parochial approach has been largely superseded by the 'New Military History', with its increasingly inter-disciplinary perspective on 'War and Society' – encompassing international relations, the social sciences, anthropology, gender and media studies – as well as revising aspects of economic, political and constitutional history.

Although these studies have added much needed diversity and breadth to the history of the British army, exponents of this 'New Military History' have not sufficiently challenged the existing views of older generations of military historians. Furthermore, instead of developing a unique approach of their own, advocates of the 'New Military History' have sought instead to borrow ideas and theories from other historical fields. As one historian has noted, 'The Army', has become, 'a test subject for a variety of different theoretical schools'.[8] This view is echoed by Joanna Bourke, who has suggested that military history has attracted the interests of a wide range of scholars from outside the traditional military history fraternity.[9] What links these approaches together is that they have tended to emphasise the importance of social aspects and the history of war from below.[10] Approaches which, as Jeremy Black has noted, have tended to 'de-militarize' the study of military history.[11]

Recently published examples, based on these varied approaches, about the British army in the Napoleonic period include Kevin Linch and Matthew McCormack (eds), *Britain's Soldiers: Rethinking War and Society, 1715–1815* (Basingstoke: Palgrave Macmillan, 2014); Catriona Kennedy, *Narratives of the Revolutionary and Napoleonic Wars: Military and Civilian Experience in Britain and Ireland* (Basingstoke: Palgrave Macmillan, 2013); Mark Wishon, *German Forces and the British Army: Interactions and Perceptions, 1742–1815* (Basingstoke: Palgrave Macmillan, 2013); Catriona Kennedy and Matthew McCormack (eds), *Soldiering in Britain and Ireland, 1750–1850: Men of Arms* (Basingstoke: Palgrave Macmillan, 2012).

These historians owe a great deal to the work of an earlier generation of scholars who pioneered the study of war from social and cultural perspectives during the 1980s and 1990s. One of the most important studies produced in this period, which paved the way for further research, was John Brewer's *The Sinews of Power: War, Money and the English State, 1688–1783* (New York: Alfred A. Knopf, 1989). Although writing about the development of the fiscal-military state, Brewer placed the traditional military history of the period within its wider social and political context. This approach, which some have likened to the Early Modern Histories written by Michael Roberts and Geoffrey Parker, widened the study of war and encouraged historians from other fields to turn their attention to the study of eighteenth-century military history.[12]

Traditional military historians of the period, meanwhile, have been mixed in their response to these developments although some, such as Bruce Collins, Rory Muir and Jeremy Black, have incorporated social and cultural aspects into their wider histories.[13] In doing so, these historians have provided a broader sense of perspective to the history of the British war effort in the period 1793 to 1815. Naval historians such as Roger Knight and David Andress have adopted a similar approach to John Brewer and have compared and contrasted military, naval, economic, social and political factors in order to evaluate the impact of the war on the development of the British state and its war fighting capabilities.[14] Andrew Bamford and Carole Divall, meanwhile, have created both traditional campaign histories and social studies.[15] This approach has, however, not been replicated by the majority of traditional military historians who have otherwise been content to write about the same limited range of topics and have not sought to question, or revise, established arguments.

Instead the traditional, and popular, history of the British army in the French Revolutionary and Napoleonic Wars has come to be dominated by a 'heroic narrative' based on the study of British victories, and or, 'Dunkirk'-style defeats which supposedly led to later victory;[16] by far the most popular subjects being Trafalgar and Waterloo.[17] Regimental historians of the British army in this period have furthered many of these national myths. As Michael Howard has noted, the 'Historiographical tradition' of the British army, 'is that of a regimental history writ large, a rather selective regimental history at that. The regimental historian … is expected to chronicle triumphs, not disasters. His purpose is morale building, not dispassionate analysis.'[18]

The history of the British army in this period has become synonymous with the study of British victories and the career path of the Duke of Wellington. The following (somewhat exhaustive) list of books provides a mere snapshot of the more recent published material about Wellington, his generals and their major campaigns (notably Waterloo): Phillip J. Haythornthwaite, *Picton's Division at Waterloo* (Barnsley: Pen & Sword, 2016); Rory Muir, *Wellington, Waterloo and the Fortunes of Peace* (New Haven and London: Yale University Press, 2015); Tim Clayton, *Waterloo: Four Days that Changed Europe's Destiny* (London: Abacus Books, 2015); Robert Kershaw, *Twenty-Four Hours at Waterloo: 18 June 1815* (London: W.H. Allen, 2015); Nick Lipscombe, *Wellington's Guns, The Untold Story of Wellington and his Guns in the Peninsula and at Waterloo* (Oxford: Osprey, 2013); Rory Muir, *Wellington, The Path to Victory, 1769–1814* (New Haven and London: Yale University Press, 2013); Raymond P. Cusick, *Wellington's Rifles, The Origins, Development and Battles of the Rifle Regiments in the Peninsular War and at Waterloo From 1758 to 1815* (Barnsley: Pen & Sword, 2013); Huw J. Davies, *Wellington's Wars, The Making of a Military Genius* (New Haven and London: Yale University Press, 2012); David Buttery, *Wellington against Junot, The First Invasion of Portugal 1807–1808* (Barnsley: Pen & Sword, 2011); Peter Snow, *To War with Wellington, From the Peninsula to Waterloo* (London: John Murray, 2010); T.A. Heathcote, *Wellington's Peninsular War Generals and Their Battles* (Barnsley: Pen & Sword, 2010); Ron McGuigan, Howie Muir and Rory Muir, *Inside Wellington's Peninsular Army* (Barnsley: Pen & Sword, 2006).

Indeed, such is the proliferation of books on Wellington that students new to the subject might be forgiven for thinking that he, rather than York, was Commander-in-Chief of the Army and that the forces he commanded, in the Iberian Peninsula and at Waterloo, constituted 'the' British army. On the contrary, Wellington did not become Commander-in-Chief until 1842 and neither did he command 'the' British army in the Iberian Peninsula or at Waterloo – these armies were in fact expeditionary forces which were despatched for specific purposes.

Moreover, in focusing so much attention on Wellington's Iberian victories, historians have largely ignored the poor record of the army in other theatres of war over the course of the wider period 1793 to 1815. Unlike their victorious record in Spain and Portugal, the British struggled to achieve success in the Low Countries and were defeated on several occasions over the course of the period.[19] Characteristic failings made by the British in the Low Countries in 1793 to 1814 included: lack of coherent strategic thinking regarding aims and means; poor military planning; over reliance on unreliable intelligence reports; lack of accurate maps; breakdowns in civil-military relations; disrespect on the part of the British army for the actions and fighting qualities of Allied forces; and the inability of the British officer corps to identify, analyse and learn from past mistakes.

One of the problems for historians interested in the other campaigns fought by the British army in the period 1793 to 1815 is that there are significantly fewer printed primary source materials available than for those scholars interested in the Peninsular War. Most of the well-known soldiers' accounts used by historians of British army in the Peninsular War were printed after the publication of Major General William Napier's six-volume *History of the Peninsular War* between 1828 and 1840. Napier's history greatly popularised the genre of military memoirs amongst the general public and helped lay the foundations for the development of popular history.[20] After years of military defeats, British triumph in the Iberian Peninsula captured the imagination of the general public and encouraged further interest in the subject. Furthermore, with the general public eager for tales of British victories and adventures in Spain, Portugal and at Waterloo, interest in the less successful campaigns fought by the army in earlier years did not attract or stimulate the same level of interest. The relative lack of printed sources is particularly acute for the scholar of the British army in the Low Countries in the campaigns fought from 1793 to 1795 – one of the only memoirs in print being *Corporal Brown's Campaigns in the Low Countries, Recollections of a Coldstream Guard in the early campaigns against Revolutionary France 1793–1795.*[21]

The Transformation of the British Army, 1795 to 1815?

> The steady, knowledgeable and thorough-going reform that was carried out by Frederick, Duke of York between 1798 and 1809 transformed the British Army and laid the basis for its series of victories in the Peninsular War that contributed so significantly to the downfall of the Napoleonic Empire. Rightly, may the Duke of York be called the Architect of Victory.[22]

This view by John Peaty is based heavily on Richard Glover's *Peninsular Preparation, The Reform of the British Army 1795 to 1809* (Cambridge: Cambridge University Press, 1963).[23] Glover argued that, after the British defeat in the American War of Independence (1776–83) the British army suffered a decade of neglect and decay which contributed to several poor British military performances in the early years of the French Revolutionary Wars, most notably in the Low Countries in 1793–5. Despite this Glover contended that, over the course of the following years, the army was transformed by a series of reforms instigated by the new Commander-in-Chief of the army, His Royal Highness Frederick, Duke of York and that these changes enabled the army to improve its performance and achieve a series of decisive victories against the French during the later years of the Napoleonic Wars.[24]

Despite the major developments in the field of military history since *Peninsular Preparation* was published, military historians have never sought to evaluate Glover's arguments and have gradually woven his 'transformation thesis' into the fabric of the dominant historiography of the British army.[25] John Houlding, for example, has tried to place York's reforms into the wider context of British military developments in the eighteenth century, whilst Piers Mackesy pointed to the British victory in Egypt in 1801 as proof of the reforms' transformative effects on British military performance.[26] Recent academic studies have further reinforced and bolstered these existing arguments.[27]

Not only are several aspects of this argument flawed, but none of these historians has produced a generally accepted explanation of what is meant by the term 'transformation'. Although there have been detailed descriptions of the reforms themselves, there has been little attempt to question to what extent these reforms actually led to transformation. Historians have not identified criteria by which to analyse whether, and to what extent, the reforms were transformative in nature. Before considering a set of criteria for transformation, it is necessary to define terms.

Definition of Terms

According to the *Oxford English Dictionary*, transformation is defined as the process by which something is changed from one state of affairs to another: a 'considerable change' or 'metamorphosis' in 'form, character and appearance'. For a transformation to occur in an organisation something more profound than incremental reform is required – its members should think, act and perform in a noticeably different manner from before. In order to evaluate the transformation thesis more critically it is necessary to place Glover's thesis in the context of wider arguments about transformation and the nature of change in military affairs.

Evaluating the significance of change in military affairs has been a constant thread in the work of historians. For example, Michael Roberts coined the term 'Military Revolution' to describe many of the major military changes which occurred in European warfare in the early modern period.[28] Other historians have further refined and critically evaluated the validity of this concept.[29] Although this may be the case for the term 'Military Revolution', some of the other terms used by historians to describe military change are not as well defined or understood. Military historians have often used the term 'transformation' to describe the process of military change, but have not sought to explain the concept itself.

Furthermore, much of what has been written about the scope of transformation in military contexts has been generated by current debates between Western defence analysts about future war. During the 1990s American and British military thinkers developed a new conceptual framework in order to understand and evaluate military changes more rigorously. At the heart of the new framework was the idea that the post-Cold War American military was experiencing a technology led 'Revolution in Military Affairs' (RMA) one which would alter the way future wars would be fought.[30] Since the idea of an RMA was postulated, the subject has gained in popularity amongst military analysts, historians, journalists and even politicians, and has been more widely applied to encompass other aspects of military change.

One idea which developed out of the wider RMA debate was that, since the beginning of the twenty-first century, the armed forces of the United States and Great Britain have been undergoing a technology led transformation.[31] Although it is not the purpose of this book to analyse in detail modern theories about transformation in current military affairs, it is important to demonstrate the absence of any similar analytical thinking or framework in the work of military historians of the Napoleonic period. Therefore, the concepts and criteria developed for transformation by current analysts provide a useful comparator by which to examine whether the changes made by York to the British army in 1795 to 1809 were truly transformative.

In the modern debates, Paul David has pointed out that the process of transformation should not be confused with that of reform. According to David, transformation is a significant change in the way an army functions and operates, brought about by a series of dramatic developments. In contrast, reform is merely a gradual process of improvement made to existing practices.[32] Similarly Leonard L. Lira has argued the need for a clear distinction to be made between transformative change and the process of reform. Influenced by the work of social scientists, such as K.K. Smith, Amir Levy and Uri Merry, Lira has argued that military thinkers need to take a more nuanced approach to the subject of change and the value of social theory.

One of the ideas borrowed by Lira from social science is that change can be split in two and analysed as either first or second order change.[33] 'First order change', according to Lira, can be of great benefit to an organisation since it can iron out teething problems and lead to improved performance. Lira, however, is keen to stress that first order change can only go so far because it does not bring about a change of mind-set or culture. According to Lira, 'Second order change' transcends functional aspects and alters the 'Founding assumptions, concepts, values and practices' which define how members of an organisation operate.[34] Lira's analysis aptly describes the distinction which should be made by historians between military reform and transformation.

For transformation to occur, therefore, the personnel within an organisation must alter their ethos and core values and be ready to make major administrative and functional changes over time –administrative and organisational changes on their own are not enough to bring about transformative change. The changes made must transcend incremental reforms and lead to self-sustaining improvements in functions and performance. The changes made to the British army between 1795 and 1809 were incremental and did not alter the ethos or culture of the Army in the ways required for the changes to be transformative in nature. As this book demonstrates, although York's reforms led to some improvements, they did not lead to improved military performance which must surely be the test of whether an army has been transformed.

Methodology and Structure

This book started as an MPhil dissertation about the disastrous British expedition to the Scheldt in 1809. The initial assumption was that this defeat was an atypical experience for the British army. However, further research into British military campaigns in the Low Countries in 1793 to 1815 revealed that the British army had suffered more than its fair share of defeats in this 'Cockpit' of Europe. It gradually became apparent that these defeats were caused by errors of judgement on the part of British commanders and that these mistakes were repeated by the British in other theatres of war.

This discovery demonstrated the need to question the validity of Glover's transformation thesis and the impact of the reforms and to place greater emphasis on Britain's military experience in the Low Countries. Instead of focusing on just one campaign, the scope of the research was broadened in order to study the conduct and performance of the British Army in four campaigns in the Low Countries over the course of 1793 to 1814. Additionally, it was also necessary to place British military culture, and the character of York's reforms within the context of wider military developments and European military culture. Only then would it be possible to pronounce on the relative quality of the British army and the impact of the reforms.

The book is structured as follows: the first chapter outlines the state of the army in 1793 and its poor performance in the Dunkirk campaign of that year. Chapter two briefly analyses the British defeat in the Low Countries in 1794 and 1795 and evaluates the subsequent reforms made to the British army by York. Chapters three, four and five analyse three further British defeats in the Low Countries, between 1799 and 1814, demonstrating the lack of impact of the reforms and the Army's inability to learn. The concluding section summarises the main points raised and confirms the argument that the British army was not transformed by York's reforms. Given the lack of research that has been undertaken into the campaigns of the British army in the Low Countries it was essential to place each of the campaigns within a wider context. Thus, in addition to the focus on operational military history, each chapter also includes a discussion of Anglo-Dutch relations and wider British strategic aims and objectives. This extended line of inquiry required research in a range of archives and museums across the British Isles as well as a review of the relevant secondary literature.

Source Materials

Because this book is predominantly about British military culture and operational performance the primary sources materials used in its creation were those of the senior politicians and diplomats who framed British strategy and the military figures who were tasked with its execution. It is not about the conduct and experiences of the 'ordinary soldier'. This approach is also reflected in the choice of secondary source material, with the emphasis being primarily placed upon political, strategic and military histories rather than social studies or the surviving letters of individual soldiers.

Such a study would not have been possible without regular visits to read the personal papers and official military reports housed at The National Archives (TNA). Indeed the bulk of the official military documents relating to British military operations in the French Revolutionary and Napoleonic Wars are stored at TNA within the War Office (WO) collections. Other items located at the TNA that have proved useful are the maps and plans stored in the Map Room, the many naval intelligence reports located within the Admiralty Office collections (ADM) and the letters and correspondence of officials at the Foreign Office (FO).

Alongside TNA, the British Library (BL) has also provided a rich source of primary and secondary material; particularly for the personal papers of British politicians, such as William Huskisson and Lord Auckland, and for more obscure journal articles, such as the *Consortium on Revolutionary Europe*. The Templer Study Centre at the National Army Museum (NAM) also provided a large number of important manuscript materials, such as those of Captain Peter Bowlby. The Caird Library at the National Maritime Museum (NMM) also provided useful source material, especially the personal papers of Vice Admiral Sir Richard Goodwin Keats.

Due to the large number of Scottish officers in the British army during the period in question, it was also necessary to visit both the National Archives of Scotland (NAS) and the National Library of Scotland (NLS) in Edinburgh. Both of these provided source materials which were not available south of the border: most notably 'the Military Notebook and Papers of General Sir Thomas Graham'. Alongside trips to both London and Edinburgh, the secondary source materials and unpublished dissertations located at the Bodleian Library and at All Souls College Cambridge have also been of use. Similar research was also undertaken at Warwick University, the Cadbury Research Library at the University of Birmingham and at Birmingham Central Library.

The Internet has also been an invaluable tool, especially the Internet Archive with its ever expanding collection of digitised books, military manuals and personal papers, such as the Dropmore Papers. Other useful electronic sources include the online versions of the Parliamentary Papers (PP), older editions of newspaper articles and the online depository for journal articles, JSTOR.

Chapter 1

The British Army and the Dunkirk Campaign, 1793

The Ministers and the Military

Unlike the Royal Navy, which was administered and directed in wartime by the Cabinet, the First Lords of the Admiralty and the officials in the Admiralty office, the army did not possess a clear chain of command. The symbolic and ceremonial head of the British army was His Majesty King George III. Despite being refused the chance to gain active military experience during the Seven Years War (1756–63) the king nurtured a keen interest in political and military affairs and was the commanding officer of both the Foot Guards and the Household Cavalry. Over the course of the Napoleonic period, the king played a key role in the management of promotions and his powers of patronage allowed him to maintain an influence over appointments.[1] That all major military and strategic decisions needed royal approval also meant that the king was always well informed about the war effort and this enabled him to influence wider political and military aspects.[2]

Directly answerable to the king and to Parliament was the C-in-C who was chiefly responsible for the upkeep and organisation of the regular forces, both at home and abroad. The C-in-C was supported in these tasks at the Horse Guards by the Adjutant (AG) and Quartermaster Generals (QMG) – the former was tasked with the upkeep of the army whilst the latter was responsible for its movements and supply. The Royal Artillery and Engineers benefitted from being administered separately by the Ordnance Department, headed by the Master General who was also responsible for the procurement of military equipment and ammunition.[3] The C-in-C also relied on a number of other administrative officials and organisations, such as the medical officials of the Army Medical Board and the military representatives at the Treasury. But, although influential in military administrative affairs, the C-in-C had relatively little influence over British strategy and the planning of military expeditions. Instead, the key persons who were responsible for the direction of British strategy and the deployment of the army were the senior politicians based at Whitehall, in particular the Prime Minister and the Secretaries of State for War and Foreign Affairs.[4]

During the early years of the French wars the incumbents of these key positions were William Pitt the Younger, Sir Henry Dundas (later Lord Melville), and Sir William Grenville. Pitt had risen to power in 1783, thanks largely to the support of the king, who deeply disliked the opposition Whigs and their leader Charles Fox. From 1783 to 1801 Pitt, Dundas and Grenville formed the key triumvirate in British political and strategic circles alongside the king.[5] The king continued to play a formative role in British politics and the conduct of the war during the period 1793 to 1810, a period which witnessed a range of governmental changes as British military fortunes went from bad to worse in Europe. Despite the political turmoil, however, the key British government posts largely remained in the hands of a small group of ministers, many of whom were Pitt's friends and protégés.[6] Indeed, as Jennifer Mori has suggested, during the 1790s Dundas and Grenville were more akin to being Pitt's political 'creatures' than his friends.[7] Over the course of the following decades, the king's grip over British politics gradually waned, due to a combination of the deterioration of the king's mental health and an increase in the power of the executive, with its growing emphasis on Cabinet politics.[8] Thus the British war effort in the years 1793 to 1815 was managed and maintained by a small number of people. It must be remembered that the creation of a dedicated civil service and the development of professionally trained government officials was still some way in the future.[9] In the political realm, it was not unusual for a senior minister to hold a number of different and complex governmental posts at the same time. For example, Henry Dundas, Britain's first Secretary for War in the period 1793 to 1801, was also Home Secretary and the President of the Board of Control.[10]

The British Army on the Eve of War

> Our army was lax in its discipline, entirely without system, and very weak in numbers. Each Colonel of a regiment managed it according to his own notions, or neglected it altogether. There was no uniformity of drill or movement; professional pride was rare; professional knowledge still more so.[11]

This statement, written by Henry Bunbury, highlights some of the British army's significant weaknesses at the start of the French Revolutionary Wars. Dejected after its defeat in America, the army had returned to Britain with little to show for its endeavours. Despite some battlefield success, particularly in the early years of the war, the increased scope and scale of the conflict after 1778 had stretched British military and naval resources to breaking point.[12] Although other factors played a part in British defeat in 1783, poor strategic and military planning were major factors, particularly in the humiliating defeats suffered by the British at Saratoga in 1777 and Yorktown in 1781.[13] Furthermore the lack of popular support for the war in Britain hindered recruitment levels and necessitated the use of German mercenaries in British service. Naval recruitment had also proved difficult during the early years of the American war and only gained in popularity after the French declared war on Great Britain in 1778.[14]

The crushing military and naval defeat of British forces by the combined American and French armies at Yorktown in 1781 was a strategic hammer blow for the British war effort and hastened calls for an armistice, which was negotiated at Paris in 1783.[15] The reputation of the British army, which had been high since the Seven Years War, had been turned upside down and the force which returned from America needed drastic reform. War weary and financially exhausted, however, the British government was in no position to undertake costly reform and the politicians eschewed the need for change and demobilised the bulk of the army.[16]

Demobilisation was rapid as the army shrank in size from its wartime strength of over 90,000 officers and men to well below 50,000 in a year.[17] The remaining regiments were redeployed across the globe to guard what remained of the British Empire, leaving a skeleton force in the British Isles. The British army at home continued to be reduced, save for a brief period around the time of the Nootka Sound crisis in 1790 and by 1792 there were barely 13,092 officers and men fit for service out of a total garrison of 15,919. The British army as a whole, including the garrisons in the Caribbean, Canada, Australia, India, Gibraltar and the Bahamas, officially numbered 43,717, of whom 36,557 were listed as 'effectives'.[18] These numbers were in keeping with the strength of the British army in the period 1775 to 1777.[19]

The meagre size of the army in Great Britain was necessitated by both cultural and financial factors. The British public had long been averse to the existence of a large standing army because of the perceived threat that this would pose to British liberty; sentiments which could be traced back to the English Civil Wars' and to the aftermath of the Glorious Revolution of 1688.[20] The general public was also opposed to the creation of barracks, fearing that these would enable the government to gather troops together in order to impose their will on the populace. This latter concern had little merit since in the absence of purpose-built accommodation and an official police force, soldiers were both billeted with civilians and employed to maintain order, factors which increased existing tensions.[21]

The lack of a nationwide system of barracks, combined with the need for British troops to be dispersed across the country in small groups to keep the peace, greatly hindered the effective training of the troops. Unlike the French and Prussians, who regularly staged large peacetime training camps, it was usually only in times of war that the British were able to gather large numbers in camps.[22] The multiplicity of roles which the army was expected to perform, combined with the need to spread the forces across the globe, militated against the development of standard drills and training methods for the infantry and cavalry.

The lack of training opportunities not only hindered the drilling of the troops, but also hampered the development of higher command skills amongst the officer corps. With few opportunities to train in camp, veteran officers had to rely on what they had previously experienced, which generally meant the skills cultivated in America during the War of Independence. A major problem with this approach, however, was that the skills that had proved useful in American conditions were not necessarily good preparation for European war.[23] Few British officers had experience of European warfare or indeed knew what it was like to command large forces on a European battlefield.

The forces involved in the War of Independence were pitifully small by European standards. For example, Cornwallis's army in the campaigns in the Carolinas and Virginia in 1780–1 was no bigger than around 8,000 men at the peak of the fighting. On many occasions such as the Battle of Green Spring Farm, during the Yorktown campaign in 1781, the number of British troops involved did not exceed 2,500.[24] In contrast, York was expected to command around 35,000 troops in 1793, 5,000 more than the entire British military presence in the American Colonies in 1776.[25]

The small-scale nature of the armies in America meant that the majority of the officer corps of the British army, save those of Dundas's generation, went to war in 1793 with as J.A. Houlding notes 'Little or no experience of manoeuvring in brigade, let alone in the lines and columns adopted on campaign' and the majority were forced to 'learn their business on the spot'.[26] Lack of training in large formations, combined with the small-scale character of the war in America, meant that the British officer corps in 1793 was largely bereft of generals who had the necessary skills to command large formations on campaign. This continued to hinder the improvement of the British army throughout the conflict and, as Wellington later noted of his colleagues, 'I have often said that if there were eight to ten thousand men in Hyde Park, it is not every general that would know how to get them out again …'.[27]

The continued rotation of battalions to and from different parts of the British Isles and the globe was also disruptive, with different types of drill favoured in different climes. The movement of officers also hindered training techniques, especially if a regiment received a change of commanding officer. It was customary for colonels to train their men according to their own methods. The result was chaotic with regiments being drilled in a variety of different ways.[28] Although there was some form of official guidance, in the form of the *King's Regulations* of 1728, 1764 and 1778, these had not been made compulsory.[29] It took until 1792 for a standardised drill manual for the infantry to be introduced, in the form of Colonel Sir David Dundas's *Principles of Militarily Movements, Chiefly Applied to Infantry*.[30] Although York has been accredited as a keen supporter of Colonel Dundas's drills, Dundas's *Principles* had first been published in 1788 when he was QMG in Ireland. Dundas's drills were known at the Horse Guards before York assumed office and had caught the attention of Lord Jeffrey Amherst when he was C-in-C and it was Amherst who had made *Principles* the basis of the 1792 regulations.

The adoption of a standard system of drill in the British army was long overdue, especially given that the Europeans had experimented with standard drills for many years. The army of the Dutch Republic, for example, had created a set of standard drills during the Eighty Years War (1568–1648). In Prussia the first official regulations for the training of the infantry emerged as early as 1714. These were updated at regular intervals during the years that followed.[31] The French also experimented with a variety of drills during these years and gradually standardised them. Even the Americans, during the War of Independence, showed a desire to create greater uniformity of drill than their British opponents. George Washington famously enlisted a Prussian drill master, Baron von Steuben, to train the Continental Army in European methods.[32]

Although the adoption of a standardised system of drill was a necessary step for the British army, *Principles* was far from innovative because Dundas's tactical ideas were chiefly based on the dated training methods of Frederick the Great.[33] Unlike some of his contemporaries, who had made names for themselves fighting colonial wars in North America and the West Indies, Dundas was a European soldier who had served under the Duke of Cumberland in the Low Countries and Germany during the Seven Years War. It was during this conflict that Dundas had developed a keen appreciation of the rigorous and methodical drills used by the Prussians.

Crucially, Dundas was not interested in assessing the recent tactical developments which had been undertaken by the army in North America, such as the greater use of light infantry. His aim was to prepare the troops for the type of linear warfare that he had experienced in Europe during the Seven Years War.[34] By adopting Dundas's *Principles*, both Amherst and then York remodelled the British army on a military system which had changed little in fifty years; the Prussians did not perform well in the early campaigns of the Revolutionary Wars and the weaknesses of Frederick's system were to be cruelly exposed by Napoleon in 1806.[35] Neither did Amherst or York heed calls from those who suggested that the army needed greater numbers of light troops.[36]

The British cavalry were also deficient in a number of aspects, not least in terms of recent military experience having played only a very limited role in the American war.[37] Although the British raised a number of provincial loyalist cavalry units for service in America, only two regular regiments were despatched from Great Britain. The regiments that did serve, namely the 16th and 17th Light Dragoons, also suffered greatly from the loss of mounts on the long voyage to the colonies.[38] Such was the lack of combat experience amongst the British cavalry in the period 1776 to 1793 that when a considerable number were deployed to Flanders in 1793 they could not perform even the most basic task of placing mounted sentries.[39]

Since 1715, Britain's artillery had been maintained on a permanent footing. Before this point the only permanent force of artillerymen had been the gunners of the Tower of London who had trained at the grandly titled 'Artillery Garden' in Spitafields since the sixteenth century.[40] Over the course of the 1700s the administration of the artillery had become more sophisticated. In 1716 the Ordnance had started manufacturing its own artillery pieces and in 1741 had opened its very own training centre for junior officers – the Royal Military Academy based at Woolwich.[41] This emphasis on education marked artillery and engineer officers out from the rest of the British officer corps whose members, unlike their European counterparts, generally entered the military without the benefit of formal military education or any encouragement to develop a cognitive approach to their profession.[42] Learning in the military was not a British forte.

Another area of the British military machinery which was deficient during this period and which continued to be so throughout the French wars was British intelligence. Lack of reliable intelligence about the Low Countries and the state of the French army was a recurrent problem for the British. Whilst the French employed a number of experienced staff tasked with intelligence gathering, the British had no such organisation at their disposal.[43] A further impediment to the gathering of reliable intelligence was the fact that British diplomats, the main source of British intelligence during the French Revolutionary Wars, were evicted from the Continent after the French conquest of the Low Countries in 1795, which closed off a vital avenue of intelligence for the British.[44] Shorn of diplomatic intelligence gathering and lacking in trained staff officers the British were forced to rely on untrustworthy sources, such as smugglers and deserters.

Lack of adequate maps was another problem, with the Horse Guards possessing scant topographical knowledge of the coast and hinterland of the Low Countries. Throughout the period, British generals often found themselves operating in alien conditions without any clear understanding of what they faced or where they were supposed to advance. Official guidance was not of a high order – indeed, it was not until 1805 that a 'Depository of Military Knowledge' was created by York at the Tower of London to store the various maps and reports gathered over the years.[45] However, despite its grand title, the Depository was little more than a glorified storeroom and lacked many items. Additionally, there was no process by which lessons from past campaigns could be identified and until 1857 there was no official journal for the development of military thinking.[46]

To sum up – on the eve of war the British army was reduced in number, poorly trained and deficient in light infantry and experienced cavalrymen. The majority of its officer corps lacked recent European military experience and, ordnance officers aside, had not had the benefit of formal military education. For both the rank and file, the Flanders campaign of 1793 was to be a true baptism of fire.

Reasons for British Intervention in the Low Countries

> The English ... only make up their minds to fight when their interests seem absolutely threatened ... Their history is full of alterations between indifference which makes people think them decadent, and a rage which baffles their foes. They are seen, in turn, abandoning and dominating Europe, neglecting the greatest continental matters and claiming to control even the smallest, turning from peace at any price to war to the death.[47]

These words, by Albert Sorel, perfectly describe the oscillations in the British approach to Continental affairs in the decade leading up to Britain's involvement in the War of the First Coalition in 1793. For much of this decade, the government of Pitt the Younger pursued a policy of isolation from European affairs following the British defeat in the American War of Independence.[48]

Ousted from America and unpopular in Europe, isolation from European affairs had been a popular and prudent choice, the prime minister seeking to use the peace to rebuild the British economy and the Royal Navy.[49] However, events in the Low Countries during the 1780s gradually drew the British towards intervention once again. The cornerstone of Britain's strategy in North-West Europe, as envisaged by Pitt and his colleagues, was the existence of strong ties between the British and Dutch governments and the maintenance of Austrian rule over the Southern Netherlands. Before analysing the British position regarding the Habsburgs, it is necessary to outline the formative influence that Anglo-Dutch relations had upon British strategic thinking in Europe.

Above all other considerations in Europe, Pitt aimed to secure good Anglo-Dutch relations and cultivated a close relationship with the House of Orange. There was nothing new about this strategic vision. Since the middle of the sixteenth century, the English had sought to secure close relations with the Dutch in the face of Spanish expansionism in Northern Europe.[50] The close proximity of London to Amsterdam also provided the English with a ready-made market for goods on the Continent. The Dutch, in this period, used their powerful fleets to carve out a great trading empire overseas, which at its height incorporated trading stations in New Guinea, China, Ceylon, the Cape and North America and enjoyed a golden period of population growth.[51]

Anglo-Dutch relations turned sour during the 1650s due to the development of an intense trade rivalry between the two states. Fierce Anglo-Dutch economic competition eventually gave rise to three 'Trade Wars' between the two states in 1652–4, 1661–7 and 1672–4 respectively.[52] Although ultimately more destructive for the Dutch economy in the long term, the English suffered several major defeats at the hands of the Dutch fleet during these years. None was more humiliating than that suffered by the English in June 1667 when, with the English preoccupied in dealing with the aftermath of the Plague and the Fire of London, the Dutch Fleet under Admiral de Ruyter successfully forced the River Medway and severely damaged the anchored English fleet.[53]

Frictions between the two states continued and in 1688 Stadtholder William I of Orange, with the aid of English Protestant rebels, successfully invaded the British Isles in the event known as the 'Glorious Revolution'.[54] William cemented his victory when he defeated James II at the Battle of the Boyne in 1690. William's successful invasion ushered in a period of stability and renewed goodwill between the British and the Dutch and, although this proved short-lived, the rule of the House of Orange contributed to the development of the belief in British political circles that the future strength of the United Provinces required the Dutch state to be governed by a member of the House of Orange. The British also hoped that a rejuvenated Dutch state, under a stable government, would be able to act as a bulwark against the gradual growth of French power in Northern Europe.

These hopes proved short-lived, however, when William died childless in 1702, leaving the Dutch without a leader. Although Queen Anne ruled over the British Isles for a brief period, her death twelve years later further distanced the British from the Dutch and, with the accession of the Hanoverian George I, ushered in the Georgian period. For the next forty years the British sought to maintain friendly relations with the Dutch amidst fears of the growth of French power in North-West Europe.[55]

During the War of the Austrian Succession (1740–8), the British and Dutch fought alongside the Austrians against the French. However, the British grew increasingly alarmed during these years at the lack of strong Dutch leadership. British fears regarding the strength of their Dutch ally peaked in 1747 when, faced with the prospect of a French invasion of the United Provinces, the British actively advocated the need for the Dutch to restore the Orangeist party to its former position of strength at The Hague and that a member of the House of Orange be elected to the post of Stadtholder.[56] The British even went as far as to deploy a naval force to the River Scheldt in order to show their support for the Orangeist cause. A successful Orangeist coup quickly followed, the news of which was greeted with scenes of great joy amongst the ministers in London.[57]

Over the course of the following decades a growing number of Dutchmen and women came to detest the level of influence exercised by the British over Dutch affairs. By the 1770s the most vocal opposition to the House of Orange came from the self-styled Dutch 'Patriot' party, whose members resented the close ties which had developed between the British and the House of Orange.[58] Eager for change, especially the reform of the armed forces, the Patriots were also heavily influenced by the ideas of the American Revolution.[59] The American War of Independence, meanwhile, had also heightened existing Anglo-Dutch tensions, especially over mercantile interests.[60] Matters eventually came to a head in 1780 when the Patriots forced William V to support the American colonists in the war with Great Britain.[61] Over the course of the following years the Patriot movement gained greater strength throughout the United Provinces.[62]

Considerable frictions also existed between the Dutch and the Austrians over the subject of trade access to the North Sea, via the River Scheldt. The

Austrians wanted to see the Scheldt opened to trade, so that Antwerp could reap the benefits of increased access to the North Sea, whilst the Dutch sought to keep the river closed, a right which they had been given in 1648.[63] A mini crisis ensued in 1784 when the Austrian Emperor Joseph II claimed Maastricht as an indemnity for the closure of the Scheldt.[64] All-out war was averted but British influence over Dutch affairs was further weakened when the French mediated between the Dutch and Austrians at the subsequent political negotiations at Fontainebleau in November 1785.[65]

The Dutch continued to argue amongst themselves and the internal divisions in Dutch politics finally came to a head in September 1786 when the Patriots forced the Stadtholder to relinquish command of the armed forces.[66] Over the course of the winter months and into the New Year the Orangeists lost control of Holland, along with several other provinces, as the paramilitary forces of the Patriots seized power.[67] Panic-stricken by these events, Pitt's newly appointed government had flirted with the idea of British military intervention, but instead negotiated for a Prussian force, under the Duke of Brunswick, to invade the Dutch Republic and restore the House of Orange.[68] Challenged by disciplined Prussian troops, the Patriot forces were defeated and scattered. Subsequently, the British reclaimed the strategic initiative and negotiated for the Dutch and Prussians to join them in forming a new Triple Alliance.[69] Despite this victory for British diplomacy the Patriot cause did not die out in 1787 and neither did the House of Orange gain in strength. Pleased with the Prussian invasion and subsequent negotiations, the British allowed themselves to slip back into their former policy of isolation.

During the same period the British were also concerned about the political instability of the Southern Netherlands, particularly in the years immediately before the outbreak of the French Revolution. At the same time as the Dutch Patriot movement had been growing in strength in opposition to the dynastic rule of the House of Orange, the people of the Austrian Netherlands had begun to demonstrate their increasing dissatisfaction with Habsburg rule and, more specifically, the sweeping reforms of Emperor Joseph II.[70] Like the Dutch Stadtholder, the Austrian Emperor came to be viewed as an enemy of the people and was targeted politically by groups, such as the radical Vonckists, who sought to establish an independent Belgium.[71] Following the fall of the Bastille, the people of Brabant revolted against the Austrians and a Belgian 'Patriotic Army', which had been readied across the border in the United Provinces, invaded the Southern Netherlands and seized Brussels.[72] These events precipitated a general revolt which culminated in the formation of a short-lived independent Belgium in 1790.[73] During the same period the Belgians also cultivated closer links with the French, much to the concern of the British government, who feared for the future security of the Low Countries.[74] Although these fears were allayed in July, when the Austrians reconquered the Southern Netherlands, the outbreak of the French Revolution temporarily drew British attention to the events in France.

Unlike the Germanic powers, the British initially did not see the need to intervene in the French Revolution, nor did they involve themselves in the diplomatic disagreements which eventually brought about the outbreak of another European War in 1792. Indeed, throughout the opening years of the new decade, Pitt remained optimistic that Britain was on the verge of an extended period of peace.[75] Pitt's dreams of peace in his time proved short-lived and the British were eventually forced to intervene in the Low Countries following the French invasion of the Southern Netherlands in 1792.

The situation in the Low Countries in 1792 greatly concerned the British. Not only did the Belgians welcome the French with open arms, but the Dutch also showed signs of renewed discontent with the Orangeist government.[76] For example, the British ambassador at The Hague, Sir William Eden (Lord Auckland) wrote to Grenville in June to state that Patriot 'cabals' were rumoured to be forming in towns and cities throughout the republic.[77] The political situation worsened over the course of the following months and Auckland wrote again to Grenville in late November to say that the political situation in Amsterdam was 'critical' and that the Patriots had 'become noisy and impudent' there being scarcely 'a village, or an ale house … in which the language is not seditious'.[78] Auckland even suggested that a small squadron of British naval vessels should be readied for operations in the Scheldt, in case of a sudden French invasion.[79] Auckland's advice was not heeded, however, and although the events in the Low Countries made war between Great Britain and France increasingly likely, the diplomats of each nation carried on working towards the continuation of peaceful relations. Grenville, in particular, held out a hope that hostilities could be avoided.[80] However, after months of negotiations, it was the French who finally decided to act and on 1 February 1793 the regicidal members of the French Revolutionary Convention declared war on Great Britain and the United Provinces. The British responded in kind two weeks later.[81]

The situation at The Hague was chaotic. The Dutch government showed little sign of urgency, whilst a resurgent Patriot party welcomed the French as liberators. Flooded with messages, and fearful of the French advance, Auckland feverishly asked Grenville for British military and financial support for the Dutch. Auckland demanded, 'Men, Commanders, Ships and

Money', and, more specifically, that 'The Duke of York' and 'some English battalions' be despatched to Holland.[82] The British had already hired some 13,000 Hanoverian troops to be used in Holland against a potential French invasion, but it would be several months before this force was ready.[83] Auckland also echoed the comments of Edmund Burke, made over two years previously, by stating that the beleaguered Dutch state should be viewed by the British government as being of similar importance as one of its own counties.[84]

Auckland's request clearly made an impression upon Grenville and, in just over a week, a small convoy of British troop-transports carrying three battalions of His Majesty's brigade of Foot Guards, under the Duke of York, sailed for the Dutch coast.[85] The British force landed on Dutch soil at Hellevoetsluis on 4 March. York proceeded to The Hague to meet with the Dutch government and Auckland. In the meantime, the Guards, under a future hero of the British army in India Major General Gerard Lake, were divided and positioned along the coastline.

On 18 March 1793 the Austrians decisively defeated the French, under Dumouriez, at the Battle of Neerwinden. Battered and bruised, Dumouriez's army was sent into a headlong retreat through the Austrian Netherlands to the French border fortresses. The Low Countries were saved. Shortly before Neerwinden ministers in London and the senior figures in the Low Countries had started to consider how best to proceed in the war against France. Foreseeing a French defeat and eager to see the United Provinces secured for the future, Auckland had suggested to Grenville that the British should consider commencing an offensive to secure the United Provinces and the Austrian Netherlands.[86] News of Neerwinden convinced Auckland of the benefits of such a campaign:

> The interests of Holland, as well as of the allies cannot be better served than by now sending towards the frontiers of France all the troops that are able ... the Duke of York is strongly of this opinion, and left The Hague tonight, in order to proceed with the brigade of Guards to Bergen-op-Zoom ... If the campaign can be successfully maintained, possibly it should be wished to use every effort to gain possession of the principal places on the French frontier, such as Lille, Valenciennes, Conde (and even Dunkirk and Calais) with the intention either to keep them or to demolish them.[87]

That Auckland mentioned York is significant because historians of the period have generally argued that the subsequent British operations in Flanders were devised solely by the politicians.[88] Over the course of the following weeks, the king and Grenville also warmed to the idea of swift military action.[89] Aside from aiding the Dutch there were other reasons why the British welcomed the idea of an advance into the Southern Netherlands. For instance, the British were keen to restore Austrian rule to the Southern Netherlands and rebuild the old barrier fortresses which had previously protected the Low Countries against French expansionism. The problem facing the British was that over the course of the late eighteenth century the Habsburgs had gradually lost interest in the Low Countries and longed instead to exchange their lands in North-West Europe for Bavaria.[90] This so-called 'Bavarian exchange' naturally concerned British strategists, but the apparent weakness of France in the spring of 1793 and the belief that the war in Europe would be short-lived made them think that the time was right for them to find a solution. The British, like the other European powers, were eager to secure indemnities of their own.

Strategic Planning Process

Uneasy about the war aims of the Austrians, York was ordered by Henry Dundas to despatch one of his aides-de-camp (ADCs), Captain Crauford, to the Austrian headquarters to ascertain Austrian strategy.[91] Crauford's report stated that the Austrians were keen to work with the British and that the Austrian commander, Prince Frederick Josias of Saxe-Coburg-Saalfeld, proposed a conference of the Allied commanders, including York, the Stadtholder, Count Starhenburg, the Prince of Orange, Brunswick and General Knoblesdorf, the Prussian commander in the Low Countries, to be held at Antwerp on 7 April.[92] Crauford was also able to confirm that the commander of the *Armée du Nord*, former French Minister for War, Charles François Dumouriez, 'was ready to turn his arms against the Convention and lend his aid to the re-establishment of the monarchy in France'.[93] With the French seemingly in disarray, the British were further emboldened to take action in order to secure their own primary strategic objectives on the Flanders coast before the end of hostilities.

The conference was the first time that the main military representatives of Great Britain, Austria, Prussia and the United Provinces had met since the decision to despatch British troops to support the Dutch. The result was to prove significant and in a little over a week Dundas instructed York to suspend purely defensive operations and to advance in support of the Austrians before striking out to the north to seize Dunkirk. Dundas, like Auckland before him, hoped that the subsequent Allied offensive would ensure 'The Security of the Netherlands as a barrier to the ambitions of France, and a frontier to the United Provinces'.[94] Pitt and Dundas also reasoned that by committing to the offensive they would be in a position to dictate Allied strategy and ensure British interests were secured before the French were defeated.[95] The ministers also believed that conquests on the seacoast would provide them with a valuable bargaining chip, which could then be offered to the Austrians, in the hope that the Habsburgs would retain the Southern Netherlands after the end of hostilities.[96] Operating with the Austrians also made military sense until British reinforcements were available.

The decision to commit the British army to the offensive changed the nature of the British commitment to the war in Europe. Until this point the British intervention in the Low Countries had been strictly limited to support of the House of Orange and the Dutch government with a small contingent of British soldiers. Following the Antwerp conference the role of the British army was widened to include not only participation in a major Allied offensive but one which required greater British military presence on the ground. York's force was to be increased from just over a thousand British regulars to include several thousand British, Hanoverian, Hessian, Austrian and Prussian troops. It was to be a truly multi-national force which, although fighting for Allied objectives, was forged to secure British interests.

What is particularly striking about the British decision to increase their involvement in Europe was that the ministers and the generals involved made up their minds in just a matter of a few days without fully considering the potential consequences of their decision. Important questions were not raised. For example, nobody recognised the need to ask whether the army was capable of fighting a major European war. Perhaps the reason why the ministers did not spend time considering the finer details of their decision was because they were already thinking about where they would strike next.

As the Antwerp conference was taking place, Pitt, Dundas and Grenville were thinking about other expeditions and were not short of ideas. Pitt was eager to attack the French coast, believing that the French would be unable to protect their vast coastline from British amphibious raiding.[97] In suggesting such a strategy Pitt, whether consciously or not, advocated a return to the type of military enterprises employed by his father, William Pitt the Elder, during the Seven Years War.[98] This approach had many admirers. Several military and political figures believed that British interests were best served by the deployment of Britain's limited military resources in raiding the French coast, rather than in support of 'untrustworthy' Continental powers. The Master General of the Ordnance, Charles Lennox, Duke of Richmond, was a known supporter of this approach.[99]

There was also a small group of politicians, outside Pitt's inner circle, who wanted the government to support French counter revolutionary groups by sending arms and equipment to the French coast, notably royalist heartlands like Brittany and the Vendée; the chief advocate of this policy was William Wyndam.[100] Although initially unwilling to give in to these suggestions, the growing zeal and radicalism inherent in French politics and foreign policy would later convince Pitt of the benefits of this stratagem. The government sanctioned the despatch of troops to support a Federalist rising at Toulon in August–September 1793 and launched an émigré expedition to Quiberon in 1795 to support French royalists in Brittany.[101]

Alongside Pitt, Dundas played a key role in major policy decisions and was entrusted with the task of acting as unofficial war minister, a role he performed whilst also Home Secretary, President of the Board of Control and Treasurer of the Navy. These wider responsibilities no doubt influenced Dundas's outlook regarding the war effort, Dundas placed increased emphasis on the need for regular military and naval activity to protect Britain's trading empire. Like Pitt, Dundas also firmly believed that France was on the verge of defeat and that the war would be short-lived, a belief which contributed to his desire to despatch a sizeable British expedition to secure the West Indies and capture as many French-controlled Caribbean islands as possible before the end of hostilities.[102] The ministers' assumption that the war in Europe would be short-lived would come to undermine British strategy and contribute greatly to British defeat in 1793.

The 1793 Campaign and the Road to Dunkirk

Following the Antwerp conference, the British agreed to advance south to Tournai in order to link up with Coburg's army.[103] This decision appears to have been taken without much thought as to whether the British forces in the Low Countries were up to the task. Apart from the weaknesses inherent in the British military establishment at the time, the British forces in the Low Countries were so few in number that they could hardly be referred to as an army. For instance, before the arrival of the first contingent of Hanoverians in late April, York's 'army' was made up of barely six infantry battalions, comprising the three strengthened Guards battalions under Lake and a further three battalions of line infantry under the newly arrived Major General Ralph Abercromby.[104] Excluding the Guards, the quality of York's force was not of a high order. Abercromby's brigade, which was composed of the 14th, 37th and 53rd Regiments of Foot, was barely fit for service having absorbed several hundred new recruits from a series of independent companies before it had embarked for the Continent.[105] Of the three newly arrived regiments, the 53rd was in the worst condition and, although York received an apology from the Horse Guards for the condition of Abercromby's force, he was forced to leave the 53rd at Bruges where it was to be made ready for action.[106]

Due to the limited number of British troops the Austrians had generously given York control over a force of Austrian cavalry, whilst the Prussians had also provided two battalions of infantry; these troops were to stay with the British until the arrival of Marshal Freytag's Hanoverian forces.[107] With the British likely to be involved in siege work, York's unofficial chief of staff, Colonel Sir James Murray asked for a 'Train of battering cannon and other requisites for a siege'.[108] Murray failed to list any specifics at this stage, the British concentrating instead upon making arrangements for the arrival of the Hanoverians.

As Hanoverian reinforcements began to arrive, the British generals spent much of late April and early May discussing the advance with the Austrians.[109] Coburg's plan was not a bold one, the Austrian commander favouring a limited offensive in order to seize a number of fortresses instead of a bold advance to destroy the French forces. A cautious stratagem which somewhat typified the ponderous nature of Hapsburg military planning during the *Ancien Régime*.[110] This limited form of warfare was not unique to the Austrians and had been developed by others during the previous century, as a means to safeguard the professionally trained soldiery of the European great powers. Expectations of what could be achieved by pitched battles were low and many thinkers believed that the risks involved in fighting a major battle were too high for it to be actively sought. Furthermore, the fact that most armies generally did not live off the land during the period before the Napoleonic wars, meant that it was imperative for generals to secure enemy cities in order to feed and reequip their troops. As R.R. Palmer has argued, prior to the French Revolution several important considerations encouraged military leaders to advocate a guarded approach to war and warfare:

> Wars were long, but not intense; battles were destructive (for the battalion volleys were deadly), but for that reason not eagerly sought. Operations turned by preference against fortresses, magazines, supply lines, and key positions ... war of positions prevailed over war of movement, and a strategy of small successive advantages over a strategy of annihilation.[111]

Although Lille was initially earmarked as the next objective for the Anglo-Austrian armies, alongside Condé, the Allies quickly changed their minds when it was discovered that a sizeable French army had taken up a defensive position to the south of the city of Valenciennes.[112] Eager to retain the services of the British for as long as possible, the Austrians managed to convince York that the French forces on the coast were too strong to be attacked until after the French army at Valenciennes had been dealt with. Once Valenciennes was captured, Coburg promised York that he would not object to the Anglo-Hanoverians marching to besiege Dunkirk.

York was happy with these changes, Murray exclaimed to Dundas that 'Every professional man acquainted with the fortress in question is decidedly of the opinion that Valenciennes will be a much easier conquest than Lille', and that until Valenciennes fell and French troops were drawn away from the coast 'There was an evident impossibility in any separate enterprise whatever being undertaken by His Royal Highness.'[113] As York and Coburg marched to Valenciennes another Austrian army, under the command of General Clerfaiyt, was to besiege Condé. With the campaign decided upon, the British generals were happy to forget temporarily about Dunkirk and placed the thought of a coastal campaign to one side. Their failure to plan for the advance to the coast at this stage would later prove significant.

Over the course of May the Anglo-Hanoverian forces participated in a series of engagements in support of the Austrians at the minor battles of Vicogne, St Armand and also in the Allied attack on the entrenched camp at Famars on 23 May. In each instance, the Anglo-Hanoverians performed well, although the Coldstream Guards suffered heavy losses.[114] At Famars, York's forces were largely spectators when the cautious Austrians forced the French to abandon their positions outside Valenciennes.[115] With the French secure inside the city, the Allies readied itself for a long siege.

Remarkably, given the number of times British troops had served in Flanders over the course of the eighteenth century, the siege of Valenciennes was the first occasion since the War of the Spanish Succession (1701–14) that the British army had participated in besieging a major European fortress.[116] However, British inexperience in European siege warfare, combined with the small scale of British forces, meant that York's troops played only a minor role in the siege. With little to do save oversee the digging of trenches and the construction of earthworks, the British high command turned their thoughts to Dunkirk.

Planning and Preparation

Alongside the desire to retain the strategic initiative over the French and secure their own aims at the expense of the Austrians, the British were eager to secure Dunkirk for a number of other reasons. Chief amongst these was the fact that the French had long used the port as a staging area for an invasion of the British Isles and in 1744 Marshal de Saxe had gathered over 70,000 men in the environs of Dunkirk for this very reason and had only been unable to put his plans into effect because of poor weather in the English Channel.[117] Whilst in 1773 a plan had been mooted to close the port of Dunkirk to French vessels in the event of the outbreak of another war with France.[118] Dundas and York also believed that a victory on the coast would provide them with the means to restore some pride to the army and enable them to destroy one of the last known safe havens of privateers in Western Europe.[119]

However, what is striking about the correspondence between the generals and the ministers in these weeks is the overconfidence displayed by York and Murray regarding the siege of Dunkirk. Despite the British army's lack of experience in European siege warfare Murray made it clear to Dundas that the weak state of the French army practically made it inevitable that the British would be able to achieve a swift victory on the coast and stated that '40,000 effective men were, in the present situation of the French army, a force fully adequate to the reduction of Dunkirk'.[120]

This belief in the weakness of the French army was central to the British mind set, for the generals, like the politicians before them, believed that France was on the brink of defeat and would not be able to reinforce the Flanders coast. Murray wrote to Dundas that, 'in the present distracted state of France,' there was no reason to believe that the French would be able to make 'any great augmentation of force' upon the coast.[121] Once the Anglo-Hanoverian forces reached Dunkirk the 20,000-strong British contingent, under York, would besiege Dunkirk whilst the Hanoverians acted as an 'Army of Observation.'[122] Murray also suggested to Dundas that York aimed to follow-up the siege of Dunkirk with operations against Bergues and St Venant.[123]

Although seemingly well-thought out, Murray's plan did little more than set out how the British were to march to the coast and that the British and Hanoverian forces would operate separately when they reached Dunkirk. Nothing was done to secure accurate intelligence about Dunkirk's defences or the condition of the French forces in the region, whilst nobody sought to gather information about the character of the roads or the layout of the Flanders canal network. At no point did York, or Murray, see the need to conduct a thorough reconnaissance of the area in question. Instead, Murray had the audacity to ask Dundas if the minister could make enquiries about the logistical situation on the coast, specifically whether vessels could transport the siege train via the canal network from Nieuport to Dunkirk.[124] Asking Dundas to perform such a basic military task was perverse, given the close proximity of the British forces to the Flanders coast. The generals also ignored the need for naval support. This was bizarre given that one of the main reasons for the coastal campaign was that the British could nullify the threat posed by French privateers based at Dunkirk. The port needed to be sealed off from both land and sea if the British wanted to invest the town and conduct a swift siege. That such a fact went unnoticed by the British generals as they planned the siege illustrated their incompetence.

The one aspect which the British spent time trying to organise was the procurement of a siege train. Murray finally forwarded an extensive list of requirements for the siege to Dundas and Pitt. This had been drawn up by York's senior ordnance officers, Major William Congreve and Colonel Moncrief.[125] The requirements were disproportionate to the task; for instance, Congreve wanted over 130 pieces of artillery, thousands of round shot, mortar shells and the all-necessary waggons, horses and drivers. Moncrief also demanded several hundred tons of oak planks for the construction of the siege works plus thousands of spades, pickaxes and sand-bags.[126] The scale of the list no doubt shocked Dundas, but instead of questioning York's judgement he placed the task of procuring the necessary materials in the hands of Richmond. Murray also informed Dundas that it was York's intention to reach the coast by about the beginning of September which gave the government, and the Ordnance, roughly two months to ready and ship the siege equipment.[127]

This was a mammoth task and one which angered Richmond, who had little sympathy for Pitt and Dundas's Flanders strategy.[128] Despite these reservations, Pitt managed to convince the Master General of the need to keep up to date with York's expected arrival time on the Flanders coast.[129] From this moment onwards every arrangement, contract and preparation was made with September in mind. Time was of the essence. The generals' failure to gather up-to-date information about the situation on the coast was further compounded by the failure to use existing sources of information. On several occasions in the 1700s the British were given responsibility for dismantling Dunkirk's defences and in 1773 an ensign based at Dunkirk made a series of observations regarding the ports defences and layout.[130] By the early 1790s these reports, alongside several maps, were stored by the Ordnance Office. As will become apparent later in the book, however, the British army's lack of a culture of knowledge sharing meant that these documents were forgotten by the time of the Flanders campaign and thus were not presented to York for the Dunkirk campaign.

Valenciennes surrendered to the Anglo-Austrian besieging forces on 28 July 1793. The sudden fall of Valenciennes was greeted with jubilation by the British. Murray wrote excitedly to Dundas that York's army would now be able to reach the Flanders coast by the end of August.[131] Murray did not ask Dundas whether this change would affect the movement of the siege train. Instead he carried on with readying the Anglo-Hanoverian forces for the march north. At the same time, the British commanders in the Low Countries were made an offer by the Austrians which promised to alter the course of the campaign. Keen to capitalise on French defeats, and no doubt eager to prevent the British from moving to the coast, Coburg suggested that the Allied forces advance to destroy the French forces in central Flanders, followed by an aggressive final offensive to crush the revolutionaries in Paris.[132]

The response of the British high command to Coburg's suggestion was highly questionable and bordered on unprofessional. Instead of thinking through the positives of the Austrian plan, York and Murray dismissed Coburg's plans out of hand. Murray even wrote to Dundas to state that he did not think it necessary to 'Trouble you [Dundas] with the particulars of this plan'.[133] Nor did they alter the expected arrival date of the army on the coast. By not informing Dundas and Pitt of the 'particulars' of the new Austrian proposals both York and Murray acted far beyond their authority and may have let slip a golden opportunity to end the war.

Over the course of the next few days York met with Coburg to decide when the British could be released to march to the coast. After much discussion, York informed the politicians that his Anglo-Hanoverians would reach the coast by 22 August.[134] As the British rushed to prepare their forces further planning errors ensued. The most significant related to Murray's request to Dundas for information about the Flanders canal network. Dundas was a busy man and was greatly preoccupied with overseeing preparations for the siege of Dunkirk and was also monitoring the situation at Toulon.[135] Weighed down by an increasingly unhealthy workload and lacking detailed knowledge of the Flanders coast, Dundas instructed General George Ainslie, the British commander at Ostend, to assess whether it was possible for a siege train to be transported by canal from Nieuport to Dunkirk.

Seeking to keep matters as secretive as possible, Ainslie organised a night-time spying mission. The conditions did not suit the task in hand and in the darkness each of the canals must have looked identical to Ainslie's agent, something which made the correct identification of the right canal impossible. The presence of French patrols also hindered the spy's task resulting in his having to hide in a marsh to avoid capture.[136] Cold, soaked and tired from the experience, the spy reported to Ainslie the following morning, but owing to the general lack of knowledge about the area in question and the difficulty inherent in working at night in hostile terrain, the spy had in fact reconnoitred the wrong canal. The mission having failed, York and Dundas chose not to sanction any further missions, a decision which left Ainslie embarrassed and the British none the wiser.[137] Despite the many questions left unanswered by this fiasco, York and Murray seem to have been unperturbed by the events in question and focused instead on readying the troops for the march north.

On 21 August, the Anglo-Hanoverians reached the Flanders coast. The journey from Valenciennes had not been without incident. Having set off on 15 August in several columns, the Anglo-Hanoverians parted company with Coburg after defeating a French force at the Battle of Caesar's Camp on 7–8 August. This victory was quickly followed by another, this time for York, at the minor Battle of Lincelles on 18 August. This action was a rare victory for the British against the French. Having arrived on the field after a force of Dutch had been pushed off a hill near the village of Lincelles, Lake and his Guardsmen proceeded to advance, in parade ground fashion, up the hill and into the fire of over 6,000 French infantry and their supporting artillery. Bayonets fixed, the guardsmen drove all before them and cleared the road to the coast in the process.[138]

Lake's charge at Lincelles deserves to be remembered as one of the finest military exploits of the French Revolutionary Wars and remained the greatest single victory for a force of British infantry over their French counterparts until the Egyptian campaign in 1801. The conduct of the guards at Lincelles epitomised all that was good about how British troops were prepared for small-scale tactical operations, ones in which the regimental values of the British army could come to the fore. It was fortunate, therefore, that the task of attacking the French forces at Lincelles fell to Lake's troops, the guardsmen being the finest British troops under the York's command. The victory at Lincelles generated overconfidence on the part of the British high command. For example, Murray boasted to Dundas shortly afterwards that he believed that Dunkirk would surrender the moment that the British siege train arrived.[139]

On reaching the coast, the Anglo-Hanoverian forces pushed back French outposts and prepared the ground for the siege train. To the south of Dunkirk, Freytag's 'Army of Observation' screened the British positions, the Hanoverian forces forming a defensive arc 10 miles to the south-east of Dunkirk between the French-held town of Bergues and the village of Poperinghe. British intelligence regarding the strength of the French on the Flanders coast was sketchy at best. The British were aware that a sizeable French garrison protected Cassel and that Dunkirk and Bergues were garrisoned but, other than this information, little was known about French troop movements behind the lines.

No sooner did the British arrive outside Dunkirk than things started to go wrong. The first issue was the appearance off Dunkirk of French gunboats. Fast moving and agile in shallow coastal waters, the gunboats immediately began to bombard the British troops that were stationed in the sand dunes and in the main camp.[140] The British had not thought to organise a naval force of their own before marching to the coast and, in the end, it was Dundas who took it upon himself to gather a force of naval vessels to support the army. On 31 August Dundas instructed Rear Admiral John MacBride to prepare a squadron to support York's operations.[141] This was a sound decision because a naval force would not only provide the British with a means to combat the French gunboats, but would also enable them to blockade the port. Disdainful of what he believed to be ministerial meddling, Murray's response to Dundas's decision was short-sighted, 'Upon the subject of naval cooperation … tho' it is no doubt proper upon many accounts to send the squadron you have announced, I do not look upon it to be very material towards the siege'.[142]

Why Murray did not recognise the 'material' value to be gained by having a naval force stationed off Dunkirk is unclear given that Murray was no stranger to amphibious operations, having participated in a number of combined operations earlier in his military career, in both North America and the West Indies.[143] Furthermore, although he disregarded the merits of having a naval squadron stationed just off the Flanders coast, Murray had previously asked Dundas for sailors to transport the siege train from Nieuport to Dunkirk.[144] Why Murray had only wanted sailors and no other naval force to support the army was strange and highlights the peculiar nature of Murray's thinking at this point in the campaign. The fact that York placed great trust in Murray's military thought is indicative of his limited military knowledge at this time.

The character of the coastal terrain was also something of a surprise for the British. York and Murray only realised the importance of the canal system as a means of defence when they arrived on the coast. The canals and dykes provided ideal defensive lines for the French whilst the broken country between the dykes suited the fleet-footed tactics of the French light infantry and hampered the movement of the large British baggage train. It was also not until the British arrived that they realised that by cutting the sea dykes and opening sluice gates the French could inundate the area between Dunkirk and Bergues and flood the fields to the east of Dunkirk. The British did not recognise the danger until it was too late. The French commander at Dunkirk, Jacques Ferrand, had instantly cut the sea dykes when it was clear a British force was intent on attacking the port.[145] The wet summer weather did not help the situation either, the summer rains having already flooded some of the fields before the sea water began to rise. Despite these problems, York and Murray remained confident of a quick victory and Murray told Dundas that, 'The inundations will have no effect in preventing the siege'.[146] As will become clear, the British would come to rue the French decision to cut the dykes.

In the meantime, other problems needed to be overcome if the siege was to be a success. A more important problem for the British at this stage was logistics. Since arriving on the coast, the British had expected the siege train to arrive promptly, but there was little sign of the convoy. Ten days after York's troops had reached the coast the first convoy of vessels carrying part of the siege train finally arrived at Ostend and Nieuport, aboard were twenty-four mortars and thirty-six 24-pounders.[147] Further delays ensued however due to the fact that the British port authorities had packed vital engineering equipment, which was needed by York before the guns could be placed in position, underneath the siege guns. This dilemma forced the seamen at Ostend and Nieuport to unload all of the cargo before they could transport the guns to Dunkirk.[148] The arrival of the first batch of artillery was greeted with relief by the British high command, but concerns remained, notably that not all of the requested ordnance had arrived. Nevertheless, the British worked quickly over the course of the first week of September to prepare the batteries to bombard Dunkirk. British enthusiasm would prove short-lived, however, thanks the efforts of a rejuvenated French army and the over-confidence of Freytag and York.

Before analysing the French preparations for a counter-attack, it is necessary to outline the nature of the Hanoverian forces and their dispositions. Freytag's 'Army of Observation' was located 10 miles to the south of York's camp at Dunkirk, the Hanoverian forces deployed in a defensive cordon 20 miles long and several miles deep. The first outpost line covered the villages of Wormdhout, Herzeele, Houtkerque and Poperinghe; a stronger second line guarded the villages of Bambecque, Rousbrugge and Quaedypre. If the distances involved were problematic enough, the existence of a large area of marshland, immediately east of the French-held town of Bergues between the British camp and the Hanoverian outposts, was a serious impediment to swift communication between the Anglo-Hanoverian forces.

The French inundations and limited number of dyke roads also made communication between the British and the Hanoverians difficult. The broken nature of the Flanders countryside did not suit the Prussian-style tactics of the Hanoverians. The French, by contrast, were much better equipped to fighting on the coast, the canals and dyke roads providing them with a series of ready-made earthworks, a perfect setting for French light troops to operate. French control of the canal networks also gave their troops an advantage and enabled them to maintain speedy communications and an efficient supply system. The British and the Hanoverians struggled to drag supplies to the front from Ostend and found it problematic to source adequate forage and drinking water in their flooded positions.

The actual strength of the Anglo-Hanoverian force was also an issue, with Freytag having barely 12,000 troops at his disposal, whilst the majority York's force at Dunkirk was tied down. Freytag's contingent consisted of four regiments of line infantry, one of light infantry, a guard's battalion, three divisions of artillery, eight cavalry regiments and a force of horse guards.[149] The quality of the Hanoverian contingent was good; Freytag's cavalry and artillery were highly rated by the British.[150] Despite the quality of the Hanoverians, the large area of ground which York had expected Freytag to cover meant that the Hanoverians were too widely dispersed to resist a major French attack without British aid. The French *Armée du Nord*, in contrast, was concentrated and ready to strike.

By the spring of 1793 French defeats coupled with the outbreak of insurrection in the Vendée had resulted in the creation of a new government organisation which was tasked with the direction of the war effort and the maintenance of public order – the Committee of Public Safety (CPS).[151] Driven by a determination to regain the strategic initiative and save France from invasion the CPS alongside the Committee of General Security (CGS) orchestrated the mass conscription of French citizens into the armed forces. The first of these major levees in 1793 was known as the February *Levée des 300,000*; followed in August by the more famous *Levée en Masse*.[152] Further measures were also taken to try to improve the fighting quality of the French armies and the Republic's officer corps, such as the reorganisation of the French infantry into demi-brigades and, with reference to new ideas and older French military theorists, combat divisions.[153] As the new formations integrated, the CPS also took the decision to send representatives to each of the French armies, with orders to inform the government of the quality and conduct of the various French commanders in the field.[154]

Further actions taken by the CPS and CGS included the cultivation of a greater revolutionary zeal amongst French troops in order to attain new heights of bravery and aggression in the defence of France. The hostile European powers such as Austria, Prussia and Great Britain, and the internal opponents of the revolution were to be terrified into submission. With this vision in mind, the CPS sought to reclaim the initiative against the coalition powers with the French being especially eager to strike against the Allied forces in the Austrian Netherlands and restore their so-called 'Natural Frontier' in the Low Countries.

Even before the French had been aware of the Anglo-Hanoverian advance to the coast, Carnot himself had decided that the French forces in Flanders needed to strike at the weak Allied positions on the coast and Ostend was singled out as a prime target. The raiding force assembled for this task, under Generals Jean-Baptiste Jourdan and Antoine de Béru, had moved north from Douai and Lille in mid-August. But they were surprised and defeated by Lake's guardsmen at Lincelles.[155]

The presence of York's Anglo-Hanoverians on the Flanders coast had forced Jourdan to retreat to the relative safety of Cassel and Dunkirk. Carnot had responded by rapidly readying Dunkirk for a siege and reinforcing the French forces at Cassel. Throughout August and early September 28,250 men were sent from the French armies of the *Moselle* and *Rhin* whilst a further 2,750 men were sent northwards from the *Ardennes*.[156] The French forces on the coast were then reorganised into several different interdependent commands. The *Groupe du Nord*, comprising 23,500 men, under General Nicolas Barthel, was stationed at Cassel. To the east, was the *Mauberge* with a fighting strength of 18,000. Finally, in the centre, was the 58,900 strong *Corps Principal* under Houchard, making for a total of 100,400 effective men. Once assimilated into the various garrisons across French-held Flanders, including Dunkirk, the operational combat strength of the *Nord* amounted to around 50,000 officers and men.[157]

Changes were also made to the French chain of command. Jourdan, who was already a divisional commander, was chosen to command the garrisons at Dunkirk and Cassel in place of Barthel. General Joseph Souham was also replaced by Jacques Ferrand, whilst further down the chain of command some future heroes of Napoleon's *Grande Armée* were given their first chance to shine, most notably a young Captain Édouard Mortier who found himself promoted to the rank of Lieutenant Colonel Adjutant General, based at Dunkirk.[158] Mortier would prove to be a wise choice. Other future Napoleonic officers who would distinguish themselves in the Dunkirk campaign included Lieutenant Michel Ney, Lieutenant Colonel Jean-Victor Moreau, who commanded a volunteer battalion, Captain Jean-Baptiste Bernadotte, General of Brigade Jacques MacDonald and Lieutenant Colonel Dominique Vandamme.[159]

Despite possessing the element of surprise and having the benefit of numerical superiority, Houchard was not the most aggressive of French generals and his plan erred on the side of caution. The Nord was to advance in six columns, five of which were to push back the Hanoverians, whilst another was to force

York to abandon the siege of Dunkirk. Houchard did not desire a decisive battle, but simply wanted to protect French Flanders, before planning a new offensive to strike back at the Austrians.

The French dispositions prior to their advance on 6 September were as follows: 3 columns, with a combined strength of 20,800, under the command of Pierre Dumesny and Vandamme, were stationed to the west of Cassel and had instructions to advance to the north against the enemy outposts stationed in the villages of Poperinghe, Proven, Rousbrugge and Oost-Cappel. In the French centre, Jourdan, with 13,000 troops, was to strike Wormdhout and Herzeele, which, unbeknownst to the French, was the centre of Freytag's outer line of outposts. To Jourdan's left were a further 12,000 French troops, formed in 2 columns; the closest to Jourdan, under General Jean Noel Landrin, was positioned on high ground just to the north of Cassel. Landrin was ordered to strike at Wormdhout. The other column, under Theodore Leclaire at Bergues, was to advance eastwards against the British forces to the south of the swampy ground. Finally, Ferrand was to attack York's siege works with 6,000 men.[160]

Despite being aware of the movement of sizeable French reinforcements to the coast, York and Freytag were not aware of the full scale of the French force marshalled before them. The accuracy of reports regarding French troop movements was sketchy at best. Murray knew that French reinforcements were gathering at Cassel and near St Omer, but he did not know how many troops were involved nor what the French intended.[161] Yet, despite the French troop movements, York apparently did not think it necessary to send out further scouts or send reinforcements to Freytag.

The key battle for the fate of Dunkirk was fought to the south-east of the port as Houchard's attacking columns made several deep indentations into Freytag's defensive cordon between 6 and 7 September; Vandamme's column seized Poperinghe, Landrin halted at Wormdhout, whilst Jourdan pushed through the centre, only to be halted by several counter-attacks.[162] Ferrand's garrison also conducted a spirited sortie against the British trenches on the evening of 6 September which, though bravely conducted, made little headway.[163] However, with the cordon punctured and no sign of reinforcements from York, Freytag ordered his troops to withdraw. The retreat was not without incident and at Rexpoede, York's brother, Prince Adolphus Duke of Cambridge and Freytag were wounded.[164] The two commanders were eventually saved by the arrival of Count Walmoden who led the battle-ready Hanoverians to the village of Hondschoote.

On 8 September Houchard threw caution to the wind and attacked Walmoden's 14,600 Hanoverians with around 22,000 French troops.[165] A bloody battle of attrition ensued and despite brave Hanoverian resistance the French were victorious.[166] Informed of Walmoden's defeat and fearful of being encircled, York abandoned the siege of Dunkirk and retired in the evening of 9 September. Such was the speed of the British retreat that two battalions of infantry were almost left behind at the village of Tetteghem.[167] In the rush to escape York decided not to save the siege guns and also abandoned the army's stores, equipment and baggage; something which would be repeated by the British at Dunkirk just under a century-and-a-half later during Operation DYNAMO in June 1940.

Aftermath

Murray was quick to inform Dundas of the unfortunate events and stated 'With extreme sorrow' that following the defeat of the Hanoverians at Hondschoote, York was 'reduced to the necessity of collecting his whole force by abandoning the position he had taken near Dunkirk'. Murray was also sad to point out that in the process the British had been forced to leave 'Thirty-two of the heavy guns and part of the stores provided for the siege'.[168]

The sudden retreat was not a pleasant experience for the British troops due to the wet summer weather which had churned up the already muddy roads. The Royal Artillery and the cavalry also found it tough going, with gun carriages and horses often getting stuck in the mud, whilst both services also lacked the quantities of forage necessary to feed their horses adequately. In scenes not dissimilar to those which British soldiers would later experience on the Western Front in the late summer of 1917, York's troops slogged their way through the mud to safety. Perhaps the most harrowing example of the suffering experienced by the British in the retreat occurred on the beach at Nieuport when, in the rush to escape the French, almost an entire waggon-load of sick and wounded soldiers was drowned by the incoming tide.[169]

The lack of a dedicated military transport service in the British Army was also a cause of considerable frustration. The British had hired civilian carts and drivers earlier in the campaign and found that, under pressure, the drivers were not suited to the task in hand and neither were the carts. The few carts that the British brought back from the siege were so overloaded that many simply fell to pieces as they were dragged through the many quagmires which covered the roads. Dead and exhausted horses also littered the route of the British retreat. Furthermore, with much of the baggage left behind, many of the British troops were also without their tents and blankets. As one officer recalled:

> The army, it may be supposed, is not well satisfied: but in the anguish
> of their disappointment and distress they know not who to blame,
> the difficulties under which they labour are truly pitiable. Scarcely

can even the officers obtain the necessities of life; and many of them are without a change of linen. What then must be the situation of the poor soldiers? In the brigade of guards, which we may conclude to be as well provided at least as the others, there is only one tent to every ten men; and they have not a single truss of straw to save from entering contact with the cold, damp ground. Add to this the present heavy rains, and then conceive what sickness and mortality may close the miseries of the present campaign![170]

The conditions accelerated the onset of disease amongst the cold and hungry soldiers. The troops had started to fall ill in the swampy conditions before Dunkirk and many more cases emerged as the Allied forces retreated. The worsening state of the Anglo-Hanoverians was of great concern to Murray whom, in a letter to Henry Dundas, expressed the fears of the British high command at what might happen if the weakened Allied forces were attacked by the French:

The state of this army is very distressing. The troops being too much dispersed … I cannot give you an exact account of the numbers either of sick or of the fit for duty, which I am sorry to find vary considerably from what they were … I understand that we have in all, Austrians included 8 or 9,000 sick and wounded. Garrison men be left and posts maintained, so that after the departure of the four regiments, there will not be above 12,000 … men in camp, so that if the enemy should direct their principal effort against us … I fear it will be necessary to give up Ostend.[171]

Murray and York were also concerned about the withdrawal of four infantry regiments, the British government having requested earlier in the campaign for York to spare a brigade of infantry for service elsewhere. With the Anglo-Hanoverian forces close to breaking point, it was fortunate that the other Allied forces were still relatively fresh and the French were eventually checked by the determined Austrians at the two-day Battle of Wattignies fought on 15–16 October.[172] The campaigning season ended with both sides poised to make a bid for a decisive action the following year.

In late November 1793, the Anglo-Hanoverian army entered winter quarters. At long last the York and his subordinates had an opportunity to rest, take stock and prepare for the next campaign. The British officer corps and the senior generals in British service certainly had much to learn about how to operate in European conditions, whilst a period of rest and recuperation was also exactly what the British and Hanoverian soldiers needed.

In spite of the poor showing in Flanders, neither York nor any of his subordinate officers sought to undertake a thorough review of the campaign in order to try to highlight errors of judgement and identify potential lessons to be learnt. As far as York was concerned the failure at Dunkirk and the Anglo-Hanoverian defeat in the wider campaign in Flanders were not of his or his soldiers making. Although he opted to keep silent in public, in private York was all too eager to lay the blame for the defeat upon the British politicians, the Hanoverians and the Austrians. Indeed, no sooner had the British been forced to retreat from Dunkirk than York wrote to his father, the King, to exonerate himself and blame others for the defeat.[173]

Despite having every right to be frustrated with the conduct of the politicians, York's letter to his father was riddled with fabrications designed to shift the blame. York argued that 'Sir James Murray applied in My name to Your Majesty's ministers for … a sufficient naval force to co-operate with me, and to protect me against the enemy's vessels'. York also argued that Freytag had repeatedly disobeyed his instructions.[174] York clearly did not request naval support when he claimed to have done so, nor is there evidence to suggest that Freytag acted in any less a professional manner than any other officer might have done in the circumstances. Freytag's instructions were vague at best and York expected Freytag to defend a very wide area, with barely enough troops for the purpose. Although Freytag underestimated the strength of the French forces in the area, it is unlikely that any of the British generals would have acted differently, since both the British and the Hanoverians believed the French to be poor soldiers in the wake of Lincelles.[175]

It was also highly misleading for York to suggest that he was aware of the French troop build-up before Freytag was since it was from the Hanoverians that York received much of his information. Indeed, Freytag's outposts stretched almost to Cassel itself, this town known by the British to be one of the main staging areas for French forces in northern Flanders.[176] Although Freytag was certainly foolhardy in disregarding many of the reports that indicated that sizeable French reinforcements were nearby, it must be remembered that it was York who had the final say when it came to the deployment of the Allied troops on the coast. If York had feared for his left flank and wanted Freytag to keep in close contact with the British camp at Dunkirk, he could have ordered Freytag to concentrate closer to Dunkirk or sent a force of British troops to support the Hanoverians. By not doing so, York isolated Freytag just at the moment when he most needed to concentrate his forces.

The main reasons for the British defeat at Dunkirk, namely poor planning on the part of York and his senior commanders and lack of accurate intelligence information, thus went unrecognised. The British habit of blaming their Allies did little to aid faltering coalition relations. Freytag, for all his experience, lost control of his Hanoverian forces in the retreat and was somewhat foolhardy prior to the French attack. Nevertheless, Freytag and Walmoden put up a sound defence during the initial French offensives on 6–7 September. York and Freytag were lucky to have a general of Walmoden's quality on whom they could rely. Walmoden acted with great courage and skill in both the retreat to Hondschoote and during the battle. Indeed, if York had acted with greater calm during the initial French attacks, he could have sent reinforcements to support Walmoden, since the British troops at Dunkirk were hardly engaged until Ferrand's sortie.

If York had sent reinforcements to Walmoden at Hondschoote, the outcome of the battle might have been different given the fact that, despite possessing a numerical superiority over the Allies in the wider theatre of operations, Houchard's troops had suffered greatly during the earlier battles and were dispersed over a wide area. Although the terrain made the use of Walmoden's cavalry almost impossible, reducing the Hanoverians' effective strength to 9,000 infantry, Walmoden's soldiers were better trained and equipped than their more numerous French opponents and the Hanoverians were also in possession of a strong defensive position.

Thus, despite the French numerical superiority, Walmoden's troops provided stubborn resistance. If York had opted to rush to Walmoden's aid, the Anglo-Hanoverians might have been able to achieve a much needed victory. Eager to save the British troops under his command, however, York left the Hanoverians to keep the French at bay whilst the British extricated themselves from Dunkirk. By the end of the battle Walmoden's force was spent and, in the words of one Hanoverian officer, the Hanoverians could 'no longer to be depended upon'.[177] In leaving the Hanoverians to fight the French alone at Hondschoote, York sacrificed his German allies in order to save his British troops. That the Hanoverians performed this thankless task exemplified their fighting spirit and professional pride whilst, in contrast, the British retreat was uncoordinated and confused.[178]

Fundamentally, poor planning on the part of the British high command led to the failure of the coastal campaign in 1793, but as the following chapter demonstrates the British learnt nothing from this defeat and repeated many of the same mistakes during the following campaign in the Low Countries.

Chapter 2

British Defeat in the Netherlands, 1794–5 and the Duke of York's Reforms

Following their defeats at Dunkirk and Hondschoote York's forces had continued to retreat until the onset of extreme cold forced a halt to active operations and the British entered winter quarters. Not only did this offer the British a golden period of rest, but it also presented them with an opportunity to review what had gone wrong in 1793 so that they could fight more effectively the following year. However, although the British busied themselves with administrative tasks, nobody recognised the need to evaluate the past campaign or to analyse why things had gone so badly wrong at Dunkirk. The situation was further compounded by the fact that many senior officers, including York, spent the winter on leave in London and command of the army in Flanders was temporarily handed to the newly promoted Lieutenant General Sir William Harcourt.[1] With few senior officers on hand to help him in his new role, Harcourt was content to merely work on administrative issues and thus the lessons of 1793 were not identified.

On his return to the Low Countries in January 1794, York also eschewed the need for any kind of review and focused instead on preparing the army for active operations.[2] There was one notable personnel change with Murray being appointed to take command of a brigade of infantry in order to make way for Colonel James Craig to act as York's senior ADC.[3] Administrative aspects apart, the Duke also made contact with the Austrians and the Dutch in order to ascertain what they sought to achieve in the new campaign. During these discussions, the British were aided by a former French officer, Major General François Jarry de Vrigny de la Villette, whose knowledge of the French army and local topography was highly regarded.[4] After several meetings with the ambitious Austrian chief-of-staff, Colonel Karl Mack von Leiberich, York accepted the new Austrian strategy, which again called for an Allied offensive in Flanders to drive the revolutionaries back to the frontiers of France.[5] As with the previous campaign, the Austrians did not desire a decisive engagement with the French, but favoured a new thrust to seize a series of apparently vital strategic positions.[6]

After being reviewed by the Austrian Emperor at Le Cateau on 16 April the Anglo-Hanoverians and their Austrian counterparts launched their new offensive.[7] As in the early stages of the previous campaign, the Allies achieved some early successes and were quick to encircle the French-held fortress of Landrecies.[8] Over the course of the rest of April a French relief force, under Souham, tried repeatedly to break through the Allied advanced position in order to lift the siege. Despite Souham's best efforts, the French were defeated at the battles of Vaux, Villers-en-Cauchies, Beaumont and Willems.[9] The Anglo-Hanoverian army played a prominent role in each of these engagements and the infantry were well supported by the British and Austrian cavalry.

Following the capture of Landrecies, which fell to the Austrians on 30 April, the Allies advanced to the north-west and took up a series of positions between Courtrai and Menin.[10] The French, under Pichegru, were concentrated in the vicinity of Lille, but French troops also held positions as far north as Dunkirk and to south-west of Landrecies. Meanwhile, following the failed attempt to break the siege of Landrecies, Souham had tried to retire to Lille, but had been partially overtaken by Clerfaiyt's advance guard and had taken up a defensive position several miles to the east of Lille on the right bank of the River Lys. Although the Lys provided some protection from Clerfaiyt, the presence of the main Allied army to the south of this position greatly concerned Souham and Pichegru.

With the French forces divided, Coburg and York decided to attack the French before their forces could reunite. Under the supervision of Mack the Allied forces were divided into six attacking columns and ordered to converge to the west of Tourcoing in order to keep Souham away from Lille. Once this was achieved the Allies would then attack Pichegru and force Souham to surrender.[11] The success of the plan depended on the ability of the Allied commanders to cooperate effectively and coordinate the timing and speed of each of their respective attacks so that they reached their objectives in good order and with enough strike power to make a decisive blow. What Mack and his colleagues had not bargained for, however, was that the French had also planned to make a general attack and had positioned the bulk of their finest troops in close proximity to the planned Allied line of advance.[12]

Thus when the Allied columns began their narrow advance towards Tourcoing on 17 May they met with little resistance. However, unbeknownst to the Allied high command, the French had started their own advance and had made several major gains at the expense of the Allied troops on either flank. By the time Coburg was fully aware of the danger the Allied columns were already fully engaged and could not easily be coordinated. Over the course of the following day the main Allied attacks lost their impetus and the battle gradually degenerated into a number of confused engagements before Coburg and York were forced to order a general withdrawal.[13]

Although the Allies were able to make an orderly withdrawal after defeat at Tourcoing, the British ministers were alarmed by the defeat and feared a sudden French advance to threaten Ostend. With York unable to reach the coast, Henry Dundas despatched another expeditionary force of around 10,000 men, under the command of the highly experienced Major General Francis Rawdon Earl of Moira, to safeguard the Flanders coast.[14] Moira's force had spent much of December aboard ship in the English Channel, having failed to support the Royalist cause in Normandy and Brittany, and were thus on hand to be deployed to protect Ostend.[15] After having made a successful landing at Ostend, Moira was forced to move inland following news that the Austrians had been forced to withdraw towards Maastricht after the decisive French success at the Battle of Fleurus on 26 June 1794.[16] With the Austrians in full retreat, and the Dutch offering scant resistance, York and Moira retired from Flanders; the French secured Brussels and the great Belgic port of Antwerp in the process. The loss of Antwerp was a major blow for the British war effort, but with the survival of York's army at stake, the Prince had no choice but to abandon the city and its dockyards to the French.

During the late summer of 1794, the Anglo-Hanoverian army snaked its way through the United Provinces in search of a new defensive position.[17] This retreat was similar to the one which the British had conducted after Dunkirk and, yet again, it was far from well managed. 'O dear, O dear' wrote the commander of the newly arrived 85th Regiment of Foot, Lieutenant Colonel Edward Paget, brother of Lord Paget, 'We lost a waggon full of baggage in the last march'. The villains of the piece, according to Paget, were the inefficient and unprofessional commissary services: 'the Commissary Department want a great deal of scouring' and wrote further that his men were 'cheated' of their food and pay in the process.[18] Tired and hungry, Paget and the rest of the army were forced to keep on the run, the wet roads making progress slow. As a lieutenant in Paget's regiment noted, the veterans in the ranks also found it tough going: 'even old campaigners of America declared they never underwent a march of such exertion and fatigue'.[19]

Having crossed the frontier between the Southern Netherlands and the Dutch provinces in early September York decided to defend the River Maas.[20] The Duke's hopes were scuppered on 14 September when the French outflanked the Anglo-Hanoverian positions and captured the important village of Boxtel.[21] Although Abercomby reclaimed the village, by way of a bold counter-attack the following morning, York's faith in the river defences had been greatly shaken and he ordered the army to take up a new defensive position beyond the River Waal at Nijmegen.[22] The British reached the Waal several days later and spent the following two months creating what York hoped would be an unassailable defensive position behind the strong-flowing waters of the Waal and the River Lek.

Despite high hopes of being able to hold the French until the winter forced a halt to operations, the French continued to make offensive preparations and surprised the British by launching a number of attacks across the frozen Waal during the last days in December and into early January.[23] The British again made attempts to push the French back but, with French advancing in ever greater numbers, the British decided to fall back upon the River Lek and to the River Yssel. By this point the British forces were under the command of Harcourt, York having been recalled in December, due to political pressure.[24]

Over the course of the spring the Anglo-Hanoverian army made its sorry way across the heart of the United Provinces. Freezing in the winter cold and ravaged by sickness, hundreds of British and Hanoverian troops fell in droves by the roadside.[25] Ensign St George, a junior officer in the 80th Regiment of Foot, noted the harrowing account of the retreat:

> The cold was so intense on the march … (that) our breath was freezing as soon as emitted … The wind was so excessive high it drifted the snow and together so strong that we could hardly wrestle against it … Some so exhausted with fatigue were obliged to lie down … but when they woke they found their blood almost instantly congealed in their veins and so frost bitten as not to be able to stir … In one place 7 men, 1 woman and a child were found dead … A few men were found alive, but their hands and feet were frozen to such a degree as to be dropping off at the wrists and ankles.[26]

The hospital conditions that awaited those who were rescued from the roadside often proved to be as deadly as the frozen ground, as frostbitten men were laid side by side with those suffering from fever. The men of the 85th were also plagued by Caribbean fever, having sailed to the Low Countries in a transport which had previously been used to carry infected troops to Great Britain from the West Indies.[27] As Corporal Robert Brown noted, the hospital staff showed wanton disregard for the welfare of the sick and wounded:

> Removing the sick in waggons, without clothing sufficient to keep them warm in this rigorous season, has sent hundreds to their

eternal home; and the shameful neglect that prevails through all that department, makes our hospitals mere slaughter-houses; without covering, without attendance and even without clean straw and sufficient shelter from the weather, they are thrown together in heaps, unpitied, and unprotected, to perish by contagion.[28]

As conditions deteriorated so too did British discipline and the troops pillaged and raped their way across the Dutch landscape.[29] The increasingly despicable behaviour of the British towards the local population accentuated anti-British sentiment amongst the Dutch peasantry, who welcomed the French as liberators.[30] With little reason to remain in the United Provinces, the British hastened to the neutral city of Bremen, where they were finally evacuated by the Royal Navy.

Scratching the Surface: York's Reforms and the British Army

At the beginning of 1795 it became obvious that the war could be carried on in no satisfactory way by the system of temporary expedients and makeshifts which had hitherto been the only resource of the government. A step was therefore taken towards the re-establishment of the Army's discipline and efficiency by the appointment of the Duke of York to be Field Marshal Commanding-in-Chief.[31]

The promotion of York to the post of C-in-C was not greeted with any great fanfare and neither was it thought that much good would follow his appointment. As Lord Cornwallis noted, 'Whether we shall get any good by this, God only knows, but I think that things cannot change for the worse in that department'.[32] Furthermore, York was only appointed to the post in order to save face and placate the king's desire for his son to play a prominent role in the military establishment.[33] York's rise to the top of the command pyramid was not due to his skill as a commander or to any plan he had for the future of the army but was simply a case of the ministers seeking to safeguard the reputation of the Crown. Although some historians have suggested that York possessed 'an active appreciation of what was wrong with the Army', his knowledge of the key weaknesses was limited.[34] York did not have a reform 'blueprint' outlining the changes that needed to be made. Nor were the reforms motivated by any great desire on the part of the York, or his colleagues, to alter the status quo.

The reform process was triggered because the British army was clearly unready to meet the threat of French invasion. The duke thus found himself in a position of authority when changes were needed and the government was clearly concerned at the weak state of the nation's defences. York, therefore, set about his reforms because the situation of the nation's armed forces necessitated change at a time of crisis. The reforms were merely a reaction to the prevailing circumstances, rather than a product of constructive thinking based on lessons learnt from the campaigns in the Low Countries. Although some improvements were made, notably in the form of administrative changes, the reformers did not seek radical reform and neither did they transform the British army.

The Main Reforms and Their Impact

Administration

York's first act was his creation of a new post of Military Secretary, the inaugural appointee being Colonel Robert Brownrigg.[35] Until this point, all of the correspondence relating to the office of the C-in-C at Horse Guards had passed through the hands of a civilian official in the form of the Secretary at War.[36] This change was greatly welcomed because the previous Secretary at War, Sir George Yonge, had damaged the quality of the officer corps through the unregulated sale of commissions.[37] Despite the benefits of this reform, a less positive result of the creation of a new Military Secretary was that it distanced the office of the C-in-C from the rest of the political administration.

Over the course of his first five years in office, York stamped his authority upon the administration of the army by making a series of personnel changes, designed to place like-minded officers in key positions. Alongside Brownrigg, York appointed Major General Henry Fox to act as the first Inspector General of Recruiting, a position which was eventually subsumed into the AG's department. The latter position was held by Lieutenant General Sir William Fawcett, until 1799, when another acolyte of York's, Lieutenant General Sir Harry Calvert, assumed the role. Calvert, like Brownrigg and Fox, had come to the duke's attention in the Low Countries in 1793 to 1795 and remained in post until long after the end of the Napoleonic Wars.[38]

Others to hold positions of authority at the Horse Guards included: Colonel George Morrison; Colonel William Clinton; Lieutenant General Sir David Dundas; Major Generals George Hewett; John Whitelocke; John Willoughby Gordon and Sir Harry Torrens. The last two officers are perhaps the best known, as it was they who had most dealings with Wellington, during the latter years of the Peninsular War. The most controversial of the group was Whitelocke, whose career was cut short following his mishandling of the British expedition to Rio de Plata in 1807.[39]

Although some of these officers remained in their initial posts for the entirety of the period, there was some notable overlap in terms of responsibility. Brownrigg, for instance, vacated the post of Military Secretary in 1803, only to be appointed Quartermaster General (QMG). Willoughby Gordon shared the same career path as Brownrigg, the former replacing the latter as QMG in 1809, having first served in Brownrigg's old post of Military Secretary after taking over from Clinton in 1804.[40] These key individuals apart, the bulk of the administrative work was done by a small number of clerks.

At the War Office, the number of clerks rose steadily as the wars with France developed. In 1797 the Secretary at War, William Windham, could call on the services of 58 clerks, a number which swiftly grew to 208 by 1815. York never had more than 29 clerks at his disposal at any one time. Of all the military departments, the best staffed in numerical terms was the Ordnance, the Master General being able to call upon the services of 353 clerks in 1797 and up to 886 by 1815. By way of contrast, the Foreign Office was never served by more than 34 clerks, a number which although far smaller than the Ordnance, was still superior to the number available to York. Although the small number of staff at the Horse Guards meant that close working relationships developed, the reform process was not subject to the scrutiny of others and neither was there much scope for civilian input.

Although military historians tend to suggest that civilian influence upon military matters is not beneficial, recent research into the subject of military change has suggested otherwise. Instead of hindering the process of military change, those without close ties to the military, or those in positions of authority, are often better placed to provide an impartial perspective upon the need for political and military change and are more likely to pursue transformative developments than those with a vested interest in the existing system.[41] In 1810, for instance, the prominent Whig statesman and future Prime Minister, Sir Charles Grey, proposed a series of sweeping changes to the military establishment to improve the workings of the British military bureaucracy and to provide greater unity and purpose to British strategy.

Grey's plan was to amalgamate the various departments, such as the Ordnance and Horse Guards, into a single 'Board of War.' Grey envisaged that the new board would be modelled on the system used by the Admiralty and would be controlled by a First Lord who would be aided by a panel of four military commissioners. These senior figures would preside over the smooth running of seven administrative departments, organised according to their specific functions, such as the Medical Board and the office of the Adjutant General.[42] Despite the potential merits of these proposals Grey did not greatly publicise his ideas and it is also highly questionable whether they would have been accepted by the conservative-minded Portland administration.[43] What is significant about all of this is that York did not make anything like the changes

proposed by Grey during the period, changes which might have had a transformative effect on the British army. As it was those in power were content to
maintain the status quo, an approach which was repeated by Wellington when
he was C-in-C in 1827–8 and 1842–52.[44]

Much has also been made of the importance of York's decision to establish
a Depot of Military Knowledge in 1803.[45] Despite its grand title the depot was
little more than a cluttered store room, into which a series of miscellaneous
maps and plans were placed. Nor was the depot a new idea, something similar
had existed for several years in the form of the Tower of London Drawing
Room which had been created by the Ordnance Office in 1717.[46] The Drawing
Room had also a larger number of personnel working at the Tower in the years
before it was replaced.[47] The depot was not as effective as it could have been
and, on several occasions during the war years, commanders suffered from a
lack of adequate maps. The lack of improvement in this area was due to the
fact that, instead of changing the way the existing Drawing Office operated,
York simply gave the office a new name and did not impose a new rationale
or set of procedures for improvement. The Depot of Military Knowledge was
simply a place where dusty maps were stored, rather than a centre for the
development of military knowledge.

The Training of the Infantry

Although some historians have credited York with the decision to adopt David
Dundas's drills throughout the line regiments of the army, it has already been
noted that Amherst was first to recognise the potential of Dundas's training
methods; Dundas's drills were used by every regiment in Flanders in 1793–5.[48]
The reform of the training of the line infantry, therefore, was a gradual process
and one in which York played only a minor role.[49] Of greater significance for
the tactical flexibility of the British army in the period was the development
of light infantry.

Some historians, such as Mark Urban, have suggested the reforms made to
light infantry by officers such as Sir John Moore and Calvert stemmed from
the many 'lessons learned' in North America.[50] Although there is evidence to
suggest that the British did adopt looser tactics in America, due to the terrain,
and the general lack of heavy cavalry and massed artillery on American battlefields, it is highly questionable whether the British 'learnt' anything of any
great use from this conflict.[51] Not only was there no official review of the war
in the months after the signing of the Treaty of Paris in 1783, but few senior
British officers documented their experiences.[52] Furthermore, no official government inquiries were established to evaluate the tactical developments of

the American War and, over the course of the following years, British officers largely forgot what they had experienced.[53]

The situation was not helped by the fact that York did not see the need for a large body of light infantry until Britain was faced with invasion in 1803. There were also only a few officers who had detailed knowledge of light infantry tactics: these being Moore, Coote Manningham, William Stewart and Kenneth Mackenzie.[54] However, although these officers had some knowledge of light infantry, the lack of emphasis on the development of light infantry over the course of the previous years had left the British far behind their European rivals. With no official history or collective memory of the American War to rely on, Moore and his acolytes relied heavily on the technical knowledge of several foreign experts.[55] The creation of the famous 95th Rifles was also guided by foreign expertise, in the form of the Baron de Rottenburg, who had made a name for himself in the 60th Royal American Rifles and was the author of an influential English-language light infantry manual.[56] Without men like Rottenburg, the British army would not have been able to field light infantry of the quality for which they came to be known.

The Reform and the Officer Corps

One of the first steps taken by York was to impose stricter controls over promotions.[57] The motivation for this decision stemmed from the fact that during the campaigns in the Low Countries in 1793 to 1795 the quality of many of the regimental officers in the British army had been below par. As far as York and his colleagues at the Horse Guards were concerned, the main reason for the shortfall in quality of regimental officers stemmed from the dysfunctional nature of the system by which budding officers could gain a commission and progress up the command structure. During these years, aspiring officers and those already in the system had a choice when it came to how to gain a promotion. On the one hand, the individual could seek to gain promotion through many years of hard service and the approval of senior officers, whilst on the other those with the financial means and a powerful and wealthy patron could simply purchase promotion.[58]

Although the purchase system did enable some good officers to rise to higher levels in the officer corps, the system had been much abused by Yonge, who in the years before 1793 had made a fortune via the sale of commissions. York's former ADC, Craig, was particularly scathing in his criticism of Yonge's conduct and its effects upon the quality of the officer corps:

> There is not a young man in the Army that cares one farthing whether
> his commanding officer, the brigadier of the commander-in-chief

approves his conduct or not. His promotion depends not on their smiles or frowns. His friends can give him a thousand pounds with which to go to the auction rooms … and in a fortnight he becomes a captain. Out of the fifteen regiments of cavalry and twenty-six of infantry which we have here, twenty-one are commanded literally by boys or idiots.[59]

York therefore set about tightening the rules governing how the purchase system operated. Regimental colonels were instructed to draw up detailed lists, naming the officers under their command and outlining their record and years of service. A new set of rules was also introduced to govern how and when officers could apply for promotion. For example, a subaltern who wished to be a captain had to have served for at least a year before he could seek to gain a captaincy, whilst anyone wishing to rise to the rank of major had to have served at least six years in order to be eligible.[60] Further regulations were also introduced over the course of the period but the premise remained the same: all officers had to have served for a specified period of time before they could seek higher appointments.

Although the changes instigated by York removed some of the problems inherent in the way in which officers gained promotion, the system of purchase remained until 1871 when it was finally abolished, after much debate, by the then Secretary for War, Edward Cardwell.[61] York's reforms certainly made it harder for junior officers to rise swiftly through the officer corps, but they did not prevent the wealthy from continuing to purchase their way to the higher levels after they had served the minimum years required of them. The pressures of war also had an impact on the new system and on campaign it mattered less if a junior officer had served the full five years if a place needed to be filled.

Officer Education

One of the harshest critics of the British officer corps of the age was Sir Henry Dundas, who spoke of his concern regarding the lack of training for younger officers to Grenville, in a letter dated 21 July 1798:

The education of our young military men is an object calling loudly for attention … It is impossible they can know the duties of subalterns, or of course, of their profession, for they are hurried through inferior situations into the rank of field officer before they have either studied or practically exercised the elements of their profession. [62]

The first official school for the training of junior regular officers in the British army opened in the back room of the Antelope pub in High Wycombe in 1799.[63] The brain behind the idea was not York, but an enterprising young cavalryman, Lieutenant Colonel John Gaspard Le Marchant.[64] The initial success of the project convinced York of the value of the project and, after having moved to new premises and divided into junior and senior departments it was granted the title of Royal Military College (RMC) in 1801.[65]

The supporters of the transformation thesis claim this development was a major improvement to the British military system. However, the creation of the RMC was not as radical a change as has been suggested. Firstly, although several graduates of the school eventually found themselves in administrative posts in Wellington's headquarters in the Iberian Peninsula, the fact that the school could only cater for around thirty cadets at any one time meant that it took many years for the benefits to be felt.[66] Secondly, despite creating a college to educate a small group of junior officers, neither York nor Le Marchant sought to make the course compulsory, whilst the high entrance fees also served to limit rather than encourage potential entrants. Thirdly, beyond this small beginning nothing was done by the reformers to encourage a widespread awareness throughout the army of the value of learning as a gateway to improving strategic and operational planning and military thought. As a result, for many years only a handful of serving officers recognised the value of studying military theory.

The British Approach to Military Education in a European Context

One of the problems with the transformation thesis is that its proponents have tended to analyse York's reforms in isolation. This is particularly true of the way in which military historians have assessed the reforms made by York and Le Marchant to military education in the British army. Richard Glover, for example, devoted an entire chapter to the study of York's reforms to military education in the British army, but made only a passing reference to the more extensive changes that had already been made to military education in Europe.[67] The same Anglo-centric approach can be found in the work of those who have subsequently built upon Glover's thesis.[68]

When placed within the wider context of European military developments over the course of the previous centuries, the changes made to education in the British army by York and Le Marchant in the period 1799 to 1803 appear limited and long overdue. Also, far from being on the cutting edge of military thought, the British lagged far behind their European rivals. Essentially, unlike the Europeans, the British had not yet developed a cognitive approach to war.

The European Military World and the British Army

Long before York set his reforms in motion, the French had recognised the need to train junior army officers. In 1679, for instance, the French had established a cadet school for the training of junior engineer officers at Douai and, over the course of the following decade, experimented with the training of young infantry officers in a series of new cadet companies.[69] By way of contrast, the British equivalent of the school at Douai, the Royal Military Academy at Woolwich, would not be built for another eighty years. The French continued to experiment over the course of the seventeenth and eighteenth centuries, a process which culminated in the creation of the prestigious *École Militaire* in Paris in 1750. By this point, however, the French were not the only ones to have recognised the need to develop a cognitive approach to war.

The Prussians, under Frederick the Great, had gradually sought to develop cadres of educated junior officers, whilst the Austrians and Russians had also sought to create a series of military schools of their own.[70] The Russians, in particular, had made a major effort to keep abreast of developments in Europe and in 1698 Peter the Great had established a rudimentary military school for aspiring officers of the Guards and Artillery as part of a wider series of military reforms.[71] An Artillery school was added in 1701, an Engineer school in 1712, whilst many garrison schools were also constructed. In 1758, a Russian 'École Militaire' was formed entitled 'The Artillery and Engineer Noble Cadet Corps'. This institution quickly became famed throughout Europe and by the Napoleonic era had been responsible for the education of many thousands of Russian generals, including Mikhail Kutuzov, Fedor Büxhowden and Aleksey Korsakov.[72] Thus, by the end of the Seven Years War, each of the Continental European powers had recognised the value of military education for the young entrants to their respective officer corps.[73]

With their initial advantage lost, one of the last great military changes made by the Bourbons was to update the system of military education in France, with the aim of placing the French army at the forefront of European military development once again. The French system of military education in the period before the French Revolution was the most advanced in Europe. After passing a testing examination officer cadets were expected to attend civilian school to hone their reading and writing skills. These 'Finishing Schools' fostered an appreciation for intellectualism amongst new entrants to the officer corps. Graduates of this system included a young Napoleon Bonaparte, who attended the school at Brienne.[74]

The idea behind this scheme was that the new entrants would learn both intellectual and practical skills before being sent to their respective regiments.[75]

Graduates of this system could then study at the *École Militaire* and, when officially commissioned into the French Army, might also seek further instruction by attending a more specific military academy. Napoleon, for instance, went from the *École Militaire* to a specific gunnery school at Valence, whilst Lazare Carnot, attended a Finishing School before he went on to the engineer school at Mézières.[76] Other specific schools included the geographical school for engineers in Paris, the cavalry schools at Bescançon, Metz, Douai and Angers, and those for gunnery at Bescançon, Metz, Douai, La Fère, Auxonne and Grenoble.[77]

Not all of the entrants to this new system were French and a few British officers attended French schools during these years. Indeed, it is interesting to point out that arguably Britain's best generals of the Napoleonic Wars in Wellington, Rowland Hill and William Carr Beresford attended one of the French schools in question. Although it is difficult to establish what they learned from their experiences in France, save for a better grasp of French, it is possible to say that, unlike their contemporaries, Wellington, Hill and Beresford would have been made aware of the existence of the wider European military world, one in which military thought was as highly prized as regimental responsibilities and values.

In the short term, the elaborate system of military education in France suffered greatly during the early years of the French Revolutionary Wars but nevertheless the French were able to reap the benefits of the previous reforms. During the Revolutionary Wars the French Army fielded no less than 255 generals and admirals who had had the benefit of military schooling.[78] Many of those who had received a military education went on to distinguish themselves on the battlefields of Europe. Of Napoleon's Marshals eight had attended a military academy including: Davout, Grouchy, Kellermann, Marmont, Macdonald, Perignon, Poniatowski and Serurier.[79] Napoleon also took a keen interest in military education and in 1802 created the *École Speciale Militaire de Saint-Cyr* which, over the course of the Napoleonic Wars, educated over 4,000 junior officers.[80]

The British army also lagged behind the Royal Navy in the development of education for its officer corps. Since 1677, junior naval officers had been ordered to attend training sessions in navigation and tactics, followed by an examination aboard ship.[81] Despite these developments, the French were more advanced in their educational thinking and had opened two naval academies at Rochefort and Toulon in 1670.[82] Soon the other European naval powers followed suit and created naval academies of their own: the Danish 'Sea Cadet Academy 'opened in 1709, whilst the Russians established a Naval Academy at St Petersburg in 1715. In 1699, a British civilian schoolmaster, Lewis Maidwell, had called on the Admiralty to create a similar institution and in 1705 also argued the need for a Naval Mathematical School.[83] Although the Admiralty warmed to Maidwell's proposals, the plan was later shelved, and the British remained without a Naval Academy until the mid-eighteenth-century.[84]

Though the British had been slow to emulate the Europeans, the Naval Academy at Portsmouth, which eventually opened in 1733, became the jewel in the British naval crown and offered its entrants a first-rate education as part of a broad-based curriculum ranging from navigational skills, gunnery and fortification to geometry and foreign languages. Following a year of this rigorous and largely academic introduction to life on the ocean waves the young cadets were then instructed in practical and technical skills aboard a training vessel.[85] Although not all aspiring naval officers opted to attend the new academy, the foundations had already been laid for the benefit of future generations, many of whom appreciated from an early age the value of study and learning from past experiences.

Running in parallel to, and underpinning, the new military developments in France and Europe during the 1750s to 1780s was a pan-European military intellectual ferment. During this time many of the great enlightenment thinkers had turned their attention to military thought. Philosophes such as Jean Jacques Rousseau devoted a great deal of effort to the study of war and its social implications.[86] Other military specialists from across Europe included the Frenchman Jacques Antoine Hippolyte Comte de Guibert and the German intellectual duo of Gebhard von Scharnhorst and Fredrick von Bülow.[87] The major theories about the art of war written by these individuals shaped the approaches taken by many of the European armies and existed side by side with the many thousands of military pamphlets, drill manuals and tactical treatises which were also produced during these years. Many of these publications also crossed the Atlantic and found a ready audience with the officers of the American Continental Army during the American War of Independence.[88] Indeed, a German in British pay later recalled that during operations in America his troops routinely seized large numbers of military books from captured American officers, whilst his British colleagues largely read works of fiction.[89]

In contrast to the Europeans, and their American cousins for that matter, the British officer was expected, above all, to lead from the front and uphold the paternal ethos of the regiment; book-learning and intellectualism were simply not on the agenda.[90] The British aversion to the development of new military thinking, as opposed to the educated, free-thinking attitude in the armies of Europe, is best illustrated by the overwhelming disparity in the number of works of military theory produced by Europeans, as opposed to the limited number of works written by British military thinkers.

The types of books available by British authors included titles about the general responsibilities expected of officers such as: Charles James's *The Regimental Companion: containing the relative duties of every soldier in the British Army* (London: 1800); Robert Donkin's *Military Collections* (New York: 1777); Thomas Simes's *Military Medley* (1768). Several officers also carried with them memoirs of past campaigns. These works of history tended, however, to be less about the study of past conflicts and more about the personal exploits and arguments of the author, a prime example being Colonel Banastre Tarleton's *History of the Southern Campaigns of 1780 and 1781, in the Southern Provinces of North America* (1787). Others used the opportunity to publish works that called for the reform of the tactics of the infantry. The majority of these works tended to be written by advocates of light infantry tactics, a good example being Brigadier General William Stewart's *Outlines of a Plan for the general Reform of the British Land Forces* (second edn, 1806). Although a couple of officers did argue that a focus on military education was necessary, the vast majority were more concerned with drill and fostering the regimental ethos.[91] This mentality has been well described by Corelli Barnet, who noted that 'In Great Britain the preference for character over intellect, for brawn over brain, has always taken the form of denigration of the staff-college graduate and apotheosis of that splendid chap, the regimental officer'.[92]

The authors of drill manuals aside, the only famous British military theorist of the period who had a European readership was Henry Lloyd, whose main intellectual work was his history of the Seven Years War, entitled *The history of the late war in Germany between the king of Prussia and the empress of Germany and her allies* (1766). Lloyd, however, was relatively unknown in Britain and spent his formative years in the service of both the French and Austrian armies; he also saw active service against the Dutch in the Low Countries at the siege of Bergen-Op-Zoom in 1747.[93] That the British themselves had little knowledge of Lloyd's work highlights the general ignorance of the British officer corps in relation to the study of war and military education in this period.

Perhaps the most important theorist of the late eighteenth and early nineteenth centuries was Scharnhorst. An inspiring theorist, Scharnhorst devoted his career to the study of war. He entered a military academy at an early age and went on to teach in a regimental school, before being appointed head of a military school in Berlin which sought to teach junior officers core skills in the art of staff work. One of Scharnhorst's protégés was the future military theorist and philosopher Carl von Clausewitz.[94] Scharnhorst was also a senior member of the Berlin 'Military Society', an organisation in which Prussian army officers and government officials met to discuss new developments in the context of military history.[95] The existence of this discussion group is evidence of the development of a more analytical approach to the conduct of war in mainland Europe. The absence of such a discussion group in Britain is demonstrative of the gulf which separated the learned and increasingly professional European military community and the generally unintellectual and amateurish approach of the British officer corps.

The French, like the Prussians before them, were also keen to put theory into practice. On numerous occasions they created various camps in order to put their new theories to the test. At the camp at Vassiuex in 1778, for example, the senior commanders of the French army tested the tactical ideas of a number of different theorists, including Guibert and other French writers, such as Mensil-Durand, so as to assess their practicality and see which was more suited to the abilities of the troops in conditions similar to those they would likely encounter on a European battlefield.[96] That Guibert's ideas were proved sound and Durand's heavily criticised was important at the time, but what is historically significant is the fact that the French had decided to undertake the experiments in the first place.

Placed in this European context, York's creation of the RMC was far from progressive. Although several graduates of the RMC performed well on Wellington's staff during the Peninsular War, the slowness of the British to create a school, combined with the young age of the entrants, meant it was not until late in the Peninsular War that the British were able to employ more of its graduates. Furthermore, in the period after the end of the Napoleonic Wars, both the Royal Military Academy and the RMC suffered from reduced funding and a shortfall in both quality teaching and thus talented graduates.[97]

Hew Strachan has noted that the RMC produced few senior officers in the years after the end of the Napoleonic Wars, the period 1832 to 1851 was particularly poor for the RMC; during these years only 3 graduates, out of a total number of 420, made it to the rank of Lieutenant Colonel.[98] Although the college created a means by which the British could develop young staff officers, something which the British had not had before, the return of only three senior regimental commanders for the number of entrants to the RMC was not impressive. The situation in the post-Napoleonic years was not helped by the fact the majority of senior officers and politicians, including Wellington, did not see the need for further reforms to education and viewed the graduates of the RMC with disdain. The Iron Duke later referred to the studious types in the Army as, 'coxcombs and pedants'.[99] Although some officers did advocate the need for a more European approach during these years, such as the lieutenant governor of Portsmouth in the 1840s, Lieutenant General Lord Frederick Fitzclarence, the senior figures at the Horse Guards did not respond favourably to such calls for change and nothing was altered.[100]

Ultimately the creation of the RMC was far from transformative. Until the British created the means to emulate the French and Prussians and place an emphasis on institutional learning, they would continue to operate in much the same way as before. Even as late as 1870 the British army did not fully acknowledge the need for effective military education and training for officers. As Captain James Walter wrote in 1883:

> Before the year 1870 it seems to have been, with few exceptions, an article of English faith that the trade of soldiering was one which required no apprenticeship ... and that when he donned a red coat he at once became ... impregnated with those qualities and that knowledge of which in other professions had to be learned by hard work and study.[101]

York's reforms to administration, training methods and light infantry and the officer corps were limited in scope and conception. Missing from the reforms, but crucial if the changes were to have a transformative impact, was an attempt to cultivate in the officer corps a more intellectual mind set, one which recognised the value of learning from past experiences and the benefit of regular discussions between both army and navy personnel in order to improve performance. As the following campaign case studies demonstrate, the changes made did not greatly improve British military performance and nor did they bring about a transformation in the British army.

Chapter 3

The Expedition to the Helder, 1799

The Anglo-Russian expedition to the Helder in 1799, which sought to liberate the Dutch and oust the French from the Low Countries, was Britain's main military effort of the War of the Second Coalition. Despite high hopes, British strategic and military planning blunders ultimately undermined the Anglo-Russian expedition and led to the near destruction of the British and Russian expeditionary forces. As in 1793–5, the main British failings were their inability to undertake effective operational planning and their over-reliance on unreliable intelligence reports. The British also greatly overestimated the willingness of the Dutch to support their operations and blamed the Russians for the defeat, much as they had the Austrians in 1795. Dejected by the outcome of the expedition and concerned for the safety of their colonial possessions, the British reverted to a policy of strategic isolation. In doing so the British abandoned the Austrians, who were eventually defeated the following year by a young Napoleon Bonaparte at the Battle of Marengo.[1]

The architect of the Anglo-Russian intervention in the Low Countries, and the wider alliance, known as the Second Coalition, was Grenville. An ardent opponent of French expansionism, Grenville sought the overthrow of the French directory in order to forge a new European balance of power.[2] Grenville's plans for the future of Europe, however, did not immediately endear him to the more pragmatic Prussians and Austrians. The German powers had viewed the British with suspicion ever since the breakdown of Allied relations at the end of the War of the First Coalition in 1795. Neither was Grenville's plan welcomed by all in the British Cabinet – its most vocal opponent was Sir Henry Dundas who believed that British interests would be better served if British military, naval and financial resources were used to seize French colonial possessions.[3] Although Dundas would eventually have his way, his arguments were overruled in 1798 by the weight of support for Grenville's proposal for a renewed British commitment in Europe.

Despite Grenville's high hopes, the fact remained that in the spring of 1798 a feeling of mutual distrust lingered over European politics. The British, for instance, had felt betrayed by the Austrians who had failed to repay two substantial loans that had been granted to them by the British during the previ-ous conflict.[4] Instead of seeking to better Anglo-Austrian relations, Grenville looked to Berlin for support. However, the Prussians were far from eager to engage in a new offensive war with France and wanted instead to rebuild their armed forces in order to keep both France and Austria in check.[5] Frustrated, Grenville looked to the Russians for support. Tsar Paul's intentions were not well known and the British hoped to curry favour with the new Russian mon-arch as a means to build Europe-wide support for a new campaign.[6]

However, Paul was greatly impressed by Grenville's idea for a new coali-tion and shared the foreign secretary's desire to punish the French for their aggressive polices.[7] The Tsar also sought to defend the smaller states of cen-tral Europe from French aggression and was particularly concerned about the future of Malta since this was home to the Order of the Knights of St John of whom he was Grand Master.[8] Russia's stance greatly pleased the British who had come to view the Russians as natural allies. However, before the British could make any further negotiations, news reached Grenville that several Swiss cantons had revolted against the French.[9] Although the Swiss insurgents were defeated, the events in the Swiss cantons furthered Grenville's desire for a new European alliance. Simultaneously, the British were also surprised by a series of fresh Austrian proposals. The Habsburgs had warmed to the idea of a new alliance with the British, and suggested that the British government furnish a new loan in return for renewed Austrian military commitment. The Austri-ans also wanted the British to send a fleet into the Mediterranean to support Austria's Neapolitan allies against the French.[10] They also suggested that they would support the Swiss in the event of a future Swiss revolt in return for fur-ther British funds and supplies. Although this suggestion was later accepted by the British, Grenville did not agree to this proposal until July.[11]

The British dedicated a great deal of thought to the new Austrian requests and, although Grenville refused the idea of a new loan agreement, the British agreed to commit a large fleet to the coast of Naples under Nelson.[12] This was a major strategic decision and one which was motivated by the British govern-ment's desire to both destroy the French Mediterranean Fleet and safeguard British interests in the Mediterranean and across the globe.

The British were also wary of invasion and the French had come close to doing so on two occasions prior to 1798: in 1796 the French had almost succeeded in landing an army in southern Ireland only for their fleet to be destroyed by a storm off Bantry Bay, whilst in 1797 another French naval force managed to evade the clutches of the Royal Navy and landed a small army on the Pembrokeshire coast, near Fishguard.[13] Although the latter invasion attempt was quickly defeated by the local yeomanry, both invasion scares demonstrated that the British Isles were vulnerable and that the Royal Navy could not always be trusted to defend the approaches to the British coast.

Swift action was clearly needed and Henry Dundas suggested a policy of coastal raiding in order to destroy French naval stations in Flanders and along the Dutch and French coasts. In 1798 the British launched a daring raid to destroy the lock gates at Ostend in order to prevent the French from using the Flanders canals to prepare an invasion.[14] Although the raiding force of 1,400 British troops, under Major General Sir Eyre Coote, destroyed the lock-gates and blocked the canal to the enemy in an operation similar to the Zeebrugge Raid in 1918, bad weather prevented the navy from being able to evacuate the British troops and Coote was forced to surrender.[15] The debacle at Ostend put Dundas's raiding on hold and persuaded the Cabinet of the merits inherent in Grenville's Continental strategy. Thus, as Nelson's fleet moved into the Mediterranean in mid-August, Pitt and the Cabinet promised the Foreign Secretary that major funds would be provided in order to secure a Russian alliance.[16]

It was to this end that Grenville instructed the British minister at St Petersburg, Sir Charles Whitworth, to enter into negotiations with the Tsar. This Whitworth did and, after much deliberation, the Tsar agreed to provide the British with an army of 45,000 Russian troops in exchange for a series of monthly payments of around £50,000.[17] With relations developing Grenville despatched his elder brother, Thomas, to Berlin in January 1799 to oversee diplomacy on the Continent, renew negotiations with the Prussians and to open discussions with the Dutch-Orangeist émigrés based in Berlin.[18] In going to Berlin Thomas was following a similar course to his brother, Grenville having been sent to The Hague and Versailles in the aftermath of the Dutch political crisis in 1787.[19]

After a period of complex negotiations between the Tsar and the Habsburgs both parties agreed to form a new coalition against the French and readied their forces.[20] What made matters confusing was that no treaty existed to link Britain to Austria, the British had only sought to agree matters with the Russians and still did not fully trust the Habsburgs. The Second Coalition was thus a fragile entity and its fate rested on the willingness of the Russians to support both the British and the Austrians and carry the fight to the French in Europe.

With the new coalition formed, Grenville met with Thugut and various Russian representatives in order to set out Allied aims and objectives. Initial Allied strategy for the new campaign was as follows: the bulk of the Russian army, and perhaps the Austrians, under the Archduke Charles, would take to the offensive in Switzerland and support a planned revolt.[21] Concurrently another force, preferably under Russian command, was to clear Northern Italy and advance to the French border. Finally a third Russian force, drawn from the main army, was to advance into the Netherlands to support the Dutch Orangeists. Grenville also firmly believed that victory in Holland would be all that was required to persuade the Prussians join the coalition and the following year would witness the final invasion of France.

Although this strategy seemed promising on paper, strategic, political and logistical problems soon forced the Allied leaders to deviate from this strategy. For instance, Thugut disliked the idea of the Archduke Charles fighting for 'British' objectives in Switzerland, when his forces could so easily be deployed in Italy or on the Rhine; the Austrians eventually found a way to pursue this aim as the war progressed.[22] Furthermore, it would take many weeks for the Russians to reach Switzerland, let alone the Dutch border, and after considering various options, Grenville decided against the deployment of Russian troops from the main army to Holland and that a new deal needed to be struck with the Tsar, so that more troops could be made available for an amphibious assault against the Dutch coast. Given the time it would take for the Russians to be shipped to the Dutch coast, Grenville also came to the conclusion that a British army would need to be deployed to the Low Countries in order to spearhead the Allied campaign.[23]

Rationale for Intervention

'The object of England is ... what is has been for a century. To see in that country a rational, free, and efficient government, capable of providing for its domestic happiness and of maintaining a real independence with respect to all its neighbours'.[24] This statement, written by Grenville to the American ambassador in London in November 1798, encapsulated the official aim of the British government regarding the future of the Dutch state. In order to forge 'a solid and efficient government in that country' and 'consolidate the tranquillity of Europe' Grenville sought to restore the House of Orange and the office of Stadtholder.[25] The stage was thus set for a frenetic period of diplomacy, as Grenville attempted to piece together this strategic vision for the future of the Low Countries and continued negotiations with the European powers.

Before Grenville despatched his brother to Berlin, the Foreign Secretary had received an unexpected communication from William Murray, an American dignitary at The Hague, who claimed that the Dutch-Batavian government was willing to support a British invasion if the British promised to abandon their support for the exiled Orangeists.[26] Despite this offer, Grenville refused to negotiate and dismissed the idea as 'Wholly inadmissible'.[27] In refusing the Batavian overtures for cooperation, Grenville placed his faith in the views of his brother regarding the willingness of Dutch Orangeists to support a British intervention.

During the spring months of 1799, Grenville sought to piece together plans of his own and sought the views of the exiled Stadtholder William III, who had taken residence at Hampton Court. The picture painted of the Batavian Republic by the Berlin Orangeists and agents in British pay was favourable to British plans. These various sources suggested that the Dutch were disaffected with the Batavian government and that the Batavian army and navy were mutinous. Most encouragingly of all, however, the French army was said to be in a poor state, with thousands of troops having been sent to combat the Allies in central Europe. Everything seemed to point to the need for military plans and Grenville accelerated negotiations with the Russians.

The British had been in discussion with the Russians regarding an Anglo-Russian expedition since mid-May and the British secured the services of a further 17,000 Russians on 22 June.[28] Grenville also despatched the experienced General Stamford and Captain Sir Home Riggs Popham to St Petersburg in order to discuss the finer details of the Anglo-Russian expedition with the Tsar.[29] Stamford was to piece together the military aspects whilst Popham was tasked with organising the means by which the Russians were to be transported to the Low Countries.[30]

Popham reached St Petersburg first and set about outlining the shipping timetable with the Tsar.[31] With Prussia resolutely neutral, the British could not simply rely on the Russian force marching across north-west Germany and into the Batavian Republic. A maritime solution had to be found. Time was of the essence, in that the season for expeditionary warfare in late spring and mid-summer was already passing. Popham was chosen for this task due to his nautical and logistical skills; he was also a keen administrator, having worked as a transport agent at Hamburg in 1795.[32] It was hoped that his knowledge of the transport system would help to speed up the process of procuring shipping. At Popham's request Grenville also instructed the Transport Board to secure adequate shipping for as many of the Russian troops as possible.[33]

Boats, however, were not immediately available to the British and Popham chose to secure auxiliary shipping from the Russians themselves, leaving the British to organise their own transport methods. Popham relied on the use of the Russian navy's Baltic galley fleet to transport the Russian contingent to Holland. This plan was soon scuppered, however, when Popham discovered that the Russian galleys were no longer available.[34] With time running short and the campaigning season fast approaching, Popham chose instead to reconfigure several aged Russian warships for use as transports. Furthermore, in order to furnish enough shipping for the initial landing force of 12,000 British troops, the British Transport Board, which had been created in 1794, was forced to negotiate with several prominent North-Eastern British coal merchants for the use of their seaworthy vessels, known as colliers.[35] The use of British merchant vessels also enabled the Royal Navy to free up the necessary military transports for the Russians and the second British force. The British were also short of flat-bottomed boats, which were used as landing craft, but had little choice but to make do with what they had at their disposal.[36]

As the British finalised their negotiations, the French were readying themselves for the Allied onslaught. Although suffering from the effects of wear and tear, the troops that remained in the ranks were mostly battle-hardened veterans whilst the French commanders were ambitious and aggressively minded.[37] What concerned the Directory was not the fighting spirit of the troops, or indeed the quality of the generalship, but the fact that the French military was overstretched; the French army was expected to protect a much-enlarged empire which stretched from the coasts of the Batavian Republic to the shores of the Mediterranean and the Pyramids of Egypt. The fact that over 30,000 troops, under Napoleon Bonaparte, were stranded in Egypt did not help matters and in each campaign theatre the French were outnumbered by the Allies. In the Rhine valley, for instance, Jourdan commanded 25,000 men, but was opposed by a force of over 70,000 Austrians, under Archduke Charles. Meanwhile in Switzerland, André Massena's 26,000 men were outnumbered by more than two to one by another Austrian army. Even in Italy, where the French had 70,000 men under Macdonald and Barthélemy Schérer, they were outnumbered and faced over 100,000 Austrian and Russian troops under Marshal Suvorov.[38] Thousands of French troops were also stationed in the rear of the main battle areas in order to maintain supply lines and keep order; whilst in France itself thousands of troops were tied up policing the royalist stronghold of the Vendée and other volatile regions, such as the Dordogne and the Basque Country.[39]

With typical revolutionary zeal, however, the French Directory wanted a decisive victory and in mid-March 1799 all of the French armies were ordered onto the offensive.[40] French confidence was quickly rocked by a series of defeats. Particularly crushing was the Archduke Charles's victory over Jourdan at Stockach on 25 March.[41] The Allies also made a series of quick gains in Northern Italy and on 27 April the Russian Field Marshal Alexander Suvorov defeated a French army at the Battle of Cassano d'Adda.[42] Suvorov's forces used this victory to their advantage and, over the following weeks, made themselves masters of Milan, Turin and Alessandria.[43] By the end of July 1799 the French had been forced back to the Swiss frontier and the stage was to be set for the next Allied attack. Whilst the Austrians and Russians readied their forces, the British turned their attention to the Low Countries. Before analysing the British planning process it is necessary to outline the readiness of the British army in 1799.

The British Army: Fit for Service?

As the Allied war machine pushed into the French occupied zones in central Europe and Northern Italy, the British began to make military preparations of their own. Dundas had been informed of Grenville's scheme for the Dutch expedition in early June, giving him barely two months to ready one of the largest expeditionary forces ever raised in Britain. Decimated by yellow fever whilst campaigning in the West Indies in the mid-1790s, the British army was a mere skeleton of its former self. As Michael Duffy has noted, out of the 89,000 British regular officers and men who served in the West Indies between 1793 and 1801, 43,750 died during this period of campaigning.[44] These dreadful losses had forced the British to reduce the army at home.[45] Recruitment had also slumped during this period, a fall which was tied to the widespread fear of service in the West Indies amongst potential recruits. Thus, in October 1798, the combined strength of the regular army and militia forces in Britain totaled 67,000 officers and men. Only 12,700 of these troops were regular infantry, however, and this figure also included the 5,700 officers and men of the Foot Guards.[46] More troops were needed quickly given that Grenville had promised Tsar Paul the support of a British expeditionary force of 25,000 men.[47] The lack of vessels for the shipment of the troops also meant that the British forces would need to be transported to the Low Countries in two batches. Finding troops for the initial British landing was relatively easy, with Dundas able to despatch some 12,000 officers and men from the regulars for this task.[48] Dundas's main problem was what to do in order to find enough men for the second wave of British troops, a force which was supposed to number around 10,000.

There were only a couple of options open to Dundas. He could seek to incorporate émigré regiments into the British contingent. This was difficult given the fact that several thousand émigré troops had been lost to British service following the defeat of the French Royalist expedition to Quiberon Bay in 1795.[49] Dundas therefore resorted to increasing the size of the Army. What made Dundas's task particularly difficult was the fact that the British recruiting system for the regular Army was based on volunteerism, rather than the

French practice of conscription.[50] This led to an uneven pattern of recruitment. In 1797, for instance, the British army was 30,000 men short of the number Dundas thought necessary for the defence of the British Isles.[51] Men were desperately needed for offensive operations, but the British recruitment system was not up to the task. A dramatic overhaul of this system was not a viable option, however, because conscription was perceived as the arch-enemy of British values and 'unpalatable' to British cultural sensibilities.[52]

Consequently, Dundas was forced to turn his attention to the militia. Based on conscription by ballot, recruits to the militia served for five years, but could only serve in the British Isles.[53] Another characteristic of the recruitment process for the militia was that there existed a loophole in the balloting process which allowed men to avoid service by paying for a substitute.[54] This process was rife in a number of militia regiments in 1798 and most notably in the Buckinghamshire militia, with 90 per cent of its new draft of 129 men being made up of substitutes.[55]

Facing a manpower crisis, Dundas persuaded the government to make an alteration to the Militia Act on 12 July which made it possible for militiamen to transfer into several existing regular infantry regiments.[56] In order to attract as many militiamen as possible Dundas was wise to ensure that those who volunteered could only be deployed in Europe and not to the dreaded West Indies.[57] By enabling militiamen to transfer to the regulars, Dundas had found a feasible solution to the manpower crisis and by the end of the year he was able to persuade over 26,000 militiamen to join the regulars.[58] Dundas's system would continue to provide soldiers throughout the Napoleonic wars.[59] In the meantime some 10,000 militiamen were drafted into 10 existing but understrength infantry regiments and ordered to Barham Downs in preparation for active operations.[60]

With the Militia Act passed, the British expeditionary force was finally able to take full shape. Over the course of early August the commandant of the southern district, General Sir Charles Grey, oversaw the process of rebuilding the understrength regiments.[61] On 14 August, the total strength of the 10 regiments numbered 8,927 officers and men.[62] On 18 August, the force peaked at 12,734 officers and men and was organised into 5 brigades.[63] The man tasked by Dundas with preparing the initial British assault force was Abercromby. An experienced senior officer, Abercromby had served with distinction in both Ireland and the West Indies during the 1780s–90s but had not seen active service in America due to his political support for the Colonists.[64] Abercromby had little experience of amphibious operations in Europe. Although a skilled administrator, he had a somewhat alarming tendency in battle to place himself in the thick of the action at the expense of maintaining order. He would lead the initial assault force with success in 1799, but his failure to plan effectively would hinder the expedition's long-term chances of success.

The other commanding officers of the initial landing force were some of the most experienced in the British army and included future divisional and army commanders such as Sir Harry Burrard, Moore and Coote, whilst at the lower levels battalion and company commanders included many future Peninsular War generals, notably Sir Andrew Barnard, Sir Robert Craufurd, Sir John Hope, Sir Alexander Howard, Sir George Murray, Sir Brent Spencer and George Ramsey Ninth Earl of Dalhousie.[65]

Dundas's initial instructions to Abercromby emphasised the need for, 'the greatest promptitude and vigour' owing to 'the advance season of the year'.[66] Abercromby's first task was to lead the initial landing force and seize a beachhead on the Dutch coast. Once this force had established itself, the Duke of York would land with the second wave of British troops, made up of the five British infantry brigades encamped on Barham Downs, under the command of Generals John Pitt Second Earl of Chatham, Prince William Duke of Gloucester, Robert Manners, Sir George Don and Sir Richard Earl of Cavan.[67] The Russian contingent was also scheduled to arrive at this time. York's appointment as the overall commander of the expedition, although liked by the Cabinet, was not considered a good appointment by all. The Tsar, in particular, had serious reservations about York's military skills due to the Duke's poor handling of the Anglo-Hanoverian army in 1793–5.[68]

Planning and Preparation

Piers Mackesy has argued that 'the strategic intention to seize the United Provinces was settled without seeking the advice of a British soldier: so was the operational plan which the Tsar had accepted'.[69] Contrary to Macksey's assessment of the planning process, no operational plan was ever created to guide the Anglo-Russian forces in the initial stages of the expedition. No fine-tuned landing plan was made and neither did the politicians or generals make it clear how the army was to operate once ashore. All the British did was to consider a vague series of locations for a landing. Planning how the Anglo-Russian forces were to cooperate was equally vague, with the only discussion between the two states on military matters having taken place several months earlier and, even then, the only things discussed were Popham's shipping arrangements. Little else had been done. Thus, on the eve of the largest British military expedition since 1793, all that the British and Russians had agreed upon was that their combined forces would land somewhere between the rivers Emms and Scheldt.

Although the ministers were to blame for many aspects of the poor planning process, York, who was placed in command of the whole expedition, also did nothing. The only officer who thought it necessary to consider the difficulties involved in the enterprise was Abercromby, who also consulted the expeditions QMG Colonel Sir John Hope. Despite writing a brief memorandum, which Hope forwarded to Grenville, the Foreign Secretary ignored the officer's comments.[70] Desperate for the expedition to set sail, Grenville was supremely confident in the expedition's chances of success and had complete faith in intelligence which he had received from his brother in Berlin, which suggested that the French forces in Holland were very weak. Grenville informed Abercromby that the French were weak in number and oblivious to the impending threat:

> You know that we have, down to this very hour, accurate intelligence of the amount of French force in Holland. You are aware that it does not amount to 6,000 men, and those too, dispersed ... from Delfzijl to Antwerp ... the accurate intelligence received last night of the state of Walcheren and of the Eastern Provinces affords a strong confirmation of the former accounts as to the weakness of the enemy and appears also in a very satisfactory manner that they have not yet turned their attention to our intended point of attack.[71]

Other reports meanwhile, notably from the Orangeist agent, Robert Fagel, convinced Grenville that the Dutch-Batavian army would disintegrate, once the Anglo-Russian forces stormed ashore.[72] It was on the strength of these intelligence reports that Grenville told Dundas that, 'Were all the Generals on earth assembled ... nothing they could say would weigh a feather in my mind'.[73] Satisfied with this response Abercromby and York did not question the ministers any further.

Unbeknownst to the British, much of the Orangeist intelligence was wildly inaccurate, most notably regarding the strength of the French garrison which actually numbered some 16,000 men under the gifted General Guillaume-Maria-Anne Brune.[74] The Batavian army was also much stronger and amounted to 20,000 men under the able Dutch Lieutenant General Herman Willem Daendels.[75] Reasons for the inaccuracy of British intelligence varied. Perhaps the most prominent factor was the willingness of Berlin Orangeists to bend the truth in order to convince the British to support their cause. This was not the first time that British intelligence had been found wanting. Nonetheless, bad intelligence or not, it was Grenville and his brother Thomas who were chiefly at fault for not scrutinising the quality of the reports.

Hope's memorandum may not have resulted in an operational plan, but it did raise a couple of important points. One of the most significant was that Hope did not think that the landing sites outlined by Popham would be suitable. Whilst the lack of Prussian aid also meant that a landing further south, closer to Amsterdam and the heartland of Orangeist sentiment, would be more promising.[76] Confronted with these new doubts, Henry Dundas belatedly convened a meeting on 6 August and invited Abercomby, a naval officer named Captain Flynn, and a Dutch officer called Sontag, to discuss potential landing sites.[77] Although lacking much in the way of detailed information, Flynn managed to persuade Dundas that landing on the islands of Voorne and Goeree would be time-consuming and difficult and that the Helder peninsula would be a better location.[78] With little known about the nature of the Dutch defences at the Helder or the size of French forces in the area in question, Dundas changed Abercromby's instructions and told him to decide where to land when his fleet reached the Dutch coast. Abercomby would be aided in this task by the naval commanders chosen for the expedition, these men being Admiral Viscount Adam Duncan and Vice Admiral Andrew Mitchell.[79]

The haphazard manner in which Dundas and Abercromby went about finalising the landing plans for the expedition encapsulates the ad hoc nature of British military planning during this period and portrays both politicians and generals in a bad light. Instead of making every effort to plan carefully as soon as Dundas and Abercromby were informed of the expedition, the British high command allowed itself to become so distracted by the task of readying the new force at Barham Downs that it neglected the most important task of all, the creation of a detailed operational plan. Contrary to Macksey's portrayal of the situation, in which Grenville is singled out for criticism, Abercromby, Dundas and York were also at fault in failing to plan effectively. Despite having reservations regarding the expedition, Abercromby's failure to create an operational plan outlining how the British were to operate once ashore would prove to be a major error and would return to haunt the British. As A.B. Rodger has noted, the ensuing campaign was 'An ill-conceived, ill-planned, muddle-headed fiasco … an abject lesson in how not to carry on combined operations'.[80]

Execution

The British fleet carrying Abercromby's assault force finally sailed on 13 August, with Abercromby having decided that it would sail for the Helder, a sand-dune-backed peninsula to the immediate south of the Zuyder Zee at the mouth of the River Texel.[81] No sooner had the British put to sea than the weather took a turn for the worse. Gale-force winds and a heavy swell made the crossing particularly uncomfortable and threatened the cohesion of the fleet.[82] Thankfully the British were able to keep the transports in line and arrived off the Dutch coast after a few hours sailing from England. Hopes of a quick landing were dashed as the poor weather continued for a further thirteen days. Poor visibility also meant that Duncan and Mitchell were unable to assess the movements of the Batavian-Dutch fleet under Rear Admiral Samuel Storij.[83]

These delays thus enabled Daendels to ready his division to meet the British. Daendels concentrated 5,400 Dutch infantry and 597 cavalry behind the sand dunes of the Helder peninsula. Of this force, two battalions of Chasseurs were to act as a forward screen between the coastal hamlets of Groote Ketten, Callanstoog and Petten to disrupt the initial British advance and shield the main force of the Batavian army. Behind this line and east of Callanstoog Daendels positioned the 1,756 officers and men of the 5th Batavian Demi-Brigade at the village of Oudesluis. Daendels posted the 2,072 officers and men of 1/4th Demi-Brigade, 3/6th Demi-Brigade and 1/3rd Demi-Brigade 5 miles to the south-west, straddling the villages of Warmenhuizen, Bergen and Schoorl. Two squadrons of light cavalry were then placed in the rear, whilst the 1st Batavian Dragoons were positioned in the rear of the Dutch defensive position. A further force, the 1st Demi-Brigade, numbering 2,032 officers and men, was positioned just over 10 miles away in Alkmaar. Daendels positioned his headquarters just behind the front line at the village of Schagenbrug, whilst a further force, comprising the 7th Demi Brigade and numbering some 1,715 troops under General van Guericke, garrisoned the town and arsenal at the Den Helder.[84]

The wind and rain eased on the night of 26 August and the British readied themselves to land the following day. At 5 o'clock in the morning, following the collection of the rowing boats of the ships of the line, the assault formations rowed ashore in flat-bottomed boats.[85] The initial assault wave totalled 3,000 men and comprised the brigades of Coote and Moore, whilst a detachment of Colonel Macdonald's brigade under the command of Major General Sir James Murray-Pulteney was also present.[86] Coote and Murray-Pulteney's forces were landed to the right of Moore's brigade, with orders to secure the beachhead and clear the sand hills of enemy troops. Moore, meanwhile, was ordered to land closer to the Den Helder and to besiege this position once the beachhead was won.

The lack of army/navy cooperation in thinking through the finer details of the landing quickly became apparent when, in the rush to get the troops off the boats, neither Abercromby nor Mitchell made sure that the British battalions were correctly organised into their respective brigades. Instead, companies and battalions were jumbled together and the landing quickly degenerated into a chaotic mess.[87] The rough surf also forced several battalions off course and many troops were crowded into a small space of ground opposite the hamlet of Petten.[88]

Gradually the British went about reorganising themselves and, luckily, were not faced with an immediate attack by the Dutch. Unwilling to linger too long in such a cramped position, Murray-Pulteney ordered his two battalions to advance and clear the dunes.[89] The British infantry duly advanced into the warren of sand dunes, only to be halted by the aggressive fire of the Dutch chasseurs, whose fleetness of foot and use of cover contrasted sharply with the stolid tactics of the British line infantry. The battle in the dunes was a confused affair with the British gradually pushing the Dutch forces back only for their advance to be halted on meeting Daendels's troops on the edge of the dunes.[90] Dutch counter-attacks forced the British back into the dunes but, with reinforcements arriving, in the form of the crack Guards brigade, the beachhead was made secure by 3 o'clock in the afternoon.[91]

Although the British losses had been slight, Abercromby's penchant for leading from the front had resulted in the wounding of his primary staff officers, Sir John Hope and George Murray, whilst Murray-Pulteney was also wounded. The biggest loss of the day, however, was Colonel Hay, Abercromby's chief engineer, who was killed in the initial assault.[92] Despite not making a landing plan, the bravery of the British infantry had again saved the day, although it remained to be seen how they would fare against the French regulars, rather than inexperienced Batavians.

Events now moved quickly. Moore moved against Den Helder, expecting a difficult fight, but was amazed to discover that the Dutch garrison had abandoned its positions and he quickly captured the guns covering the mouth of the Texel.[93] The loss of the Helder was a major blow for the Dutch, especially the Batavian Fleet, which was now stationed in the exposed inner waters of the Zuyder Zee and at the mercy of Mitchell. Several Dutch ships, including a couple of warships, had already been seized by the British, a situation which persuaded Storij to retreat into the dangerous coastal waters of the Vlieter, between the Helder and the Dutch naval base at Marsdiep. Mitchell sailed into the Vlieter in the early hours of 30 August and blockaded the Netherlands navy. Storij refused to surrender but, on the raising of an Orangeist flag aboard the British flagship, Storij was unable to prevent the crews of two of his vessels from mutinying. In the ensuing panic, Storij chose to surrender rather than be branded an Orangeist traitor.[94] In the space of barely a few hours, the British had destroyed the last vestige of Dutch naval power; the greatest individual prize was the Koninklijke Marine's flagship *Washington* (74).[95]

As Grenville had hoped, the initial operation had been a resounding success. Not only had the British secured a vital foothold on the Dutch coast, but the mutiny of the Dutch fleet greatly pleased the naval officers. Jubilant, Grenville and Dundas firmly expected a swift British offensive, with both Alkmaar and Amsterdam apparently within reach of Abercromby's men. Lacking maps to assess the ground, cavalrymen to scout ahead and, most importantly, a detailed plan to execute, Abercromby was less sanguine and opted instead to wait for York and the Russians and established a defensive position on the nearby Zype canal.[96] Abercomby was also concerned by the strength of the French and Dutch forces, with the French clearly not as weak as Grenville had suggested. The terrain beyond the sand dunes was also rough and did not suit the rapid movement of formed infantry. All this was explained by Abercromby to Dundas on 4 September:

> The enemy occupies Alkmaar and its vicinity, the Dutch troops are on the right ... and the French in Alkmaar, Bergen and Egmont. The French may be estimated at six thousand men and the Dutch at nine or ten thousand. On the 27 of Aug they had 7,000 men in the field and at the Helder and they have since drawn from Friesland, Groningen, Overjissel and Gelderland, everything they could collect. The country between us and the enemy is entirely intersected with ditches and canals, except on the right opposite Petten, where the sand hills of the Camperdown begin. In this situation I have judged it better not to risk an action, until the arrival of reinforcements.[97]

Inter-service relations were also strained. Abercromby had not had any word from Mitchell, who appears to have concerned himself solely with the acquisition of the Dutch fleet following the initial landings. Devoid of naval support to his flanks and rear and lacking up-to-date naval intelligence of the Dutch coast, Abercromby was unsure of the strength of the enemy and whether the Dutch Orangeists had risen in the coastal towns around the Zuyder Zee. Blind to the situation facing him to his front, rear and along the Dutch coast, Abercromby complained to Dundas at the poor conduct of the navy and of the need for Mitchell to strike at Amsterdam 'Since the 1st I have had no communication with Admiral Mitchell. I have repeatedly urged him, in the strongest terms ... to threaten Amsterdam".[98]

Despite the surrender of the Dutch fleet, the situation was not particularly favourable for the British. Poor weather was also a hindrance, causing delays to the transport of York's forces and the Russians. Captain William Young, a transport agent at Ramsgate, noted that 'The weather ... continues so very unfavourable it will be impossible to embark the troops intended for reinforcement so early as was yesterday expected'.[99]

On 3 September Abercromby was reinforced by the arrival of two brigades of infantry from Barham Downs, under Don and the Earl of Cavan and by the first Russian contingent.[100] With the Russians tired from their long voyage and the ex-militiamen having had no active military experience, Abercromby decided to remain on the defensive until York and the rest of the British and Russian forces arrived. As the British waited, however, the weather showed no signs of improvement and Brune and Daendels gathered their forces in preparation for an attack upon the British lines. The attack was to be made in three columns. Daendels was to advance with a force of Batavian infantry against the village of St Martins on the British left. In the centre another Dutch force, this time under General Jean Baptiste Monceau, was ordered to advance upon the village of Krabbendam, whilst a third column, composed entirely of French troops, was to assault the village of Petten on the British right.[101]

At dawn, on 10 September, the French and Dutch attacks managed to catch the British by surprise, with shots being exchanged as the British sentries fell back upon the villages along the Zype. Crucially for the defenders Moore was able to remove a series of makeshift bridges, which had been laid by the British, in front of the Zype.[102] This quick-thinking on the part of Moore's men delayed the French advance long enough to allow Moore to ready his troops to receive the enemy onslaught.[103] The Franco-Batavian attack was repulsed along the British line. The fighting was fierce, but the British infantry were more than a match for the enemy, blending guile with a stern, bulldog-like determination not to be forced back into the sea.[104]

With the repulse of the main French and Batavian forces, the battle for control of the Zype was effectively over. The battle had been a test of British mettle and the British infantry had withstood the onslaught. What was encouraging for Abercromby, however, was the conduct of the ex-militiamen, under Don and Cavan, particularly the four battalions of the 20th and 40th infantry regiments. The former, under the command of Lieutenant Colonel George Smyth, had held Krabbendam against Monceau's column, whilst the latter, under the bold leadership of future Peninsular War General Brent Spencer, had held St Martin against Daendels.[105] These two regiments had withstood their baptism of fire and come out victorious.

The battle for the Zype drew the initial stage of the campaign in north Holland to a close. Tactically it had been a success for the British; strategically, however, the British had failed. Poor planning and the underestimation of the strength and commitment of the enemy were the chief reasons for this scenario and meant that the British were given little choice but to wait for reinforcements before commencing an advance. This lack of impetus on the part of the British suited the French and Dutch defenders, with general Brune able to gather fresh troops and galvanise local support against the invaders.

Breakout

The British brigades from Barham Downs and most of General Ivan Hermann's Russians disembarked at the Helder, alongside York, between 13 and 15 September.[106] Whilst the Russian contingent was given time to rest after their long voyage, York met with Abercromby, to assess the situation in Holland.[107] The duke was eager to take to the offensive in the knowledge that the longer the Allies remained on the Helder, the easier it would be for the enemy to contain them, gather reinforcements and strengthen their defensive positions in readiness to mount an offensive of their own. Aware that the politicians expected a swift advance upon Amsterdam, York had little choice but to break free from the Zype.

Ideally, York would have liked to have had the task of planning the forthcoming operation himself but instructions from Henry Dundas stipulated that all major decisions were to be made by a Council of War. The council comprised York, Sir David Dundas, Lord Chatham, Hermann, Abercromby and Pulteney.[108] In spite of Henry Dundas's clear instructions, York decided to create a private plan of his own and only called a Council of War, on 18 September, to tell the gathered generals what he wanted them to do in the forthcoming battle. No aspects of the plan were discussed and nothing was altered. Neither did York provide his subordinates with much time to prepare their troops, having informed them that he wished an attack to be made the following morning.[109] Before analysing the battle that followed, it is necessary to outline what York proposed.

York's plan was as follows: the army was to be split into four attacking columns. Three were ordered to seize a number of villages which commanded the main roads leading to Alkmaar. Unfortunately for the Allies the enemy also recognised the importance of these roads. Brune and Daendels concentrated their forces at a number of key road junctions located in a series of villages. Brune placed the bulk of the French forces in the villages of Bergen, Schoorl and Schorldam with the reserve at Alkmaar. Daendels's Batavian division meanwhile held a defensive arc facing the Allied centre and right at Warmenhuizen, Enningberg, Zuyder Sluys, and Oudkarspel.[110] The French and Batavians were reinforced with the arrival of Vandamme's force at Schorl-dam, which meant that by 18 September there were around 8,000 French and 10,000 Batavian troops in the area of operations. By contrast, the Allies could put up to 30,000 troops into the field and, on paper at least, this numerical superiority should have given them a major advantage over the enemy. A number of factors combined to weaken the Allied forces, none more so than the character of York's plan and the poor calibre of Allied generalship.

The largest of the Allied columns totalling nearly 10,000 British veterans and ex-Militiamen, under the command of Abercromby, was instructed by York to advance the evening before the battle to flank the enemy positions by marching across the muddy fields to the town of Hoorn on the banks of the Zuyder Zee. From here, Abercromby was then to march towards the village of Purmerend to the rear of the Franco-Dutch army. Over to the other side of the front an advance was to be made along the sand-dunes next to the sea-shore at 4 o'clock in the morning by Hermann's Russian division, comprising twelve Russian infantry battalions under Essen and Schutorff, with the support of Manners's brigade. This column was to clear the French forces along the coastal road at Camperdown and Schoorl, before pressing on to attack Bergen. To Hermann's left, Sir David Dundas's British division was to strike down the Great Road to Alkmaar at first light, seize Zuyder Sluys and Schoo-rldam and turn onto the coastal road to support Hermann. To David Dundas's left and in the centre of the Allied line, Murray-Pulteney's division, with the support of Coote's brigade, was to begin its march at around half-past 4 in the morning, seize Enningberg and then Warmenhuizen before pressing on to attack Oudkarspel.[111]

The biggest problem with these instructions to commanders was that they were too vague. The instructions given to Abercromby are a case in point, going no further than to order his column to march to Hoorn and push on to Purmerend. At no stage was Abercromby instructed to march to the sound of the guns, or of what to do if he decided to advance upon Purmerend. York does not appear to have recognised the importance of the distances involved. For instance, Hoorn was 10 miles from York's headquarters in the centre of the British position and nearly 20 from Bergen, which meant that if the Allies achieved a breakthrough at Bergen it would take much of the day for news to reach Abercomby and for the British general to march to the sound of the guns if necessary.

Another important flaw was that, despite possessing a numerical superior-ity of about 10,000 men over the enemy, York's decision to send Abercromby with a third of the army on a semi-independent operation deprived the Allies of their extra manpower at the point of engagement with the enemy. As one of the duke's aides later noted, the plan was deeply flawed:

> The most unaccountable mistake, the great military blunder (which drew after it all the subsequent misfortune) was the plan of attack upon the 19th of September. A resolution having been taken to bring the enemy to battle, our best General and 10 or 12,000 of our best troops were detached to Hoorn ... Abercromby's column never fired a shot or saw or attracted the notice of the enemy.[112]

Abercromby's column left its cantonments on the evening of 18 September. Progress was slow, however, with the muddy ground, waterlogged fields and occasional broken bridges forcing him to halt and take several detours. These obstacles meant that, instead of a swift advance, Abercromby's march turned into a near 20-mile slog, with his brigades forced to zigzag across the terrain. William Surtees recalled the sluggish and treacherous nature of the British advance 'We moved off as it became dark, such was the state of the roads that it became the most trying and distressing march ... the roads were literally knee deep in mud in most places', while every now and then they were rendered nearly impassable'. [113]

By the time Abercromby's troops arrived at Hoorn, at half-past 2 in the early hours of 19 September, his troops were exhausted.[114] Bunbury noted the fatigued nature of the troops upon reaching Hoorn 'Our men had been under arms twelve hours: they were dead tired; nor could they have been fit to resume their march much before midday.'[115] Hoorn quickly surrendered and over the course of the next few hours all Abercromby could do was to wait for further instructions. The Allied defeat on the right, however, would lead to the recall of Abercromby's column, which thus neither threatened the enemy rear nor protected the Allied left.

The official signal for the main Allied advance to begin was scheduled to take place at around 4 o'clock in the morning. At about half-past 2, however, Schutorff was unable to prevent his impatient troops from beginning their advance.[116] Once the initial advance was made, the Russian high command was powerless to halt it, despite the fact that the Russians could not see where they were going. Captain Herbert Taylor, another of the Duke's ADCs, recalled the confused nature of the initial advance 'The signal gun was fired when it was still impossible to distinguish any object, but Lt. General Hermann said that altho' the attack was certainly beginning too soon, the impatience of the troops was such that he could not delay it.'[117]

It was about this time that Hermann called on a couple of squadrons of the 7th Light Dragoons and a battery of Royal Horse Artillery to move forward and take up position in reserve. With his rear protected, Hermann's advance guard and supporting grenadiers overran the outlying French positions along the dykes. However, the ill-discipline and impatience of the Russian infantry to get into the action, combined with the poor visibility, soon meant that all sense of cohesion was quickly lost. In addition, there were several instances of friendly fire as the impatient Russian infantry inadvertently began to fire upon their own troops:

> To the fire from the troops to the rear I must principally attribute the very great loss which the Russian troops sustained and I was confirmed in this impression at the attack of the village of Groet where the resistance of the enemy was by no means obstinate, but where the shot was certainly flying in all direction.[118]

The fighting along the coastal road soon alerted the attention of Brune at Alkmaar who reinforced Vandamme at Bergen with the 49th, 42nd and 72nd demi-brigades.[119] General Rostallant, meanwhile, was left with the 54th demi-brigade to hold Schoorl for as long as possible. Before the French could put their main body into the field, the Russians seized Schoorl after some bloody fighting. The battle for the village of Schoorl was a confused affair, a situation which was not helped by the fact that Hermann had disappeared from the head of the column after his horse was shot from underneath him in Groet. With a general officer nowhere to be seen, the Russian infantry refused calls to halt:

> Such was the confusion that prevailed that more than one officer could not find their regiment. I shouted repeatedly to those who understood German and French that their troops were firing upon each other, and that if those to the rear would be formed … but took no steps towards effecting … no general officer was with them and they repeatedly expressed in strong terms their anxiety.[120]

As the dawn fighting continued into mid-morning, the British columns also advanced. The premature nature of the Russian attack, however, had made General Dundas's task in the centre particularly difficult as his troops needed decent visibility in order to cross several muddy fields and water-logged ditches before engaging the enemy. Despite the early morning gloom, Dundas's troops crossed the swampy ground in quick time by using a number of makeshift portable bridges.[121] Despite the darkness, the British infantry captured Zuyder Sluys at about half-past 4 in the morning. At the same time Murray-Pulteney's division, comprising Coote and Don's brigades, began their advance to Oudkarspel. Murray-Pulteney's division was supported at first by several Royal Navy gunboats, under the command of Popham, whose guns peppered the Dutch positions but appear not to have had much impact on proceedings.[122] Before the full force of Murray-Pulteney's division could reach Oudkarspel Coote had to seize Warmenhuizen.[123] The Batavian defence of this village proved more stubborn than the British had expected and they were forced to send reinforcements in the form of three Russian infantry battalions under General Sedmoratzky to support Coote's brigade.[124]

With Coote's advance having been slowed by the battle for Warmenhuizen, Murray-Pulteney ordered Don to commence his attack upon Oudkarspel before Coote arrived.[125] This task would be a major test for Don's troops because 'The head of the village was strongly fortified with a double line of entrenchments, containing eight or ten pieces of artillery.'[126] Making the most of the cover provided by the Lange dyke, Murray-Pulteney swiftly ordered the three companies of light infantry, the first battalion of the 17th Foot and the 40th Foot under Spencer, to commence an attack upon the village.[127] As Spencer advanced, his force was bolstered by Murray-Pulteney who also sent forward two regular infantry battalions in the form of the first battalion of the 3rd Guards and the second battalion of the 5th Foot and two pieces of artillery. Murray-Pulteney, meanwhile, sent Don with four companies of the 40th to reconnoitre the left flank of the village. Spencer's raw troops advanced in good order but soon came under a heavy fire from the Dutch guns. With Spencer's attack stalling, the Dutch launched a couple of audacious counter-attacks but they were pushed back by the British.[128] Spencer's ex-militiamen had done themselves proud in seizing Oudkarspel but, despite forcing the Dutch into a retreat, the events on the Allied right soon forced a halt to the British advance.

Several hours before Murray-Pulteney's division attacked Oudkarspel, on the Allied left, Hermann's Russians had reached Bergen. The Russian forces were now by far the most advanced of the Allied forces and several miles ahead of the nearest British troops at Schorldam. The Russian infantry had also neglected to place troops to guard their flanks, with the troops hemmed in by the enclosed fields and sand dunes. On reaching the village, the Russians were immediately confronted by the French, who quickly surrounded the Russian forces and poured a deadly fire into them from almost all sides. As Taylor noted:

> As we advanced ... the fire of musketry from both flanks and the village in our front was extremely serious ... the troops however proceeded ... but here they were checked by the fire of the French

artillery which was now directed against the head of the column, and by the appearance of the cavalry and infantry drawn up upon the left. The troops were crowded together in a most confused mass.[129]

Hermann finally reappeared and, under heavy fire, formed up a body of grenadiers in front of the village church in the centre of Bergen. The divisional commander left his subordinate, Essen, to oversee the church whilst he moved to one of the nearby side streets in an attempt to shore up the flank.[130] The French advanced, but the ensuing battle for control of the village was a chaotic affair with the French fighting street for street and house for house against the beleaguered Russians and, after a 20-minute struggle, the Russians were encircled and Hermann taken prisoner:

> In this situation we remained about 20 minutes losing men very fast ... the enemy appeared in our rear and we received their fire upon the right. Almost at the same time the enemy were penetrating through the opening upon our left ... every spot in the village was exposed to their fire.... At this moment the enemy penetrated into the village upon the right and front and the Russian troops after firing ... gave way and fell back in the greatest confusion into the avenue. Lieut. General Hermann was taken prisoner.[131]

With the loss of Bergen, the Russian forces were sent into a headlong retreat to their cantonments at Petten, with only Essen able to restore order for a short while. Before the troops broke fully he despatched Taylor to York and asked for Manners's brigade to make a stand.[132] The crowded state of the roads and speed of the French advance, however, meant that the village of Schoorl was also lost before the British troops could be ordered forward. Thus, in the space of barely an hour since the Russian infantry had reached Bergen, almost the entire right wing of the Allied army was broken and in full-blown retreat. This left York with little option but to shore up the Allied right by ordering General Dundas to send Prince William's brigade and a detachment of Burrard's brigade to support Manners. The rest of his division was ordered back to the Zype. Although a necessary, the movement of the British battalions to Schoorl deprived the Allied army of its strike power.

With Dundas's and Murray-Pulteney's attacks having ended prematurely, the focus was once again upon the Allied left. Here Manners, Burrard and Prince William were given the unenviable task of holding back the French attacks until dark. Despite stern resistance, the weight and ferocity of the

French attacks forced the militia and guards back and by the evening the situation on the Allied right had reached a critical point:

> The enemy had followed up the retreat of our troops with great activity and such boldness, and the French now showed themselves in such numbers opposite the right of our position, and to the village of Krabbendam, that we began to feel apprehensions of their making attacks on the lines ... a great part of our army was in sad confusion. Of the Russians there remained only three battalions under Sedmoratzky in a condition to fight ... some of the newly formed Militia regiments of the English were in great disorder; a large proportion of their officers had fallen; and the men were panic stricken by this result of their first encounter with the enemy.[133]

With the Allied right about to crumble and the Zype position under threat, York despatched Bunbury, in a last gasp mission, to rally as many troops as he could and, after several trials and tribulations, Bunbury was able to persuade the weary guardsmen of Colonel Frederick Maitland's battalion, part of D'Oyley's guards brigade, to make a stand.[134] In the resulting engagement the dogged spirit of the guards saved the day, but it had been a close run thing. This was reflected in the losses of both sides, with Allied losses totalling somewhere in the region of 4,500 officers and men, 1,414 British and 3,017 Russian, the latter included 1,300 prisoners. The Franco-Batavian army lost a total of 3,427 officers and men, with the Batavians alone suffering 2,591 casualties, of whom 1,052 were captured.[135]

As the sun set in the evening of the Battle of Bergen, both sides counted the cost of the fighting. The battle had been a disaster for the Allied army and, despite high expectations of a breakthrough, the offensive had petered out. The Allies had blundered into the Battle of Bergen without thinking through how best to maximise their initial numerical superiority over the enemy. However, in his official despatch York viewed the result of the battle with little disappointment, save for the losses sustained:

> The well-grounded hopes, I had entertained of complete success in this operation, and which were fully justified by the result of the three and by the first success of the fourth attack upon the right, add to the great disappointment I must naturally feel upon this occasion, but the circumstances which have occurred, I should have considered of very little general importance, had I not to lament the loss of many brave officers and soldiers who have fallen.[136]

Crucially York did not seek to analyse the battle in any detail and nor did he seek to conduct a review of the engagement in order to identify potential lessons. Blind to his own failings, just as he had been in 1793, York blamed the Russians for the defeat and did not consider himself, or his British troops, to have acted poorly.

The Allied defeat at the Battle of Bergen on 19 September marked a turning point in the character of Allied relations in Holland. Before the battle, expectations had been high that a breakthrough would be won and the road to Amsterdam opened. Instead, the Allied army failed to achieve its objectives, with the British and Russians being forced back to their starting positions. The British were quick to lay the blame upon the Russians who, according to the York, had undermined the success gained by the British.[137] Unfortunately for the working relations of the coalition, York did not hide his frustrations. As Henry Bunbury noted, 'The Duke of York took up a violent contempt, as well as dislike of the Russians. He ridiculed them at his table, and talked of them disparagingly.'[138]

York was not alone in openly criticising the conduct of the Russians. Stories of Russian cowardice and incompetence quickly spread throughout the British army. However, many of the surviving British accounts of the Russian attack on the right were based on the word of others, rather than the result of first-hand experience. A typical British account of the conduct of the Russians is that of the Lieutenant Colonel of the 49th Foot, Isaac Brock, the future British commander in North America in the War of 1812. Despite being on the other side of the battlefield from the Russians and thus unable to have witnessed the events as they unfolded, Brock was all too eager to blame the Russians for the Allied defeat, arguing that the Russians' decision to plunder the villages proved to be their downfall.[139] Similar comments to those made by Brock can be found in many of the British memoirs and diaries regarding the campaign. Surtees, posted with Abercromby on the opposite side of the battlefield to the Russians, felt qualified enough to describe how the 'grotesque' Russians had failed to operate effectively and had naively allowed themselves to be surprised by the French.[140]

Bunbury was also critical of the Russians, both of the rank and file and the officer corps. Of the Russian generals, Bunbury labelled Hermann a 'bad general' and Essen as both 'false' and 'intriguing'.[141] The overriding image of the Russian army in Holland which emerges from the British sources is that of an ill-disciplined and poorly led army, equipped in out-dated attire and lacking all sense of tactical flexibility. The most scathing criticism of the tactical capability of the Russians at Bergen was made by Brock:

The Russians in their persons are rather short of stature, and very thick and clumsy; they having nothing expressive in their features … The officers in general are the most despicable wretches I ever saw: accustomed as they have always been to fight with troops much inferior to themselves, they thought themselves invincible … and … never dreamed it possible, from their former experience, for troops to rally after being once beaten. This fatal security was the cause of the misfortune which befell the allies on the 19th.[142]

Brock's analysis of the Russian defeat at Bergen typified the manner in which the British perceived the Russians. The British viewed the Russian rank and file as physically and socially backward, whilst the Russian officers were typecast as incompetent commanders who were unaccustomed to the 'serious' type of warfare fought in the Western world. This latter point is particularly interesting, in that Brock's analysis of the campaigns fought by the Russian army totally ignored the hard fought victories won by the Russians against Frederick the Great during the Seven Years War and in its clashes with Turks.

The Russian army was far better than Brock and his British contemporaries gave it credit for. The Russian conduct at Bergen, although poor, was not the result of the overall quality of the Russian army per se, but was instead due to a number of interrelated factors, the majority of which were not of the Russians' making. What is also clear from the British source material is that the British actually knew very little about the quality and operational skills of the Russian army. At no point prior to the Helder campaign had the British actually had first-hand experience of a Russian army, a lack of experience which gave rise to myth-making amongst the British forces.

One myth, which no doubt had played a part in convincing the British government to seek an Anglo-Russian alliance, held that the Russian army was the largest in Europe and could thus afford heavier rates of loss than other European armies. In reality the Russian army, although large by British standards, was not that much bigger than those of the French, Prussians and Austrians. One of the main reasons for this was that the Russian army drew its manpower from Russia's serf population. The Russian state could not afford to recruit large numbers of serfs for fear of crippling the Russian economy and risking provincial discontent. The situation was compounded further because once enlisted the Russian soldier was effectively taken out of civilian society for the rest of his life, with soldiers expected to serve in the army for twenty-five years. The low life expectancy of the age, combined with the attrition of war, meant that in Russia the act of 'going for a soldier' was viewed with dread by the serfs.[143]

The Russian army in this period was not the vast 'Nation in Arms' that it would become in later years.[144] In the case of the campaign in 1799, for instance, the total Russian military commitment to the war in Europe totalled about 70,000 men, of whom barely 12,000 were sent to aid the British in Holland. In comparison, the Austrians fielded around 84,000 men in Germany and Switzerland, not to mention a further force which operated on the Rhine; in April 1800 the Austrians and their Piedmontese Allies were able to field 2 armies, each of over 100,000 men.[145] The Russian army which fought in Holland and in central Europe in 1799 was an expeditionary force and one which could not easily be reinforced.

The British were also unaware that deep divisions existed in the Russian officer corps between those who favoured Prussian-style tactics and others who advocated the adoption of the type of tactics and training which the Russian army had employed in its many wars with the Ottoman Empire.[146] This 'dualism', to quote Mark Melenovsky, within the Russian officer corps prevented the establishment of a commonly agreed Russian 'way of war'.[147] Russian troops often fought in different ways depending on the ethos and views of the officer commanding. Perhaps the best known advocate of 'Ottoman' tactics in Russian service during these years was Suvorov who defeated the French in Northern Italy in 1799. Suvorov's grasp of mobile operations and recognition of the need to foster them amongst the Russian army encouraged him to write several military books, the most famous being *How to Win* (1795) and *Art of Victory* (1798).[148] Other notable Russian generals of the Napoleonic wars who also began their careers against the Turks included Kutuzov and Bagration.[149]

Under pressure to reform, the Tsar, an ardent admirer of Frederick the Great, refused to implement radical reforms and instead introduced conservative change in the form of Prussian-style infantry drills. He also purged the reformist element in the officer corps.[150] However, the coming of war in Europe forced the Tsar to reinstate many of the reformists and many, such as Suvorov, openly ignored the Tsar's Germanic drills in favour of mobile 'Ottoman' tactics.[151] The presence of a dual set of ideas within the Russian officer corps explains why Russian military performance varied from one theatre to the next in 1799. For instance, as Suvorov's Russian force was sweeping the French back in a series of dashing victories in northern Italy, the Russian forces in Holland 'Waddled slowly forward to the tap-tap of their monotonous drums' and 'if they were beaten they waddled slowly back again'.[152]

Thus, Russian forces sent to Holland were not of the same fighting quality as those that had been sent to Northern Italy and they also lacked cavalry, artillery and a supply train.[153] Exhausted after their long voyage and without adequate supplies, it was not surprising that the Russian infantry took to plundering their way through North Holland, whilst both Hermann and Essen failed to control their men. The speed with which the Russians withdrew after being counter-attacked, combined with Hermann's capture, was humiliating for the troops and the officers alike. Despite these issues, the Russians had showed considerable tenacity and had done well to drive the French forces from the villages to Bergen. It should also be pointed out that the Russian troops had never fought in the Low Countries before, whilst their position on the extreme left of the Allied line prohibited any tactical flexibility. Furthermore Hermann's Russians had never faced the French in battle before and perhaps acted as rashly as they did because they wanted to test themselves against the vaunted French army. All of these factors meant that once the Russians advanced it was impossible to stop them. Similarly, once broken, the Russian troops lost all cohesion and could not be prevented from falling back in chaotic fashion. With the French at their backs and with little British support, it is little wonder that the Russians fled as they did.

Tactically the Allies had fought with energy and vigour, but operationally the four Allied attacks were badly coordinated and lacked the reserves to enable a breakthrough to be supported and exploited. York's failure to concentrate the full striking power of the Allied army against the enemy was central to their lack of success. It meant that at crucial moments the Allied columns strike power was blunted by the need to redeploy troops to support hard-pressed commanders in other sectors. Once again this situation was of York's making, with several thousand veteran British troops having spent the day with Abercromby at Hoorn, powerless to influence events.

If Abercromby had been held in reserve behind General Dundas, then the Allies could have supported both the Russians earlier in the day and then thrust down the great road to Alkmaar, splitting the enemy line. Who knows what the Allied commanders might have achieved if this had been the case? Instead, York committed the cardinal sin of dispersing his forces in the face of the enemy, a decision which York surprisingly viewed in a positive light after the battle. He argued to Sir Henry Dundas that the Allies had almost won a breakthrough even though 'nearly 15,000 of the allied troops had unavoidably no slice in this action'.[154] Although it is conceivable that York simply sought to shift the blame for the defeat from himself to 'unavoidable' factors, his correspondence with the minister was remarkably optimistic throughout, giving the impression that he simply did not recognise his planning blunders.

York's second error was to underestimate the problem posed by the terrain. Lacking maps, the Allied infantry was left with little choice but to advance and overcome the obstacles that confronted it piecemeal. Nor did the infantry possess any knowledge of the strength of the enemy forces that awaited them. The timing of the attack was also crucial, in that the different routes allotted to the different Allied formations had their own distinctive geographical features which would require the assaulting columns to set off at a variety of different times. The eagerness of the Russians to advance at 2 in the morning, however, forced both Generals Dundas and Murray-Pulteney to set off too early on their divergent routes. The holding of Manners in reserve of the Russian advance was perhaps the only sound decision of the day, for if Manners had been attached to one of the other columns it would have been more than likely that the Russian retreat later in the day would have seen the French drive a wedge between the two Allied armies.

The Allied defeat at the first Battle of Bergen was a crushing blow to the Allied chances of success. Not only had the Allies failed to achieve the breakthrough they wanted but Allied relations had also taken a major turn for the worse. The lull over the course of the following few days played into the French and Dutch hands and enabled them to strengthen their forces.[155] As the French and Dutch readied their forces, York once again took it upon himself to plan the next offensive and instructed his commanders to prepare for another attack to propel the Allied army towards Amsterdam. A further factor which influenced York in his decision to attack again was the growing shortage of food and forage, with the Allies having overestimated the quantity of grain and fodder which they could procure from the Helder peninsula itself.[156] The bad weather also meant that the fleet had been unable to resupply the army for several weeks, whilst the fields around the Allied camp had turned into a swamp. As E. Walsh noted, 'The storms and rains were violent and incessant the roads became impassable … and the fields might be easier navigated than marched through'.[157]

York opted to pursue a tactical plan of attack in which the bulk of the Allied army would advance against the enemy on the morning of 2 October 1799. York's instructions were as follows: Abercromby was ordered to advance with a column of around 8,500 British troops from Petten, along the sea shore, to the village of Egmond-aan-Zee so as to envelop the French positions on the sand hills.[158] To Abercromby's left and in the Allied centre, Essen's 8,000 Russians were to advance along the same route as they had undertaken in the previous battle, pushing along the sand hills to Schoorl and then on to Bergen. In the meantime, General Dundas, with around 7,000 British troops, was to advance alongside Essen's Russians, whilst Murray-Pulteney with the remainder of the army was instructed to advance on the extreme left of the Allied line towards the village of Oudkarspel. Finally a force of around 2,000 Russians were to be kept in reserve at the village of Krabbendam.[159] Popham and a squadron of British gunboats were also ordered to sail down the Alkmaar canal and provide fire support for the Anglo-Russian columns.[160]

As with the previous Allied attack, the initial British and Russian advance on the morning of 2 October was successful, with Abercromby's troops advancing quickly along the undefended sea-shore at half-past 6 in the morning, whilst Essen's Russians and David Dundas's British infantry also made good progress in the Allied centre. Surtees, whose regiment was part of Dundas's column, recalled the scene on the Allied right as the Allied forces began to advance:

> On ascending a small eminence, we got a view of the village of Old
> Petten, where we discovered about 10,000 or 12,000 of our army
> drawn up near the sea beach. We passed them, and moved forward
> in direction of a high range of sand-hills, which commenced about
> a mile from the village, and which overlooked all the plain below.[161]

Within a few hours, the Allies had swept all before it along the beach and inland. York's forces, however, struggled to clear the French and Batavians from their strong defensive positions in the sand dunes which separated Abercromby's column from the rest of the Allied army.[162] As long as the French held the sand-dunes, Abercromby's troops would be stranded on the beach, unable to turn the French flank or support the rest of the army. There was also the impact of the incoming tide to consider, with the danger that, if the British troops remained on the beach, they risked being swept away. The fight for control of the sand dunes was intense, and one which saw the slow-moving British regulars struggle forward against the flexible tactics of the more fleet-footed French and Dutch light infantry:

> The French had now lined some high sand hills with a body of rifle-
> men, who began to keep up a very smart fire upon the British; shortly
> they were considerably reinforced, and they galled our troops from
> almost every eminence and outlet of the multitude of sand hills. In
> spite of all, our troops advanced with that ardour and perseverance
> which so eminently distinguish the British soldier. Though perfectly
> unacquainted with the system of sharp-shooting (and it is impossi-
> ble not to lament the want of that species of warfare in our army),
> though galled on all sides by offensive weapons that did their mis-
> chief partly unseen and always at a distance; though momentarily
> deprived from the encouraging presence of their officers by wounds

they received, and though they were themselves neither equipped for light service, not had the advantage of a light body for that purpose … our brave countrymen persevered and fought their way for four miles.[163]

The French control of the sand dunes caused major delays to the Allied advance. Not only did the rough, broken ground favour French and Dutch light infantry tactics, but the high ridge of dunes isolated Abercromby's column from the rest of the Allied army and allowed Brune and Daendels to contain Abercromby's flank attack and maintain a steady fire upon the other Allied columns.[164] One of the reasons why Abercromby was unable to force his way through the dunes was due to the fact that the officer tasked with protecting Abercromby's enveloping manoeuvre, MacDonald, advanced too eagerly with his brigade of 2,500 British regulars and lost contact with the rest of Abercromby's force. As Bunbury recalled:

> Abercromby had reckoned on his protégé, Colonel MacDonald, for the security of his left flank during the march along the beach … But MacDonald was a very wild warrior. On first entering the hills, he met with small parties, afterwards with larger, of the enemy; he got excited, followed them up, met with more, entangled himself in the waves of these great sand-downs … had a battle to himself, and so completely lost sight of Sir Ralph's column which he did not re-join until dark.[165]

What began as an orderly advance on the Allied left quickly degenerated into a somewhat chaotic series of skirmishes for control of the sand hills. On the beach the British regular line infantry had the advantage, with Abercromby able to advance some 6 miles before turning to his left so as to assault the French forces in the sand hills just to the north of the village of Egmond-aan-Zee. The fighting here was intense and confused, as Abercromby's brigades pushed forward into the sand hills, only to be met by determined French resistance. One of Abercromby's commanders was Moore. The experience of his brigade, comprising the 25th, 49th and 79th Regiments of Foot, was typical. In the morning, Moore's troops had been unopposed on the beach and had quickly marched the 6 miles from Petten to Egmond without suffering any losses. However, on reaching their destination, Moore's regiments were then ordered to clear the sand hills north of the village and duly hurried forward only for his advance guard to be engaged by a force of French hussars and light infantry.[166]

With his usual bravery and disregard for his own safety, Moore then led the main body of his brigade forward with fixed bayonets. Although initially successful in driving the French back, Moore's brigade quickly lost all sense of cohesion, with each of his regiments becoming separated in the maze of sand hills and it was not long before each of his isolated battalions were counter-attacked by French reinforcements. Brock recalled the confused nature of the fight:

> It is impossible to give you an adequate idea of the nature of the ground, which I can only compare to the sea in a storm … the instant I came up to the 79th I ordered a bayonet charge, which … was exe-cuted with the utmost gallantry, though not in the greatest order, as the nature of the ground admitted none … our loss would have been trifling had the 79th charged straightforward; but unfortunately it followed the course the 49th had taken, thereby leaving our right entirely exposed.[167]

Luckily for Brock, the French were driven back in confusion as a result of this attack, but it had been a chaotic affair and one which had dramatically showed up the British lack of tactical flexibility when it came to fighting in broken, hilly terrain. If Brock's battle had been confusing, Moore's was totally chaotic:

> My brigade, as a consequence of five hours' constant movement and action in so broken a country, were dispersed and infinitely fatigued and from the absence of some of the regiments which had not been able to keep up on the left, the enemy had struck upon the flank of the 25th Regiment, which was the most forward. The fire was extremely galling. Three companies of the 92nd regiment were sent to their support: but coming so incautiously into so hot a fire, they suffered prodigiously, and the whole began to give way … I saw myself on the point of being surrounded, when turning round to get back, I was knocked down by a shot, which entered behind my ear and came out at my cheek under my left eye. Just before I received this shot I saw the impossibility of rallying or stopping my men under such hot fire.[168]

Shortly after Moore received his wound, Paget's British light dragoons defeated a force of French cavalry on the beach next to Egmond.[169] Whilst on the other side of the sand hills, Dundas and Essen pushed the French back and, though failing to link up with Abercromby, eventually secured Bergen.[170] To the far left of the Allied line, Murray-Pulteney's column managed to fix Daendels's Batavians, but otherwise played little part in the proceedings.[171]

The Battle of Alkmaar was a pyrrhic victory for the Allies. As with the engagement at Bergen, what started as a rapid Allied attack had quickly degenerated into a battle of attrition, with the difficult terrain again causing problems for the attackers. Casualties amongst both armies were great, with the Allies coming off worse with over 2,000 losses, the vast majority British.[172] The weather in the immediate aftermath of the battle was a contributing factor in the number of deaths amongst the Allied army, with several hundred wounded British soldiers having little or no means of keeping warm, or supplies to consume, as they lay exposed on the wet and windy sand hills. As Brock recalled:

> We remained that night and the following on the sand hills; you cannot conceive our wretched state, as it blew and rained nearly the whole time. Our men bore all this without grumbling, although they had nothing to eat but the biscuits they carried with them, which by this time were completely wet.[173]

Aftermath

The Allied army was exhausted. It had fought three major battles, suffered the loss of nearly a quarter of its total strength in terms of killed and wounded, suffered also from a lack of supplies and, most importantly of all, had failed to achieve the breakthrough which the Allied high command wanted. Although the Allies had forced the French and Batavians to abandon the sand hills and relinquish Bergen and Alkmaar, they had little else to show for their efforts. If the defeat on 19 September had dented the Allies' chances of success, the bloody yet indecisive Allied victory on 2 October effectively extinguished the Allies' hopes. Until that time the Allied army as a whole had not been fully engaged whilst York had retained a numerical superiority over the French and Batavians. Allied losses, however, combined with the continued arrival of French and Batavian reinforcements, soon brought numerical parity, which enabled the French to mount a second offensive of their own.

As with the Battle of Bergen, the Allies had failed to make the most of the forces available to them and had blundered into a confused battle of attrition on their right flank. York's planning must again be called into question, in that yet again the Allied army was spread out across a wide frontage, and thus was unable to bring its numerical superiority to bear at the crucial point against the enemy. Bunbury was particularly scathing in his criticism of the plan of attack formulated by York, 'The plan of operations was complicated … intricate movements were to be executed by raw troops in a country where communications were difficult and uncertain, it is not surprising that many blunders and disappointments ensued'.[174]

What is particularly interesting about the Allied conduct of the battle is that, in contrast to the Allied experience at Bergen, it was the British and not the Russians who struggled on the right of the Allied line. It was also British, rather than Russian blunders, which contributed to the chaotic nature of the fighting on the sand hills and on this occasion MacDonald, like Sedmoratzky twelve days earlier, lost control of his troops and advanced too far forward. The frantic British advance into the dunes was also similar to the manner in which Hermann's Russians had pushed forward at Bergen and almost resulted in an exact repeat of events when Moore, in an attempt to rally his men, was almost captured by a French force.[175] It is indicative of the nature of much of British military history that the poor conduct of the British in the sand hills has not been remembered whilst, in contrast, the defeat of the Russians in the Battle of Bergen has been singled out as a significant factor in Allied defeat.

The poor conduct of the Allies at Alkmaar had proven yet again that they lacked the operational skills necessary to achieve a decisive victory. At Bergen and then Alkmaar, the Allied forces had formed up neatly and had set off with great speed and bravery but, once battle was joined, both the British and Russians proved unable to coordinate their attacks. The British lack of professional staff officers, in particular, was significant and helps explain how the Allied columns at the twin battles of Bergen repeatedly lost contact with one another. Poor Allied planning, a lack of good inter-Allied relations, combined with stern French and Batavian resistance and a lack of Orangeist support undermined the Allied effort. The Allies had also performed badly at the tactical level and specifically in their attempts to dislodge the French forces posted in the sand hills.

Although it was certainly the case that the French and Batavians had superiority in the number of light troops, the fighting in the dunes was not simply a case of light infantry against line infantry. On the contrary, the French and the Batavians had deployed all arms formations in the sand hills and defended in depth. In the Battle of Bergen, for instance, the Russian column had first met French chasseurs on the sand hills and in the outlying villages, only to run into formed bodies of French line infantry with artillery and cavalry support. Likewise, in the British advance on the beach in the battle of Alkmaar, McDonald's brigade encountered both French light troops and line infantry.

Although the Allies had won a victory at Alkmaar and advanced several miles in the process, success had been bought at a high price. Supplies, meanwhile, were running perilously short, whilst the incessant wind and rain had made the dyke roads almost impassable. Poor Anglo-Russian relations had also caused a rift between the two Allied armies, whilst there was still no sign of Grenville's promised Orangeist Dutch uprising. The conditions had also greatly worsened, the roads were in poor condition and life was also unpleasant for the troops in the wind-swept sand in the hills.[176] The situation looked bleak and, with winter on its way, it would not be long before the Texel froze over; an eventuality which would threaten to isolate the Allied army from the fleet.

Despite the near hopelessness of the situation, York still clung on to the faint hope that one last push could be decisive and therefore readied the exhausted Allied army for another attack, which was scheduled to take place on 6 October. The ensuing battle was a disaster for the Allies, as four columns, three British and one Russian, bungled their way forward amidst a rain storm. The battle followed the now familiar pattern of initial Allied success, followed by attrition. The Russians, supported by the British, at first drove all before them, but they both advanced too far and were counter-attacked by the French and Batavians. An infamous episode then took place. Following the battle, Abercromby despatched an officer, Major James Kempt, to headquarters to warn York that the French and Batavians looked to be readying a major attack of their own. On arrival at headquarters Kempt made every effort to convince the Duke of the need to ride to the front but York refused to do so until after he had finished his dinner.[177] It was to prove a fateful decision.

With the C-in-C far to the rear and bad weather reducing visibility the battle degenerated into a series of confused skirmishes until darkness forced a close on proceedings.[178] This engagement, which later came to be known as the Battle of Castricum, was the final nail in the coffin for the Allied campaign in Northern Holland. Tired, hungry and disease-ridden, the Anglo-Russian forces needed time to recuperate and resupply but the longer they remained in the flooded fields south of Alkmaar there was little hope of them achieving this. Poorly supplied and vulnerable to attack, the Allied position was desperate:

> Directly opposed to it lay the enemy, in a position almost impregnable, and confident, from an accession of strength, having just been reinforced by six thousand French troops. A naked, barren and exhausted country extended all around, thinly scattered with a few ruined villages that scarcely afforded a scanty shelter for the wounded ... the weather had set in, since the evening of the 6th October, with increased inclemency; clouds discharged themselves in torrents; and the roads were so entirely broken up, that the urgent necessities of the troops could not, with the utmost exertions, be

presently relieved. To these complicated evils the army lay exposed on unsheltered sand-hills, their ammunition spoiled, and their clothes drenched with rain water.[179]

Rough seas, particularly in mid-September, also prevented the shipment of supplies to the Helder.[180] Thus, by October, the pressing question for the British was that, if the army was forced into winter quarters, how would the troops be sustained if the Texel froze completely and the army was cut off from the fleet? It was a question for which the British had no answer and, in light of this issue and the other difficulties, the senior British generals (Abercromby, Dundas, Murray-Pulteney and Hulse) had met in the aftermath of Battle of Alkmaar to discuss the options open to the Allied army. They concluded that the situation was untenable and that there was no option but to retreat to the defensive positions on the Zype:

> Since the landing of the army in Holland it has sustained five con-siderable actions without being able to make any considerable pro-gress in the country, or to obtain any permanent, or strong situa-tion. That in these actions the Army has suffered a diminution of between 9 and 10,000 men, and a very considerable proportion of its officers, those naturally the best and bravest ... We had a large, nominal army formed of raw soldiers, hastily assembled, ill clothed, and a very great proportion of inexperienced officers ... we have no assistance, or encouragement from the country ... nor do we even obtain accurate intelligence ... From what we see, and from what we feel and have experienced: from the state of the troops, the greater part of whom have been now four days under arms in the sand hills and other situations, from the want of present, and the impossibility of bringing up future supplies: from the unparalleled inclemency of the season, and weather: from the advantage of defence the enemy possesses, his growing numbers and his absolute command of the resources of the country: from the almost impassable state of the roads, and the country from the diminished condition of our cav-alry and horses of every description: from our being now in a situa-tion which is not an advantageous military position: and from many other concurring unfavourable circumstances. We are humbly of the opinion that ... we should return to the position of the Zype ... and there await a more favourable change of circumstances.[181]

With no hope of advancing further and the army in very great danger York decided that there was little choice but to retreat back to the Helder and to seek an armistice with the French. A further factor which no doubt contributed to the British decision to retreat was that word had finally reached York regarding the weak state of the Orangeist movement in Northern Holland. Since Abercromby's landing in late August, the British had not received any form of communication from the local inhabitants or British paid agents concerning the willingness of the local population to rise up in support of the Prince of Orange. As a result the British had despatched Sontag, a Dutchman, to act as a commissary to the Dutch troops whom the British thought were located in the islands north of the Texel. Delivery of Sontag's report was crucially delayed because he had been wounded on his return to the British lines during the Battle of Alkmaar. When his report eventually reached York it did not speak positively of the Orangeists, stating that though around 5,000 men had declared for the Prince of Orange (roughly half were Storj's ex-sailors) they were in a bad state and had low morale:

> They are in want of necessities of all kind, of clothing, of arms and accoutrements. They are divided in different places … that the retrograde movement of the troops has alarmed those men, who according to the decree of the Batavians as well as their officers are not to expect mercy should the chance of war put them into their hands.[182]

A further aspect which hampered the Orangeist forces was that the areas in which they had gathered were largely inhospitable, with the people of the coastal towns and villages suffering from famine. It would thus have been almost impossible for the British to concentrate the Orangeist troops in one place for fear of starvation.[183] Faced with their poor state and the logistical problems inherent in gathering the Dutch troops together for training and supply purposes, the British opted not to transport them to the Helder but instead discussed the best way of evacuating them.

Another factor which (perhaps) contributed to the Allied decision to retreat and seek terms was that news had reached Holland in early October of the crushing defeat of Korsakov's Russian army at the second Battle of Zurich on 25 September. Although the Russians had not performed to the best of their abilities, the Allied offensive in Switzerland also failed because the Austrians had not supported their Russian Allies. Indeed, long before Suvorov's army reached the Swiss frontier, the Austrians had transferred their main army to Northern Italy and left the Russians in the lurch. With fewer troops available to them and lacking in artillery, cavalry and supplies, it was only a matter of time before Korsakov was defeated and forced to retreat. Angered by the conduct of the British and the Austrians, Tsar Paul I pulled out of the coalition, leaving the British and the Austrians to their own devices.[184]

With the Allied cause in tatters in both Switzerland and Holland, York instructed Knox to meet with Brune and an armistice was duly signed. The British were granted permission to evacuate the remainder of the Anglo-Russian army, with its artillery and horses, in exchange for the release of 8,000 French prisoners of war.[185] Interestingly, Brune clearly did not feel it essential to reclaim the Dutch fleet, a decision which no doubt angered the Batavian government.

So ended the Anglo-Russian expedition to Northern Holland, a campaign in which the British had lost nearly 5,000 men killed, wounded and missing, whilst the Russian contingent had suffered around 6,000 losses. The campaign had been a battle of attrition, with the Allies suffering around 11,000 casualties, roughly a third of their combined strength, in the period from 19 September to 6 October. This was a heavy price to pay for a narrow slice of Northern Holland and even this hard-fought area of territory was lost to the Allies at the armistice. Ultimately, therefore, the Anglo-Russian expedition to Northern Holland was a comprehensive failure.

Chapter 4

The Expedition to the Scheldt, 1809

The expedition to the Scheldt in 1809 was the greatest amphibious expedition mounted by Britain before the Crimean War. Its architect was the Secretary of State for War and the Colonies, Robert Stewart Viscount Lord Castlereagh. Like Grenville before him, Castlereagh wanted to re-establish a foothold on the Continent and restore a balance of power to Europe. The expedition had two principal objectives. The first was to destroy French naval power in the Low Countries, via the destruction of the naval dockyards at Antwerp, and the second was to provide military support to the Austrians.

The expedition, however, was undermined by a number of factors, most notably by poor strategic and operational planning on the part of Castlereagh and the main British military and naval officers. Inclement weather and stern enemy resistance also hampered the expedition, which ended in failure. The spread of a deadly epidemic amongst the British soldiers on the islands in the Scheldt decimated the British expeditionary force and the island of Walcheren became 'The Grave of the Army.'[1] The political ramifications of the debacle were quickly felt back in Britain as the government of the Duke of Portland collapsed and a Public Inquiry was initiated.

Although largely forgotten today, due to the popularity of Wellington's campaigns in the Iberian Peninsula, the expedition to the Scheldt was a serious debacle and marked the nadir of the British war effort against Napoleon.

The British Army: Fit for Service?

Following the year-long Peace of Amiens, which collapsed in 1803, the British army increased in size to meet the demands of the next conflict with France.[2] Renewed fears of French invasion during the period 1803–5 also served to galvanise British public support for the war effort and encouraged thousands of civilians to volunteer for part-time military training.[3] As the conflict with France intensified over the course of the following years and more British troops were sent on active operations in Europe and across the globe the British struggled to find enough new recruits to make good on past losses.[4] In 1809, for example, the British army suffered over 25,000 casualties but was only able to recruit around 12,000 men.[5]

Furthermore, although the reforms made by York had improved the administration of the army, British military performances continued to disappoint. One of the main reasons for this was the military's inability to learn from the past and to plan operations effectively. For example, poor strategic and operational planning were hallmarks of the disastrous British expeditions to South America in 1806–7.[6] The first expedition was the brainchild of the rash adventurer, Popham, who after the successful British mission to capture the Cape from the Dutch in 1806 persuaded Major General Sir David Baird to send a small force, under Brigadier General Beresford, to seize the Spanish cities of Buenos Aires and Montevideo.[7] Although initially successful, this unofficial enterprise suffered from poor planning and inaccurate intelligence and ended with Beresford's capitulation to a mixed force of Spanish militia and civilians.[8] Although Popham was recalled to face a court martial, he was not forced to resign and continued in the service.[9] In 1807 a second expedition was launched, under the command of Whitelocke, but again poor planning greatly undermined the ensuing campaign which came to a disastrous end when Whitelocke's forces were forced to surrender at Buenos Aires.[10] Defeated and dejected, the British were forced to evacuate the region, the reputation of the British army in tatters.

In Europe Napoleon's victories over the other European powers over the course of 1805–7 had isolated the British from the continent of Europe and meant that the British army had had relatively few opportunities to conduct large-scale operations on the Continent.[11] A rare success for the British was achieved in Italy in 1806 when a small British expeditionary force, under General Charles Stuart, defeated a small French army, commanded by General Jean Reynier, at Maida.[12] Stuart was also successful in conducting operations in the Kingdom of Naples in 1809 and defeated the French invasion of Sicily in 1810. Other small-scale expeditions were also mounted in the Mediterranean and the British established garrisons on the Ionian Islands and Cephalonia.[13] Troops were also sent to Hanover in 1805, Stralsund in 1807 and Sweden in 1808.[14] However, none of these expeditions placed serious pressure on France and Napoleon's economic policies soon forced the British to act far more ruthlessly.

Following the end of the War of the Fourth Coalition in 1807, which witnessed the near destruction of the Kingdom of Prussia by the French, Napoleon and Tsar Alexander I had signed the Treaty of Tilsit. This realigned the Russians and Prussians with France and enabled Napoleon to isolate Britain further and reduce her influence over European affairs.[15] It also reinforced Napoleon's Continental System which since 1806 had sought to exclude British goods from European markets in response to the British blockade of France.[16]

Napoleon also hoped to pressure the smaller maritime states of Europe to exclude British shipping from their ports, forge a grand alliance of the other naval powers in opposition to Great Britain and rebuild the French navy following its humbling defeat at Trafalgar in 1805.[17] Napoleon also tightened his grip over the Low Countries when he transformed the Batavian Republic into the Kingdom of Holland and placed his brother, Louis Bonaparte, upon the new Dutch throne in June 1806.[18] The British were also concerned by reports which suggested that Napoleon wanted to seize the neutral Danish fleet and about the implications this might have for British trade.[19]

Locked in a new naval arms race, the British desperately sought a means to strike back and did so with a vengeance in August 1807 when the Royal Navy launched a surprise attack upon the great Danish naval base at Copenhagen.[20] The ferocity of the British attack caught the Danes completely by surprise and greatly weakened the Danish fleet.[21] The same year Napoleon also tried to seize the Portuguese fleet following the Franco-Spanish invasion of Portugal, only for the British to rescue the Portuguese navy and royal family at the last minute.[22] This was only the start of a general crisis in the Iberian Peninsula and in 1808 the French ousted the Spanish Bourbons and subsumed the former Spanish state into the French Empire. Horrified by the French betrayal, the Spanish people duly rebelled against the French in May and defeated a French army at the Battle of Bailen in July.[23] This rare French defeat provided a great piece of propaganda for the rebel cause and helped convince the British to despatch troops to support the Spanish. British confidence received a further boost in mid-August 1808 when Sir Arthur Wellesley defeated the French at Vimeiro.[24]

Although this success was later marred by the controversial Convention of Cintra, the British remained committed to the war in the Iberian Peninsula and in October they despatched Moore to command in Spain and Portugal.[25] Once again, however, the ensuing campaign in Spain was poorly planned and badly executed and resulted in Anglo-Spanish defeat at the hands of Napoleon.[26] Although Moore fought the French to a standstill at Corunna and managed the British evacuation, he was mortally wounded in the process. The army Moore commanded at Corunna had also suffered terribly in its retreat to the coast of northern Spain and was thus a shadow of its former self.[27] The largest British military expedition to the Continent since 1799 had almost witnessed the destruction of a British army and the campaign was labelled a 'shameful disaster' by the *London Times*.[28] Despite suffering badly during this campaign, many of the same soldiers who fought with Moore in Spain would find themselves bound for the Scheldt only a few months later.

Rationale for British Intervention

In the late summer of 1809 British troops were once again despatched to the Low Countries, the catalyst for a new British expedition to the region being the renewed hostility between Austria and Napoleon. Since signing the humiliating Treaty of Pressburg in 1805, following the Battle of Austerlitz, a small group of Austrian diplomats headed by Count Phillip Stadion had watched events in Spain and Portugal with interest.[29] This 'war-party' became increasingly vocal and managed to persuade the emperor and his inner circle within the Habsburg court that war with France was essential for the future of the Empire.[30] The head of the Austrian army, the gifted Archduke Charles, sided with the more cautious elements at court and impressed upon the emperor the need for a breathing space so as to make the army fit for service.[31]

Before committing themselves to another major conflict the Austrians set about finding potential allies. The first port of call for Austria's diplomatic agents was St Petersburg. Following negotiations at Tilsit and Erfurt, Tsar Alexander I had agreed to support Napoleon if France was attacked by Austria or Prussia.[32] Austrian fears regarding Russian intervention were soothed, however, following reports from St Petersburg that Russia was unlikely to provide the French with military aid in the event of a new European war.[33] However, military and financial support for Vienna would not be forthcoming.

The Austrians now turned their attention to Great Britain. In October 1808, a secret message was received by the Foreign Office from Vienna asking for financial assistance. The Austrian proposal was audacious. The Austrians wanted an initial loan of £2.5 million and a further £5 million over the course of 1809. In return the Austrians promised to put almost half a million men into the field against Napoleon.[34] The British were sceptical of the Austrians because of their previous poor relations, especially regarding financial matters.[35] During the following weeks, the Secretary of State for Foreign Affairs, Sir George Canning, discussed matters with his Cabinet colleagues and much to the Austrians' frustration the British refused the proposals.[36]

In March 1809 the situation changed markedly. Instead of witnessing a major victory in Spain, the British were counting the cost of the disastrous Corunna campaign and Canning was eager to secure better Anglo-Austrian relations.[37] This time the British promised to provide both financial instalments and military support and, after a last-minute declaration of hostilities, the Austrians advanced into French-held territory on 12 April 1809.[38] Before the Austrian declaration of war, the British had started to consider where to strike at the French. Although the Habsburgs had suggested the Weser estuary, the British focused their attentions upon the Scheldt with a view to striking at the French naval base at Antwerp.[39]

Since the French defeat at Trafalgar and Napoleon's creation of the Continental System, the British had been watchful of Napoleon's efforts to rebuild the French navy.[40] Despite suffering heavy shipping losses at the great naval battles of the Nile and Trafalgar, the expansion of the French Empire in the period following Trafalgar meant that by 1809 the French navy had increased in size. The key to France's naval regeneration was the French possession of a number of well-protected deep-water harbours, from Antwerp to Genoa, where they were able to construct ships-of-the-line unmolested by the Royal Navy.[41] The Royal Navy, by contrast, was suffering from the pressures of war. Forced to patrol the oceans and blockade French ports, the Admiralty's main concern after Trafalgar was the battle against the scourge of wear and tear. In addition, manpower shortages posed serious problems for the Royal Navy, with losses being compounded by a decrease in recruiting.[42] Although Napoleon's plans had received a set back at Copenhagen, the British were adamant that the French naval establishments in the Low Countries needed to be destroyed. The British had long contemplated mounting such an expedition. As early as 1798, for instance, the First Lord of the Admiralty, George Second Earl of Spencer, had discussed at length a scheme put forward by Popham to seize the smuggling port of Flushing on the island of Walcheren and the British had also toyed with the idea of seizing Flushing by a *coup de main* in 1799.[43] The British were also wary of the invasion threat posed by the presence of a French fleet at Antwerp. As General Craufurd noted:

> From the Scheld he will be able to combine a formidable invasion with the greatest facility ... with invasion, certain invasion, of the most formidable description, approaching, the success of which would be attended with every horrible calamity that could possibly befall this great and prosperous and happy country ... the destruction of all its power and consequence, of every species of property, of all domestic comfort, of all personal security, the annihilation of our liberties and our whole political existence ...[44]

These sentiments expressed by Craufurd a year after the Scheldt expedition mirrored those of the Admiralty in 1809. Since the recommencement of hostilities in 1803 the Admiralty had maintained a constant sentinel over the Scheldt, with the estuary being watched by a small squadron under the command of Admiral Thomas Russell.[45] Information regarding the French naval establishment at Antwerp flooded into the Admiralty office both from blockading British vessels and also from less trustworthy sources, such as smugglers. An example of a typical report received by the Admiralty from the British naval forces off the Scheldt reads as follows:

> At Flushing there are ... seven 74 gun ships, a frigate, and 7 gun boats, on the stocks two 74 gun ships, a frigate and a brig. In the roads a frigate and a brig. Among all the vessels at Flushing not more than 800 men. At Ramaskins 7 gun boats. At Caampveer about 40 sail of smugglers ...[46]

Over the course of 1805 to 1809, numerous reports such as this were received by the Admiralty from vessels off the Scheldt. Many reports not only gave information about the ever changing strength of the French naval forces at Antwerp and Flushing, but also advised the Admiralty of the need for an expedition to be sent to the region. One such call for military action was received by the Admiralty from an anonymous source on 7 March 1808 which stated that 'It would be advisable for the present moment to get possession of the town and port of Flushing – and of the whole island of Walcheren as there is in the port 6 sail of the line and 16 smaller vessels which are meant for an expedition.'[47] By 1809 the Admiralty and the ministers of the Portland government were convinced that Antwerp posed a major threat to British interests. The First Lord of the Admiralty, Lord Mulgrave, stated in a speech to the Cabinet on 25 March 1809 that:

> the formidable Naval Force assembled in the Scheldt and its rapid increase is of more importance ... to this country than any naval force, that is, or can be assembled by the enemy ... that the Scheldt fleet is within a short distance of the vulnerable ports of the coast of England ... that the British fleet in the Baltic could be exposed to an attack from the Scheldt, and the existence of a strong fleet there would place in jeopardy all our blockading squadrons from Brest to Toulon ...[48]

What is important is that Antwerp, rather than Flushing, was the principal target of the British strategists. For the Admiralty, the destruction of the dockyards at Antwerp promised to cripple Napoleon's ship-building plans, whilst the forcing of the Scheldt would also offer the potential for the possible capture or destruction of the French squadron stationed there.

Planning and Preparation

At the centre of initial planning for the new Anglo-Austrian alliance had been Canning.[49] When Canning had suggested the idea the ministers had been unsure of whether to support the Austrians. However, when news reached London that the Austrians had defeated the French at the Battle of Aspern-Essling on 21–2 May the government unanimously supported the need for a new British intervention in the Low Countries.[50] By this point, Canning's main rival in government, Castlereagh, had assumed responsibility for the expedition. A gifted protégé of Pitt the Younger and a former head of the Board of Control, Castlereagh had been readied by Pitt for high office and was the natural successor to both Lord Grenville and Sir Henry Dundas.[51]

Before gaining the Cabinet's official approval of the scheme Castlereagh sought the advice of the newly appointed C-in-C of the British army Sir David Dundas.[52] Dundas had only been appointed to the post in March, after the resignation of York, following the latter's embroilment in a scandal regarding the sale of commissions.[53] Dundas quickly put his thoughts to paper and also called on several officers at the Horse Guards to do likewise.[54]

The generals agreed that the operation would be difficult and that success would depend upon tight army and navy cooperation. They also agreed that troops would need to land on the islands on both sides of the Scheldt before an advance to Antwerp could be made. The words of Calvert can be taken to sum up the general feeling of those consulted, 'The service would be arduous, and the troops employed on it must undoubtedly be exposed to considerable risk …'.[55] These opinions should have warned Castlereagh against launching the expedition, but the Austrian victory at Aspern-Essling convinced him that the expedition had to be launched.[56]

The Admiralty was also asked to provide its opinion of the operation and the First Lord Henry Phipps (Lord Mulgrave) was consulted about the practicalities of transporting a large military force to the Scheldt. Mulgrave in turn also sought the advice of Captain Sir Home Popham. When questioned at the Parliamentary Inquiry following the expedition to the Scheldt in 1810, Popham recalled his meeting with Mulgrave:

> as nearly as I can recollect, my Lord Mulgrave said there was a large disposable force, and that as the French had a very strong fleet in the Scheldt and were still building more ships, it would be very desirable to make an effort to destroy them, and he requested that I would turn my thoughts to that subject, as it would be very desirable that I should see Lord Chatham and Lord Castlereagh in the course of a day or two.[57]

Popham's tasks were to assess the topographical, tidal and climatic conditions in the Scheldt and to procure transports for the expeditionary force – Popham having performed the latter role before in 1799. Popham was quickly made aware of the topographical difficulties which an expedition to the Scheldt would encounter. The River Scheldt did not flow in a single course from Antwerp to the North Sea, but instead broke into two channels bypassing the islands of North and South Beveland and Walcheren.[58] These two channels were known as the West and East Scheldt, the entrance to the West Scheldt was known as the Wielingen Channel, whilst the entrance to the East Scheldt was known as the Veere Gat, the former was reached by the deep anchorage known as the Stone Deep whilst the latter was entered from the Roompot.[59]

The West Scheldt was the larger of the two channels and was the most direct route to Antwerp. The West Scheldt, however, was bordered by high sand dunes and dykes, which obscured much of the French and Dutch coastal defences, whilst the presence of the French squadron also meant that it was almost impossible for the British to gain a clear view of the Franco-Dutch positions around Antwerp. This meant that Russell could give little information to the Admiralty as to the precise location of the French ship-building centre at Antwerp.[60] The lack of information posed another serious question: how would the British navigate their way up the Scheldt? As one of the navy's best pilots Popham was one of the few men available to the Admiralty who could answer this question, but given the lack of information about the conditions in the Scheldt the only way Popham could provide a definite answer was if and when the British fleet sailed into the Wielingen Channel.

The first problem facing Popham with regard to naval operations was how to nullify the French gun batteries along the banks of the Scheldt, whilst also steering a course that kept the fleet safe from the West Scheldt's turbulent currents and shifting sandbanks. Faced with similar circumstances in previous operations the Royal Navy had achieved mixed results. In the forcing of the Sound at Copenhagen in 1801, the British warships had managed to silence the Danish gun batteries but had suffered severe losses in the process.[61] The British had faced a similar set of problems again in 1807 when Admiral Sir John Duckworth's squadron attempted to force the Dardanelles.[62] In the case of the Scheldt, the British were faced with a difficult series of operations. This time the navy would have to work closely with the army, as British troops were scheduled to land on the banks of the Scheldt to capture the enemy gun batteries. The act of forcing a heavily defended coastal position would pose problems for the Royal Navy for many years to come, with the expedition to the Dardanelles in 1915 being a case in point.

Tidal and climatic conditions were also important. Popham was aware that the British needed to commence the navigation of the Scheldt when the tide was high, if the British waited too long and went at low tide they risked being stranded on the many sandbanks of the West Scheldt. With late summer fast approaching and daylight hours shortening, Popham advised Castlereagh that time was once again of the essence, 'I see the season advancing fast; and, if we are imperceptibly led on till the midsummer fine weather is past, we shall have the most dreadful of all difficulties, the elements to encounter'.[63] Like Calvert before him, however, Popham's warnings fell on deaf ears and Castlereagh ploughed on with preparations.

With transport issues likely to consume precious time, Popham again stressed the need for the expedition to be despatched as quickly as possible, 'Transports are the greatest clog to every sort of expedition, particularly those in which promptness and celerity are so essential to success.'[64] With no dedicated military transports of their own, military and naval officials were forced to hire secure civilian vessels for several months at a negotiated rate; the net result of this haphazard system was that the cost to hire greatly fluctuated.[65] With so little time to work with, Popham advised Mulgrave to convert several old warships into troop transports instead of relying on civilian vessels.[66]

Whilst Popham pieced together a memorandum about transport issues and assessed the obstacles and dangers the navy would encounter, Castlereagh continued to urge the Cabinet to launch the expedition. Prior to the Austrian victory at Aspern-Essling, Castlereagh had been buoyed by intelligence reports which stated that French troop strengths in Holland and Flanders were particularly low:

> The intelligence received from the northern parts of France, from Flanders, and from Holland, although not such as will enable me to furnish you with any precise statement of the enemy's force ... represents them as drained as low, if not lower than at any former period, of regular troops, and I apprehend it may be generally assumed, that we can never expect to find the enemy more exposed or more assailable in that quarter nor is it probable that Great Britain will ever have a large disposable force applicable to such a service than at the present moment.[67]

The apparent weakness of the Dutch and French forces in the region, combined with Austria's victory over Napoleon and the eagerness of the Admiralty to attack Antwerp, convinced Castlereagh that the operation had to be launched quickly.[68] However, the quality of British intelligence was patchy. As Carl A. Christie has noted, the British lacked accurate information about enemy activity in the Low Countries, 'Reliable intelligence about the upper reaches of the Scheldt was virtually unobtainable. Nothing was known about Flanders or Brabant, both of which could send reinforcements if they were available.'[69]

Flushed with news of Aspern-Essling Castlereagh failed to question the quality of British intelligence or fully consider the doubts of the military.[70] Throughout June, Castlereagh worked feverishly to prepare the armed forces, with the help of Dundas, whilst also spending considerable time in finding a command pairing for the expedition. Castlereagh's choice for commander of the army was the Master General of the Ordnance John Pitt, Second Earl of Chatham and brother of the late Pitt the Younger. A senior Lieutenant General, Chatham, was also a former First Lord of the Admiralty and had commanded a brigade in Holland in 1799.[71] Although Chatham was not the most experienced front-line general, he was available for command which was more than could be said for many of his contemporaries. Indeed, for the first time in the conflict there was a serious shortage of senior military commanders available to Castlereagh. For instance, Sir John Moore had been killed at Corunna; York had only recently resigned, whilst generals Burrard and Dalrymple had had their careers cut short following the Convention of Cintra in 1808.[72] Wellington, meanwhile, whose reputation had also been tarnished by Cintra, was already employed commanding British forces in the Iberian Peninsula. With so few candidates for the role, Castlereagh had little choice but to appoint Chatham as the commander of the expeditionary force.

By contrast, the Navy had a wide range of officers available for appointment as commander of the naval force. The Admiralty's decision to appoint Admiral Sir Richard Strachan was surprising for he had no experience of amphibious operations.[73] Like the army, promotion in the navy was a potentially difficult business. Although rewarding service and experience, this could be problematic, an example being if the Admiralty wanted to promote a gifted captain to the rank of Rear Admiral, it had to promote all officers above the chosen captain in the naval officer list to a higher rank. Another problem for the navy was that, despite there being many gifted junior commanders there was not the same number of gifted admirals; by 1809 many senior naval leaders had either retired or been killed including Collingwood, Nelson and Vincent.[74] This left Strachan as the only viable option. Strachan's role in the forthcoming expedition was to be a man-manager, overseeing a wide spread of interdependent naval and amphibious operations, without necessarily having to take an active role in any of them. Like Chatham, he was to pull the strings whilst junior commanders carried out the plans.

The Admiralty's choice of Rear Admiral Sir Richard Keats, a dynamic naval commander to serve under Strachan was consistent with its selection policy. In previous joint operations older commanders such as Admiral George Elphinstone, later Lord Keith, and Admiral James Gambier had been appointed to command the overall naval force, leaving more dynamic commanders, such as Nelson and Cochrane, to oversee more active operations. Despite this, Strachan's lack of experience in amphibious warfare should have sounded a warning to the Admiralty before it appointed him to command the naval forces for the expedition. Brave and headstrong 'Mad Dick' Strachan, as the sailors refereed to him, also lacked detailed knowledge of the Scheldt estuary.[75] Strachan's lack of experience in coordinating naval action with military operations, coupled with his ignorance of the Scheldt, would severely hamper the expedition.

Chatham was appointed, with the king's blessing, in early June and Strachan's appointment came at the same time.[76] With the king's acceptance of the expedition, all that remained was for the Cabinet to offer its approval, which it gave on 21 June.[77] Whilst Castlereagh consulted with key figures in London, the final preparations were made and the south coast of England, from Portsmouth to Ramsgate, became a hive of activity. From the middle of June onwards regiments stationed across the British Isles were to be seen marching towards the coastal towns of the south east. Rifleman Benjamin Harris recorded the sight of an army on the move on the road to Dover:

> From Hythe to Deal was one day's march: and I remember looking along the road at the good appearance the different regiments made as we marched along. It was as fine an expedition as ever I looked at, and the army seemed to stretch, as I regarded them, the whole distance before us to Dover.[78]

The coastal towns were soon swamped by thousands of soldiers. An anonymous officer of the 81st Regiment of Foot recalled the scene he found on arriving in Ramsgate: 'Everything is bustle, agitation, running backwards and forwards. The place is full of wives, friends, and daughters of the officers about to embark'.[79] The generals also received their marching orders. One such commander, General William Dyott, noted his surprise on receiving his orders to prepare for active operations: 'The move from Winchester turned out what I little expected ... I was to go without delay to the Isle of Thanet, to take the command of a brigade consisting of the 6th, 50th, and 91st regiments...'.[80]

Whilst the British readied their forces Napoleon managed to outmanoeuvre and defeat the Austrians at the battle of Wagram on 5–6 July.[81] The Austrians opted to seek an armistice with the French and the news of these negotiations reached London roughly two weeks later.[82] Despite Napoleon's victory over the Austrians, Castlreagh remained hopeful about the prospects of the expedition and continued to oversee preparations. Of vital importance at this stage was the need for a clear and precise operational plan, but in the hectic rush to get the expedition underway, the British failed to create anything remotely resembling a sound plan of operations.

Castlereagh, Chatham and the naval representatives met over the course of June and early July to finalise the objectives of the expedition, assess transport issues and plot where the army would be landed. What was lacking in these meetings was a discussion of what the troops would do once they had disembarked on the islands in the Scheldt and ultimately upon the Continent. Chatham knew that somewhere in the vicinity of Antwerp the French navy was constructing ships-of-the-line. His task was to force the Scheldt by landing troops along its banks, capture the French gun batteries there and then land a force close enough to Antwerp to destroy the French ships. What was not clear was how the troops would actually operate beyond their beach heads. How would commanders communicate with one another? Would the army need to storm Antwerp? These questions needed answers. Chatham and Strachan, however, appear not to have deemed it necessary to raise them. As Chatham recalled to the Scheldt Inquiry, once the guns along the Scheldt had been captured by a series of landings, there was no plan of operations to guide the British troops who would land near to Antwerp. Commanders were simply expected to react to the circumstances, 'No plan in detail was ever concerted for the attack on Antwerp: it must have depended entirely on circumstances after we had landed on the continent.'[83]

Not only did no plan exist for the crucial later stage of the campaign, in which Chatham sought to land two divisions of British troops at Sandvliet near to Antwerp, but even the initial landings to be made on the islands in the Scheldt (Walcheren, Cadsand and South Beveland) were not part of a clear plan of operations. In effect, once the troops had landed, the British commanders had no guidance other than to advance and clear their respective beachheads of enemy troops and artillery. Once this task was completed, they had no other instructions. Chatham really had no idea of what he wanted his troops to do once they had landed save advance beyond the sand hills and neither did he understand, or claim to be aware of the actual location of the dockyards, 'I was not distinctly apprised of the situation of the docks, nor do I know that there were any docks at Antwerp ... I had no distinct knowledge before I left England where the arsenals were'.[84]

Instead of making a clear plan of operations and gathering together accurate intelligence about Antwerp and its environs, Chatham relied instead on his ability to make things up as he went along and react to the circumstances, 'The duty of the Admiral and General [is] to decide according to circumstances and information on the spot'.[85] Confident in his and his naval counterparts' ability to find a way to Antwerp, Chatham eschewed the need to create an operational plan and concentrated instead on readying the troops for active service.

Execution

After weeks of preparation, in which British troops had to wait aboard ship for long periods, the British expedition to the Scheldt finally set sail at 5am on 28 July 1809.[86] The initial British landing plans were as follows. Sir Eyre Coote, Mackenzie Fraser and Thomas Graham's divisions, comprising just over 12,000 men, were to land at Zoultand Bay on the south-west coast of the island of Walcheren in waves of 3,000 men at a time and with orders to clear the landing beaches. Whilst this operation was being undertaken, a smaller landing was to take place on the Bree Sands, on the north-west coast of Walcheren, in order to clear the French forces covering the Veere Gat, a small waterway separating Walcheren from South Beveland.[87] Once these operations were completed Sir John Hope's division was to make its way along the East Scheldt and through the Veere Gat to South Beveland. Finally, General Huntly's division was to land on the island of Cadsand, with orders to clear the beaches of French gun batteries in preparation for the fleet to move up the West Scheldt. Once these landings were complete, the British would then be in a position to seize Flushing and move towards Antwerp.

Before the fleet sailed, however, a series of developments combined to affect the character of the initial British operations on the Scheldt. Whilst final preparations were being made, the British were forced to alter the location of their main landing on the island of Walcheren. This change of plan was brought about as a result of a number of factors: the first was the result of a last-minute council of war which met on 24 July. Attended by a number of senior commanders, the meeting had been called by Strachan who wanted to shift the main landings from Zoutland Bay to the Bree Sands in order to land the main body more efficiently. Strachan also suggested that if this operation was to be undertaken, it would be best for Hope's division to wait until the British were in a position to land on the Bree Sands before sailing through the Veere Gat and on to South Beveland.[88] After a brief consultation the council accepted Strachan's proposal. Following the meeting, Strachan received word from Captain William Bolton, of HMS *Fishguard*, who reported that the French had moved their naval squadron from Antwerp to Flushing.[89] Strachan reinforced Admiral Gardiner's squadron and informed Chatham that the main landings were to be switched from Zoutland Bay to the Bree Sands and that the fleet would move from its current anchorage to the Roompot.[90] This decision was welcomed by Chatham who was happy to shift the main landing to the north of the island on account of the rough sea:

> The wind shifted to the westward, and continued to blow very fresh. The anchorage of the Stone Deep being much exposed to the heavy sea which this wind occasioned, it became necessary to secure a [move] to leeward, in which the fleet, particularly the small craft, might ride in safety and … as the surf rendered a landing … at West Capelle or Domburg impracticable, the Left Wing of the Army, destined for the reduction of Walcheren should be put on shore at the Bree Sand out of range of shot of the Fort Ter Haak. The Roompot off the S.West end of the island of Schouwen affords the best shelter.[91]

Anchored safety in the Roompot, the British high command seemed content with the smoothness of the initial operations off the Scheldt. Despite this, however, the decisions made on 24 July, and the willingness of Chatham to accept these decisions, were to have major consequences for the expedition. By landing on the northern shore of Walcheren, Strachan, with the compliance of Chatham, had inadvertently added to the obstacles facing the expedition in that, instead of being able to make a swift advance upon Flushing, the British now had to undertake a potentially difficult advance across the island.[92] Thus in the space of barely a few hours, the British high command had dramatically altered the dynamics of the military operation from a potentially fast-moving series of attacks into a drawn out advance.

Whilst the final preparations were being made, the embarkation of the expeditionary force was also completed. The embarkation of the expeditionary force was a major achievement for the Admiralty owing to the limited number of transports which had been available to the British in May and July. The initial shortfall in the number of transports resulted from both the unprecedented number of transports required for the Scheldt expedition and the fact that several hundred had already been despatched to the Iberian Peninsula. The Transport Board solved the problem by converting several of the fleet's versatile seventy-four-gun ships-of-the-line into troop transports, which saw the ship's gun decks cleared in order to provide space for the soldiers and stores.[93] William Thornton Keep, an officer in the 77th Foot, recalled the commotion and excitement during the embarkation of the regiment at Spithead:

> I suppose there is about 14 hundred on board now we are embarked, as she carries the whole of our regiment in addition to her own complement of seamen, and I leave you to judge what an animat-

ing scene it is, to see so many red coats and blue, thus assembled together, with a large body of the largest fleet that ever was seen on the coast of Old England![94]

Although providing a quick fix to the transport shortage, the cramped conditions experienced by the soldiers aboard ship were not conducive to a long voyage, with the soldiers crammed together in conditions not too dissimilar to those of a slave ship. Private William Wheeler aboard HMS *Impetueuse* recalled:

> I descended by the main hatchway, all was darkness, and the deck completely covered with the troops. The first step I took off the slips was some one's leg, the second on an Irishman's face ... I made another stride and found there was nothing but living bodies to walk on, I was soon arrested in my course for someone seized hold of my leg and down I threw myself across half a dozen of my comrades ...[95]

Overcrowding also threatened to accentuate another common issue affecting combined operations: inter-service friction. The scourge of many a combined operation, inter-service friction could be sparked by a number of factors, such as the lack of respect between the two services, particularly of the navy towards the army, this being perhaps a by-product of many years of naval success which contrasted sharply with military failure. During the voyage to the Scheldt, the overcrowded conditions aboard many of the line-of-battle-ships resulted in tempers flaring in a few cases between soldiers and sailors.[96] An officer of the 81st Foot later recalled how the overcrowding aboard ship affected the work of the sailors and frustrated the soldiers who were eager to land, 'The men having been some days on board, had already enough of the sea, and were seemingly panting for breath on the crowded decks. The sailors had no room to execute the necessary work of the ship.'[97] Another instance of inter-service friction en route to the Scheldt occurred aboard the frigate HMS *San Lorento*, with tempers flaring between soldiers and sailors owing to the conduct of army Captain Peter Bowlby who, on feeling sea sick, decided to lie down on the quarterdeck.[98] Unbeknown to Bowlby, such an act went against naval regulations and was seen as a mark of disrespect by the ship's crew. Thankfully for all concerned the voyage was of short duration.[99]

Following the changes in the British landing plans the final orders were completed. The left wing of the army comprising Paget, Fraser and Graham's divisions, under the overall command of Coote, was to land on the Bree Sands, with the support of Admiral Robert Otway's warships. This force was to be supported by the gunboats of Admiral Lord Beauclerk, whom Strachan had tasked with providing fire support for Coote's landings.[100] Whilst Otway undertook the landings on the Bree Sands, the right wing comprising Hope's Division was to be transported by Keats's squadron, with the aid of Popham, towards the Veere Gat with orders to wait at anchor in the Roompot in preparation to land on South Beveland.[101]

Another force under the command of Commodore Edward Owen carrying the Marquis of Huntly's Division was to land on the island of Cadsand. Finally, the reserve, comprising Sir James Erskine Second Earl of Rosslyn's Light Division and Lieutenant General Thomas Grosvenor's Division, under the naval direction of Captain Robert Barton, were ordered to the coast of Walcheren.[102]

One of the first problems which the British experienced concerned communications. For despite thinking through when and where to land, Chatham had not planned how he would communicate with his subordinate commanders when aboard his flagship. The mechanics of the landing, such as timing and the organisation of the various waves of rowing boats, were the responsibility of Strachan rather than Chatham.[103] Thus until Chatham could land he had little or no control over events. Indeed when asked at the Scheldt Inquiry as to whether he had been able to have any control once aboard ship over the navigation of the Scheldt and the landing of the troops, Chatham was forced to state that he had no such authority.[104]

Chatham was faced with the prospect of attempting to oversee several major landings over an extended area of operations amounting to roughly 700 square miles. Not only was his line of sight affected by the weather but, having left England with a shortage of adequate maps and inadequate military intelligence, he also lacked in-depth knowledge of the strength of the enemy and the local topography. Unsure of the true strength of the French forces in the area, concerned perhaps by the movement of the French naval squadron and lacking recent experience of combat, Chatham was faced with two immensely difficult tasks of attempting to control and then coordinate the landings. Chatham found that not only could he not coordinate the landings, but neither could he have much influence over the deployment of the assault forces on their landing beaches. Only when Coote's forces had cleared a beachhead could the commander of the army take command. Fortunately for the British, the main landings on the Bree Sands were led by Coote and Hope, officers who had extensive experience of amphibious operations: Coote, for instance, had commanded the Ostend raid in 1798 and had spearheaded the landing at the Helder in 1799. Hope was equally well versed in beach assaults. Both commanders were fortunate to be in command of the two landings which were to take place in close proximity to the main part of the fleet, thus benefiting from superior fire support and from their numerical superiority to the weak enemy forces that were guarding the beaches north of Walcheren.

The most significant landing to be made at this stage was on the island of Cadsand.[105] Cadsand's importance to the expedition owed itself to the fact that the islands northern shore formed the south bank of the all-important West Scheldt, the main route by which the British fleet was to sail to Antwerp. The north shore of the island was not without its defences, however, with French artillery positions being located at various points along Cadsand's coast. It was imperative that the British cleared these artillery batteries before the fleet attempted to sail up the West Scheldt, as fixed shore batteries would have a distinct advantage over warships in a gunnery duel, owing to the fact that the roll of the ship would greatly reduce the potential accuracy of a vessels guns.[106] If the British failed to achieve this, they would be forced to besiege Flushing before being in a position for the navy to cooperate fully with the army and move up the West Scheldt towards Antwerp.[107]

The British landing on Cadsand was the responsibility of Lieutenant General George Gordon, Marquis of Huntly.[108] An experienced commander, Huntly knew the dangers inherent in amphibious warfare, having served in the failed expeditions to Flanders in 1793–5 and the Helder in 1799 where he was wounded.[109] Before meeting with his military superiors Huntly journeyed to Deal and met with Captain Edward Owen to discuss the transport arrangements for the impending operations against Cadsand. During this meeting Owen had informed the general that, owing to the limited number of flat-bottomed boats available, he could only land 600 to 700 troops at a time.[110] Huntly's instructions from Brownrigg were vague at best and stated that:

> The possession of the batteries established by the enemy on the Island of Cadsand being judged essential to the free navigation of the entrance of the West Scheldt, I have the honour to acquaint you, by Lord Chatham's directions, that this service is to be executed by such proportion of the 2nd Division of the Army under your Lordships' command as you may judge, on a personal view of these defences, and in conjunction with the opinion of Commodore Owen, who commands a division of the Fleet to cooperate with you in this service.[111]

Not only did Brownrigg say nothing of how Huntly was to land but neither did he tell Huntly what resistance he should expect. The only other point Brownrigg made to Huntly was to state that 'It would appear that 2,000 men …

will be a sufficient force'.[112] This suggestion concluded Brownrigg's instructions to Huntly and left the general with the belief that his orders were to land 2,000 men in one wave on Cadsand, but only to land these troops if the conditions enabled him to do so.[113] Once aboard ship Huntly and Owen discussed matters more closely, 'A question arose as to the number of men that could be landed; … Huntly's instructions supposed that I had the means of landing 2,000 men at one operation; I had not the means for that number; the number for the Men of War was 615 … that number was carried to 700'.[114]

Lack of sound information about the enemy was also an issue for Huntly. With little knowledge of the strength of the Franco-Dutch forces on Cadsand, Huntly was unwilling to risk landing batches of 700 men at a time. Huntly's lack of knowledge about the enemy was again the result of a poor planning on the part of the British high command, with Chatham having told Huntly nothing about the strength of the enemy's forces on the island.[115] With time of the essence and a lack of inter-service communication causing confusion, Huntly set sail aboard a brig on the afternoon of 28 July in order to try to reach Chatham aboard HMS *Venerable* and clarify his instructions. Despite his best efforts rough weather and thick fog forced Owen to recall the general.[116]

With Huntly unable to reach Chatham, Owen took it upon himself to procure extra shipping from Strachan and wrote to the admiral on 29 July to state that, 'I must … press upon you the usefulness of the boats of Gardiner's squadron to us, both in the power of landing men quickly and in covering their landing to their launches'.[117] Strachan's reply arrived on the evening of 30 July and in it the admiral notified Owen of the need to wait upon better weather, but suggested that Gardiner would be in a position to help with the landings.[118] At this point, the weakness of the British communication network was fully exposed when Strachan's message to Gardiner failed to arrive.[119] The failure of this order to reach Gardiner meant that the admiral remained fixed to his position off the mouth of the West Scheldt, so near yet so far from Owen. What made the situation all the worse was the fact that Strachan assumed that Gardiner had received his message and did not deem it necessary to repeat his instructions. Thus both Owen and Huntly remained stranded off Cadsand and blind to the state of the French defences. It was at this point, when all else had failed, that a contingency plan would have been of great use to Huntly and Owen. Lacking such a plan, and not possessing a decent map of the island, Huntly had little choice but to remain in wait off Cadsand.

As Dyott recalled, Huntly's troops were anxious to land but from what could be seen of the French defences an attack by a battalion sized force might have led to disaster:

We were kept in a state of hourly suspense from the 29th July until the 4th August … the constant state of suspense we had been kept in was irksome in the extreme. Three of four times we had made every preparation to land, the boats alongside and the troops all prepared; but as the enemy appeared in great force, and were strongly defended by cannon and works, it was fortunate we did not attempt to get on shore, as in all probability the six hundred men we embarked would have been sacrificed".[120]

Owen had also received reports of enemy troops arriving in force upon Cadsand from the mainland, but had failed to see anything for himself owing to the height of the sand dunes. Deserters meanwhile also stated that there were over 1,400 French troops on the island and with more arriving daily.[121] Continued bad weather, meanwhile, combined with French reinforcements meant that the British hopes of conducting a landing lessened by the hour. Indeed, if at this point the British had finally been able to land, there are considerable doubts that they could have held on to Cadsand, given that by the last day of July there were close to 6,000 fresh French troops, albeit of middling quality, on the island with more troops continuing to arrive.[122] With the situation clearly beyond them, Strachan finally called a halt to the Cadsand operation.[123] Although affected by poor weather, Huntly's landing on Cadsand was the product of poor planning and the fragile British communication system. Lacking enough boats to land his entire force, bereft of intelligence about the strength of the enemy forces and isolated from both Chatham and Strachan, Huntly and Owen had little choice but to abandon the Cadsand landings and take part in the operations to the north.[124]

The ramifications of this decision were significant in that by leaving the French batteries intact, the navy would find it difficult to sail up the West Scheldt without suffering heavy losses. This complication made it necessary for the British to secure a new passage to Antwerp and forced them to lay siege to Flushing. If they failed to find a new passage, they risked running up the West Scheldt with Flushing intact, which would have risked the loss of much of the fleet.[125]

A further unforeseen development was that with the main British force now landing far from Flushing, the French were free to ferry troops and supplies from Cadsand to Flushing, a vital lifeline which would enable the French forces on Walcheren to withstand the British onslaught for longer. Blame for the confused state of affairs which affected the British operations against Cadsand can also be levelled at Strachan, who, as the man responsible for coordinating the British landings and naval operations, failed to coordinate his forces, 'His intelligence was too narrow to grasp the full purport of his task, or to comprehend the multitude of complicated operations by which it was to be accomplished ... he appears not to have possessed the ability or the greatness to act solely as director in chief'.[126]

The British failure at Cadsand, resulting from poor planning and poor operational decision making, was a major blow to the expedition's chances of success. As the Cadsand operation ground to a halt, the main British landings on Walcheren and South Beveland got underway. Before the troops landed, they were greeted with a view of the coastline. An anonymous officer of the 81st Foot recalled the scene awaiting the British, 'The Dutch coast lies extremely low. When seen at a distance, the sea seems to overhang it. The tops of the trees are first seen, and the land appears as if it were rising from the bosom of the ocean'.[127]

On the afternoon of 30 July the British troops under Fraser and Graham stormed the beaches of the Bree Sands. The decks of the warships provided the men of the other divisions a fine view of the landings. As Wheeler noted:

> The Gunboats had taken up their position along the shore, the flats full of soldiers and towed by the ships boats, formed in the rear of the Gunboats. On a signal the flats advanced. All now was solemn silence, saving the gunboats, who were thundering showers of iron on the enemy. Their well-directed fire soon drove them to shelter, behind the sandbank. The flats had now gained the Gunboats, shot through the intervals and gained the shallow water, when the troops leaped out and waded ashore, drove the enemy from behind the hills where they had taken shelter from the destructive fire of the Gunboats.[128]

With the supporting fire of the gunboats scattering enemy resistance, the British assault force quickly brushed aside the enemy troops on the sand dunes and moved inland.[129] With the French and Dutch forces in retreat the 71st Regiment of Foot, under the command of Colonel Dennis Pack, drove the enemy eastwards along the coast and silenced the guns at the weakly defended Fort Ter Haak.[130] Pack was an ideal choice as leader of the first landings on Walcheren having commanded the regiment throughout the campaigns in South America, Portugal and Corunna.[131]

Eager to oversee the advance of Pack and the remainder of his brigade, Picton quickly advanced to aid his subordinate at the head of the first battalion of the 36th Foot.[132] On their arrival, Picton found that the fort had already surrendered. With the threat from Fort Ter Haak nullified, Pack advanced with the 1/36th to mount an attack on Veere. By now the light was fading and with darkness quickly covering the dykes and fens the British were forced to call a halt to the day's proceedings. Whilst Fraser's division had moved to the right of the Bree Sands, the rest of Coote's force was landed on Walcheren. By nightfall the British army on Walcheren numbered roughly 12,500 men.[133] At daybreak on the morning of 31 July the British advanced on Veere in two columns.[134] William Thornton Keep recalled the character of the countryside as the British advanced:

> I took the Colours and fell in, and we moved forwards in the best spirits, towards Fort [Ter] Haak. It had been taken by our light troops at the point of the bayonet overnight and the guns spiked. After a fatiguing march of several hours through deep sands we halted on the dike to refresh the men and wait for orders. We were soon however in movement again, and towards evening reached Veere, which we found to be a strongly fortified place on the margin of the sea.[135]

Whilst the main body of the army on Walcheren advanced southwards, Fraser's Division, with the aid of Beauclerk's gunboats, attacked Veere.[136] After a day-long bombardment the 500-strong garrison of Veere surrendered.[137] Despite the weather and the lack of information about the enemy, the fall of Veere capped what had been a successful couple of days for the army on Walcheren, proving that at the tactical level at least the British were capable of swift action and successful inter-service cooperation.

The following day was one of steady progress for the British, as the army moved towards Flushing, with Graham's and Paget's divisions encountering pockets of resistance around the various villages between Middleburg and Flushing. As Wheeler recalled, the wet roads were a major nuisance:

> We could not form into any other order ... neither could we render much assistance to the advance as there were deep ditches full of water, each side [of] the road. A few of us did manage to get across into the field on our left, but was soon obliged to return for we met other ditches, wider and deeper, than those beside the road.[138]

After navigating the muddy conditions, the British eventually ended the day on the outskirts of Flushing.[139] Graham's division also made gradual progress and eventually captured a series of French naval gun batteries at the villages of Dishoek, Vygenter and Nolle along the shoreline to the south of Flushing.[140] In the meantime, Fraser's division, which was fresh from seizing Veere, advanced along the eastern side of the island to Fort Ramaskins.[141] Like Veere,

Sir Arthur Wellesley, 1st Duke of Wellington by Thomas Lawrence. (Reproduced with kind permission of the Taylor Library, Pen & Sword)

King George III and the Prince of Wales reviewing the 3rd (or the Prince of Wales's) Regiment of Dragoon Guards and the 10th (or the Prince of Wales's Own) Regiment of (Light) Dragoons, *c*. 1797. Oil on canvas, attributed to George Beechey (1798–1852), *c*. 1830, after his father, Sir William Beechey (1753–1839), *c*. 1797–8. (Reproduced with kind permission of the National Army Museum)

Frederick Augustus, Duke of York, reviewing troops in Flanders, *c.* 1794. Oil on canvas by William Anderson, signed lower right. (Reproduced with kind permission of the National Army Museum)

Sir David Dundas, KB, Commander in Chief. Coloured etching by and after Robert Dighton Snr, published by Robert Dighton Snr, London, April 1810. (Reproduced with kind permission of the National Army Museum)

Lieutenant General (later General Sir) Robert Brownrigg (1759–1833), *c.* 1810. Oil on canvas by Sir Thomas Lawrence (1769–1830), *c.* 1810. Half-length portrait of subject, bare-headed, facing forward, Lieutenant General's coatee, cloak over left shoulder. (Reproduced with kind permission of the National Army Museum)

The British landing at Callantsoog in August 1799 by Dirk Langendijk. (Reproduced with kind permission of the Taylor Library, Pen & Sword)

The landing of British troops, under General Sir Ralph Abercromby, on the Texel, Holland, 27 August 1799. Oil on canvas attributed to Robert Dodd (1748–1815), *c.* 1799. Officers direct lines of British infantry into action at left, while two military and naval officers are in discussion on the right, soldiers and stores disembarking beyond. (Reproduced with kind permission of the National Army Museum)

Lieutenant General Sir John Moore, KB (1761–1809), *c.* 1805. Oil on canvas, by Sir Thomas Lawrence (1769–1830), *c.* 1805; half-length, full face, dressed in Lieutenant General's coatee, with Bath Star. (Reproduced with kind permission of the National Army Museum)

The 28th Regiment at Quatre Bras, 1815 by Elizabeth Thompson (1875). (Reproduced with kind permission of the Taylor Library, Pen & Sword)

GRENADIERS & LIGHT INFANTRY
OF THE 29TH OR WORCESTERSHIRE REGIMENT OF INFANTRY
ON DUTY AT HOME.

London Pub.d May 1.st 1812 by Colnabi & C.o 23 Cockspur Street

Grenadiers and Light Infantry of the 29th or Worcestershire Regiment of Infantry, 1812. (Reproduced with kind permission of the National Army Museum)

Ramaskins was a strategically important position and the fort's guns commanded the navigable Slough passage, which divided Walcheren from South Beveland. It was vital for the British to seize Ramaskins because Chatham hoped to use the Slough passage in the future advance upon Antwerp.[142] With time of the essence, the British swiftly erected a heavy artillery battery about 700yd from the fort.[143] After a brief bombardment, supported by rifle fire, the garrison surrendered:

> At daylight [3 August] the garrison directed a good deal of fire on the battery, till the 95th Rifle corps were pushed forward close to the ramparts, wherever an individual could find cover; and one or other of these cool fellows fired at such of the garrison as showed themselves above the parapet … till they had silenced the fort. In the afternoon, the battery being nearly complete, the garrison, consisting of 127 men, surrendered.[144]

As the main body of Chatham's army advanced across Walcheren, Sir John Hope's division landed on South Beveland and established a camp at Goes.[145] With much of Walcheren and South Beveland under British control, Chatham and the British senior commanders turned their attention to Flushing.[146] As far as the British were concerned Flushing needed to fall, and fall quickly, if they were to maintain their tight schedule and seize Antwerp before the wet late summer weather deteriorated any further. But as with the operation on Cadsand, poor planning would again undermine British operations, this time with fatal consequences.

A Ruinous Seige: The Siege of Flushing

Although not the principal town of Walcheren, that honour going to Middleburg, the port of Flushing was the focal point of trade and military activity on the island. With direct access to the North Sea, via the West Scheldt, Flushing was the gateway to Antwerp and was a famous smugglers' haunt. As with all the ports along the Dutch coastline, Flushing was well defended. During the Eighty Years War Flushing's defences had been tested on a number of occasions and the port had been taken from the Spanish by the Dutch in 1572.[147] Flushing's defences had been improved after this siege and were greatly added to during the subsequent decade and had been strengthened by the French as recently as 1807.[148] Not only had the main walls been strengthened but the French garrison also had a network of defensive canals at their disposal. Not only did these waterways allow for the movement of troops throughout the islands, but they could be also be used to inundate the surrounding countryside. Thus, despite not being a major fortress, Flushing could not be taken lightly.

On 1 August a scouting party of Royal Engineers had assessed the state of the town's defences and advised Chatham that an assault of the town was not practicable owing to the strength of its defences. Instead of immediately assaulting the town, the engineers told Chatham that a bombardment was needed, one which if well managed might force the garrison to surrender before an assault was made.[149] The British troops soon found themselves organised into working parties and ordered to prepare the necessary offensive works, with work commencing on the first battery of guns and the first trenches, on 3 August.[150] Wheeler recalled the scene before Flushing:

> The enemy is completely shut up in Flushing, and we are going on with the necessary work for the destruction of the town. There is not an idle hand to be found, some are building batteries, digging trenches, filling sand bags, making large wicker baskets, carpenters making platforms, Sailors bringing up guns, Mortars, Howitzers, ammunition, Shot shell etc.[151]

As Michael Duffy has noted, sailors played a vital part in amphibious operations on land and were used to drag guns, stores, supplies and to man naval gun batteries.[152] As an officer of the 32nd Regiment of Foot recalled, the sailors of the fleet worked hard in helping the troops prepare their positions around Flushing, 'A strong division of sailors was landed, when we appeared before Flushing, to assist in the erection of the batteries. Their station was on the extreme right; they threw up a considerable work, armed with twenty-four pounders.'[153]

Whilst the British worked feverishly to erect their siege works, the French commander of Flushing, General Louis-Claude Monnet, continued to ready the town for the impending siege. Since the British landings, Monnet's first priority had been to reinforce the garrison; this he had been able to do as a result of the failure of the British to seize Cadsand and their inability to cut Flushing off from Antwerp. By leaving the West Scheldt free for shipping, the British had left a lifeline open for Monnet, whose call for aid resulted in French reinforcements being ferried across the West Scheldt to Flushing between 4 and 7 August. In this way, Monnet received around 4,000 extra troops, bringing his force to around 8,000.[154] The British high command seem only to have realised the significance of their failure to seize Cadsand at this point, with Chatham suddenly calling on Strachan to 'bring in the ships of war without a moments loss of time, as the enemy might easily be reinforced from Cadsand'.[155] The navy however was not yet in a position to accede to Chatham's request, with the general being forced to step up preparations for the siege as best he could, ordering a party of engineers to work on the first of many mortar positions, located at Nolle House.[156]

Poor inter-service relations were already having a profound effect on the conduct of the expedition. Lack of communication had already resulted in the failure of the operations against Cadsand, whilst the British attempts to force the garrison of Flushing to surrender were being undermined by the fact that the navy had so far failed to force the West Scheldt and cut Flushing off from reinforcement. Both Chatham and Strachan were to blame for this situation, with a lack of effective planning prior to the launch of the expedition combined with tunnel vision with regard to their own areas of operation. Strachan was blinded by concerns about the movement of the French squadron, to the detriment of both Huntly's and Coote's initial landing plans, whilst Chatham and his QMG Brownrigg, had been guilty of over eagerness with their desire to land the troops on Walcheren. Both lacked an understanding of the likely, catastrophic, effects of a failure to secure Cadsand. Before the British could prepare their gun batteries the French were preparing a strike of their own and, after a detailed consultation, Monnet decided to inundate the flat ground around Flushing.[157] French engineers promptly began to cut holes in the many sea dykes and to open the defensive sluice gates that ringed the town's outer defences. Many of the British troops were forced to leave the trenches momentarily so as to avoid drowning.[158]

This stratagem had two advantages: by flooding the low-lying land around Flushing, the French were able not only to hamper the British as they prepared their siege works but were also able to reduce the points from which the British could mount an attack. With a potential British advance now forced to move along a limited series of uncut dykes, the French commander succeeded in limiting the number of troops which the British could use at any one time to attack Flushing and enabled his troops to pinpoint where a potential British attack was most likely to be launched. The delays made to the construction of the British siege works were particularly frustrating for the Royal Engineers who were forced to devote precious time and effort to shoring up existing positions and clearing excess water out of the flooded British trenches. As Colonel William Fyers recalled, 'Great exertions were required … to preserve the communications from being inundated by the sudden rise of the water. Parties were everywhere at work to let off the water from the trenches, and to prevent its further entry … The Artificers were kept constantly at work'.[159]

With a prolonged siege now on the cards, the British were faced with the fresh problem of how to transport a heavy siege train quickly across the muddy hinterland of the island. It was an issue which the British had not thought about before and stemmed directly from the British decision to land the bulk of the army at the Bree Sands, instead of Zoutland Bay. Had the British decided to land at Zoutland Bay, the artillery would have only had to make a short journey to Flushing. As it happened, however, when the British shifted their landings to the Bree Sands they failed to consider the logistical difficulties inherent in transporting their heavy guns from such an exposed beach to any future destination. It was only on reaching Flushing that Chatham realised the full extent of the problem but by that point in time he could do little except invest the town and wait upon the guns to be moved from Veere to Flushing; a distance of nearly 13 miles. As Fortescue has noted, once the guns were landed, the British struggled to move them across the island, 'This work was found to be too heavy for the artillery-horses, the roads being so narrow and the ditches so numerous that accidents were frequent; and, accordingly, the whole of the guns were hauled over a deep soil, soaked with constant rains, by a huge team of men'.[160]

By landing the siege train miles from Flushing, Chatham and Strachan increased the pressure on the engineers to transport the siege train to Flushing and also jeopardised the speed of the British advance; the lack of wheeled transport also greatly delayed the movement of the siege train.[161] The navy, meanwhile, was not without blame in its handling of the situation and instead of landing the siege train and equipment in an orderly fashion, the train had simply been dumped in a mess upon the beach.[162] Precious time was thus taken up sifting through the equipment before it could be used. Chatham should have known better given that he was the Master General of the Ordnance and had been First Lord of the Admiralty when York had made a number of similar mistakes before the siege of Dunkirk in 1793. Chatham, like many of his contemporaries, clearly had learnt nothing from his previous experiences.

Over the course of early August, the engineers supervised the construction of the British works before Flushing. It was back breaking work for the troops involved and the hours were long and intense; on 4 August, over 600 men worked through the day, and into the early hours of the following morning, to construct a mortar battery and a communication trench.[163] As Captain William Paisley of the Royal Engineers noted, however, many of the senior engineers were incompetent:

> In six days since the Trenches were opened we have made only one
> 6 Gun one 6 Mortar Battery with a parcel of infernal ins and outs
> from 8 to 1100 yards from the place ... The Corps of Engineers is

disgraced and damned for ever. The Cry of the whole Army & Navy is against us. I found Jones when I landed in a state of despair. Boteler wished that the first shot might take off his head. The French are making counterworks & do them faster than we do ours. We were offered the whole Army to act under us ... but what could we do with a parcel of old men or rather old women at our head, with fellows without Souls to direct the operations of Armies. With fellows old in years, poor in spirit, beardless in military experience, destitute of knowledge, not merely block heads but block bodies ... Gen. Brownrigg says that the Engineers are not fit to be employed in war.[164]

This damning attack upon the senior engineers attached to the expedition highlights that poor operational command was not confined merely to Chatham and Strachan, but affected the lower levels of the command hierarchy. Poor senior command at the highest level of the expedition had already taken its toll, the fact that the two senior engineer commanders were also lacking in command skills was still more alarming. Alongside a lack of urgency on the part of the senior commanders was the fact that both D'Arcy and Fyers exhibited equally poor skills in coordinating the siting of the offensive artillery batteries:

To the Left of our Lines, a Battery had been made of 3 24 Pounders, so distant that it could not reach the place, nor injure the Enemy in any way. This was again owing to the ignorance of the Engineers I mentioned who had the chief direction, & placed their works by guess, instead of measuring distances which is, or ought, always to be done in placing batteries.[165]

These elementary failings on the part of the two senior engineer officers encapsulate the unprofessional and shoddy manner in which the British conducted the siege. Paisley's account of the conduct of his superiors also provides an important insight into the conduct of the expedition at a lower level. Another target of Paisley's criticism was Coote:

Sir Eyre Coote however wanting to improve upon my plan, ordered us to keep possession of the French Battery if possible, he was also anxious that I should fill up the cut that the Enemy made to let in the seawater.... both these things were impracticable till we had entrenched properly ... but a Commander-in-Chief must have his way.[166]

Paisley's account of the expedition to the Scheldt is an important source and one which serves to highlight the many faults in the British army's conduct of the campaign, not only at the highest level but also further down the command chain. Although no doubt eager to make sure that his reputation was left untarnished by the failings of the expedition, Paisley was an astute engineer officer who went on to establish a fine reputation within the Ordnance Department.[167] His comments, therefore, should not be taken lightly.

Before the British bombardment could finally open, the French made a desperate bid to spike some of the British guns. On the night of 7 August a French sortie was launched against Graham's Division, which was entrenched on the right of the British line near the Nolle Battery.[168] The French force was not the most experienced and suffered from a lack of coordination, owing to the difficult nature of the flooded terrain and the fact that the attacking troops were mostly drunk.[169] The French were quickly pushed back, leaving the British battery at the Nolle position unmolested.

Another reason for the sluggishness of the British siege preparations was because Chatham and Strachan had fallen out with one another. Chatham had grown frustrated by the disorganised fashion in which the navy had dumped the siege train upon the Bree Sands, whilst Strachan was upset by Chatham's criticism of the navy in its apparent unwillingness to force the West Scheldt. A proud defender of the values of the Royal Navy, Strachan was greatly displeased with his army colleague and reacted badly to Chatham's views. As Chatham and Strachan's relationship deteriorated, so too did relations between the services.[170] Following the French sortie, Chatham reminded Strachan of the need for the navy to cut Flushing off from Cadsand, so that no more fresh enemy forces could be used to bolster the garrison. On 11 August, Strachan decided that enough was enough and forced the West Scheldt, 'Yesterday afternoon Lord William Stuart with 10 frigates availed himself of a light wind from the westward and though the tide was against him passed the batteries between Flushing and Cadsand nearly two hours under the enemy's fire'.[171]

By moving up the West Scheldt, Strachan was able to inform Chatham that Flushing was completely isolated from the mainland. This not only prevented the French from gaining reinforcements from Cadsand, but it also provided the British with an opportunity to bombard Flushing from both land and sea and, on 13 August, almost all of the British batteries received the signal to commence the bombardment.[172] In a matter of minutes the ground trembled as twenty-six 24-pounders, eight 8in howitzers, and sixteen 10in mortars sent their deadly projectiles shrieking through the sky towards the spires and rooftops of Flushing.[173] For the tired working parties of British troops the spectacle of over fifty heavy guns firing, both day and night, was awe inspiring. As Keep recalled:

> The shells sent an immense height aloft into the air appeared like falling stars, producing on their descent into the town a distinct

reverberation, and the Congreve Rockets with their trains of fire crossing each other illuminated the Heavens, the whole of which was reflected in the waters around us … our fire kept increasing, until showers of rockets and shells … set the town in flames![174]

The ferocity of the initial British bombardment greatly weakened the French defences and, following this show of force, Chatham instructed Graham to destroy a French battery, which had lobbed several shells into the British lines from atop one of the nearby dykes. With fire support from Nolle position, Graham instructed the 3rd Battalion of the 1st Regiment of Foot and the first battalion of the 14th Regiment of Foot, alongside a detachment of the light infantry of the King's German Legion (KGL), to advance and attack the French position. The 3/1st cleared all before them along the dyke, whilst the 1/14th and the KGL moved against another dyke close to the outskirts of Old Flushing.[175] The commanding officer of the 1/14th, Lieutenant Colonel Jasper Nicholls, distinguished himself at the head of his troops and captured both thirty French troops and an artillery piece.[176]

Over the course of the day both sides traded shells, but the longer the duel went on the more accurate the British shelling became and by the end of the day Flushing had been set alight. Buoyed with these events and eager for the town to surrender, Chatham boldly called on the French to surrender for the sake of the civilian population:

> It being manifest that the present, and well directed fire, both of His Britannic Majesty's Sea and land forces, now before Flushing, has been so effectual, that if continued much longer the town will be a perfect ruin. The General Commanding is induced by feelings of humanity to summon you to surrender.[177]

The French had other ideas and refused Chatham's request. This rebuttal greatly frustrated Chatham who was now very anxious to push on to the dockyards at Antwerp. Chatham's anxiety about the situation was raised following the receipt of a number of intelligence reports from Hope, between 6–12 August, which suggested that the French and Dutch had gathered 40,000 men at Antwerp and had moved several warships down the Scheldt in order to defend the approaches to the dockyards.[178]

Chatham again called on Strachan for aid but, before the British ships could commence their deadly work, the rising water forced Chatham to take action and the situation became so perilous on the night of 14 August that a force under Pack was ordered to advance and repair the dykes to the front of the flooded British positions.[179] Pack once again excelled himself, advancing in the face of enemy fire several hundred metres to the site of the cut dyke. The British commander not only stormed an enemy battery, but also managed to shore up the cut in the dyke and return with a large number of prisoners of war.[180]

With the British position secure, the stage was set for the navy to bring the bombardment to its climax. At 11am on 15 August seven warships sailed up the West Scheldt and proceeded to pound Flushing with a number of thunderous broadsides.[181] Faced with the prospect of Flushing's total destruction, Monnet quickly changed his mind about the whole situation, and surrendered to the British. With the support of the navy, Flushing fell only 38 hours after the start of the British bombardment.[182] Napoleon was not best pleased when he heard the news of the capitulation.[183]

With Walcheren secured, the bulk of the British forces were transported to South Beveland in preparation for the final descent upon Antwerp. Chatham displayed little desire to join the troops and spent the next ten days trying to rebuild civil relations with the people of Flushing. As the British dallied, the French continued to bolster their garrison at Antwerp and, by 22 August, almost 60,000 Franco-Dutch troops and national guardsmen were stationed in the vicinity of Antwerp, whilst there were also 22 large ships in the West Scheldt.[184] It was later also discovered that Marshal Bernadotte was in command of the French force at Antwerp.[185] Additionally, British troops on South Beveland had started to suffer bouts of fever, which rendered an increasing number of soldiers unfit for duty.[186]

With the fate of the expedition in the balance, Brownrigg came to the conclusion that there was little hope of success; a view which was accepted by several other senior commanders. With sickness ravaging the troops and his subordinates unsure of success, Chatham met with the other commanders on 27 August and it was decided to cancel the final advance to the dockyards.[187] Before news of this decision reached London, the British press had already suggested that the expedition was doomed to failure. *The London Times* argued that 'No achievement of magnitude' was likely and as every hour passed by 'hopes of a successful issue' greatly diminished.[188] These were prophetic words.

With active operations at an end, the next question facing the British was what they were to do with Walcheren? Once again poor planning returned to haunt the British high command in that it had failed to assess what it would do if they failed to seize Antwerp but still had possession of the islands in the Scheldt. On paper, Walcheren was a potentially useful site for a minor naval base. But in reality, with Flushing's dock having been badly damaged and with British troops dying of fever in and around the town, such an idea was not particularly welcomed by the British. However, Castlereagh instructed Chatham to retain Walcheren as a potential bargaining piece whilst negotiations between Austria and France continued.

This decision, like many made by Castlereagh during the campaign, was made without any personal experience of the situation on the ground. By ordering Chatham to retain the island, Castlereagh effectively condemned many thousands of British soldiers to death. Chatham meanwhile returned to England, leaving Coote in command of 16,500 troops on Walcheren. Austria eventually agreed to Napoleon's harsh peace terms on 14 October 1809, signing the Treaty of Schoenbrunn, which brought an end to the campaign of 1809. Peace was of little consolation for Coote's men who were instead engaged in a desperate battle against the deadly 'Walcheren fever'.

'Wasting Fever'

FEVER

The epidemic which ravaged Chatham's army on the islands in the Scheldt was the worst medical catastrophe experienced by the British army during the Napoleonic period.[189] Medical expert Dr Martin Howard has suggested that Walcheren fever was not one disease but was in fact a deadly cocktail of illnesses, the chief components being malaria, dysentery, typhus and relapsing fever. In a matter of a few short weeks almost half of Chatham's army was suffering from the effects of the epidemic.[190] Understaffed and ill-prepared, the medical services struggled to cope with the epidemic and could not halt the spread of the disease. As with the Walcheren expedition in general, there was plenty of blame to go around, not least for Castlereagh who had not informed the Medical Board of the expedition's destination.[191]

Once again Castlereagh's decision-making must be called into question with his role in the medical preparations having consequences not merely for the progress of the expedition but also for the health of the British army itself. The Medical Board also attracted criticism in that they failed to make sure that the 'attached' medical men actually sailed to the Scheldt. As McGuffie has noted, out of the official number of some ninety-six medical officers and hospital mates officially attached to the expedition, a figure which was supposed to have included thirty-seven surgeons/physicians and sixty hospital mates, only sixty-three men, comprising thirty-three surgeons/physicians and thirty hospital mates actually sailed with the force.[192]

With barely sixty medical men of varying degrees of skill and experience to care for a force of nearly 40,000, the Board can be said to have failed to prepare the medical arrangements effectively. A further area in which the Board acted poorly was in the procurement of transportation. Like the rest of the expedition, space for wagons and carts was limited. For the medical officers this meant that they would need to procure the necessary transport they required from the local population. The French, by contrast, had found a solution to the problem of how to move the wounded quickly away from the field of battle with the creation of dedicated military ambulances.[193] It would be a long time before the British followed suit and this meant that, in the case of expeditions like that to the Scheldt, sick and wounded men were often forced to huddle together until some form of transport was procured, a policy which increased the spread of infection. Given the fact that the British military had a long history of campaigning in the Low Countries, it is surprising that past experiences were not taken into account by Castlereagh and the leading military figures.

With the Medical Board kept in the dark, Castlereagh and his military commanders were the ones who should have made every effort to assess the medical problems that the British force would likely encounter. As recently as 1747, for instance, a British force sent to Walcheren had been decimated by fever, an episode which had been well documented by Dr William Pringle.[194] Not only did Castlereagh fail to take this into account but he also failed to study the events of the Flanders campaign of 1793 in which York's army suffered dreadfully from fever.[195] Castlereagh also failed to read a memorandum written in 1799 by Abercromby about the practicality of military action on Walcheren. If Castlereagh had taken time to read this document he would have been apprised of the medical issues inherent in mounting such an operation and read Abercromby's warning that the islands in the Scheldt were 'Extremely unhealthy.'[196] The French had also suffered from disease on Walcheren; in the autumn of 1808, for instance, seventy French soldiers had died of fever, whilst four more died from the disease in January 1809.[197] Unlike the British, however, the French were quick to learn from this experience with the majority of French troops remaining on the mainland during the campaign. Once medical experts reached Walcheren it soon became clear that the islands were unhealthy. As Dr Webb noted in his journal:

> The bottom of every canal … is thickly covered with an ooze … Every ditch is filled with water, which is loaded with animal and vegetable substances in a state of Putrefaction; and the Whole island is so flat, and so near the level of the Sea that a large Proportion of it is little better than a Swamp, … The effect of these Causes of Disease is strongly marked in the appearance of the inhabitants, the greater part of whom are pale and listless.[198]

Surrounding Webb, but unnoticed by the doctor as a threat to his health, would have been millions of mosquitoes which had found a perfect home in the swampy ground found on the islands of Walcheren and South Beveland. British medical officers such as Webb believed that the disease was caused by the spread of unhealthy vapours, emanating from the putrid substances which filled the canals. Picton noted in his diary, like Webb, that the disease was spread by putrid substances contaminating the air.[199]

Once the vapour had infected the victim, medical officers were to employ a variety of procedures designed to cleanse the patient's infected blood. These techniques ranged from the deliberate bleeding of a patient, to the prescription of cigars so as to clear the air from harmful vapours, as well as the much more successful use of Peruvian bark.[200] However, this latter substance was in short supply. Lack of knowledge about how diseases were spread greatly hindered the medical response and large numbers of sick men were placed alongside the wounded in dreadfully unhealthy conditions. As surgeon John Wrangle recalled, 'I passed a barn where about … 100 poor fellows lay suffering from this dreadful calamity'.[201] Unbeknownst to Wrangle, the crowding together of the sick accelerated the spread of the epidemic and also enabled it to mix with a variety of other illnesses, such as dysentery, which affected the British troops – factors which meant that the hospitals were breeding grounds for the disease.[202]

The government in London first received reports of the fever from Dr Webb on 11 September.[203] Within the space of a couple of weeks Castlereagh, urged by reports from Walcheren to despatch extra medical staff, called on medical men from across Britain to volunteer to serve on Walcheren.[204] Castlreagh particularly hoped that a senior physician and two respected doctors could be sent at once to the region. However, on being asked to go to Walcheren, the Physician General, Sir Lucas Pepys, stated in no uncertain terms that he had no experience or in-depth understanding of military medicine.[205] There was even less enthusiasm on the part the civilian medical profession who mostly felt that to volunteer to serve would increase their chances of getting the disease; those who did eventually volunteer included Dr Gilbert Blane and Dr James Borland. As Elizabeth Crowe has noted, however, these men were also advocates of reforming the Medical Board and may well have gone to Walcheren more in order to fulfil their political ambitions.[206]

Understaffed and unprepared for such large numbers of sick, the medical department was simply not up the task of caring for the thousands of sick and dying. The ordinary regimental surgeons, the front-line medical men attached to the expedition, had to work within a limited framework of understanding and with inadequate supplies at hand and this challenge was beyond them. Reports of sickness surfaced on South Beveland. Here one of the first soldiers to encounter it was Harris:

> The first I observed of it was one day as I sat in my billet, when I beheld whole parties of our Riflemen in the street shaking with a sort of ague, to such a degree that they could hardly walk; strong and fine young men ... seemed suddenly reduced in strength to infants, unable to stand upright – so great a shaking had seized upon their whole bodies from head to heel.[207]

Following the capture of South Beveland in early August, Sir John Hope's Division had seen little active service and the presence of thousands of inactive troops on a mosquito-infected island meant that the fever quickly engulfed Hope's troops.[208] An unidentified soldier of the 38th Foot recalled the speed with which his regiment succumbed to fever on South Beveland:

> We had not been many days upon the island before our men began to fall bad of the Ague and fever and so fatal did that disorder prove that in less than a month we buried more than 600 men so that out of the 1000 ... that we took out with us we did not bring 400 back.[209]

Battalions were quickly reduced in size to a few hundred healthy men, whilst whole companies were wiped out; such was the virulence of the epidemic and the inability of the medical department to stem the rising number of cases. The general officers were just as vulnerable as the rank and file. Picton recorded in his diary the harsh conditions and the anger he felt towards the ministers in London:

> The climate is to the full as destructive as that of the West Indies and will be the Grave of the Army ... we are already beginning to be sickly to an alarming degree ... The Regiments in my brigade have already above 100 each in hospital and the Artillery 80 out of four companies. If ministers are suffered to persist in their quixotic measure of attempting to retain this Golgotha it will be the most costly and disgraceful enterprise which the country was ever seduced into by Empirical Politicians.[210]

Such angry words highlight the growing resentment amongst many of the lower echelons of the high command against the commanders in chief and the politicians in London. Unfortunately for the British, the conditions were to get worse long before they got better, with many officers dying before they could be granted sick leave to return to Britain.[211] One of the unlucky ones who died was Lieutenant General Mackenzie Fraser, whilst many of Wellington's best generals in the Peninsula, such as Charles von Alten and Picton himself, also fell ill. By the start of September the situation had reached a crisis point, with thousands sick and many already dead. The symptoms varied depending upon which of a number of diseases the victim caught; common symptoms included having bouts of extreme heat and then terrible chills, trouble with breathing, loss of strength and appetite, and inability to walk.[212]

Such was the scale and virulence of the epidemic that, as late as February 1810, long after the expedition had returned to Britain, some 11,513 officers and men were still suffering from fever, whilst a total of 3,960 officers and men, some 10 per cent of the expeditionary force, died from the disease. By contrast, the total number of British deaths sustained in combat was just 106.[213] The dead were so plentiful and the disease so virulent that the British medical officers were forced to bury the dead in a series of mass graves around Flushing, as one soldier later recalled, 'They would take them [the dead] to the outside of the town and empty them down into a very large hole … and when the hole was full they would fill it up and make another so that many were [buried] in one grave'.[214]

With conditions deteriorating the British decided to evacuate the worst hit regiments, whilst a garrison of 15,000 men, under Coote, was to be maintained on Walcheren.[215] This decision was long overdue, but by embarking both the ill and the healthy aboard transports, the disease continued to spread, meaning that healthy soldiers who boarded the boats on Walcheren were often struck down with fever when they reached the coast of England. On the English coast, many of the beaches were strewn with the sick, whilst the local inhabitants refused to harbour the returning officers.[216] Bowlby recalled the number of losses sustained by his regiment and also noted the death of one of his comrades at Colchester barracks:

> We had a fair wind to Harwich where we landed … One of the Captains who had been detained in Harwich overtook the regiment and seeing the corporal of his company said 'where is the company?' 'I am the only man left sir' was the reply, 'and the other companies are not much better off'. Lieutenant Cunninghame was one of the merriest of t[he] party, next morning he was taken ill and died after a short illness. Man[y] officers were down with the fever and two-thirds of the men in the hospital.[217]

It would be a very long time before the final effects of Walcheren fever ceased to have an effect on those who took part in the expedition to the

Scheldt. What made Walcheren fever all the worse, besides the high number of deaths that were directly caused by the disease, was its relapsing character. This meant that survivors were often subjected to bouts of fever later in life. Two of the most famous examples of soldiers who suffered throughout their lives from the effects of Walcheren fever were Keep and Harris, both of whom were forced to retire from the army owing to its effects. Keep remained in the army a good deal longer than Harris before finally deciding that he could not face up to a hard life of campaigning whilst still suffering relapses of fever.[218]

Other more prominent sufferers from relapses of fever included none other than future Peninsular War generals Graham, Picton, Charles Von Alten, Sir James Leith and Sir William Stewart. This list could be extended to include many other junior commanders who would also engage the French in Spain and Portugal. Several battalions in the British army were plagued with the disease for the rest of the war, with heavy rain and extreme heat often triggering renewed bouts. Wellington famously complained in 1811 that his 'Walcheren battalions' were a major liability.[219] The failure at Walcheren lived long in the memory of the British army and civil society and spawned many cartoons and works of poetry; the following extract written in 1812, is a particularly poignant example:

> Ye died not in the triumphing
> Of the battle-shaken flood,
> Ye died not on the charging field
> In the mingle of brave blood;
> But twas in the wasting fevers
> For full three months and more
> Britons born,
> Pierc'd with scorn
> Lay at rot on the swampy shore[220]

The Scheldt Inquiry: Lessons Unidentified

As the remnants of Chatham's army struggled to survive the winter months on the disease-ridden shores of the Scheldt, the Portland government was subjected to intense political pressure amidst calls from the press for a full governmental inquiry into the expedition.[221] The government had also been rocked by a personal feud between Canning and Castlereagh, the latter having caught wind of Canning's plot to oust him at the next reshuffle.[222] This rivalry was only resolved when Castlereagh fired a pistol-ball into Canning's thigh in a duel at Putney Heath on 21 September 1809.[223] Shortly afterwards the Portland government collapsed and a new Tory administration was formed under

Spencer Perceval.[224] Although the old leadership had made way for new, the Whigs were not satisfied and lobbied for a full public inquiry into the disaster. Despite losing an initial vote on 23 January 1810 the Whigs won a second vote in the commons three days later, thanks in part to the surprise support of Castlereagh, and it was agreed that a Committee of the Whole House would be created to conduct a formal investigation into the Scheldt expedition.[225]

The Inquiry opened on 2 February 1810 and was initially chaired by the former Chief Justice of Bengal and member of the Privy Council, MP Sir John Anstruther.[226] In order to develop a clear picture of how the expedition had been created and conducted, the inquiry was organised in a chronological fashion, with each of the key persons being called to give evidence of their role and involvement in turn. Thus the first witness was David Dundas because he had been the first military official to have been involved in the preliminary planning process by Castlereagh.[227] Over the course of the following months over forty key witnesses were interviewed by the committee drawn from both the political world and the armed forces. Howard has noted, 'It was intended that the enquiry focus on the wider questions such as whether the expedition should have been undertaken, rather than it being a means of attaching guilt to individuals.'[228] Crucially, although the committee wanted to know what had happened and why, they were not interested in identifying potential military lessons. Furthermore, the Inquiry was the result of political and press pressure and was not inspired by the military or a desire on the part of Horse Guards to learn lessons. Despite the importance of the press in generating pressure for a public inquiry the general public and press were excluded from the proceedings and the proprietors of Fleet Street were forced to publish only from official government reports.[229]

As the Inquiry progressed over the course of the spring its ability to conduct an objective review of the expedition was greatly undermined by the actions of Lord Chatham. Shortly after his return from Walcheren, in October 1809, Chatham had drafted a personal account of the expedition in which he heavily criticised Strachan and the Royal Navy for not forcing the West Scheldt when the fleet arrived off the coast of Walcheren.[230] However, instead of sending the draft to the Secretary for War, Chatham had controversially forwarded two drafts to the king; the first on 15 January and the second almost month later on 14 February 1810.[231] Although the king instructed the general to send the second draft to the Secretary at War, the damage had already been done as news of Chatham's private dealings with the monarch had leaked to the press. As a senior Cabinet minister Chatham's actions were placed under intense scrutiny by the Whigs and the press, the general public meanwhile were eager to blame someone for the catastrophe and Chatham was the perfect target. Slow and cautions, both as a general and politician, Chatham was placed under intense pressure. Whig statesman William Pleydell-Bouverie Lord Folkestone, for example, described Chatham's actions as, 'Inconsistent with the constitution', a view which was shared by a number of other opposition politicians, such as George Tierney and Samuel Whitbread.[232]

The politicians were not alone in venting their anger with Chatham; Strachan was also displeased with his former comrade in arms and viewed Chatham's actions as a slight against his reputation. Strachan had been oblivious to Chatham's politicking and had only caught wind of the general's actions by reading about it in the newspapers and through society gossip.[233] Eager to defend his own reputation, Strachan penned a guarded narrative of his own and blamed Chatham and the weather for the disaster.[234] Strachan was even told by the Committee not to answer any questions which might incriminate him.[235]

The heated nature of Chatham and Strachan's personal vendetta, combined with existing inter-service tensions, meant that none of the senior military and naval commanders approached the Inquiry with a desire to identify lessons. Just as his inability to plan had compromised the expedition, Chatham's wanton disregard for official procedure, combined with his selfish desire to blame Strachan, undermined the Inquiry.[236] Additionally, the failure of the British military and naval establishments to conduct reviews of their own meant that another golden opportunity for the British to learn from the past was squandered. Thus, unlike the deliberations in Whitehall following the Iraq War in post-Blair Britain, there was to be no 'Chilcot-style' review of British strategic and operational planning in the years after 1809–10.

Chapter 5

The British Army and the Debacle at Bergen-Op-Zoom, 1813–14

On the night of 8 March 1814 a small and inexperienced British army, under the command of Peninsular War and Walcheren veteran Lieutenant General Sir Thomas Graham, attempted to seize the French-held fortress of Bergen-Op-Zoom. Despite some initial success, the lack of detailed operational planning on the part of Graham and his senior commanders meant that the British assault was a muddled affair. The quality of the British generalship was also particularly poor. Not only did two of Graham's senior subordinates fail to follow their orders but the experienced commanders of the Guards column also proved overly cautious under fire and did not secure the situation when the circumstances presented themselves. After having been 'Fairly out-generalled and disgracefully beaten' in the battle for control of the town, the surviving redcoats were then forced to surrender.[1] Before analysing the British defeat at Bergen-Op-Zoom it is necessary to place the campaign in the context of the events in Europe after 1810 and to analyse the reasons why the British returned to the Low Countries in 1813–14.

British Strategy, the European Powers and the Invasion of France in 1813–14

The destruction of the *Grande Armée* in the snows of Eastern Europe, following Napoleon's ineffectual capture of Moscow in 1812, precipitated the near collapse of the Confederation of the Rhine.[2] It was against this backdrop that the British Foreign Secretary, Castlereagh, started to plan the creation of a new coalition to restore the balance of power in Europe. In other words, Castlereagh sought to adopt Grenville's 1798 scheme for a 'Grand Alliance', except on this occasion the aim was the overthrow of Napoleon rather than the Parisian revolutionaries.[3]

As Grenville had done fifteen years before, Castlereagh first turned to Russia for support and in January 1813 Lord William Cathcart was instructed to open negotiations with the tsar about a possible alliance.[4] Eager to strike a decisive blow against Napoleon, Tsar Alexander I welcomed the British proposals and agreed to an alliance.[5] Castlereagh was also anxious to gain Prussian backing, the British having received reports which suggested that Prussian public opinion was deeply anti French. Ultimately it was the tsar who was best placed to influence the Prussians and after a series of secret negotiations he persuaded the Prussian King, Frederick William III, to join the alliance.[6] In return for their military and diplomatic support for the new coalition, the British promised to provide both the Russians and the Prussians with substantial financial assistance and armaments. By September the Prussians had received over 100,000 muskets, whilst the Russians had been provided with thousands of muskets and over 100 pieces of artillery.[7] With the Russians and Prussians ready for war all that was left for Castlereagh to complete his strategic vision was to win the support of Vienna. Unfortunately for the British, the Austrians were not as war-minded as their Russian and Prussian counterparts and were unwilling to enter into a new round of hostilities. The Habsburgs chief strategist, Prince Klemens Wenzel von Metternich, was wary of the Russians and their long-term aims in central Europe.[8] For the time being the Allies would have to make do without the Austrians.

Despite hopes of a decisive victory, the Russian and Prussian armies struggled to cooperate fully in the ensuing campaign and a rejuvenated Napoleon eventually inflicted two defeats upon the Allies at the battles of Lutzen and Bautzen in May 1813. Whilst both sides licked their wounds and considered their next moves, the Austrians decided to act and offered Napoleon the chance to negotiate a lasting peace at the Congress of Prague in August.[9] Unwilling to settle for anything less than supremacy, however, Napoleon refused the Austrian peace plan and continued to ready his forces for the next round of hostilities. This was a fatal decision on the part of the emperor and the Austrians viewed Napoleon's intransigence as a sign that peace was unlikely unless he was defeated. Convinced that a victory was needed over the French for a settlement to be concluded, the Austrians abandoned their neutrality and opted to join the Allies.[10]

With such a large injection of fresh troops at their disposal the Allied generals, who were under the overall command of the Austrian Field Marshal Karl Phillip von Schwarzenberg, eventually achieved a decisive victory over Napoleon at the three-day Battle of Leipzig in mid-October 1813.[11] Napoleon's reputation was severely dented by this defeat and with French troops again in retreat the bonds of unity which had held together Napoleon's Empire gradually disintegrated. The Bavarians were first to display disloyalty and mobilised an army to confront the retreating French, only to be defeated by Napoleon at the Battle of Hanau on 30 October.[12] Despite this reversal the Allied armies remorselessly pursued the broken *Grande Armée* as the Confederation of the

Rhine gradually splintered in the wake of the French retreat. Faced with the prospect of a power vacuum in central Europe the Allied leadership met, at the beginning of November, at the city of Frankfurt-am-Main in order to outline what was to be done about Napoleon and the French state.[13]

Although having come together to defeat Napoleon in the previous campaign each of the Allied powers continued to have different views about what needed to be done about the French Emperor. As far as the Russians were concerned Napoleon could not be trusted and the tsar was adamant that the only course of action was the invasion of France and the root and branch destruction of the Napoleonic system.[14] Although Frederick William III was more cautious than the tsar, he was eventually persuaded to support the Russians by General Gneisenau and several other hawks in the Prussian military, who wanted revenge for the humiliation of 1806–7.[15] In keeping with their earlier neutrality, the Austrians were less openly belligerent whilst Metternich remained unsure about Russia's long-term strategic aims and intentions and was determined to control the spread of Russian influence in central Europe.[16] Thus, whilst the Russians and Prussians prepared invasion plans, the Austrians offered Napoleon one final olive branch in the form of the Frankfurt Proposals. The proposals offered Napoleon the chance to negotiate a new peace treaty and to remain master of a new French state which would be enclosed within it's so called 'Natural Frontiers', including the Southern Netherlands.[17]

The fact that the Austrians offered Napoleon the Southern Netherlands and the vital port of Antwerp in return for peace greatly concerned the British government.[18] Indeed, before news of the Austrian plans reached London, Castlereagh had been working on a strategic plan of his own for a post-war Europe based upon the ideas of his former political master, Pitt the Younger. This plan assumed that a defeated France would be contained by a number of powerful neighbour states and stripped of the Low Countries.[19] Aside from the Austrians, the main impediment to Castlereagh's scheme was Napoleon himself. The French Emperor firmly believed in the need to retain the Low Countries and later stated to his close confidant, Armand A.L. de Caulaincourt, that 'France without its natural frontiers, without Ostend or Antwerp, would no longer be able to take its place among the States of Europe.'[20]

Napoleon had tightened his control over the Low Countries in 1810, when he dismantled the Kingdom of Holland and incorporated the former Dutch lands into the French state.[21] Therefore, as far as Castlereagh and the British government were concerned, Metternich's offer of natural frontiers constituted a major threat to Britain's long-term security. The British were thus greatly relieved when Napoleon rejected the initial Austrian proposals and, although he later tried to make a new agreement with Metternich, the Habsburgs refused further negotiations and readied their forces for the great Allied invasion of France.[22] Wary of a French popular revolt, akin to the one which had greeted the troops of the First Coalition in 1792, the Allied leadership was at pains to stress to the French people that their enemy was Napoleon and that they would not rest until a secure peace was restored:

> The Allied Powers do not wage war against France but against the preponderance that has been so loudly proclaimed; that preponderance, which for the misfortune of Europe and France, the Emperor Napoleon has too long exercised beyond the limits of his Empire ... They will not lay down their arms until the political state of Europe is re-established; until solid principles have resumed the ascendancy over vain pretensions; finally, until the sanctity of treaties has established a solid peace in Europe.[23]

In order to achieve these aims the Allies had decided upon a general plan of campaign. In the north the 30,000 strong Army of North Germany under Bernadotte with III Corps of the Prussian Army of Silesia was to drive the French from the Low Countries. In the centre Marshal Gebhard von Blücher at the head of the 100,000-strong Army of Silesia was ordered to cross the Rhine into Alsace. In the south Schwarzenberg and the 200,000-strong Army of Bohemia was to strike deep into southern France via Switzerland. The three armies would then make a coordinated thrust to seize Paris.[24] In total the Allied powers assembled 327,000 troops and 1,106 pieces of artillery for the invasion of France, not to mention Wellington's 68,000 Anglo-Portuguese troops which had already crossed the Pyrenees. Indeed, once all the garrison troops and reservists are added to the front-line forces gathered for the invasion, the Allies had over 1,000,000 troops at their disposal in December/January 1813–14.[25]

The French were not in a strong position. Although Napoleon had sought to raise a new *Grande Armée* in the aftermath of the Leipzig campaign, the emperor had only been able to secure a further 120,000 conscripts out of the 936,500 Frenchmen he had hoped to incorporate into the ranks.[26] Napoleon distributed his meagre forces in three defensive sectors from North to South: guarding the Low Countries was Marshal Étienne Macdonald with around 15–20,000 troops. Although this force was expected to defend a wide expanse of country, a large number of MacDonald's troops were stationed at Antwerp under General Nicholas Maison; the bulk of the French army in Holland, under General Gabriel Joseph Molitor, was poorly disciplined and plagued by desertion. South of the Low Countries, between Koblenz and Landau, were a further 40,000 men, under Marmont. In the south, Marshal Claude Victor had barely 10,000 troops to oppose Schwarzenberg and the massive Army of Bohemia. Other than the veterans of the Imperial Guard, under Marshal Édouard Mortier, the only other troops available to Napoleon were 30,000 National Guardsmen. It must also be remembered that around 100,000 French veterans, under Marshal Nicholas Soult, were needed to hold the southern front against Wellington.[27] The stage was thus set for the invasion of France.

Rationale for British Intervention in 1813

In the meantime the British received intelligence reports from Holland in early November which suggested that the Dutch were on the verge of revolution. These reports were confirmed on 21 November when two Dutch dignitaries arrived in England and informed the British government that the people of Amsterdam had declared their independence.[28] The leading Dutch dignitary, Gijsbert Karel Van Hogendorp, requested British military support and proceeded to meet the Prince of Orange in order to secure the former Stadtholder's return.[29] The Prince of Orange duly informed the British government that he intended to return to Holland in order to mastermind the fusion of both the Southern and Northern Netherlands into a new 'United Netherlands'. He also suggested a marriage alliance between his heir and the daughter of the Prince Regent, Princess Charlotte of Wales.[30]

Eager to provide aid for the Dutch, the Secretary of State for War and the Colonies, Earl Henry Bathurst, despatched Major General Sir Herbert Taylor and Dutch Colonel Robert Fagel to The Hague with weapons for the rebels (over 20,000 muskets) and orders to 'collect the most correct circumstantial information' about the Dutch rebels.[31] The British were also informed that elements of the Army of the North already en route to support the Dutch and that a mobile force of Cossacks, drawn from Lieutenant General Ferdinand Fedororich von Winzegorode's Russian Corps, under Major General Alexander Benckendorff, had arrived at Amsterdam.[32] Bathurst was pleased to discover that the III Corps of the Prussian Army of Silesia, under Lieutenant General Friedrich Wilhelm Freiherr von Bülow, was also bound for Holland.[33] With Allied troops already in the Low Countries, the British opted to place 'boots on the ground' and despatched a small force of Royal Marines to the Scheldt and a contingent of Foot Guards to Holland.[34] Plans were drawn up for the despatch of a much larger British force to be sent to support the Army of the North and Bathurst also ordered the commander of the British garrison on the island of Stralsund, Major General Samuel Gibbs, to ready several of his battalions for service in the Low Countries.[35]

The man chosen to command the Guards was Major General George Cooke. A veteran of the French Revolutionary Wars, Cooke had seen extensive service in the Low Countries, serving in all three expeditions to the region in 1794–5, 1799 and 1809. He had been wounded in the fighting on the Helder peninsula in 1799 and was one of the many thousands to contract Walcheren fever during the expedition to the Scheldt in 1809.[36] Cooke's initial instructions were to proceed to the coast of Holland and then to Amsterdam in order to support 'The efforts made by the people of Holland to re-establish their independence under the auspices of His Serene Highness the Prince of Orange.'[37] Despite the circumstances, Bathurst did not entirely trust the Dutch rebels and provided Cooke with a second set of orders, which the general was to follow if the Dutch proved incapable of defending themselves. These were as follows: if Amsterdam was recaptured by the French, Cooke was to move his command to the Scheldt and to make contact with the marines and Gibbs.[38] Once the two British expeditionary forces were united, Cooke and Gibbs were to 'Undertake any operation which may appear to you advisable for the purpose of gaining security to Rotterdam, The Hague and Amsterdam; or if your force be equal to it of expelling the enemy from any other position which they may occupy.'[39] Unlike Cooke, who had extensive military experience in the Low Countries, Gibbs had served there on only one occasion, having participated in the bungled raid on the lock gates at Ostend in 1798.[40]

Although Bathurst can be applauded for his swiftness of action in response to the events in Holland, his decision to send two different sets of instructions no doubt confused the commanders. These criticisms aside the British government had at least shown an element of daring and it must be recognised that Bathurst's main goal was simply to have British troops on the ground at a time when the fate of the Low Countries was in the balance. Cooke's small flotilla reached the Dutch coast on 6 December 1813.[41]

Whilst Cooke's force was en route to the Low Countries, Bathurst had been busy making preparations for the despatch of the main expeditionary force under Sir Thomas Graham. A seasoned campaigner, Graham had entered the army late in life but had quickly demonstrated his quality, later commanding a sizeable portion of Wellington's army at the decisive Battle of Vittoria.[42] Unlike many of Wellington's generals Graham had achieved a victory of his own at the Battle of Barrosa in 1811.[43] Suffering from eye problems, however, Graham had returned to England after Vittoria and was thus available for active service just when Bathurst needed a veteran commander. However, if anyone was ready for another chance to strike at the French it was Graham, the general having harboured a deep hatred of the French following the death of his wife and the mistreatment of her coffin by a mob at Toulouse. Having served as a volunteer at the siege of Toulon in 1793, Graham had returned to Scotland and raised the 90th Regiment of Foot 'Perthshire Volunteers'. Graham also had some good connections in both political and military circles; his father-in-law being Lord Cathcart, whilst his cousin was Sir John Hope.

Graham received his marching orders on 4 December and, like Cooke before him, was informed of the utmost importance of the need to support the Dutch Orangeists. Despite the importance of the mission, Graham was informed that few troops could be spared for the Low Countries and that he would simply have to make do with what he was given.[44]

The British Army: Fit for Service?

The British forces commanded by Graham were of mixed quality. Gathered together at the last minute from garrisons across the British Isles the majority were raw recruits and, although Bathurst later provided four further battalions, Graham had barely 7,604 effective men at his disposal at the start of the campaign.[45] Graham's force was not the finest:

> The number of fit men available fell short of Bathurst's expectations by nearly one-third, and the total deployed – which, by default, must therefore have included men deemed unfit for their units – still fell short by nearly a quarter. What was more, over and above the units' being understrength, the state of these battalions was frequently poor, with many lacking much of a cadre of old soldiers, and many having particularly young NCOs.[46]

Attrition, combined with a shortfall in recruitment, were the main reasons why there were so few troops to send to the Low Countries in 1813. As Linch has noted between 1808 and 1813 an average of 15,000 men joined the army every year, although fewer than 10,000 joined in 1810.[47] During the same period the army suffered on average 22, 695 casualties per year or 10.8 per cent of the total strength of the British army.[48] Some years were worse than others, particularly 1809 when the army suffered around 25,000 casualties as a result of the fighting in the Iberian Peninsula and the Walcheren malarial epidemic.[49] As a consequence the British opted to deploy second and even third battalions on active service, a measure which had not been countenanced earlier in the war due to the fact that the entire point of second battalions had been for them to remain at home in order to form a nucleus of recruits. By 1812, however, the losses sustained in Spain and Portugal prompted Wellington to create experimental battalions of his own and York also formed a number of second, third and even fourth battalions for active service.[50] Graham was mostly provided with second and third battalions; the majority of his troops were either completely new to soldiering or had been encouraged to join the regulars from the militia, veterans were few and far between.

This was not the first time that former militiamen formed the bulk of a British expeditionary force; Henry Dundas had used such a scheme to provide extra manpower for Ireland in 1798 and for the Helder expedition a year later.[51] Although militiamen were often fit and hardy, they were often thrown into action before they were fully ready for the rigours of campaigning. But, in spite of this, the British army absorbed over 110,000 militiamen into regular service over the course of the Napoleonic Wars; 16,000 of whom transferred in 1809 alone.[52] The fact that Graham's expeditionary force was chiefly formed of second, third and even fourth battalions explains why his force was so inexperienced.

Alongside Cooke and Gibbs, Graham could count on the services of the experienced Major Generals John Byne Skerret and Kenneth Mackenzie. Mackenzie, the older of the two, had joined the army at the age of 13 in 1767 and saw active service in the West Indies and Flanders during the early years of the French Revolutionary Wars. Mackenzie had met Graham in 1794 when Mackenzie was appointed to serve in Graham's newly formed light infantry regiment. A close friend of Sir John Moore, Mackenzie made his name as a skilled drill master of light troops and played a formative role in the creation of the Light Brigade at Shorncliffe camp in 1803. He commanded a brigade under Graham at Cadiz in 1810 but was ordered back to England due to ill-health and only returned to active service when he was ordered to the Low Countries in 1813.[53] Skerret, in contrast, had only reached the rank of Major General in 1813 having entered the army in 1783 and had held a number of administrative and active commands in the Iberian Peninsula before being ordered to the Low Countries.[54] Despite their experience, both men would find the challenge of war in the Low Countries to be particularly difficult.

Planning and Preparation

Despite knowing that only a small force could be spared for service in the Low Countries, Bathurst was eager to strike at the French as soon as the circumstances permitted. On 5 December 1813, the Prince of Orange had chaired a meeting of the representatives of the Allied powers in the Low Countries. Although each of the various persons present had different strategic ideas about the future campaign, Taylor had been instructed by Bathurst to talk up British commitment to the war with France and the Major General promised the Allied leadership that Graham would support the Allied advance. In doing so the British won a firm friend in Bülow. The Prussian commander was delighted with the news of British support and made it clear that he intended to advance into the Southern Netherlands as soon as his full force was assembled.[55] With Graham still en route, Bathurst ordered Cooke to support the Prussians.[56] Cooke decided to move against the French-held port of Willemstadt and to place a garrison on the Island of Tholen.[57] As Sergeant Thomas Morris recalled, the winter conditions did not make for a pleasant march, 'There was a partial breaking of the frost; and our first day's march was the most miserable I have ever experienced. The roads were literally knee-deep in mud; many lost their shoes and boots. After toiling all day, we were only able to accomplish a distance of ten miles.'[58]

As the British troops acclimatised to the wintry December weather, Taylor worked alongside the British ambassador, Richard Trench, Second Earl of Clancarty, to rearm the Dutch. The Prince of Orange also faced the difficult task of trying to instil a fighting spirit amongst a Dutch population which, during the years of French occupation, had eschewed violent popular protest in favour of peaceful demonstration.[59] Whilst these matters were being dealt with Bathurst turned his thoughts to the coming offensive.

Bathurst was eager to secure British interests and turned his attention to the great French naval dockyards at Antwerp: 'Our great objective is Antwerp. We cannot make a secure peace if that place be left in the hands of France.'[60] Since the failed expedition to the Scheldt in 1809, the British had harboured the desire to destroy the French vessels based at Antwerp once and for all. In the intervening years, Napoleon had strengthened Antwerp's defences and, although the British had succeeded in burning the port facilities at Flushing in 1809, shipbuilding at Antwerp had continued unabated.[61] Flushed with excitement at the prospect of striking a decisive blow for British interests in the Low Countries, Bathurst, like Castlereagh before him, became convinced that the time was right for the British force in Holland to strike at Antwerp:

> It is now my duty to call your attention to another object in which the British interests are deeply invested. I mean the destruction of the naval armament at Antwerp. If at any time you should find it possible by marching suddenly on Antwerp to occupy such a position as would enable you to destroy the ships which it is understood are now laid up there, you would perform an essential service to your county. Always bearing in mind that it is the destruction of the

naval armament not the capture of the citadel or town which should
be the principal object of your exertions.[62]

The politicians made every effort to furnish Graham with as many resources
as could be spared, including a small train of field artillery and another 20,000
stands of arms.[63] Although bad weather delayed Graham and Gibbs' arrival
until 15 December, the Allied forces were quick to take the offensive. Russian General Benckendorff's Cossacks were the first to drive south and with
the aid of the local population seized Breda before Graham arrived in the
Roompot.[64] Once he had landed, Graham received news that the French had
abandoned the Dutch coast and he therefore decided to join Cooke at Willemstadt. By mid- to late December the Dutch port had turned into the main
British supply depot alongside the smaller dockyard at Helvoetsluys.[65] Despite
Bathurst's expectation that Graham would be able to make a quick advance in
conjunction with the Prussians, the situation on the ground was less favourable. Although Breda had been seized and the islands north of the Eastern
Scheldt secured, it soon became clear to Graham that the French were not in
full retreat and intended to defend the main fortresses in Brabant.

Before making an advance, Graham decided to organise his forces into
two divisions. The 1st Division was placed under the command of Cooke and
included Cooke's old Guards brigade, under Colonel Lord John Proby, and
the newly constituted 1 Brigade under Taylor. The 2nd Division, under the
command of Kenneth Mackenzie, also comprised two brigades, one of which
was placed under the command of Colonel John Macleod, whilst the other,
formed of the army's light troops, was handed to Gibbs. Both divisions had
a company of artillery attached to them and could call on the support of the
2nd King's German Legion Hussars. For the meantime three further battalions, including the aged men of the Royal Veteran Battalion, were left to garrison Willemstadt.[66]

With Antwerp outlined as the main objective, Graham spent much of the
rest of December and early January making the necessary preparations for
an advance. Graham was greatly aided by his close friend Lieutenant Colonel James Stanhope, who had served with Graham throughout the Peninsular
War and was appointed to act as his Deputy QMG in Holland.[67] As Stanhope
noted in his journal, although the British wanted to advance and seize Bergen-
Op-Zoom they first needed to secure Breda which, for a brief period, was in
danger of being recaptured by the French:

> You will have heard of our having landed at Tholen in consequence
> of the evacuation of Willemstadt and Breda. We made a recon-

naissance on Bergen-Op-Zoom the next day but reinforcement had entered that morning. Had the winds not detained us so long in England, I think we should have taken the place by a coup de main ... That day is however gone by. On the 18th the French pushed a strong body supposed to be from 6 to 7,000 men to and invested Breda where Benckendorff was with 1,200 Russian infantry and 3,000 cavalry ... General Benkendorff evacuates Breda tomorrow moving on Dusseldorf ... We, although not half equipped, weak in numbers and having a most extensive line to defend, nevertheless send a brigade 'pour le moment' to keep the French out if possible.[68]

Allied intelligence also indicated that a further force of 5,000 French were en route to Antwerp. With only 8,000 men under his command and the French strength increasing, Graham informed Bathurst that he could 'attempt nothing against any of the strong places in Brabant' without Prussian assistance.[69] A crisis was averted during the first week in January 1814 when the approach of the Prussian advance guard persuaded the French to abandon their plans against Breda. Graham finally met Bülow in the city on 9 January and it was decided that both armies would seek to attack the villages north of Antwerp.[70]

Bülow assumed overall control of the offensive and ordered Graham to attack the village of Merxem which was located immediately north of Antwerp. Graham's troops were to be assisted in this task by a force of Prussian infantry under General Adolf Freiderich Oppen.[71] A further Prussian force was to attack the nearby villages of Minderhout and Wuustwezel, whilst General Borstel held Westmalle. The Prussians advanced first and managed to push the French from Minderhout and Wuustwezel over the course of 11–12 January, whilst the newly organised 2nd Division advanced from Calmhout and Roosendaal to the vicinity of Merxem.[72] The British troops were heavily engaged for the first time on 13 January and after some confusion evicted the French from the village.[73] British jubilation proved short-lived for no sooner had the British seized Merxem than they were ordered to retreat by Bülow, whose own troops had been forced back by the French.[74] After the skirmish at Merxem, the British retreated to the vicinity of Bergen-Op-Zoom. Despite the withdrawal Graham maintained the desire to strike against Antwerp and tried to convince Bülow of its importance. However, what convinced Bülow to order another forward movement was the Prussian general's anger at Bernadotte who had announced in *The London Times* that he, and not Bulow, had masterminded the liberation of the Low Countries.[75]

In late January the Allied forces advanced once more against the villages north of Antwerp and pushed the French into Antwerp after a series of coordinated attacks.[76] Although keen to please his British allies, Bülow was ordered to link up with the rest of the Army of Silesia in Northern France. The Prussian subsequently informed the British that he would protect the planned British bombardment of Antwerp's dockyards for three days, but would vacate the Low Countries thereafter.[77] With little choice in the matter, Graham accepted these terms, and with time of the essence he quickly established a series of batteries north of Antwerp. With too few heavy guns of their own, the British were forced to rely on a mixed number of Dutch ordnance which, as Stanhope noted, was poor in quality:

> Our battering train was frozen at the emboucher [mouth] of the Scheldt & could not be landed & the ship with the rockets was wind bound at Harwich. We were therefore obliged to collect whatever guns could be found in Holland and they were bad in quality and inadequate in number. Several of the guns burst & the mortars never carried with a correct range with the exception of three napoleons & they had but few shells belonging to them.[78]

With the batteries built and the first shots fired those uninvolved in the bombardment made every effort to gain a good view of the events. Taylor was particularly well placed to observe the shells as they rained down upon the city of Antwerp:

> At 3 I went to the top of the church steeple of Merxem with Sir T. Graham, the Duke of Clarence, etc., to see the effects of the batteries. They opened at half-past three, but the shells in general seemed to fall short. However, towards 5 there was a blaze, and our fire continued until past dusk, when it ceased. That of the enemy, which had been very warmly kept up, ceased soon after. The buildings on fire proved to be Magasins de Comestibles, and a church this side of the arsenal. Our casualties were few, four artillerymen and a few horses wounded. Their shot and shells passed all our quarters and injured many houses of this place, also struck the church steeple occasionally while we were in it. All continued very quiet during the night, and some of our guns and mortars were moved to the right, more within range.[79]

The fire from the British batteries continued in much same manner for the next two days but, despite setting parts of the town and docks ablaze, they were unable to destroy the dockyards and the French ships moored therein. One of the main reasons for this was that, whilst the Allies had gathered their forces for a fresh advance after the first Battle of Merxem, the French had had time to prepare for the British onslaught. The garrison at Antwerp had also greatly benefited from the sudden arrival of Lazare Carnot, the fabled 'organizer of victory', who had recently been appointed by Napoleon to secure its defences.[80] A notable defensive measure taken by Carnot before the British arrival had been his decision to order that each of the French vessels in the harbour be covered by protective layer of timber and earth, which he hoped would absorb any future shelling.[81] Following the British arrival, Carnot mounted a number of sorties designed to interrupt the bombardment and spike several British batteries and encouraged the French gunners to keep up such a ferocious counter-fire that the British were forced to withdraw some of their battalions from Merxem.[82] As Smyth later reported, the British bombardment ultimately failed to achieve its objectives:

> It was impossible not to entertain the most sanguine hopes of a favourable result, notwithstanding however the utmost exertion of every officer and man in the Army and the very excellent practice made by the artillery who threw more than 2,000 shells, & a continued fire of three days we have not obtained the object in view. The ships were repeatedly on fire, several fires kindled in the buildings round them, and a large store room containing the biscuits & provisions for the fleet destroyed by being just on fire. The vessels themselves, however, have not been burnt; and I am afraid it is not possible to destroy them without much large[r] means than we at present possess.[83]

Graham had little choice but to cease the bombardment and bid farewell to Bülow's Prussians. The British had tried their best, but their best had not been good enough. Not long after Bülow had left the scene, Graham was forced to order a halt to proceedings in order to plan his next move.

Following the ineffectual bombardment of Antwerp, Graham was obliged to place his army into cantonments between Bergen-Op-Zoom and Breda.[84] As Graham considered his options, it gradually became clear to him that his force was too small to attack Antwerp until a greater array of heavy ordnance was available. With the government eager for signs of progress and having achieved little since his arrival in Holland, Graham turned his attention to Bergen-Op-Zoom:

> I am inclined to think that if the reinforcements were arrived and the weather tolerably steady we might get hold of Bergen-Op-Zoom, the garrison of which is certainly of a bad description … If we

got Bergen-Op-Zoom … we should be able to cross the Scheldt at leisure below Antwerp should there be favourable circumstances in that part of Brabant.[85]

On the following day, Graham clarified his ideas to the British representative at The Hague, the Earl of Clancarty, with a view to gaining Dutch military support for the attack on Bergen-Op-Zoom:

An attack on Bergen-Op-Zoom provided no better garrison be thrown into it, would probably be on the whole the most beneficial of anything that [we] could … undertake. There is no probability of my being able to do anything alone against Antwerp which by the last accounts must have 10,000 men in garrison, nor is it possible that I could be able to look after that garrison and carry on the siege of Bergen-Op-Zoom.[86]

Despite promising to discuss Graham's scheme with the Prince of Orange, Clancarty did not think it likely that the Dutch would be able to support Graham in the manner in which he would have liked. The Prince of Orange, Clancarty informed Graham, wanted instead to make himself master of Venloo and Maastricht.[87] The only sizeable Dutch military assistance which Graham could count upon was a Dutch infantry brigade, under the command of General Hendrik George, Count de Perponcher Sedlnitsky.[88]

Although Graham's army was strengthened by the arrival of another British infantry brigade under General Gore, Graham remained of the opinion that Bergen-Op-Zoom was the only realistic objective that his small army could hope to seize before the end of spring.[89] Despite this, Graham continued to think beyond the immediate situation he considered the possibility of bribing the French commander at Antwerp, in order to gain the dockyards without loss of life. He also gathered information about the French military situation beyond Antwerp, in particular the strength of the French garrison at Ostend.[90]

Before taking further action, Graham's time was taken up with making two important personnel changes. Graham decided that his Commissary General George Spiller and his Deputy QMG Lieutenant Colonel Frederick Trench had performed poorly during the previous operations and needed to be replaced.[91] Despite Graham's criticisms, both were experienced practioners. Spiller, for instance, had served on York's staff during the Helder expedition in 1799 and as Deputy Commissary General on the home establishment, whilst Trench had served on Walcheren in 1809 and acted under Graham at Cadiz. Nevertheless, Graham was not satisfied with their conduct. However, instead of following the official protocols and writing to York, Graham instead mentioned the problem to Wellington.

Instead of simply offering his views on the subject Wellington decided to take matters into his own hands. He informed Graham in mid-January that Lieutenant Colonel Charles Cathcart and Thomas Dunmore were willing to serve in the Low Countries.[92] Although both he and Wellington had subverted Army rules, Graham made it clear to Bathurst that the changes had been forced upon him because of the poor staff which he had been given by the administrators at the Horse Guards.[93] With the changes having already been made and with greater matters to worry about, both Bathurst and York opted to turn a blind eye to the whole episode.

As the British readied themselves for the next stage of the campaign, Graham became increasingly conscious that the war in France was not going as well as had been hoped. Both the armies of Silesia and Bohemia had driven deep into France by January 1814 but Blücher and Schwarzenberg moved at different rates.[94] With the Allied armies divided, Napoleon gathered his forces and prepared to strike against his enemies piecemeal. Although his forces were checked by Blücher at the Battle of La Rothière, on 1 February 1814, Napoleon launched a whirlwind-like offensive over the course of the following days and defeated the Prussians on three occasions at Champaubert, Montmirail and Vauchamps.[95] Napoleon then turned his attention to Schwarzenberg and the Army of Bohemia which he defeated, at the Battle of Montereau, on 18 February.[96] Despite these reverses, the Allied armies were not destroyed and both Blücher and Schwarzenberg resolved to ready their forces for another offensive.

In the Low Countries, however, a lack of up-to-date intelligence meant that Graham did not have a clear idea of what was taking place in France and as he waited for further news he gradually grew more concerned about the situation. Graham's anxiety was raised, on the last day in February, when he received word from Bathurst which suggested that his army might soon be broken to provide reinforcements for North America and Southern French theatres.[97] This new information clearly agitated Graham, who immediately started to consider whether to strike at the French before his troops were to be withdrawn from the theatre of operations.[98]

Bathurst's letter certainly confused the situation and accentuated the general anxiety of the British high command. Unsure about the fate of the Allied offensives in Champagne, perturbed by Bathurst's letter, and worried by news of French troop concentrations to his front, Graham decided that Bergen-Op-Zoom needed to be taken.[99] Before planning the operation Graham despatched

Stanhope to gain permission for the attack from the Crown Prince and to ask for reinforcements. Stanhope used all his powers of persuasion to make it clear to Bernadotte that, with the British troops likely to be withdrawn, bold action was needed to seize Bergen-Op-Zoom:

> I then brought forward the subject which was of the greatest impor-
> tance and which had not been mentioned to any of the other com-
> manders, the probability of the British corps being entirely with-
> drawn. This led me into the detail of the intended force which was
> promised, the failure of the militia bill on which those 'hopes' were
> grounded, the smallness of our corps at present, the extent of our
> cantonments, the necessity of keeping Tholen & South Beveland to
> have an eye on Flushing, the considerable numbers of the enemy
> opposed to us in Antwerp & Bergen-Op-Zoom, the necessity of
> reinforcing Lord Wellington's army and the inadequacy of the
> means without breaking up the British corps, which was therefore
> in the contemplation of our government. I then stated the anxiety
> which General Graham felt to get hold of Bergen-Op-Zoom as it
> would facilitate our operations on the other side of the Scheldt, but
> that he had not a force sufficient to cover and besiege it.[100]

By repeating the idea that Graham's force was about to be withdrawn, Stanhope managed to convince Bernadotte that it was a good idea that Bergen-
Op-Zoom was taken as quickly as possible. Stanhope also convinced the former French marshal to send General Wallmoden and a force of fresh troops
to support the British.[101] Bernadotte clearly valued Graham's presence in the
Low Countries and, although it was unclear to Graham whether Bathurst
would really divide his army, Graham had at least been provided with the
ideal means to persuade Bernadotte of the need to seize Bergen-Op-Zoom.

Another factor in Graham's decision was that the latest intelligence suggested that there were no more than 3,000 poor quality French troops in the
town and that they were also low in morale.[102] Graham was convinced of the
need to strike as quickly as possible when, on 4 March, he received intelligence
from the Duke of Saxe-Weimar that a strong French force had been observed
en route to Antwerp.[103] Graham had also been informed that, due to the thick-
ness of the ice at Helvoet, the heavy ordnance which had been shipped to the
Dutch coast for the British could not be moved until the ice had thawed.[104]
Thus, with sizeable French forces apparently preparing for an offensive to his
front, the Allies in retreat and his force seemingly on the verge of being broken
up for other operations, Graham believed he had little choice but to mount a

surprise attack on Bergen-Op-Zoom. A prominent influence over the resulting British plan of attack, Graham's chief engineer, Carmichael Smyth, later justified Graham's decision by stating that nothing else could have been done in the circumstances:

> The greatest difficulty ... in making any arrangement for forward movement was the fortress of Bergen-Op-Zoom which could not be left in the rear without a considerable corps to mask it. Its capture also with a view to the security of Holland should any reverse of affairs take place is so very evident that Sir Thomas Graham was induced to make a considerable effort to gain possession of this important fortress.[105]

The Hill Upon the Zoom

With Bergen-Op-Zoom firmly in his sights, Graham rushed to ready his forces for an attack. Bergen-Op-Zoom is one of a number of towns located on an incline known as the Brabant wal, a 20m-high ridge which runs diagonally across northern Brabant between the River Scheldt and Roosendaal.[106] The Dutch word Bergen roughly translates as 'hill' in English and thus in the Dutch language Bergen-Op-Zoom equates to 'The Hill upon the Zoom'. The Zoom, which was canalised before 1814, acted as a natural boundary between the north and south of the town.[107] The Zoom also provided water for both the harbour area and a series of defensive ditches, which ringed the eastern side of the town. Bergen-Op-Zoom's defences in 1814 were formidable and were still roughly based upon those which had been constructed, over the course of 1698 to 1701, by the great Dutch engineer Menno van Coehoorn. He had also been responsible for the maintenance and construction of the Dutch forts which had formed the old defensive barrier between Holland and France.[108] Although sacked by the French in 1747, the fortress had been completely rebuilt over the course of the following decades.

Bergen-Op-Zoom's reconstructed defences in 1814 were designed to repel an attack from the direction of France whilst the canalised River Zoom provided whoever commanded the fortress with direct access to the Scheldt estuary. Either side of the Zoom on the western side of the fortress were the sand-covered approaches to the Scheldt and, beyond that, a large area of marshland protected the western approaches to the harbour area. These natural obstacles shielded the western fringes of the town and were especially deadly at high tide when the rising waters of the Scheldt covered the sand flats. This whole area was also covered by the guns of the Water-Fort, which had been built upon the sands and was connected to the rest of the fortress by a slice of polder and to the harbour via the fortified Water-Gate. Both sides of the narrow harbour were protected by a series of water-filled ditches and earthen ramparts, features which have been described by Christopher Duffy as characteristic of Dutch military engineering.[109] The area north of the harbour, meanwhile, housed the powder magazine, whilst the southern part was shielded by an inner defensive position known as the Orange bastion.

Unlike the northern harbour walls, which were defended by stone-built angular defensive bastions linked to the rest of the northern ramparts by the Steenbergen Gate, the south-western walls were made merely of compacted earth.[110] To the south of the Orange bastion was an old fortified camp which had subsequently been incorporated into the town's southern defences and was known as the Kijk in dem Pot.[111] North of the Kijk in dem Pot was the central square at which point the Antwerp road crossed the route to Breda.[112]

As the Napoleonic engineer and historian Sir John Jones noted, the towns defences were strongest between the Kijk in dem Pot and the Breda Gate which 'Were constructed with a variety of outworks flanked by galleries for reverse fire in their counterscarps, and were extensively countermined; and further, their right was supported by a system of detached lunettes'.[113] The area between the Breda and Steenbergen gates was also strongly defended and was supported by the Lines of Steenbergen, which protruded in a diagonal line from the northeastern corner of the fortress in the direction of Breda. Bergen-Op-Zoom anchored this defensive line and, if viewed from a wider perspective, formed the southern corner of a grand defensive triangle, which had been created prior to the French Revolution to protect Brabant and Zealand from French attack.

Although well-defended, the French garrison could not make the most of Bergen-Op-Zoom's defences for a number of reasons. Firstly, the commander of the fortress, General Bizanet, had barely 2,700 raw levies men at his disposal, a force deemed too few to garrison the entire length of the town's walls.[114] Taylor certainly thought that the French were too weak defend the fortress properly and informed York on 22 January that 'A surprise would be practicable.'[115] Secondly, the French did not command the Scheldt estuary and thus could not reap the benefits of Bergen-Op-Zoom's close proximity to the river and North Sea. Indeed, had the weather been warmer, the British might have been able to sail down the Scheldt to within a close distance of the town. Finally, Bizanet did not know which direction a likely attack might come from given that the Allied forces had bypassed the town en route to Antwerp and held the surrounding countryside. The British needed to make the most of this situation.

With the decision made to attack Bergen-Op-Zoom, Graham and his senior commanders rushed to put together a plan of operations. Lacking any personal knowledge of the fortress and its defences, Graham relied on the judgement of Carmichael Smyth. Smyth, however, was no expert on the fortress and instead sought the advice of two Dutch engineers, Captains Jan Egbertus Van Gorkum and De Bère. Both had close links inside the fortress and were related.[116]

De Bère had been first to volunteer his services to the British and had made a reconnaissance of the fortress with Smyth towards the end of January. During this mission, De Bère had suggested to Smyth that the fortress could be taken by surprise and thought that an attack would best be made on the western side of Bergen-Op-Zoom. Smyth, however, did not place a great deal of faith in De Bère's technical knowledge and later informed Taylor that, despite his zeal, De Bère knew 'nothing of fortifications'.[117] Van Gorkum was thus entrusted with finalising a plan of attack.

Given the amount of intelligence work he had undertaken over the course of the previous weeks, it was no surprise that Van Gorkum was one of only a handful of officers who were called by Graham to attend a last-minute planning meeting at the village of Wouw on 7 March. What is surprising is that although Graham and his staff agreed to adopt Van Gorkum's plan, including the date for the attack which was set for the night of 8 March, they spent the rest of the meeting adapting it on the suggestion of De Bère. Thus, instead of assaulting Bergen-Op-Zoom with 6,000 men in 2 sizeable columns plus a third false attack, as Van Gorkum had suggested, the British decided that around 3,000 men were enough for the task and accepted a fresh proposal from De Bère who claimed that another attack to the east of the fortress would stretch the weak French garrison to breaking point.[118] Van Gorkum was not amused by the changes, particularly since he knew that the area chosen for the new attack was well defended. Despite making this point to Graham, the general's mind was made up and, as Van Gorkum was escorted out of the room, Smyth confidently boasted that numbers were irrelevant as British guardsmen would easily triumph over French forces three times their number![119] Although Graham eventually added a further 300 men to the attack, Van Gorkum was left angered and frustrated by the British general.

For the rest of the British commanders, the planning meeting at Wouw was the first time they had heard of the idea to assault Bergen-Op-Zoom. Although no doubt excited by the prospect, they had little time to ready their men or think through their respective tasks. In rushing the planning process and placing his confidence in questionable intelligence, Graham had inadvertently emulated the mistakes made by the other British generals who had commanded in the Low Countries since 1793 and paved the way for another disaster.

The final version of the plan of attack called for four different attacking columns to assault the defences of Bergen-Op-Zoom at 10pm on the night of 8–9 March. The so-called 'Right Attack', under the command of Skerret, Arthur Gore and Lieutenant Colonels George Carleton and Frederick Muller, was to be made against the harbour side of Bergen-Op-Zoom with a composite force of around 1,100 infantry drawn from the 21st, 37th and 44th Regiments of Foot. Led by a couple of Dutch guides and a group of engineers, the Right Attack was to begin its advance at 9pm from the village of Halsteren. From here Skerret, Gore and Carleton were to traverse the Tholendijk and cross the River Zoom close to the town walls. Skerret, Gore and Carleton were then to 'Gain the ramparts' to their right and 'proceed along it until met by the attacks made by the brigade of Guards'.[120] The soldiers of the Right Attack, as with those in the other attacking columns, were also instructed to shout out 'Up with the Orange' if they encountered any other troops in the darkness, the reply to was to be 'God Save the King'.[121] As the senior commander in the area, Skerret was also ordered to mount a diversion against the northern ramparts of the fortress. This 'False Attack' was to be made by around 250 men drawn from the flank companies of the 21st, 37th and 91st Regiments of Foot under the command of Lieutenant Colonel Benjamin Ottley.[122]

To the south side of the town the 1,000-strong 'Left Attack', under Cooke and Proby, was to advance northwards from their camp at the village of Hoogstraten and enter Bergen-Op-Zoom by way of the Kijk in dem Pot.[123] Chiefly composed of detachments from the three Guards battalions, the Left Attack also benefited from the guidance of two of the habitants of the town and Van Gorkum, Smyth and Captain Sir George Hoste. Once inside the fortress, Cooke and Proby were to advance 'To their left along the ramparts, to meet the troops under the command of Lieutenant Colonel Carleton.'[124] Last but not least, 650 infantrymen, drawn from the 55th and 69th Regiments of Foot under the command of Lieutenant Colonel Morrice, were to undertake De Bère's 'Centre Attack' against the eastern face of Bergen-Op-Zoom. Morrice did have the 33rd Regiment of Foot in reserve, although these troops were much further back. Once inside the fortress, Morrice was to establish communications with the other attackers and 'be in readiness for any further operations against the enemy which may be necessary'.[125]

What was striking about Graham's plan was its vagueness. Apart from informing each of the commanders that, once inside the fortress, they were to endeavour to link up with the other attackers no further guidance was pro-vided. Although Carleton knew that he had to link up with Cooke and that Cooke's column was to advance against the southern side of the fortress, he did not know when or where. The British also lacked detailed maps of the town and relied heavily on what the Dutch engineers said about the fortress.[126] Furthermore, Graham's underestimation of the fighting qualities of the French troops played a key part in the events of 8–9 March, events which not only tarnished Graham's reputation, but also that of the British army.

The first British troops to attack the fortress of Bergen-Op-Zoom belonged to Ottley's False Attack which succeeded in drawing the bulk of the French garrison to the northern side of the fortress.[127] Ottley's soldiers were quickly forced to retire but had achieved all that Graham had asked of them. The first troops to enter Bergen-Op-Zoom were the men of Carleton's advanced guard from the Right Attack who, after a silent march along the Tholendijk, reached the mud-laden ditches outside the walls and crossed the narrow River Zoom just as the False Attack commenced.[128]

Carleton, with the 150-strong body of troops under his command, wasted little time and quickly secured the outer ramparts near the harbour. What Carleton and Gore needed to do at this point was to wait for the rest of the col-umn so that they could push forward in a coordinated advance to link with the Left Attack in the vicinity of the Antwerp Gate. Patience, however, was not one of Carleton's virtues and he continued the rapid advance along the southern ramparts without waiting for Skerret. In their eagerness to push on, neither Carleton nor Gore decided to inform Skerret and so when Skerret and around 200 more men reached the ramparts they found no sign of the forlorn hope. By this stage, the False Attack had succeeded in drawing the bulk of the French garrison away from the harbour area and, although this feint was forced back with heavy losses, it had provided the Right Attack with a golden opportunity to push home its attack against no resistance.

Skerret, however, had other ideas. Like Carleton before him, he had only to wait for Lieutenant Colonel Frederick Muller and the reserve to appear before ordering a further advance. Skerret was motivated by a desire to achieve a notable victory of his own in order to redeem his reputation, which had been dented by his poor conduct under Graham during the bungled Tarragona expedition in 1811, under Cooke at Tarifa in 1812 and finally as a brigade commander at the siege of San Sebastián in 1813.[129] During the planning process, Skerret had spoken at length to Van Gorkum about the need to capture the French magazine and arsenal and, although the Dutch engineer had agreed with him, Graham's plan had made no mention of these as objectives.[130] Undeterred, Skerret had convinced himself that the powder magazine was vital to the success of the operation and, when he reached the deserted ramparts, he disobeyed Graham's instructions and hastened off at the head of a body of troops in the direction of the magazine.[131] Skerret also failed to inform Muller who arrived with the reserve shortly after Skerret had moved off. On seeing British troops advancing along both sides of the ramparts, Muller was unsure of which direction to take and decided to remain on the defensive.[132]

The division of the Right Attack into three independent bodies undermined its impact. As the hours passed, Skerret and Muller gradually became embroiled in a minor battle of their own for control of the harbour area and powder magazine. This battle occupied their time and efforts for the rest of the operation and left them powerless to influence the events on the southern side of Bergen-Op-Zoom, events which ultimately decided the fate of the British attacks.

Carleton and Gore, with just over a hundred men, were the only ones from the Right Attack to follow their instructions and were left to capture the entire stretch of ramparts from the harbour to the Antwerp Gate on their own. Thankfully for the British, there were only a handful of French troops stationed on the southern ramparts and both commanders were quickly able to push on to within the vicinity of the Antwerp Gate, where they expected to meet the troops of the Left Attack. Unbeknownst to them, however, the severity of the weather had delayed Cooke's advance and forced the guards to find another way into the fortress.[133] The route chosen by Graham for the guards to follow was particularly long and would have taken a while to complete even in good weather. The distance involved, combined with the terrible conditions, meant that the Guards did not enter Bergen-Op-Zoom until half-past 11, over an hour after Carleton and Gore had entered the fortress.[134] Cooke's troops might even have been delayed longer had it not been for Lieutenant Charles Abbey and his axe-wielding sappers who cleared a direct path for the Guards through an outer line of wooden palisades to the ramparts.[135]

Oblivious of the reasons for the delay, Carleton and Gore proceeded along the ramparts and tried to link up with the Centre Attack near the Breda Gate. The Centre Attack, however, had been a complete failure with Morrice and his subordinate, Lieutenant Colonel William Elphinstone, being wounded in the process. The survivors of this attack, plus the men of the reserve, under Major George Muttlebury, had then been redirected to support Cooke.[136] Carleton, therefore, had marched straight into a trap and after a quick firefight Carleton and Gore were both killed.[137] With both their commanders down, the remainder of the force retreated back along the ramparts to the Antwerp Gate, where they finally met a party of Cooke's Guardsmen, under Lieutenant Colonel George Clifton.[138] As Clifton considered his options, Van Gorkum, who had accompanied Clifton's command, tried to open the Antwerp Gate but failed to do so.[139] With no sign of any other British troops, Clifton boldly advanced into the maze of streets only to be killed by a blaze of French musketry and the rest of Clifton's force surrendered.[140]

Oblivious to Clifton's fate, Cooke despatched another party, under Lieutenant Colonel Henry Rooke, to discover what had happened to the Centre Attack and Clifton's party. Rooke found the Antwerp Gate to be back in French hands and returned to Cooke none the wiser as to Clifton's movements.[141] The fate of the Centre Attack only became clear to Cooke when Muttlebury arrived from the eastern side of the fortress with nearly a thousand infantry. Though Cooke now had roughly a third of the total attacking force under his command, the disappearance of Clifton cautioned him against making any forward movement:

> The opinion of our leaders was that we should maintain quiet during the night, and take possession in the morning. Colonel Smyth then took his leave to report to the General, Sir G. Hoste accompanying him. The plan adopted seemed unhappy. Here we were, men and officers standing about in a cold night.[142]

Having survived the various events on the southern side of the fortress, Sperling had made his way to Cooke's headquarters and was well placed to observe the discussions between the commanders of the Left Attack. As Sperling noted, the most vocal officer amongst Cooke's staff was Proby:

> Believing myself the only Engineer officer in the place, I made frequent visits to the look-out, to see if the General had any orders. Lord Proby, who commanded the Guards, was filled with melancholy forebodings. He had taken up his post with the General, and seemed occupied in instilling the diffidence with which his own mind was filled. He characterised our situation as desperate (although exactly the reverse, as any decisive measure must, humanely speaking, have insured success) and the importance of the safety of the Guards.[143]

John Proby, Second Earl of Carysfort, had been commissioned into the British army in 1795 and had spent much of his career as a staff officer. He had risen to the post of Assistant QMG to the British forces in Portugal and Spain in 1808–9 but, despite seeing active service in the Low Countries during the Walcheren expedition and under Graham at Cadiz in 1811, he had little experience of commanding troops in battle prior to being given the command of the brigade of guards in Graham's army for the campaign in Holland.[144] It is difficult to understand why Proby was so pessimistic about the situation for, although things had clearly not gone to plan, he and Cooke had nearly 2,000 men at their disposal atop the southern ramparts and would have been aware due to the firing to the north that at least one of the other columns had penetrated the fortress.

Proby's concern regarding the safety of the Guards might have been influenced by his desire to avoid a repeat of the events at Ostend in 1798.[145] Whatever influenced Proby's judgement, he convinced Cooke of the need for patience and Cooke decided to wait until dawn before doing anything else. Cooke, it must also be remembered, was without the expert knowledge of both Smyth and Van Gorkum, the former having unwisely decided to vacate his post in order to report back to Graham, whilst Cooke had foolishly sent Van Gorkum with Clifton and had not seen the Dutch officer since.[146]

Blind to the nature of the fortress, Cooke's decision to remain on the defensive enabled the French to concentrate their forces against Skerret and Muller. Skerret, like Carleton and Gore, was already mortally wounded and his post was taken by Captain James Guthrie. Under renewed pressure and without reinforcement from Muller, the survivors of Skerret's force filtered back to the harbour area. Dunbar Moodie, who had joined Guthrie's party towards the end of the night fighting, described the chaotic nature of the events that followed, 'The enemy now brought an overbearing force against us … the slaughter was now dreadful, and our poor fellows, who had done all that soldiers could in our trying situation, now fell thick and fast'.[147] The sight of Guthrie's shattered troops streaming back from the powder magazine convinced Muller that retreat was the only option and the British troops in the harbour area retreated in chaotic fashion to the Water Gate. Moodie and his comrades were subsequently forced to surrender when they unexpectedly discovered the gate in French hands, whilst Muller surrendered his command under the guns of the Water Fort.[148]

On the southern front, the situation had gradually worsened and, in the early morning, the French mounted a series of vigorous attacks which aimed to dislodge Cooke's troops. Although thwarted in these attempts, Muttlebury and the troops of the 69th and 55th Regiments thought the situation was bleak.[149] Hemmed inside a small sector of Bergen-Op-Zoom and with no word from the Right Attack, Cooke finally acquiesced to Proby's request and ordered the guards to retreat under the cover of Muttlebury's infantry. Shortly afterwards

Proby's retreat was interrupted when Cooke received official confirmation of Muller's capitulation from Lieutenant Colonel Leslie Jones who had been taken prisoner by the French and had been sent to Cooke's headquarters under a flag of truce. Bizanet called on Cooke to surrender.[150] Dejected by the news, Cooke did not hesitate and capitulated on the spot.

So ended the bungled British attempt to seize Bergen-Op-Zoom, an operation that suffered not only from being badly planned but also poorly executed. Total British losses for the assault stood at 2,552 killed, wounded and captured; the vast majority, at just over 2,000 officers and men, were those who had capitulated.[151] As 3,300 men had made the assault, the percentage of men lost, out of the total number of attackers, stood at around 77 per cent, making it the highest rate of loss experienced by the British army in the Napoleonic Wars.[152]

Aftermath

Shortly after the attack on Bergen-Op-Zoom, Graham attempted to distance himself from the events in question. Not only did he report to Bathurst that he had had little choice but to mount the attack, but he also stressed that he had been persuaded by the Dutch engineers that an attack would be successful.[153] Graham's political masters received news of the debacle at dinner in London on 13 March from Stanhope, whom Graham had despatched immediately after the defeat.[154] At a meeting convened by York on the following day, further details of the debacle were divulged by Stanhope to the assembled officers. Taylor also attended this meeting and noted that, according to Stanhope's report, the defeat had been caused by the failure of the False Attack, the insubordination of Carleton, and Muller's abandonment of the harbour area and subsequent surrender.[155] Amazingly Stanhope managed to persuade York that the defeat at Bergen-Op-Zoom had not been deserved and in light of the courage shown by Graham and his men 'It was settled that in consideration of Graham's merit in the plan, it [the defeat at Bergen-Op-Zoom] should be treated as a victory & all persons mentioned were promoted & I among the others.'[156] With this decision a golden chance to review the campaign and learn the lessons of the defeat was lost.

On 18 March Taylor received a more detailed explanation of the events from Graham himself, the general making it clear to Taylor that the defeat was due to those under his command and not to his own failings:

> The subject is still too painful to think of almost. I am, however, satisfied that if I can blame myself for anything, it is for having placed more confidence than I ought in such young troops. At the same time I considered them much improved in steadiness by the

Merxem campaign, and that they were less likely to run wild after plunder and wine than older soldiers. But above all, I could not reckon on their leaders behaving like subalterns carrying handfuls of men on without support or order to be uselessly sacrificed. It is quite heart breaking to have had such a melancholy result, instead of that which would have been that of good conduct.[157]

Although Graham had every reason to be angry with his subordinates, not least Skerret and Muller, he was not as innocent as he protested. As the C-in-C of the British forces in the Low Countries he was responsible for the attack and the manner in which it was planned.[158] Had Graham been more patient and waited just a few more days he would not have had to gamble on an attack because the Prussian and Austrian armies defeated Napoleon, at the two-day Battle of Laon, on 9–10 March 1814.[159] Even before this defeat, the French had already decided to withdraw and had concentrated their troops at Antwerp in preparation to do so.

The irony, of course, was that Graham believed these movements to be the first signs of an impending attack and became fixated with the idea that the British needed a secure base, north of Antwerp, from which they could defend the Dutch frontier. Quite why Graham believed the capture of Bergen-Op-Zoom would have aided the British position in the Low Countries if a French attack was imminent is unclear. Even if the British had made themselves masters of Bergen-Op-Zoom, the fortress would not have provided much in the way of defence if a major French counter-attack had been launched by Napoleon; Graham simply would not have had the means to defend the town against a large French army with heavy artillery. Ultimately Graham should not have panicked for, despite their defeats at the hands of Napoleon, the Prussians were not decisively beaten. Indeed, the Allied armies had suffered worse defeats during the campaign of 1813 and had still managed to regroup and defeat Napoleon at Leipzig. Graham's lack of faith in the resilience of the Allies said more about Graham than it did anything else. It would also have been unlikely that Bathurst would have depleted Graham's forces if a French counter-attack had been launched, given that the safety of Holland was still a foremost British interest.

Why Graham did not decide to retreat to his cantonments, or to the safety of the city of Breda is also hard to understand, given that either of these two positions would have placed his troops in contact with the Dutch and kept his forces close to the ice-bound supply depots at Willemstadt and Helvoetsluys. The fact that Graham decided on an attack meant that the events at Bergen-Op-Zoom were of his making and one would have expected him to have at least thought through how his troops were to operate against the fortress. It was also strange that, having decided to gamble on an attack, that Graham only deployed a fraction of the forces available to him. Although he clearly needed to deploy some troops to screen his forces, his decision to deploy Gibbs, with around 4,000 men, for this task deprived him of extra striking power. In essence, had Graham attacked with the number of men suggested by Van Gorkum, he would have had sizeable reinforcements available to throw into the assault and seize the fortress.

Much of the confusion which characterised the British assault stemmed from Graham's mishandling of the planning process, not least his decision to alter Van Gorkum's plan at the last minute in favour of De Bère's scheme for a central attack. Indeed, why Graham placed so much trust in De Bère was strange given that Smyth clearly had little confidence in De Bère's technical understanding, whilst Van Gorkum was also sceptical about De Bère's grasp of the situation. Graham's instructions to his subordinates were also vague. Instead of being provided with a detailed operational plan, outlining exactly how the various columns were to coordinate their operations and force the French to surrender, each of the commanders were simply told where to enter the fortress and that speed was of the essence.

Another crucial failing was that nobody at the planning meeting had thought to question how each of the columns was to communicate. Graham and his subordinates simply expected that each of the attacks would be made on time, arrive exactly where they were supposed to, and be in positions which would be easy for the other columns to find. As it turned out, communication between the columns was almost non-existent. Without flares or rockets to pinpoint where the various columns entered, the commanders on the ground could do little but despatch small parties into the darkness in the hope that they would stumble upon troops from the other columns. Cooke, for instance, was forced to despatch scouting parties off into the town, but fell victim to French counter-attacks.[160] Graham, therefore, played a major part in the failure.

Poor planning and insubordination aside, the British might still have achieved victory at Bergen-Op-Zoom had Cooke and Proby decided to throw caution to the wind and drive into the heart of the town when they had the chance. Although such a move would have been dangerous, by the early hours of the morning Cooke had control of much of the southern half of Bergen-Op-Zoom and also had an extra 900 infantry at his disposal after Muttlebury's arrival. Although his instructions, like those of the other commanders were vague, it is unclear what Cooke and Proby thought they could achieve by waiting on the defensive until dawn, especially given that the French were clearly still in possession of much of the town and would need to have been dislodged one way or another. If Cooke's inaction is hard to understand, Proby's defeatism is even more inexplicable given that he commanded arguably the finest troops in Graham's army and the most suited to an assault operation. As it was, however, the guards were given little opportunity to test themselves against the French. Proby rather cynically tried to save his Guardsmen whilst Muttlebury and the line troops covered their retreat. Unfortunately for Proby, Cooke was unable to guarantee the safety of the Guards and they too were forced to surrender.

In spite of the embarrassing nature of the defeat and capitulation of a large portion of Graham's army, including the guards, Graham's version of the events at Bergen-Op-Zoom was not questioned by the ministers in London, or by York. Unlike Major General Whitelocke, whose career was destroyed by his surrender at Buenos Aires in 1807, Graham was not even subjected to a court martial. Nor did the government seek to question Graham's surviving subordinates in order to piece together a clearer picture of what had gone so badly wrong. No official inquiry was established and neither was there any official debrief for Graham back in London. Matters were quickly swept under the political carpet and attention was turned elsewhere. Remarkably, Graham's military career was not jeopardised by the disaster and he was even raised to the peerage by the Prince Regent.[161]

As the British placed a positive spin on the events, the Austrians, Prussians, Russians and Wellington's army continued their relentless advance into France and Napoleon was forced to abdicate on 13 April 1814. Although the British had contributed much to Napoleon's eventual defeat, their military performance in the Low Countries in 1813–14 was poor and would have achieved little had the Allied armies failed to defeat the French. It would not be the last time in European history that a British army would so heavily rely on Allied support to defeat the French and safeguard the Low Countries.

Conclusion

A number of clear parallels can be drawn between the British defeat at Bergen-Op-Zoom in 1814 and previous British military failures in the Low Countries. All were conceived by the politicians in London as a means to secure British interests in the Low Countries and all failed as a result of rushed strategic and operational planning, based upon unreliable intelligence. In addition, Anglo-Allied relations were often imperfect and the British habitually bemoaned the fighting qualities of their European Allies, despite their own poor military record in Europe. Repeated British defeats in the Low Countries, combined with the propensity of British generals to run for the safety of the ships after defeat in battle, severely damaged the reputation of the British army. This habit almost resulted in the breakdown of Allied relations in 1815 and might have led to a completely different outcome had Gneisenau succeeded in persuading Blücher that Wellington would flee to the coast after Ligny.

As has been demonstrated, the Low Countries played a pivotal role in the British pursuit of both European and global strategies. British interest in the Low Countries, however, was not a new phenomenon. The price of British defeat in the Netherlands in 1793–5 was French dominance of the Low Countries for over twenty years and the intermittent threat of a French invasion. Although British strategists proved adept at remaining committed to the Low Countries over the course of the period 1793 to 1815, British military operations in the region routinely failed. Despite the fact that the generals were often responsible for the military fallings behind the defeats in question, the politicians were also responsible, not least for their propensity to deviate from existing strategic plans at the last minute in order to mount ambitious operations. In 1793 and 1814 the British deviated from existing aims in order to placate their Allies and secure a tangible victory of their own. Unfortunately for the British, however, military blunders and strategic mismanagement resulted in defeat at both Dunkirk in 1793 and at Bergen-Op-Zoom in 1814.

British ministers also routinely let their excitement at the prospects of victory cloud their better judgement and based their offensive strategies upon unreliable intelligence. As demonstrated by Grenville's flawed perspective and planning prior to the Helder expedition in 1799. The politicians also regularly failed to consider the practicalities of their decisions and often committed their limited military and naval resources to a number of different operations at the same time. In 1793, for example, Pitt, Grenville and Dundas simultaneously despatched British forces to the Low Countries, West Indies, India and the Mediterranean, despite having only a limited number of regular troops and vessels at their disposal. As the wars dragged on and the attrition rates increased, the British struggled to keep up the numbers by the usual means and were forced to take drastic measures in order to fill the ranks.

Manpower worries came to a head in 1799, when Henry Dundas was forced to draft militiamen into the regulars, in order to provide enough troops for the Helder expedition. Dundas's militiamen also required extra training before they could be deployed and this forced Abercomby to suspend operations until the new recruits arrived. This delay proved decisive and enabled the French and Dutch to ready their forces for the campaign. The British forces, under the overall command of York, made little headway in the ensuing campaign despite being able to call upon the services of a large Russian contingent. Defeat duly followed. A similar set of circumstances also prompted the British to draft a large number of militiamen into the regulars in 1813–14.

The only occasion when British could call upon a sizeable disposable force for active service was before the Scheldt expedition in 1809. Castlereagh's failure to forewarn the medical services of the intended destination of the expedition resulted in the near destruction of the British forces by disease on the islands of Walcheren and South Beveland and caused many thousands of troops to suffer from severe relapses of the illness for the remainder of the Napoleonic Wars. Notwithstanding the problems caused by the ministers in London, British military operations in the Low Countries also failed because British generals routinely avoided making operational plans and did not learn from their previous mistakes. For instance, in the build-up to the siege of Dunkirk in 1793, York and Murray did not consider how their forces would operate after they had invested the French fortress and nor did they consider it necessary to scout the area before they reached the coast. They also failed to plan how a siege train would be transported to Dunkirk and disregarded the value of naval support. The British also lacked maps of the area and relied heavily on inaccurate intelligence information. As a result York made few preparations for the siege, divided his forces in the face of the enemy and was defeated. Despite the defeat York and the military administration in London did not investigate what had caused the reversal. No official military enquiry was ever convened and there was no attempt to analyse the campaign for future reference. With nothing learned from the defeat at Dunkirk, the British continued to commit similar military blunders over the course of the remainder of the conflict and eventually lost the Low Countries in 1795.

In each of the major British campaigns in the Low Countries over the course of 1793 to 1814, British desire to achieve a quick victory, combined with overconfidence in the fighting qualities of British troops and a reliance on inaccurate intelligence encouraged commanders to rush through the planning process so that their forces could get stuck into the enemy as quickly as possible. As has been shown, these factors also affected British amphibious operations. In 1799, for example, Abercomby and Mitchell were given little information about the Dutch coast and only decided where to land when they anchored off the Dutch coast. Similar planning blunders jeopardised the expedition to the Scheldt in 1809 and led to the near destruction of Chatham's army. Chatham and Strachan not only failed to create a detailed operational plan for both the landings and the subsequent advance on Antwerp but also failed to consider how they would maintain good communication with their subordinates. Given the lack of preparation, things started to unravel for the British as soon they reached the Scheldt and got progressively worse until the expedition was aborted. Despite the establishment of an inquiry, no attempt was made to identify lessons from the defeat and the British officer corps was left none the wiser from the whole experience.

This pattern of defeat also blighted the British campaign in the Low Countries in 1813–14. Not only did the British fail to plan their attempt to destroy the French dockyards at Antwerp, but they also bungled their way to disaster at Bergen-Op-Zoom. Like other British generals before him, Graham rushed to attack his objective in Bergen-Op-Zoom, having hurried the planning process. The British also relied on faulty intelligence and underestimated the fighting abilities of the garrison, mistakes which greatly contributed to their defeat. British defeats which followed the same pattern also occurred in South America in 1806–7, during the Corunna campaign in 1809, at Burgos in 1812 and, finally, during the disastrous Louisiana campaign in 1815, which culminated in the crushing defeat of Edward Pakenham's Peninsular War veterans at New Orleans – clear evidence that the British never learnt from their mistakes.

Although the reforms made by York made good some of the problems which had affected the army during the early years of the French Revolutionary Wars, the administrative changes did not directly impact upon performance because there was no emphasis on the need to learn from past mistakes and no mechanism for learning existed in the British military. According to

Huw J. Davies, the British officer corps of the Napoleonic Wars was an intellectually minded body which shared ideas and was able to learn from the past:

> It is clear that military thinking took place within a defined intellectual community, which prior to 1815 facilitated the transfer of ideas, innovative practices and adaptations across the wide theatre of operations that the British Army practiced in. These can be loosely termed 'military knowledge networks' and several existed within and between theatres.[1]

Central to Davies's argument is the assumption that the British officer corps was a thinking organisation and one whose members were able to learn from the past. However, as has been demonstrated, these claims appear exaggerated given the British experience in the Low Countries and elsewhere. For instance, although Wellington famously remarked that he had 'Learnt what not to do' in the Low Countries in 1794, there is little to suggest that other British officers possessed the ability or desire to do likewise. For the most part the British military profession, to quote John P. Kiszely, 'had a highly variable attitude toward military history' and until recently has never truly been committed to the development of a culture of military thought.[2] Moreover, neither is there much evidence to suggest that the British recognised the benefit of ideas sharing and no official channels existed for officers to discuss ideas with their contemporaries.

The only occasions in which officers had a chance to share ideas was in private meetings, but there is little or no evidence to illuminate what these discussions were about, let alone to suggest that the conversations themselves ever went beyond the confines of the dinner table. Thus contrary to Davies's argument, the true British approach to military knowledge during this period was characterised by what Anthony Clayton has termed 'An anti-intellectual self-confidence' which was often fatal to British military performance and helped perpetuate the idea that 'the innate abilities of the gentleman amateur would always triumph over the professional or the native tribesman'.[3]

One of the by-products of the lack of an intellectual approach to war in the British army was that there was no official mechanism in place for collecting and collating military reports and identifying potential lessons. Despite the fact that the British created a number of Commissions of Military Inquiry over the course of the period 1806 to 1818, none of these were designed to analyse in detail recent military developments or decipher lessons to be learnt from past military operations. Instead, the Commissions were created to report on purely administrative aspects.[4] Military inquiries were not the norm and it was rare that anything could be learnt from these opportunities, owing to the fact that the participants were often chiefly motivated by the desire to save their careers than to learn from past mistakes. The inquiry which followed the British surrender at Yorktown in 1781, for example, quickly degenerated into a clash of egos between Lieutenant Generals Sir Henry Clinton and Charles Earl Cornwallis as the two men eschewed the chance to learn from the past and entered into a personal vendetta against one another.[5] The Cintra Inquiry in 1808 and the Scheldt Inquiry in 1810 were also dominated by personality clashes, instead of attempts to learn.

The absence of a culture of learning not only meant that British officers were unready for the rigours of European war but were also equally unready for amphibious operations. Despite having mounted numerous amphibious operations against the French over the course of the 1700s, the administrators at the Horse Guards had never encouraged army officers to undertake special training for amphibious warfare. In contrast, the Royal Navy had gradually developed a specialist amphibious force of its own over the course of the period, in the form of the Royal Marines. Although the Marines gained their Royal status in 1802, their origins can be traced back to an Order in Council in 1664, which called for the creation of the Duke of York and Albany's Maritime Regiment of Foot.[6] There were limited regulations for how the Royal Marines were to operate, however, so the Marines had developed their own approach to warfare and were trained according to both naval and military drills.[7] A number of specialist works of amphibious theory were also available for officers of the marines and, although these texts were not incorporated into official regulations, they served to encourage Marine officers to develop an identity and to embrace their role as specialists in amphibious operations.[8]

Further evidence that the British army did not ordinarily learn from past experience of amphibious operations is demonstrated by the fact that Abercomby needed to train his men for amphibious landings prior to the successful expedition to Egypt in 1801.[9] His death in the ensuing Egyptian campaign robbed the British army of one of its brightest talents. The deaths of Moore at Corunna in 1809 and Le Marchant at Salamanca in 1812 deprived the army of two more rare military thinkers. Neither was there a policy of official debriefings and, for example, Wellington was never interviewed after he returned from India despite having played a major role in the wars against Dhoondiah Vagh and the Marathas.[10]

This contrasted markedly with the learning ethos fostered by the Prussians after their defeats at Jena-Auerstadt in 1806 and in East Prussia in 1807. Shortly after the defeat at Friedland in June 1807, King Frederick William ordered the military high command to undertake a formal investigation into the poor performance of the Prussian army. The inquiry was organised into two military commissions. The most important of these was the 'Military Reorganisation Commission' which was placed under Scharnhorst's control.[11] The work of this commission was nothing short of remarkable. As Peter Paret has noted:

> From 1807 to 1812 the Commission reviewed the 1806 campaign in minute detail, evaluating every battle, combat and skirmish to understand the decisions made by commanders and their mistakes. Every unit commander was interviewed, with potential lessons being identified and documented for the benefit of future generals. Even the king was fully informed of the proceedings and ideas were shared for good practice.[12]

Ultimately the Prussians recognised in defeat the value of learning from their mistakes in order to improve future military performance whereas the British did not. The senior figures at the Horse Guards, and their political masters, were often all too eager to find scapegoats instead of seeking to understand what had occurred and why victory had not been secured. Prussia was not the only European power to seek lessons after defeat. Indeed, had other reviews not been undertaken by the Austrians and Russians after their defeats the French might never have been defeated at Leipzig. As it was the Austrians, Prussians and Russians eventually learnt that the way to defeat Napoleon was to emulate the French military system – especially the use of Corps – to provide strategic and operational flexibility. It was fortunate, therefore, that the British had one commander at their disposal in Wellington who thought and fought more like a European than his contemporaries in the British army.

The Wellington Factor: the Iron Duke, Waterloo and Reasons for British Victory

'A close run thing': Wellington's famous and all too brief summation of his conduct at the Battle of Waterloo provides historians with a revealing insight into the thoughts of the Iron Duke the day following the battle.[13] Waterloo was the largest, most closely fought and decisive of Wellington's career. It was also a new experience for both Wellington and the British troops who served under his command, for on the muddy fields of Belgium, both he and his men faced Napoleon for the first and last time. The enclosed nature of the battlefield, allied to the sheer number of soldiers involved (around 150,000) added to what would have been a dramatic assault upon the senses of the British commander and his red-coated contingents. Neither would the British veterans have witnessed such numbers of heavy French artillery pieces before, indeed, Napoleon's artillery at Waterloo numbered well over 100 guns; far more than the numbers used by Napoleon's marshals against the British in Spain and Portugal. Nor would they have fought alongside quite so many different European soldiers as they did in mid-June 1815.

The British forces under Wellington's command acquitted themselves well in defeating the French at Waterloo but they were by no means alone in having bested the *Grand Armée*. Wellington's victory was a truly European effort. The German contingents, notably those from Hanover, Nassau and Brunswick, fought bravely alongside their British counterparts. Contrary to the popular history of the battle, especially the Sharpe novels, Wellington was also indebted to the sterling service of the soldiers of the United Netherlands.[14] Indeed many more 'foreign' soldiers in Wellington's army became casualties at Waterloo than did their British comrades; the British and King's German Legion suffered 7,687 losses out of a total of between 14,000 and 17,000 sustained by Wellington's forces.[15]

The Dutch and Belgian contribution is particularly noteworthy primarily because the British could count upon over 20,000 well-trained and led Dutch and Belgian troops to fight alongside them.[16] Indeed, the soldiers under the Prince of Orange's command can be said to have been the living end-product of a generation of British diplomacy which since 1793 had sought to ensure the alliance of Britain and Holland. Anglo-Dutch relations in 1815, though, differed markedly from their previous experiences in the Low Countries, not least in 1799 when the British had been shorn of Dutch support and were forced to combat the local inhabitants as well as the French in their bid to liberate Amsterdam. Indeed, in each of the main operations mounted by the British to the Low Countries over the course of the period 1793 to 1809 the Dutch and their Belgian counterparts remained fairly hostile towards the redcoats. By 1814, however, the Dutch and their Belgian neighbours had grown weary of their French masters and years of economic hardship brought on by the war in Europe; Dutch merchants were also eager to resume trade relations with the British. The creation of the United Netherlands following the fall of the Napoleonic regime meant that when the French Emperor invaded France from Elba in 1815 the British could reply upon an army of Dutch and Belgian troops who were willing to fight to defend their new nation against the hated French. This change of circumstances explains to some extent why Wellington was able to succeed in the Low Countries, where others before him had failed. The difference was not that the British army was much better trained or generally better led in 1815 but that Wellington could count on the support of a disciplined allied army and the local inhabitants, a relationship which was similar to that which he and the British had enjoyed with the Portuguese during the Peninsular War.

The presence of such a large number of disciplined Dutch and Belgian troops, meanwhile, enabled Wellington to place more troops in the field than any other raised for service in the Low Countries. His soldiers could also count on there being food and supplies, which could be paid for from the local population, and were not totally dependent upon the Royal Navy and tidal conditions for the arrival of new resources. This being said the fact that the Dutch and Belgian ports were open to British goods and supplies was a real advantage enjoyed by Wellington in 1815 and one which British generals would greatly rely upon in future global conflicts on the Continent. The changed nature of the political situation in North-West Europe was vital for Wellington in 1815 and proved a crucial enabling factor for his success.

The Dutch-Belgians were not the only 'foreign' element in Wellington's army; the Iron Duke could rely upon the support of thousands of Hanoverians, Brunswickers and other contingents drawn from several small Germanic states. The Kings German Legion, meanwhile, was integrated into the British military machine. The Hanoverians of the Legion were highly professional soldiers and had served the British Crown well since their formation in the aftermath of Napoleon's invasion of their homeland in 1805. Like the Dutch, the Hanoverian presence was the result of Britain's long-maintained 'special relationship' with Hanover; Hanoverian troops had served alongside the British since 1793 from the siege of Dunkirk to the battlefields of the Iberian Peninsula. These soldiers played a vital part in the 1815 campaign, proving that the Prussians were not the only Germans to achieve a decisive blow against the French at Waterloo.

Soldiers aside, by far the most important factor in Allied success at Waterloo was Wellington's generalship. Unlike other British generals, all of whom had courted defeat and disaster in the Low Countries, Wellington was able to achieve lasting success. The fact remains that there was no other officer in British military service during the period quite like Wellington and his command of the Allied army in 1815 was based upon a learning experience of his own.

Unlike most of his contemporaries, Wellington was an educated soldier who not only developed an ability to think constructively about military affairs but also actively sought to analyse and learn from past experiences. These attributes provided him with the means to succeed where others had not. Further-more, it is possible to argue that all of Wellington's command skills, such as battlefield tactics, eye for terrain, ability to work with allies, logistical exper-tise and recognition of the value of intelligence, were products of a gradual apprenticeship in the art of war, which can be traced back to his initial baptism of fire in the Low Countries in 1794–5.

It was in the Netherlands that a young Sir Arthur famously 'learnt what not to do', evidence that there is always something to learn if one has the desire and ability to do so; traits which few British officers possessed. Wellington was also an avid reader who always tried to develop prior knowledge of the area of operations for which he was bound. As S.P.G. Ward has noted:

> When he was sent to India his library was stocked with books on India … when he was sent to the Peninsula he carried not only a Spanish prayer-book from which to learn the language, but Sir Charles Stewarts' old Portuguese letter-books of 1797 and Gen-eral Richard Stewarts' of 1803, amongst other sources from which he made his first interpretation of the form a war in Portugal would assume … Few generals have devoted their spare hours so advanta-geously to utilitarian scholarship.[17]

In the absence of a culture of learning and an official mechanism for the identification of lessons, Wellington's pursuit of professional knowl-edge marked him out from the crowd. Wellington's desire always to be well informed about the enemy, which the duke famously described as a quest to understand what was 'on the other side of the hill' was the product of per-sonal intelligence gathering and astute planning. Thus, on numerous occa-sions throughout his career, Wellington was able to learn from past mistakes when his contemporaries did not. For example, it was not merely by chance that Wellington placed great stock in the accumulation of good intelligence in the Iberian Peninsula but because he had learnt from his own failure to gather accurate intelligence during the early stages of the error strewn Deccan cam-paign against the Marathas in 1803.[18] Additionally, Wellington's eye for detail and skill at writing meticulous despatches won him admirers in high places and between 1807 and 1808 Wellington acted as an expert military advisor to Castlereagh.[19]

Wellington's ability to learn gave him a great advantage over his contem-poraries who were usually content to ride into the thick of the action with-out first thinking through how best they were to operate, maintain their forces on the march, or defeat the enemy. Wellington's hours of study also enabled him to develop a keen appreciation of both the limitations of British military power and the weaknesses of his opponents. Although he had spent his early career in India, many of the challenges he faced during this time were not unlike those which he would confront in European conditions later in his career.[20] Wellington's time at Angers also introduced him to the scientific character of European military thinking and impressed upon him the value of learning. Evidence of Wellington's ability to learn from past experiences and think constructively about the strengths and weaknesses of his own troops and those of the enemy can be found in the records of a conversation between Sir Arthur and John Wilson Croker MP prior to the 1808 campaign in Portugal.

In 1808, Wellington's knowledge of French numerical superiority prompted him to propose a scheme for the recruitment and maintenance of a remodelled Portuguese army and better logistical arrangements.[21] Additionally, although Wellington greatly valued the British regimental system, he was also quick to recognise the merits of the French divisional organisation and adopted something similar in 1809; a corps structure also gradually evolved.[22]

As well as having a keen appreciation of the strengths and weaknesses inherent in the French military system, Wellington's years of study and command apprenticeship had taught him to distrust his fellow general officers. Whether in the aftermath of the controversial Convention of Cintra in 1808, or the near disaster at the Battle of the River Coa in 1810, Wellington often displayed a general distrust of his fellow senior officers and he habitually sought to lead from the front instead of delegating tasks to others. Wellington also much lamented the inability of his subordinates to learn from their mistakes and rebuked one general as follows, 'What I cannot bear is his leaving his guns and stores; and strange to say, not only does he not think he was wrong in so doing, but he writes of it as being rather meritous, and says he did it before'.[23]

Therefore, when asked later in life how he had achieved success when others had not Wellington's responded simply by stating that, 'The real reason why I succeeded in my own campaigns is because I was always on the spot—I saw everything, and did everything for myself'.[24] Although historians have suggested that Wellington's habit of doing everything by himself marks greatness as a leader of men, particularly his hands-on approach at the Battle of Salamanca in 1812, it can also be viewed as a sign of the general weakness of the British officer corps. For example, in the aftermath of the close-run Battle of Albuera and the escape of the French garrison at Almeida in 1811, Wellington blamed himself for not having been present and lamented the incompetence of his generals and their inability to undertake effective operational planning:

> I certainly feel, every day, more and more the difficulty of the situation in which I am placed. I am obliged to be everywhere, and if absent from any operation, something goes wrong. It is to be hoped that the General and other officers of the army will at last acquire that experience which will teach them that success can be attained only by attention to the most minute details; and by tracing only part of every operation from its origin to its conclusion, point by point, and ascertaining that the whole is understood by those who are to execute it.[25]

Wellington also understood the importance of supply and logistics. He recognised, like Napoleon, that military forces can only operate effectively if well-fed. Wellington's logistical system was highly effective, not least because it was based upon cooperation with the local population; food was to be paid for and not to be looted. Wellington's emphasis upon the need for positive civil-military relations was the product of his experience in India and the Iberian Peninsula. In these hostile and climatically challenging environments Wellington needed to rely upon trade with the local populations, especially when his forces moved inland of the coast. Wellington had seen with his own eyes the potential disaster that could befall an army lacking supplies and close relations with a local population when he witnessed the British retreat through the Netherlands in the harsh winter of 1795.

Wellington was also liked by his men. He had a morale-boosting effect upon his fellow generals and even amongst the ordinary fighting men whom he famously referred to as the 'scum of the earth'. One such soldier was Edward Costello, a Rifleman, who had seen extensive service in the army during the Peninsular War and Waterloo campaign. A seasoned campaigner, Costello later served in Spain with the British Auxiliary Legion during the First Carlist War (1833–9) and returned to many of the old battlefields of the Peninsular War. On one occasion in 1835 Costello and his fellow volunteers marched across the former battlefield of Vitoria, the former Rifleman describing the experience as deeply moving and his former general as 'our immortal Wellington'. Costello also recounted a conversation with a fellow soldier in which he talked with great pride about having fought in Wellington's army and that under the Iron Duke's command failure had been out of the question: 'I replied that I had been educated in Wellington's school where we were taught to make no blunders'.[26]

This later line explains how and why the British army performed so much better in the Low Countries in 1815 than in its previous campaigns in the Netherlands – the answer was Wellington. Sir Arthur succeeded where others had failed because he was a maverick. The British soldiers who had fought at Waterloo were not much better than those which had besieged Dunkirk, stormed ashore at the Helder, died of malarial fever in the Scheldt or surrendered at Bergen-Op-Zoom. In some cases, they were the very same men. Sir Thomas Picton, who commanded the 'fighting' Fifth Division at Waterloo, had contracted fever during the Walcheren expedition in 1809; Sir Rowland Hill, whom Wellington trusted above all others, had taken part in the bungled expedition to Hanover in 1805–6; Sir Henry Clinton had served as the Duke of York's aide-de-camp in 1793–5 and went on to lead the Second Division at Waterloo; Sir Andrew Barnard had served at the Helder in 1799 and later commanded the 95th Rifles at Quatre Bras and Waterloo; Sir Charles Alten fought as a Captain in the Hanoverian contingent in 1793–5 and later led the Third Division at Waterloo.[27] Major General Sir George Cooke, meanwhile, commanded the First Division at Waterloo despite having performed so poorly at Bergen-Op-Zoom and having surrendered with his force of Foot Guards to the French. Many of these men, but especially Cooke, were fortunate that Waterloo was such a significant victory and that they had a chance to redeem themselves having suffered defeat earlier in their careers. Wellington had that effect upon subordinates. Under his command mediocre generals could rise to do great things, whilst those who had tasted success under his wing could also sink once they were tasked with independent command.

The decline and spectacular fall of Sir Edward Pakenham is a case in point. Under Wellington's tutelage in the peninsula Pakenham made a name for himself as a brave and courageous leader, most notably in command of the Third Division at Salamanca in 1812, but when chosen to command an army in North America Pakenham led his men to disaster at New Orleans on 8 January 1815. Over confident to the point of foolhardy, Pakenham believed that his small army of Peninsular War veterans would achieve a swift victory over their American counterparts. Pakenham devised no clear plan for the battle and ordered his troops to advance with parade-ground precision towards the 5,700 Americans who had formed up behind a high wall. Neither Pakenham, nor his subordinate General Gibbs, had thought to equip their 8,000 men with the means to scale the American defences and as their troops advanced across the open field they were mown down by American musketry and cannon fire. In under half an hour around 700 British troops were killed and over 1,400 were wounded. In stark contrast, the Americans suffered only 7 men killed and 6 wounded. It was like the Battle of Breeds Hill (more famously known as Bunker Hill) all over again. As for Pakenham, he paid for his errors with his life. The Battle of New Orleans remains one of Britain's worst military disasters. The destruction of Pakenham's small army was a major humiliation for the British, especially in light of the fact that Pakenham's soldiers had only recently arrived in America fresh from victory in Spain and Portugal. It can hardly be argued then that this was an army transformed. On the contrary, it served as yet another example to the British of how not to conduct military operations; lessons, though, which again went unheeded and unlearned.

This, of course, is not to suggest that Wellington did not have faults of his own. Indeed, in spite of his undoubted brilliance Wellington badly handled his army after victory at Salamanca in 1812, which led to the humiliating and destructive retreat from Burgos. British success in the peninsula was also largely founded on the support of the local population and, had the Portuguese and Spanish abandoned the British, no amount of battlefield prowess on the part of Wellington would have been able to prevent the need for a general British evacuation; the same can be said for Wellington's campaigns in India and at Waterloo. Neither did Wellington seek to codify his approach to command, nor did he seek to establish a culture of learning amongst his fellow officers. Additionally, not unlike Napoleon, Wellington's style of leadership hindered his generals' professional development; Wellington also only fully trusted Hill.[28] Wellington's opposition to reform during his time as C-in-C also hindered the development of competent British generals and many future commanders were often left asking 'what the great duke would have done' when they encountered difficulties on campaign.[29]

He could also display overconfidence, as evidence during the initial part of the 1815 campaign when his wanton disregard for Dutch and Prussian intelligence reports almost led to disaster.[30] Wellington could also be far too disparaging of the contribution made by others and made enemies at home, although given the propensity for the Horse Guards to select incompetent generals to replace seasoned campaigners in the peninsula it is perhaps easy to understand why. Wellington was also fortunate not to have to face Napoleon and the *Grande Armée* when the emperor was at the peak of his powers in 1805–10. This though is to run the risk of drifting into the counterfactual.

Wellington was unique amongst his contemporaries and the successes achieved by his troops were not replicated by other British generals in other theatres, not least the Low Countries.[31] Only Wellington was able to sustain British military success and must be praised for his achievements given the failings of almost all of his fellow commanders and the track record of the army before he was given prolonged command in the Iberian Peninsula and Flanders. Wellington, therefore, did an excellent job of making good with bad tools and in leading an untransformed British army to final victory in 1815.

Notes

Introduction

1. See Steve Pincus, *1688, The First Modern Revolution* (New Haven and London: Yale University Press, 2009); Tim Harris, *Revolution, The Great Crisis in the British Monarchy, 1685–1720* (London: Penguin, 2007); Peter Unwin, *The Narrow Sea, Barrier, Bridge and Gateway to the World, The History of the English Channel* (London: Headline, 2003), pp. 130–5.
2. G.J. Renier, *Great Britain and the Establishment of the Kingdom of the Netherlands 1813–1815, A Study in British Foreign Policy* (London: Allen & Unwin, 1930), p. 1.
3. For an in-depth study of British society during this period see Mark Philip (ed.), *Resisting Napoleon, the British Response to the Threat of Invasion, 1797–1815* (Aldershot: Ashgate, 2006); E. Cookson, *The British Armed Nation 1793–1815* (Oxford: Clarendon Press, 1997), p. 38.
4. Richard Holmes, *Marlborough, England's Fragile Genius* (London: Harper Press, 2008), pp. 324–406.
5. Rory Muir, *Britain and the Defeat of Napoleon, 1807–1815* (New Haven and London: Yale University Press, 1996), p. 1.
6. Colin S. Gray, *The Leverage of Sea Power, The Strategic Advantage of Navies in War* (New York: The Free Press, 1992), p. 165.
7. Michael Howard, 'Military history and the history of war' in Williamson Murray and Richard Hart Sinnreich (eds), *The Past as Prologue: The Importance of History to the Military Profession* (Cambridge: Cambridge University Press, 2006), pp. 12–20; Stephen Morillo with Michael F. Pavkovic, *What is Military History?* (Cambridge: Polity, 2006), p. 61.
8. William P. Tatum III, 'Challenging the New Military History: the case of Eighteenth-Century British Army Studies', *History Compass* 4 (2006), pp. 1–13 at pp. 6–7.
9. Joanna Bourke, 'New Military History' in Matthew Hughes and William J. Philpott, *Palgrave advances in modern military history* (Basingstoke: Palgrave, 2006), p. 262.
10. Peter Paret, 'The New Military History', *Parameters: The Journal of the Army War College*, 31/3 (autumn, 1991), pp. 13–36 at p. 16.
11. Jeremy Black, *Rethinking Military History* (Abingdon: Routledge, 2004), p. 6.
12. Tatum III, 'Challenging the New Military History', p. 5; Jeremy Black, 'Eighteenth-Century English Politics: Recent Work and Current Problems', *Albion: A Quarterly Journal Concerned with British Studies*, Vol. 25 No. 3 (Autumn, 1993), pp. 419–41 at p. 438; Jeremy Black, 'Historiographical Essay: Britain as a Military Power, 1688–1815', *JMHS*, Vol. 64 No. 1 (Jan. 2000), pp. 159–77 at pp. 159–60.
13. See Bruce Collins, *War and Empire: The Expansion of Britain 1790–1830* (Harlow: Pearson Longman, 2010); Rory Muir, *Britain and the Defeat of Napoleon*; Jeremy Black, *Britain as a military power 1688–1815* (London: UCL Press, 1999).
14. Roger Knight, *Britain against Napoleon: The Organisation of Victory 1793–1815* (London: Allen Lane, 2013); David Andress, *The Savage Storm: Britain on the brink in the age of Napoleon* (London: Little Brown, 2012); N.A.M. Rodger, 'Review of Roger Knight and Martin Wilcox, *Sustaining the Fleet, 1793–1815: War, the British Navy and the Contractor State* & Janet MacDonald, *The British Navy's Victualling Board, 1793–1815: Management Compe-*

tence and Incompetence', *EHR*, cxxvi. 519 (Apr. 2011), pp. 465–6; Robert K. Sutcliffe, *British Expeditionary Warfare and the Defeat of Napoleon, 1793–1815* (Woodbridge: Boydell, 2016).

15. Examples include (Traditional): Andrew Bamford, *A Bold and Ambitious Enterprise, The British Army in the Low Countries 1813–1814* (Barnsley: Frontline, 2013); Carole Divall, *Burgos 1812: Wellington's Worst Scrape* (Barnsley: Pen & Sword, 2012); (New): Andrew Bamford, *Sickness, Suffering and the Sword, The British Regiment on Campaign, 1808–1815* (Norman: University of Oklahoma Press, 2013); Carole Divall, *Napoleonic Lives, Researching the British Soldiers of the Napoleonic Wars* (Barnsley: Pen & Sword, 2012); Carole Divall, *Redcoats Against Napoleon, The 30th Regiment During the Revolutionary and Napoleonic Wars* (Barnsley: Pen & Sword, 2009).

16. This study furthers the limited argument of blaming the politicians and exonerating the generals. Phillip Ball and Kate Bohdanowicz, *A Waste of Blood and Treasure: The 1799 Anglo-Russian Invasion of the Netherlands* (Barnsley: Pen & Sword, 2017).

17. Dominic Lieven, *Russia against Napoleon, The Battle for Europe, 1807 to 1814* (London: Penguin, 2010, orig. pub. 2009), pp. 3–4.

18. Howard, 'Military history and the history of war', p. 14.

19. Some work has been done more recently to broaden studies of the army in this period, notably by Martin Howard. For example: Martin R. Howard, *Death Before Glory: The British Soldier in the West Indies in the French Revolutionary and Napoleonic Wars 1793–1815* (Barnsley: Pen & Sword, 2015).

20. Hew Strachan, 'The Idea of War' in Catherine Mary McLoughlin (ed.), *The Cambridge Companion to War Writing* (Cambridge: Cambridge University Press, 2009), pp. 7–13 at p. 13.

21. Other examples include: Captain L.T. Jones, *An Historical Journal of the British Campaign on the Continent in the Year 1794* (London, 1797); Sir Harry Verney (ed.), *The Journals and Correspondence of General Sir Harry Calvert, comprising the campaigns in Flanders and Holland in 1793–4* (London: Hurst and Blackett, 1823); Anon., *The Present State of the British Army in Flanders, with an authentic account of the British retreat from before Dunkirk by a British officer in that Army who was living on the 24th of September* (London: H.D. Symonds, 1793). Several memoirs have also been studied by historians in journal articles, i.e. Colonel H.C.B. Cook (ed.), 'The St George Diary A junior regimental officer in the Low Countries, 1794–95', *JSAHR*, V. 47 (1969). Also located at TNA: SSR/7745/14 'A Junior Regimental Officer in the Low Countries 1794–1795'.

22. John Peaty, 'Architect of Victory: The Reforms of the Duke of York', *JSAHR*, Winter 2006, Vol. 84, No. 340, pp. 339–48 at p. 348.

23. The Duke of York's reforms had already formed the subject of historical enquiry before Richard Glover published *Peninsular Preparation, The Reform of the British Army 1795 to 1809* (Cambridge: Cambridge University Press, 1963) but had not been earmarked as having had a transformative effect. Two historians to analyse the reforms before Glover were: Sir John Fortescue in his *History of the British Army* and Julia H. Macleod, 'The Duke of York's Plans for the Army', *HLQ*, Vol. 9 No. 1 (Nov. 1945), pp. 95–100.

24. Glover, *Peninsular Preparation,* pp. 12–13. The most recent study of the life and military reforms of the Duke of York maintains the same argument outlined by Glover: Derek Winterbottom, *The Grand Old Duke of York: A Life of Prince Frederic, Duke of York and Albany 1763–1827* (Barnsley: Pen & Sword, 2016).

25. John Houlding, *Fit for Service, The Training of the British Army 1715–1795* (Oxford: Oxford University Press, 1981); Piers Mackesy, *The British Victory in Egypt, The End of Napoleon's Conquest* (London: Taurus, 2010, orig. pub. 1995); Hew Strachan, 'Review of Glover, *Peninsula Preparation*, Houlding, *Fit for Service* and Mackesy, *British Victory in Egypt*', *EHR*, Vol. 112 No. 446 (Apr. 1997), p. 497. Other historians who have furthered these arguments include: Corelli Barnet, *Britain and Her Army 1509–1970, A Military, Political and Social Survey* (London: Allen Lane, 1970), pp. 239–46; Peaty, 'Architect of Victory', pp. 31–9; David Gates, 'The Transformation of the British Army 1783–1815' in David Chandler and Ian Beckett (eds), *The Oxford History of the British Army* (Oxford: Oxford University Press, 2003, orig. pub. 1994),

pp. 132–60; Mark Urban, *Generals, The Ten British Commanders Who Shaped the World* (London: Faber & Faber, 2005), pp. 95–119.

26. Bamford, *Sickness, Suffering and the Sword*, pp. xx, 3; Knight, *Britain against Napoleon*, pp. 103–4; Rory Muir, *Wellington, The Path to Victory, 1769–1914* (New Haven and London: Yale University Press, 2013), p. 289.

27. Michael Roberts, 'The Military Revolution, 1560–1660' in Clifford J. Rogers (ed.), *The Military Revolution Debate, Readings on the Transformation of Early Modern Europe* (Oxford: Westview, 1995), pp. 13–36.

28. Geoffrey Parker, *The Military Revolution, Military innovation and the rise of the West, 1500–1800* (Cambridge: Cambridge University Press, 1988); Rogers, *The Military Revolution Debate*; Williamson Murray and MacGregor Knox (eds), *The Dynamics of Military Revolution 1300–2050* (Cambridge: Cambridge University Press, 2001).

29. Williamson Murray and MacGregor Knox, 'Thinking about revolutions in warfare' in *Dynamics of Military Revolution*, pp. 1–14; Morillo with Pavkovic, *What is Military History?*, pp. 76–7; Colin S. Gray, *Strategy and History, Essays on Theory and Practice* (Abingdon: Routledge, 2006), pp. 113–19; Andrew Latham, 'Warfare Transformed: A Braudelian Perspective on the 'Revolution in Military Affairs', *EJIR*, 8:2 (2002), pp. 231–66 at pp. 231–5. Elements of this theory were linked to the development of the US Doctrine of AirLand Battle in the mid-1980s.

30. See United States Department of Defence, 'Transformation Planning Guidance', Apr. 2003, http://www.defense.gov/brac/docs/transformationplanningapr03.pdf, pp. 1–34; Robert T. Foley, Stuart Griffin and Helen McCartney, '"Transformation in contact": learning the lessons of modern war', *International Affairs* 87:2 (2011), pp. 253–70 at p. 255; Eliot A. Cohen, 'Change and Transformation in Military Affairs' *JSS*, 27:3 (2004), pp. 395–407 at p. 395; Theo Farrell, 'The dynamics of British military transformation', *International Affairs*, 84: 4 (2008), pp. 777–807. For further debates about RMAs and established military theory see David Lonsdale, 'Clausewitz and Information Warfare' in Hew Strachan and Andreas Herberg-Rothe (eds), *Clausewitz in the Twenty-First Century* (Oxford: Oxford University Press, 2007), pp. 231–50; Andrew N. Liaropoulos, 'Revolutions in Warfare: Theoretical Paradigms and Historical Evidence: The Napoleonic and First World War Revolutions in Military Affairs', *JMHS*, Vol. 70 No. 2 (Apr. 2006), pp. 363–84.

31. Paul K. David, 'Military Transformation? Which Transformation, and what lies ahead?' in Stephen J. Cimbala (ed.), *The George W. Bush Defence Program: Policy, Strategy, and War* (Dulles, Potomac Books, 2010), p. 11. Also available online at http://www.rand.org/pubs/reprints/RP1413.html.

32. Leonard L. Lira, 'Transformation and the Evolution of the Professional Military Ethic: A current assessment', a paper presented for the United States Army Command and General Staff College, Combined Arms Centre at Fort Leavenworth, Kansas and the CGSC Foundation, Inc. Conference on Exploring the Professional Military Ethic, 15–18 November 2010, www.leavenworthethicssymposium.org/resource/resmgr/2010.../Lira.pdf. Also published in Mark H. Wiggins and Chaplain (Maj.) Larry Dabeck (eds), *Symposium Report, Fort Leavenworth Ethics Symposium, Exploring the Professional Military Ethic* (Fort Leavenworth: CGSC Foundation Press, 2011), pp. 221–34.

33. Lira, 'Transformation', p. 2.

34. For a comprehensive list of the secondary sources used see Bibliography.

Chapter 1

1. Jeremy Black, *George III, America's Last King* (New Haven and London: Yale University Press, 2008, orig. pub 2006), pp. 117–19.

2. Jeremy Black, 'British Strategy and the Struggle with France 1793–1815', *JSS*, Vol. 31 No. 4 (Aug. 2008), pp. 553–69 at pp. 560–2.

3. Glover, *Peninsular Preparation*, p. 36.

4. Rory Muir and Charles Esdaile, 'Strategic Planning in a Time of Small Government: the Wars against Revolutionary and Napoleonic France, 1793–1815' in C.M Woolgar (ed.), *Wellington Studies I* (Hartley Institute: University of Southampton, 1996), pp. 1–91 at pp. 6–9.

5. Michael J. Turner, *Pitt the Younger: A life* (London: Hambledon Continuum, 2003), p. 121.

6. J. Holland Rose, *William Pitt and the Great War* (London: Bell & Sons, 1912), pp. 454–82, esp. pp. 466–7.

7. Jennifer Mori, *William Pitt and the French Revolution 1785–1795* (Edinburgh: Keele University Press, 1997), p. 270.

8. Peter Jupp, *The Governing of Britain 1688–1848, The Executive, Parliament and the People* (London: Routledge, 2006), pp. 118–21; Knight, *Britain against Napoleon*, pp. 96–121, 213–50; Muir, *Britain and the Defeat of Napoleon*, pp. 9–13; Muir and Esdaile, 'Strategic Planning in a Time of Small Government', pp. 16–19.

9. There was no such thing as a professionally minded 'Civil Service' in Britain until after the publication of the Northcote-Trevelyan Report in 1855. For more on the origins of the Civil Service see: Rodney Lowe, *The Official History of the British Civil Service, Reforming the Civil Service, Volume 1: The Fulton Years, 1966–81* (London: Routledge, 2011), pp. 17–40.

10. Holden Fuber, *Henry Dundas, First Viscount Melville, 1742–1811, Political Manager of Scotland, Statesmen, Administrator of India* (Oxford: Oxford University Press, 1931), p. 75.

11. Lieutenant General Sir Henry Bunbury, *Narratives of the some passages in the great war with France, from 1799 to 1810* (London: Richard Bentley, 1854), p. 1; G.A Steppler, 'The British Army on the Eve of War' in A.J. Guy (ed.), *The Road to Waterloo, The British Army and the struggle against Revolutionary and Napoleonic France 1793–1815* (London: National Army Museum Publications, 1990), pp. 4–15 at p. 4.

12. Stephan Conway, 'Britain and the Revolutionary Crisis' in P.J. Marshall (ed.), *The Eighteenth-Century, Volume II, The Oxford History of the British Empire* (Oxford: Oxford University Press, 2006, orig. pub. 1998), pp. 325–46 at pp. 340–1. The catalyst for the enlargement of the conflict had been the British defeat at Saratoga in 1777 and the French intervention on the side of the Colonists. For details of the immediate British response to these events and the origins of British strategic overstretch see: Gerald S. Brown, 'The Anglo-French Naval Crisis, 1778: A Study of Conflict in the North Cabinet', *WMQ*, Third Series, Vol. 13 No. 1 (Jan. 1956), pp. 3–25.

13. William B. Willcox, 'Too Many Cooks: British Planning before Saratoga', *JBS*, Vol. 2 No. 1 (Nov. 1962), pp. 56–90; William B. Willcox, 'The British Road to Yorktown: A Study in Divided Command', *AHR*, Vol. 52 No. 1 (Oct. 1946), pp. 1–35.

14. For details of the recruitment of the British armed services in these years see: Stephen Conway, 'The Politics of British Military and Naval Mobilization, 1775–83', *EHR*, Vol. 112 No. 449 (Nov. 1997), pp. 1179–1201; Stephen Conway, 'British Army Officers and the American War for Independence', *WMQ*, Third Series, Vol. 41 No. 2 (Apr. 1984), pp. 265–76; Stephen Conway, 'To Subdue America: British Army Officers and the Conduct of the Revolutionary War', *WMQ*, Third Series, Vol. 43 No. 3 (Jul. 1986), pp. 381–407, Stephen Conway, 'The British Army, "Military Europe," and the American War of Independence', *WMQ*, Vol. 67 No. 1 (Jan. 2010), pp. 69–100; Brendan Simms, *Three Victories and a Defeat, The Rise and Fall of the First British Empire, 1714–1783* (London:. Penguin. 2008), pp. 596–7, 618.

15. For a recent study of the Yorktown campaign and the siege see: Jerome A. Greene, *The Guns of Independence, The Siege of Yorktown, 1781* (New York: Savas Beatie, 2005).

16. H.C.B. Rogers, *The British Army of the Eighteenth-Century* (London: George Allen & Unwin, 1977), p. 27.

17. Figures taken from: 'Return of the number of effective men in the British army, from the 1st January 1775 to the 1st January 1783; distinguishing each year:--as far as can be made up from the documents in the War-Office' by Richard Fitzpatrick, 22nd May 1806: House of Commons, Parliamentary Papers Online (Proquest, 2006), Table 172, p. 393; Kevin Barry Linch, 'The Recruitment of the British Army 1807–1815' (Ph.D. thesis, University of Leeds, Oct. 2001), p. 21.

18. Knight, *Britain against Napoleon*, p. 51; PP: 'An account of the effective numbers and established strength of regiments of cavalry, guards, and infantry, borne on the British establishment; and the general distribution of the said forces; in the years 1791 and 1792' by Lord Palmerston, 22 February 1816: House of Commons, Parliamentary Papers Online (Proquest, 2006), Table. 40, p. 391. See also: J.W Fortescue, *A History of the British Army, Vol. III 1763–1793* (London: Macmillan, 1911), p. 526. For analysis of the Nootka Sound crisis see: Howard V. Evans, 'The Nootka Sound Controversy in Anglo-French Diplomacy—1790', *JMH*, Vol. 46 No. 4 (Dec. 1974), pp. 609–40.

19. PP: 'Return of the number of effective men in the British Army, from the 1st January 1775 to the 1st January 1783; distinguishing each year:--as far as can be made up from the documents in the War-Office' by Richard Fitzpatrick, 22nd May 1806, Table 172, p. 393.

20. Colin Kidd, *British Identities before Nationalism, Ethnicity and Nationhood in the Atlantic World 1600–1800* (Cambridge: Cambridge University Press, 1999, repr. 2004), p. 266, Hannah Smith, 'Politics, Patriotism, and Gender: The Standing Army Debate on the English Stage, circa 1689—1720', *JBS*, Vol. 50 No. 1 (Jan. 2011), pp. 48–75; Jack P. Greene, 'Empire and Identity from the Glorious Revolution to the American Revolution' in Marshall (ed.), *The Eighteenth-Century, Volume II*, pp. 208–30.

21. John Brewer, *The Sinews of Power: War, Money and the English State 1688–1783* (London: Unwin Hyman, 1989), p. 43.

22. Claus Telp, *The Evolution of Operational Art, 1740–1813 From Frederick the Great to Napoleon* (London: Frank Cass, 2005), p. 20; Christopher Duffy, *The Army of Frederick the Great* (London: David & Charles, 1974), p. 37. Several maps of British training camps are located at The National Archives and include: TNA WO 78/ 5825: – 'Plan of Encampments of Swindley Camp – (under Duke of York and David Dundas) – 29 June 1800', TNA WO 78/ 5824: 'Plan of Encampments of Bagshot Heath – 1 – Jan. 1799, 31 Dec. 1799', TNA WO 78/ 5823: 'Plan of Encampments of Windsor Forest 24 June 1799', TNA WO 78/ 5822: 'Plan of Encampments of Windsor Forest 23 July 1798', TNA WO 78/5824: 'Plan of Encampments at Bagshot Heath, on 1 January and 31 December 1799'. For example of a camp at Winkfield see TNA WO 78/ 5821, Colchester see TNA WO 78/ 5820, and Windsor Park in 1805 see TNA WO 78/ 5826.

23. Fortescue, *History of the British Army, Vol. III*, pp. 535–9.

24. Brendan Morrissey, *Yorktown 1781, The World Turned Upside Down, Osprey Campaign Series, No. 47* (Oxford: Osprey Publishing, 1997), pp. 28–9; Glover, *Peninsular Preparation*, p. 116.

25. Various historians cite that the British had around 30,000 men in the Colonies in 1776: numbers calculated from Barnet Schechter, *The Battle for New York, The City at the Heart of the American Revolution* (London: Jonathan Cape, 2003), pp. 112–14; Daniel Marston, *The American revolution 1774–1783, Osprey Essential Histories No. 45* (Osprey: Oxford, 2002), p. 41; Robert Harvey, *A Few Bloody Noses, The American War of Independence* (London: John Murray, 2001), p. 199; Mark Urban, *Fusiliers, How the British Army lost America but learned to fight* (London: Faber & Faber, 2007), p. 75.

26. Houlding, *Fit for Service*, p. 348.

27. Elizabeth Longford, *Wellington, The Years of the Sword* (London: World Books, 1969), p. 113.

28. J.W. Fortescue, *The British Army 1783–1802, Four Lectures Delivered at the Staff College and Cavalry School* (London: Macmillan, 1905), p. 12.

29. Houlding, *Fit For Service*, p. 229.

30. Houlding, *Fit For Service*, p. 238; Dundas's drills were first adopted by the British garrison in Dublin in 1789, where Dundas was stationed.

31. John Childs, *Armies and Warfare in Europe, 1648–1789* (New York: Holmes & Meier, 1982), p. 76; Anon., *Regulations for the Prussian Infantry* (repr. Westport: Greenwood Press, 1969; orig. pub. 1759).

32. Arnold Whitridge, 'Baron von Steuben, Washington's Drillmaster', *History Today*, v. 26 i.7 (Jul. 1976), pp. 429–36 esp. pp. 433–4.

33. Colonel Sir David Dundas, *Principles of Military Movements Chiefly applied to the infantry, illustrated by the manoeuvres of the Prussian troops, and by an outline of the British campaigns in Germany during the War of 1757* (London: T. Cadell, N.DCC.LXXXVIII), p. iii; Mackesy, *British Victory in Egypt*, p. 30. Dundas's manual was published again in 1796 under the title *Rules and Regulations for the Formations, Field Exercise and Movement of His Majesty's Infantry*; Keith John Bartlett, 'The Development of the British Army during the wars with France, 1793–1815' (doctoral thesis, Durham University, 1998), Durham E-Theses Online (Proquest, 2006), p. 164; Cookson, *The British Armed Nation*, pp. 30–1.

34. David Gates, *The British Light Infantry Arm c. 1790–1815, its creation, training and operational role* (London: Batsford, 1987), p. 14.

35. Brent Nosworthy, *Battle Tactics of Napoleon and his enemies* (London: Constable, 1995), p. 166; Peter Paret, *The Cognitive Challenge of War, Prussia 1806* (Princeton and Oxford: Princeton University Press, 2009), pp. 11–32.

36. Gates, *The British Light Infantry Arm*, p. 50.

37. Few books have been written on the subject of Cavalry in the American War but a rare example is Jim Piecuch (ed.), *Cavalry of the American Revolution* (Yardley: Westholme, 2012).

38. Robin May and Gerry Embleton, *The British Army in North America 1775–1783, Osprey Men at Arms Series No. 39* (London: Osprey, 1997), p. 13.

39. J.W. Fortescue, *A History of the British Army Vol. IV 1789–1801* (London: Macmillan, 1906), p. 95.

40. Stephen Bull, *The Furie of the Ordnance, Artillery in the English Civil Wars* (Woodbridge: Boydell, 2008), p. 16.

41. Glover, *Peninsular Preparation*, p. 187.

42. No equivalent of Woolwich existed for regular army officers until the creation of the Royal Military College in 1803 – military education will be analysed in greater detail later in the chapter.

43. Christopher D. Hall, *British Strategy in the Napoleonic War 1803–1815* (Manchester: Manchester University Press, 1992), p. 47.

44. Hall, *British Strategy in the Napoleonic War*, p. 48.

45. Bartlett, 'The Development of the British Army', p. 39.

46. The journal in question later became the *Royal United Service Institute Journal*. The origins of this organisation can be traced back to the creation of the Naval and Military Museum by Wellington in 1831. For more on the history of RUSI see: https://www.rusi.org/history.

47. Albert Sorel, *L'Europe et la Revolution Francaise* (1885) quoted in A.W. Ward and G.P. Gooch, *The Cambridge History of British Foreign Policy, 1783–1919 Volume I: 1783–1815* (London: Cambridge University Press, 1922), p. 144.

48. J.T. Murley, *The Origin and Outbreak of the Anglo-French War of 1793* (D.Phil. thesis, University of Oxford, 1959), p. 9; R.N.W. Thomas, 'Reponses to War: The Military Reaction of the British Government to the French Declaration of War in February 1793' in Ellen Evans, John W. Rooney jr (eds), *The Consortium on Revolutionary Europe 1750–1850 Proceedings, 1993* (Institute on Napoleon and the French Revolution: Florida State University, 1994).

49. Ward and Gooch, *The Cambridge History of British Foreign Policy, I*, p. 147.

50. Renier, *Great Britain and the establishment of the Kingdom of the Netherlands*, p. 9.

51. Tim Blanning, *The Pursuit of Glory, Europe 1648–1815* (Cambridge: Allen Lane, 2007), p. 98; Jan A. van Houtte and Leon van Buyten, 'The Low Countries' in Charles Wilson and Geoffrey Parker (eds), *An Introduction to the Sources of European Economic History 1500–1800 Volume 1: Western Europe* (London: Methuen, 1980), p. 82.

52. N.A.M. Rodger, *The Command of the Ocean, A Naval History of Britain, 1649–1815* (London: Penguin, 2006), pp. 12–18, 66–78, 81–6; Jonathan I. Israel, *The Dutch Republic, Its Rise, Greatness, and Fall 1477–1806: The Oxford History of Early Modern Europe* (Oxford: Clarendon Press, paperback edn 1998), pp. 713–27, 766–78, 785, 796–7, 812–13, 848. For more on the

Anglo-Dutch Wars see C.R. Boxer, *The Anglo-Dutch Wars of the 17th Century* (London: HMSO, 1974); Roger Hainsworth and Christine Churches, *The Anglo-Dutch Naval Wars, 1652–1674* (Stroud: Sutton, 1998); J.R. Jones, *The Anglo-Dutch Wars of the Seventeenth Century* (London: Longman, 1996); M.A.J. Palmer, 'The "Military Revolution" Afloat: The Era of the Anglo-Dutch Wars and the transition to Modern Warfare at Sea', *War in History*, Vol. 4 (2) (1997), pp. 123–49.

53. See Gijs Rommelse, *The Second Anglo-Dutch War (1665–1667): International Raison d'État, Mercantilism and Maritime Strife* (Hilversum, The Netherlands: Uitgeverif Verloren, 2006).

54. Renier, *Great Britain and the Establishment of the Kingdom of the Netherlands*, p. 8.

55. Simms, *Three Victories and a Defeat*, pp. 268–9.

56. G.J. Renier, *The Dutch Nation, An Historical Study* (London: George Allen & Unwin, 1944), pp. 227–39.

57. Simms, *Three Victories and a Defeat*, p. 348.

58. Israel, *The Dutch Republic*, pp. 1005, 1056, 1095–7, 1099, 1103, 1116, 1119.

59. Simon Schama, *Patriots and Liberators, Revolution in the Netherlands 1780–1813* (Collins: London, 1977), pp. 62–3; Maarten Prak, 'Citizen Radicalism and Democracy in the Dutch Republic: The Patriot Movement of the 1780s', *Theory and Society*, Vol. 20 No. 1 (Feb. 1991), pp. 73–102, p. 85.

60. H.M. Scott, 'Sir Joseph Yorke, Dutch Politics and the Origins of the Fourth Anglo-Dutch War', *HJ*, Vol. 31 No. 3 (Sep., 1988), pp. 571–89, p. 573.

61. Israel, *The Dutch Republic*, pp. 975, 1096–7, 1100, 1113–14.

62. Wayne P. Te Brake, 'Popular Politics and the Dutch Patriot Revolution', *Theory and Society*, Vol. 14 No. 2 (Mar. 1985), pp. 199–222, pp. 205–6.

63. For a detailed study of the political and diplomatic history regarding the opening/closure of the Scheldt look to S.T. Bindoff, *The Scheldt Question to 1839* (London: George Allen & Unwin, 1945).

64. Ward and Gooch (eds), *The Cambridge History of British Foreign Policy, I*, p. 161.

65. Raymond Kubben, *Regeneration and Hegemony, Franco-Batavian Relations in the Revolutionary Era, 1795–1803*, Studies in the History of International Law 1 (The Hague: Martinus Hijhoff, 2011), p. 156.

66. Jeremy Black, *British Foreign Policy in the Age of Revolutions, 1783–1793* (Cambridge: Cambridge University Press, 1994), p. 112.

67. J. Holland Rose, 'The Missions of William Grenville to the Hague and Versailles in 1787', *EHR*, Vol. 24 No. 94 (Apr. 1909), pp. 278–95, at p. 279.

68. Schama, *Patriots and Liberators*, pp. 129; Black, *British Foreign Policy in the Age of Revolutions*, p. 118.

69. Jennifer Mori, *William Pitt and the French Revolution 1785–1795* (Edinburgh: Keele University Press, 1997), p. 59. Although the British government was pleased with the outcome of the Prussian intervention, Pitt was criticised for his actions by some liberally minded thinkers, one of the most vocal opponents of the whole affair was Jeremy Bentham: Stephen Conway, 'Bentham versus Pitt: Jeremy Bentham and British Foreign Policy 1789', *HJ*, 30 (1987), pp. 791–809 at p. 801.

70. Adrien de Meeüs, *History of the Belgians* (New York: Praeger, 1962), p. 239.

71. Meeüs, *History of the Belgians*, pp. 240–1. For more on the Vonckists see: Geert Van den Bossche, 'Political propaganda in the Brabant Revolution: Habsburg "negligence" versus Belgian nation-building', *History of European Ideas*, 28:3 (2002), pp. 119–44, esp. p. 137.

72. E.H. Kossmann, *The Low Countries 1780–1940* (Oxford: Clarendon Press, 1978), pp. 58–9.

73. Janet L. Polasky, 'Democrats, and Jacobins in Revolutionary Brussels', *JMH*, Vol. 56 No. 2 (Jun. 1984), pp. 227–62 at p. 227.

74. Black, *British Foreign Policy in an Age of Revolutions*, p. 266.

75. Murley, *The Origin and Outbreak of the Anglo-French War of 1793*, p. 9.

76. Meeüs, *History of the Belgians*, pp. 246.

77. Auckland to Grenville, 22 June 1792, The Hague, *The Manuscripts of J.B. Fortescue preserved at Dropmore Vol. II* (being the Correspondence and Papers of Lord Grenville 1698–1820) (London: His Majesty's Stationery Office, 1894), p. 283.

78. Auckland to Grenville, 15 November 1792, The Hague, *Dropmore, II*, p. 334.

79. Auckland to Grenville, 3 December 1792, The Hague, *Dropmore, II*, p. 351.

80. Peter Jupp, *Lord Grenville 1759–1834* (Oxford: Clarendon Press, 1985), p. 152.

81. John Ehrman, *The Younger Pitt, The Reluctant Transition* (London: Constable, 1983), p. 257.

82. Lord Auckland to Grenville, The Hague, 15 February 1793, *Dropmore, II*, p. 380. Auckland had asked for military support earlier in the month, but the government had not thought it necessary to despatch British troops at this point. Instead aid had been found in the form of a force of Hanoverian troops which had been called up by H.R.H. George III, who, as Elector of Hanover, had the right to recruit Hanoverian troops if Hanover was in danger and to support the Habsburg monarchy. See TNA FO 37/44: Letter No. 25, Auckland to Grenville, 8 February 1793, The Hague.

83. Mori, *William Pitt and the French Revolution*, p. 114.

84. Auckland compared the United Provinces to Yorkshire, whilst Burke, famously argued that the British should view the Dutch Republic as being as important to British interests as Kent. Quoted in T.C.W. Blanning, *The French Revolutionary Wars 1787–1802* (London: Arnold, 1996), p. 93.

85. Sir Harry Verney (ed.), *The Journals and Correspondence of General Sir Harry Calvert, comprising the campaigns in Flanders and Holland in 1793–4* (London: Hurst and Blackett, 1823), pp. 20–2.

86. Auckland to Grenville,13 March 1793, The Hague, *Dropmore, II*, p. 384.

87. TNA FO 37/46: 'Holland, Letters and Papers from Lord Auckland at The Hague, the Secretary of State: with drafts. From March 12th: 1793 to March 31st: 1793 Volume the Fourth', Lord Auckland to Lord Grenville, The Hague, Letter no. 67, 29 March 1793.

88. Several generations of historians have pursued this line of argument, the list of historians and their woks include: Alfred H. Burne, *The Noble Duke of York, The Military Life of Frederick Duke of York and Albany* (London: Staples, 1949); Fortescue, *A History of the British Army, Vol. IV*, pp. 72, 84–5, 113, 140, 145, 149, 153, 174–8; Martha Watson, 'The Duke of York and the Campaigns of the British Army in the Low Countries 1793–1795' (M.A. thesis, University of Warwick, 2006); R.N.W. Thomas, 'Command and Control in the First Coalition: the Duke of York in the Low Countries, 1793–1794' in K.A. Roider and John C. Horgan (eds), *The Consortium on Revolutionary Europe, 1750–1850: Proceedings 1991* (Tallahassee: Institute on Napoleon and the French Revolution, Florida State University, 1992), pp. 267–73. A more balanced argument is made by Michael Duffy in his article, ' "A Particular Service": The British Government and the Dunkirk Expedition of 1793', *EHR*, Vol. 91 No. 360 (Jul. 1976), pp. 529–54.

89. George III to Grenville, 29 March 1793, Queen's House, *Dropmore, II*, p. 387; Pitt to Grenville, 30 March 1793 Downing Street, *Dropmore, II*, p. 388; Pitt to Grenville, 1 April 1793 Downing Street, *Dropmore, II*, p. 388; Grenville to George III, 3 April 1793 Whitehall, *Dropmore, II*, p. 389.

90. Mori, *William Pitt and the French Revolution*, pp. 53–5. Unlike the Dutch, whose maritime heritage had enabled them to reap the benefits of coastal trade, the Austrians' lack of naval power meant that they had been unable to maximise the potential of the Flanders coast, something which further encouraged their leaders to lobby for a the Bavarian exchange.

91. TNA WO 1/166: 'Instructions for Captain Crauford', Sir James Murray to Sir Henry Dundas, 31 March 1793 War Department-French Wars-Flanders Campaign Feb.–Aug. 1793, pp. 101–2.

92. TNA WO 1/166: 'Report of Captain Crauford who was sent by H.R.H. the Duke of York to the Prince of Coburg on the 31st of March and returned to Bergen-op-Zoom on the 4th of April', p. 119; Auckland to Lord Henry Spencer, The Hague, 6 April 1793, *The Journal and Correspondence of William, Lord Auckland, Vol. II* (London: Richard Bentley, 1861), p. 505. From this point on Prince Frederick Josias of Saxe-Coburg-Saalfeld will be referred to as Coburg.

93. TNA WO 1/166: 'Report of Captain Crauford who was sent by H.R.H. the Duke of York to the Prince of Coburg on the 31st of March and returned to Bergen-op-Zoom on the 4th of April', pp. 114–15; Fortescue, *A History of the British Army, Vol. IV*, pp. 68–9.

94. TNA WO 6/7: Sir Henry Dundas to Lieutenant Colonel Sir James Murray, 16 April 1793, Whitehall War Department and Successors: Secretary of State for War and Secretary for War and the Colonies Out-Letters. 01 February 1793–31 August 1793.

95. Thomas, 'Responses to War: The Military Reaction of the British Government', pp. 423–4.

96. Duffy, 'A Particular Service', pp. 531–2.

97. Pitt to Grenville, 30 March 1793, Downing Street, *Dropmore, II*, p. 388.

98. Erhman, *The Younger Pitt*, p. 477. For a recent study of the military policy of Pitt the Elder see Edward Pearce, *Pitt the Elder, Man of War* (London: Bodley Head, 2010); Nicholas Tracy, *The Battle of Quiberon Bay 1759, Hawke and the Defeat of the French Invasion* (Barnsley: Pen & Sword, 2010); F.J. Hebbert, 'The Belle Isle expedition of 1761', *JSAHR*, 64 (1986), pp. 81–93; W.K. Hackman, 'English military expeditions to the coast of France 1757–1761' (unpublished Ph.D. thesis, Ann Arbor, 1968).

99. J. Holland Rose, 'The Duke of Richmond and the conduct of the War', *EHR*, Vol. 25 No. 99 (Jul. 1910), pp. 554–5.

100. Boyd Hilton, *A Mad, Bad, & Dangerous People? England 1783–1846* (Oxford: Oxford University Press, 2008), pp. 82–3.

101. Jennifer Mori, 'The British Government and the Bourbon Restoration: The Occupation of Toulon, 1793', *HJ*, 40 3 (1997), pp. 699–719; Paul Kelly and Gilbert Elliot, 'Strategy and Counter-Revolution: The Journal of Sir Gilbert Elliot, 1–22 September 1793', *EHR*, Vol. 98 No. 387 (Apr. 1983), pp. 328–48; Anon., 'Her Majesty's Stationery Office, British Minor Expeditions 1746 to 1814, Compiled in the Intelligence Branch of the Quartermaster-General's Department' (London: 1884), pp. 20–7. For a study of Federalism and revolt against the Revolution, see Bill Edmonds, ' "Federalism" and Urban Revolt in France in 1793', *JMH*, Vol. 55 No. 1 (Mar. 1983), pp. 22–53.

102. Collins, *War and Empire*, pp. 94–9.

103. TNA WO 1/166: Colonel Sir James Murray to Sir Henry Dundas, 22 April 1793, Courtrai, p. 153.

104. TNA WO 1/166: General Ralph Abercomby to H. Dundas, 10 April 1793, Antwerp, pp. 121–2.

105. Verney, *Journals and Correspondence of Sir Harry Calvert*, pp. 52–3; J.W. Fortescue, *British Campaigns in Flanders 1690–1794 being extracts from 'A History of the British Army'* (London: Macmillan, 1918), p. 185.

106. TNA WO 3/11:William Fawcett to York, 27 March 1793, Horse Guards, Commander in Chief General Letters, Nov. 1792–Dec. 1793; TNA WO 1/166: Murray to H. Dundas, 19 April 1793, Bruges.

107. TNA WO 1/166: Murray to Dundas, 22 April 1793, Courtrai, p. 159.

108. TNA WO 1/166: Murray to Dundas, 22 April 1793, Courtrai, p. 158.

109. The majority of the Hanoverian army arrived at Tournai a little earlier than planned, between 26 and 31 April.

110. Gunther E. Rothenberg, *Napoleon's Great Adversaries, The Archduke Charles and the Austrian Army 1792–1814* (London: Batsford, 1982), p. 37.

111. R.R. Palmer, 'Frederick the Great, Guibert, Bulow: From Dynastic to National War' in Peter Paret (ed.), *Makers of Modern Strategy, From Machiavelli to the Nuclear Age* (Oxford: Clarendon, 1986), pp. 94–5.

112. TNA WO 1/166: Murray to Dundas, 22 April; Murray to H. Dundas, 5 May 1793, pp. 154–5.

113. TNA WO 1/166: Murray to H. Dundas, 5 May 1793, p. 201. TNA WO 1/166: '"Considerations der Armeé combines" – Frontier der France aux Pays Bas, 1793'.

114. Robert Brown, *Corporal Brown's Campaigns in the Low Countries: Recollections of a Coldstream Guard in the Early Campaigns Against Revolutionary France, 1793–1795* (London: Leonaur, 2008), p. 31.

115. Verney, *Journals and Correspondence of Sir Harry Calvert*, pp. 76–7; Burne, *The Noble Duke of York*, pp. 52–3.

116. For example although York's chief engineer, Colonel James Moncrief, had developed his siege craft during the American War of Independence he had no active knowledge of European siege warfare before Valenciennes. For more on Moncrief see: The James Moncrief papers 1710–1894, William L. Clements Library, The University of Michigan; R.N.W. Thomas, 'James Moncrief, (1744–1793)', *Oxford Dictionary of National Biography* (Oxford: Oxford University Press, 2004); David Lee Russell, *The American Revolution in the Southern Colonies* (Jefferson: McFarland, 2000), p. 115.

117. Rogers, *The British Army of the Eighteenth-Century*, p. 186.

118. TNA WO 124/ 18: Two copies of Papers proposing, in the event of war with France, (a) an invasion of Dieppe, and (b) the closure of Dunkirk harbour (1773).

119. Although Dunkirk harboured some smugglers, more came to the area later in the period when Napoleon officially welcomed English smugglers to use the nearby port of Gravelines in 1810. For further information read Gavin Daly, 'English Smugglers, the Channel, and the Napoleonic Wars, 1800–1814', *JBS*, Vol. 46, No. 1 (Jan. 2007), pp. 30–46.

120. TNA WO 1/166: Murray to H. Dundas, Letter No. 30, 12 July 1793, Estreaux, pp. 493–4.

121. TNA WO 1/166: Murray to H. Dundas, Letter No. 30, 12 July 1793, Estreaux, p. 495.

122. TNA WO 1/166: Murray to H. Dundas, Letter No. 30, 12 July 1793, Estreaux, pp. 495–6.

123. TNA WO 1/166: Murray to H. Dundas, Letter No. 39, 6 August 1793, Estreaux, p. 699.

124. TNA WO 1/166: Murray to H. Dundas, Letter No. 30, 12 July 1793, Estreaux, pp. 500–1.

125. TNA WO 1/166: 'Ordnance and ammunition for a particular service', located within Murray to Dundas, Letter No. 30, 12 July 1793, Estreaux, pp. 523–9.

126. For further details of the requests made see Duffy, 'A Particular Service', pp. 539–40; TNA HO 50/ 369: Colonel William Congreve to Sir James Murray, 2 July 1793.

127. TNA WO 1/166: Dundas to Murray, 16 July 1793, Estreaux, p. 579.

128. Holland Rose, 'The Duke of Richmond on the Conduct of the War', pp. 554–5.

129. J. Holland Rose, 'Pitt and the Campaign of 1793', *EHR*, Vol. 24 No. 96 (Oct. 1909), pp. 744–9.

130. TNA WO 124: Secretary of State, Southern Department, and Ordnance Office, Military Branch: Papers Concerning Demolition of Fortifications at Dunkirk, Ordnance Office, 22 vols. Especially TNA WO 124/ 13: Copy of a Report of the British Engineers concerning the work of demolition at Dunkirk, and two copies of an extract from it prepared specially for the French Ambassador, (1766); TNA WO 124/8: Entry Book of Correspondence of Ensign Andrew Durnford of the Corps of Engineers at Dunkirk 1 vol. 1772 Apr.–1773 Mar.

131. TNA WO 1/166: Murray to H. Dundas, 6 August 1793, Estreaux, pp. 699–700.

132. Duffy, 'A Particular Service', p. 535.

133. TNA WO 1/166: Murray to H. Dundas, 30 July 1793, Estreaux, p. 675.

134. TNA WO 1/166: Murray to H. Dundas, 6 August 1793, Estreaux, p. 700.

135. On 12 July the population of Toulon had ousted the local Central Committee and on 22 August representatives of the population asked Admiral Hood, the commander of the British Mediterranean fleet, for assistance. Over the course of August–September the British were increasingly drawn into the affairs at Toulon; eventually sending troops to defend the port against the advancing Republican forces. For a history of the siege of Toulon see: Bernard Ireland, *The Fall of Toulon: The Royal Navy and the Royalist Last Stand against the French Revolution* (London: Weidenfeld & Nicolson, 2005).

136. TNA WO 1/166: General Ainslie to Evan Nepean, 8 August 1793, Ostend; Duffy, 'A Particular Service,' p. 542.

137. TNA WO 1/166: Ainslie to Nepean, 15 August 1793, Ostend, pp. 739–41.

138. Brown, *Corporal Brown's Campaigns*, p. 61.

139. TNA WO 1/166: Murray to Dundas, 25 August 1793, Liefkenshoek, p. 800.

140. TNA WO 1/166: Murray to Dundas, No. 45, 24 August 1793, Camp near Dunkirk, p. 782.
141. TNA WO 1/167: Rear Admiral John MacBride to H. Dundas, 'Receipt of Instructions', The Downs, 2 September 1793, p. 1. MacBride's command comprised fourteen vessels, including a fourth rate, four fifth rates, and two sixth rates, two armed sloops, two bomb vessels, a floating battery and a fire ship; for full details of the MacBride's squadron see TNA WO 1/167: 'A List of His Majesty's Ships and Vessels which are to compose the squadron under the command of Rear Admiral MacBride', p. 13.
142. TNA WO 1/167: Murray to H. Dundas, Private, 3 September, 1793, p. 21.
143. Sidney Lee (ed.), *Dictionary of National Biography Vol. XXXIX Morehead-Myles* (New York: Macmillan, 1894), p. 376.
144. Murray mentioned the need for sailors in a number of letters to Henry Dundas in August, examples being TNA WO 1/166: Murray to H. Dundas, 6 August 1793, Estreaux, p. 700; TNA WO 1/166: Murray to H. Dundas, Private, 26 August, 1793, Liefkenshoek, p. 811.
145. TNA WO 1/166: Murray to H. Dundas, 24 August 1793, Camp near Dunkirk, pp. 782–3.
146. TNA WO 1/166: Murray to H. Dundas, 24 August 1793, Camp near Dunkirk, p. 783.
147. TNA WO 1/166: Murray to H. Dundas, 31 August 1793, Liefkenshoek, p. 823.
148. Duffy, 'A Particular Service', p. 546.
149. Peter Hofschröer, *The Hanoverian Army of the Napoleonic Wars, Osprey Men at Arms Series No. 206* (London: Osprey, 1989), p. 4, 8, 12–13; John Grehan, *Britain's German allies of the Napoleonic Wars: The armies of Hanover, Brunswick & the Kings German Legion 1793–1815* (Newthorpe: Partizan, Cavalier Books, 1999).
150. Brown, *Corporal Brown's Campaigns*, p. 33.
151. Simon Schama, *Citizens, A Chronicle of the French Revolution* (London: Penguin, 1989), p. 706; Richard Cobb and Colin Jones (eds), *The French Revolution, Voices from a momentous epoch 1789–1795* (London: Guild Publishing, 1988), p. 181; Blanning, *The French Revolutionary Wars*, p. 108; Robert R. Palmer, *Twelve Who Ruled* (Princeton: Princeton University Press, 1941).
152. Alan Forrest, *Soldiers of the French Revolution* (Durham and London: Duke University Press, 1990), pp. 68–76; Paddy Griffith, *The Art of War of Revolutionary France, 1789–1802* (London: Greenhill, 1998), p. 82.
153. Steven T. Ross, 'The Development of the Combat Division in Eighteenth-Century French Armies', *French Historical Studies*, Vol. 4 No. 1 (Spring, 1965), pp. 84–94; John R. Elting, *Swords Around a Throne, Napoleon's Grande Armée* (New York: DeCapo Press, 1997), pp. 33–4; Samuel F. Scott, 'The Regeneration of the Line Army during the French Revolution', *JMH*, Vol. 42 No. 3 (Sep., 1970), pp. 307–30.
154. Ian Germani, 'Terror in the Army: Representatives on Mission and Military Discipline in the Armies of the French Revolution', *JMHS*, Vol. 75 Issue 3 (Jul. 2011), p. 733.
155. Ramsey Weston Phipps, *The Armies of the First French Republic and the rise of the Marshals of Napoleon I: The Armée du Nord* (London: Oxford University Press, 1926), p. 213.
156. Phipps, *The Armée du Nord*, p. 213.
157. Phipps, *The Armée du Nord*, pp. 223–4.
158. Phipps, *The Armée du Nord*, pp. 216–17.
159. Phipps, *The Armée du Nord* pp. 193–4, 216–17, 229–31; Vandamme was local to the area having been born at Cassel in 1770.
160. For details of French dispositions on the coast see: Phipps, *The Armée du Nord*, pp. 229–31.
161. TNA WO 1/166: Murray to H. Dundas, 28 August 1793, Liefkenshoek, p. 816.
162. TNA WO 1/167: Murray to H. Dundas, 7 September 1793, Liefkenshoek, pp. 45–7.
163. TNA WO 1/167: Murray to H. Dundas, 7 September 1793, Liefkenshoek, p. 47.
164. TNA WO 1/167: Murray to H. Dundas, 9 September 1793, Furnes, p. 81.

165. John A. Lynn, *Bayonets of the Republic, Motivations and Tactics in the Army of Revolutionary France 1791–94* (Urbana and Chicago: University of Illinois Press, 1984), p. 13.
166. See B.A. Cook and I. Germani, 'The Face of Battle: Hondschoote 1793', *Selected Papers: Consortium on Revolutionary Europe 1750–1850* (Baton Rouge: Florida State University, 2002).
167. Fortescue, *History of the British Army, Vol. IV*, p. 132.
168. TNA WO 1/167: Murray to H. Dundas, 9 September 1793, Furnes, pp. 79–80.
169. Anon., *The Present State of the British Army in Flanders, with an authentic account of the British retreat from before Dunkirk by a British officer in that Army who was living on the 24th of September* (London: H.D. Symonds, 1793), p. 4.
170. Anon., *The Present State of the British Army in Flanders*, p. 8.
171. TNA WO 1/167: Murray to H. Dundas, Private, 6 October 1793, Menin, pp. 230–2.
172. Blanning, *The French Revolutionary Wars*, p. 110.
173. York to the King, Menin, 18 September 1793 in Alfred H. Burne, *The Noble Duke of York* (London: Staples, 1949), pp. 73–7.
174. Burne, *The Noble Duke of York*, pp. 73–7.
175. Duffy, 'A Particular Service', p. 549.
176. York to the King, Menin, 18 September 1793 in A. Aspinall (ed.), *The Later Correspondence of George III, Published by Authority of Her Majesty Queen Elizabeth II, Volume II February 1793 to December 1797* (Cambridge: Cambridge University Press, 1963), p. 98; TNA WO 1/166: Murray to H. Dundas, 22 April, p. 153.
177. Fortescue, *British Campaigns in Flanders*, p. 239.
178. The British made something of a habit out of abandoning their allies in order to save themselves during the period 1793 to 1814. The British abandoned their allies after the siege of Toulon, in 1793, after the failed Quiberon expedition in 1795; at the conclusion of the expedition to the Helder in 1799; at the termination of the expedition to save Hanover in 1805; in the hectic retreat to Corunna and Vigo in 1809; following the indecisive battle of Talevera in 1809; during the French invasion of Portugal in 1810 and after the failed siege of Burgos in 1812. For a complete list of the expeditions undertaken by the British army during the period 1793 to 1815 see: *Memorandum of a collection of bulletins: 1793 to 182*, Foreign and Commonwealth Office Collection (1823).

Chapter 2

1. TNA WO 1/168: 'By Order of His Royal Highness the Duke of York, Memorandum submitted to the Right Honourable Henry Dundas, etc, etc, etc, by Lieut-General Harcourt', pp. 145–56.
2. For instance, York devoted a great deal of time negotiating with Richmond so that an artillery park could be constructed in the environs of Ghent: TNA WO 1/168: 'Proposition for a park of Artillery as recommended by the Duke of Richmond for Flanders in the year 1794' included in a letter from Richmond to York, 8 January 1794, Whitehall, pp. 39–45; TNA WO 1/168: York to Richmond, 25 January 1794, Ghent, pp. 175–80.
3. TNA WO 1/168: Major James Craig to Evan Nepean, 14 January 1794, Ghent, p. 113, Burne, *Noble Duke of York*, p. 115. Burne incorrectly refers to Craig as John.
4. Hughes Marquis, 'Le Général François Jarry au service de l'Angleterre (1793–1806)', *Annales historiques de la Révolution française*, No. 356 (Avril/Juin 2009), pp. 93–118 at pp. 96–7; François Jarry de Vrigny de la Villette, or Jarry as he was known to the British, had served as a senior military engineer in both the Prussian and French armies during the period before and immediately after the French Revolution but opted to defect to the British in 1793. A keen military theorist and an expert on both light infantry and officer education, Jarry's contribution to the reform of the British army will be studied in greater detail later in the book.
5. TNA WO 1/168: York to H. Dundas, 9 March 1794, Courtrai, pp. 397–8; TNA WO 1/168: Prince of Coburg, 'Considerations sur l'ouverture et les Operations de la Campagne prochaine de la Armée 1794', Bruxelles le 4 Fevrier 1794', pp. 259–82; Mack is best known as the general

who surrendered the city of Ulm to Napoleon in the early stages of the 1805: F.N. Maude, *The Ulm Campaign 1805: Napoleon and the Defeat of the Austrian Army During the 'War of the Third Coalition'* (London: Leonaur, 2008).

6. Rothenberg, *Napoleon's Great Adversaries*, p. 36.
7. Fortescue, *History of the British Army, Vol. IV*, pp. 230–1.
8. Fortescue, *British Campaigns in Flanders*, pp. 298–300.
9. Fortescue, *A History of the British Army, Vol. IV*, pp. 232–3, 236–9, 241–3, 249–51; Phillip J. Haythornthwaite, *Die Hard!, Dramatic Actions from the Napoleonic Wars* (London: Arms & Armour Press, 1996), pp. 19–35; Richard Holmes, *Redcoat, The British Soldier in the Age of Horse and Musket* (London: Harper Perennial, 2001), pp. 224–5; Black, *Britain as a military power*, p. 195; Sir Charles Oman, 'The 15th Light Dragoons at Villers-en-Cauchies, 24th March 1794', *JSAHR*, XVII (1938); TNA WO 1/168 War Department – French Wars – Flanders campaign Jan.–Apr. 1794.
10. Lynn, *Bayonets of the Republic*, p. 17.
11. Hilaire Belloc, *British Battles: Tourcoing* (London: Steven Swift, 1912), pp. 28–48; Fortescue, *British Campaigns in Flanders*, pp. 323–6; Lynn, *Bayonets of the Republic*, p. 17.
12. Blanning, *The French Revolutionary Wars*, pp. 112–13.
13. TNA WO 1/169: York to H. Dundas, 19 May 1794, Tournai; John Grehan and Martin Mace, *Despatches from the Front, British Battles of the Napoleonic Wars 1793–1806* (Barnsley: Pen & Sword, 2013), pp. 58–61; Belloc, *Tourcoing*, p. 114.
14. Moira had served throughout the American War of Independence and played a key role in the defeat of the Americans at the Battle of Camden in 1780; he became Lord Moira in 1793 and was later appointed Governor General of India in 1812: Paul David Nelson, *Francis Rawdon-Hastings, Marquess of Hastings: Soldier, Peer of the Realm, Governor-General of India* (Cranbury: Associated University Press, 2005).
15. Fortescue, *A History of the British Army, Vol. IV*, pp. 153–6; Nelson, *Francis Rawdon-Hastings*, pp. 119–20.
16. R.N.W. Thomas, 'Wellington in the Low Countries, 1794–1795', *IHR*, Vol II No. 1 (Feb. 1989), pp. 14–30 at p. 15.
17. Fortescue, *British Campaigns in Flanders*, pp. 359–76.
18. The Marquis of Anglesey (ed.), '"Two brothers in the Netherlands, 1794–1795" Part of the Duke of York's campaign as seen through the eyes of two young commanding officers based upon hitherto unpublished letters in the "Plas Newydd papers"', *JSAHR*, Vol. 32 (1954), p. 81. Another regiment to arrive at this time was the 33rd Foot, which was commanded by Lieutenant Colonel Sir Arthur Wellesley.
19. Lieutenant Colonel R.M. Grazebrook (ed.), '"The Campaign in Flanders of 1793–1795" Journal of Lieutenant-Colonel Charles Stewart, 28th Foot', *JSAHR*, Vol. 28 (1951), p. 9.
20. For a map of the area of operations in Netherlands in 1795 see map, p. 000.
21. Huw J. Davies, *Wellington's Wars, The Making of a Military Genius* (New Haven and London: Yale University Press, 2012), p. 5.
22. Brown, *Corporal Brown's Campaigns*, p. 141; Thomas, 'Wellington in the Low Countries', pp. 18–19.
23. Brown, *Corporal Brown's Campaigns*, pp. 146–51.
24. York had been informed of the government's decision in late November 1794: H. Dundas to York, Horse Guards, November 27 1794 in Charles Ross (ed.), *Correspondence of Charles, First Marquis Cornwallis, Vol II* (London: 1859), p. 277.
25. Brown, *Corporal Brown's Campaigns*, p. 153.
26. Cook, 'The St George Diary', p. 241.
27. C.T. Atkinson, 'Gleanings from the Cathcart MSS: Part IV, The Netherlands, 1794–1795', *JSAHR* xxix (120) (1951), p. 148.

28. Brown, *Corporal Brown's Campaigns*, pp. 160–1.
29. Brown, *Corporal Brown's Campaigns*, pp. 142–3.
30. Brown, *Corporal Brown's Campaigns*, p. 142.
31. Fortescue, *A History of the British Army, IV*, p. 406.
32. Knight, *Britain against Napoleon*, p. 104.
33. Jeremy Black, *George III, America's Last King* (New Haven and London: Yale University Press, 2006, repr. 2008), p. 366; Muir, *Wellington*, p. 34.
34. Knight, *Britain against Napoleon*, p. 104.
35. Glover, *Peninsular Preparation*, p. 153.
36. Muir and Esdaile, 'Strategic Planning in a Time of Small Government', p. 6.
37. Michael Glover, *Wellington's Army in the Peninsula 1808-1814* (London: David & Charles, 1977), p. 21.
38. Bamford, *Sickness, Suffering and the Sword*, p. 5.
39. For accounts of the British defeat in South America in 1806–7 see: Ian Fletcher, *The Waters of Oblivion, The British Invasion of the Rio De La Plata 1806-1807* (Stroud: Spellmount, 2006); Ben Hughes, *The British Invasion of the River Plate 1806-1807, How the Redcoats were humbled and a nation was born* (Barnsley: Pen & Sword, 2013).
40. Knight, *Britain against Napoleon*, pp. 492–3.
41. Farrell, 'The dynamics of British military transformation', p. 782.
42. Muir and Esdaile, 'Strategic Planning in a Time of Small Government', pp. 21–2.
43. Muir and Esdaile, 'Strategic Planning in a Time of Small Government', pp. 22–3.
44. Hew Strachan, *Wellington's Legacy, The Reform of the British Army 1830-54* (Manchester: Manchester University Press, 1984), pp. 6–7, 250; Hew Strachan, *From Waterloo to Balaclava: Tactics, Technology, and the British Army, 1815-1854* (Cambridge: Press Syndicate of the University of Cambridge, 1985), pp. vii–viii; Peter Burroughs, 'An Unreformed Army? 1815–1868' in Chandler and Beckett, *Oxford History of the British Army*, pp. 161–86.
45. Peaty, 'Architect of Victory', p. 36.
46. Douglas W. Marshall, 'Military Maps of the Eighteenth Century and the Tower of London Drawing Room', *Imago Mundi*, Vol. 32 (1980), pp. 21–44 at p. 21.
47. Marshall, 'Military Maps of the Eighteenth Century', p. 24.
48. G.J. Evelyn, '"I learned what one ought not to do": The British Army in Flanders and Holland, 1793–95' in A.J. Guy (ed.), *The Road to Waterloo: The British Army and the Struggle Against Revolutionary and Napoleonic France, 1793-1815* (London: National Army Publications, 1990), p. 17.
49. For a detailed analysis of the training methods developed by Dundas and extended by York see: Houlding, *Fit for Service*. See also Chapter 1.
50. Mark Urban, Fusiliers, *How the British Army Lost America but Learned to Fight* (London: Faber & Faber, 2007), pp. 314–19.
51. Even Richard Glover has argued as much: Glover, *Peninsular Preparation*, pp. 115–16.
52. One of only a handful of exceptions being: Lieutenant Colonel Banastre Tarleton, *A History of the campaigns of 1780 and 1781, in the southern provinces of North America* (Dublin: Colles, 1787); J.G. Simcoe's, *military journal: a history of the operations of a partisan corps, called the Queen's Rangers, commanded by Lieut. Col. J.G. Simcoe, during the war of the American Revolution; now first published, with a memoir of the author and other additions* wasn't published until 1844. Although many memoirs by British, German and American officers were written, most were published in the later years of the nineteenth and early twentieth centuries, rather than in the period between the American War of Independence and the French Revolutionary/Napoleonic Wars. For a list of memoirs and their publication dates see: http://www.digitalbookindex.org/_search/search010hstusrevolutionpersonalnarrativesa.asp.
53. Piers Mackesy, 'What the British Army Learned' in Ronald Hoffmann and Peter J. Albert (eds), *Arms and Independence, The Military Character of the American Revolution* (Charlottesville: University of Virginia, 1984), pp. 191–215.

54. Gates, *The British Light Infantry Arm*, p. 106.; Phillip Haythornthwaite, *British Rifleman 1797–1815, Osprey Warriors Series No. 47* (Oxford: Osprey, 2002); Raymond P. Cusick, *Wellington's Rifles, The Origins, Development and Battles of the Rifle Regiments in the Peninsular War and at Waterloo 1758 to 1815* (Barnsley: Pen & Sword, 2013), pp. 87–118.

55. Examples include: Lieutenant Colonel A. Emmerich, *The Partisan in War: Or The Use of a Corps of Light Troops to an Army* (1789); Oberst-Leutnant von. Ewald, *Abhandlung von dem Dienst der liechten Truppen* (Flensburg, Schleswig & Leipzig: 1790); M. de Jeney, *The Partisan: Or the Art of Making War in Detachments* (1760); M. Lecointe, *The Science of Military Posts, for the use of Regimental Officers who Frequently Command Detached Parties* (1761), General P. Bourcet, *Principes de la guerre des montages* (Paris: 1775) and Jarry, *Instruction Concerning the Duties of Light Infantry in the Field* (1803).

56. Baron de Rothenberg's manual was titled: *Regulations for the Exercise of Riflemen and Light Infantry, and Instructions for their conduct in the field* (1799).

57. TNA WO/3/28: 'Army Circular of 12 March 1795'.

58. For detailed analysis of the workings of the Purchase System see Anthony P.C. Bruce, *The Purchase System in the British Army, 1660 – 1871* (London: Royal Historical Society, 1980).

59. Colonel Sir James Craig quoted in Peaty, 'Architect of Victory' pp. 339–48 ; Hugh Thomas, *The Story of Sandhurst* (London: Hutchinson, 1961), p. 20.

60. Glover, *Peninsular Preparation*, p. 152.

61. Hew Strachan, *The Politics of the Army* (Oxford: Clarendon, 1997), pp. 37–8.

62. Dundas to Grenville, 21 July 1798, *Dropmore, IV*, pp. 263–4.

63. Anthony Clayton, *The British Officer, Leading the Army from 1660 to the Present* (Harlow: Pearson Longman, 2007), pp. 71–2.

64. Glover, *Peninsular Preparation*, p. 199.

65. Peaty, 'Architect of Victory', p. 35.

66. S.P.G. Ward, *Wellington's Headquarters, A Study of the Administrative problems in the Peninsula 1809–1814* (Oxford: Oxford University Press, 1957), 'Appendix I: List of officers serving in the Adjutant-General's and Quartermaster-General's Departments in the Peninsula, 1 April 1809 to 25 June 1814', pp. 170–93.

67. Glover, *Peninsular Preparation*, pp. 187–210.

68. As demonstrated by Peaty, 'Architect of Victory', pp. 34–6.

69. John A. Lynn, *Giant of the Grand Siècle, The French Army, 1610–1715* (Cambridge: Cambridge University Press, 1997), pp. 270–3. For a discussion of the development of the French army and its administration before 1680 see Colin Jones, 'The Military Revolution and the Professionalization of the French Army under the Ancien Regime' in Clifford J. Rogers (ed.), *The Military Revolution Debate, Readings on the Transformation of Early Modern Europe* (Oxford: Westview, 1995), pp. 149–67.

70. Claus Telp, *The Evolution of Operational Art, 1740–1813 From Frederick the Great to Napoleon* (London: Frank Cass, 2005), p. 20; Christopher Duffy, *The Army of Frederick the Great* (London: David & Charles, 1974), pp. 37–9. For a more general study of reform in the Prussian army see William O. Shanahan, *Prussian Military Reforms 1786–1813* (New York: AMS Press, 1966). For the Austrians and Russians see Christopher Duffy, *The Army of Maria Theresa, The Armed Forces of Imperial Austria, 1740–1780* (London: David & Charles, 1977), pp. 28–30; Christopher Duffy, *Russia's Military Way to the West, Origins and Nature of Russian Military Power 1700–1800* (London: Routledge & Kegan Paul, 1981), pp. 142–5; John L.H. Keep, *Soldiers of the Tsar, Army and Society in Russia 1462–1874* (Oxford: Clarendon Press, 1985), pp. 242–3.

71. Andrew P. Janco, 'Training in the Amusements of Mars: Peter the Great, War Games and the Science of War, 1673–1699', *Russian History/Histoire Russe, 30 Nos. 1–2* (Spring–Summer) 2003, pp. 35–112.

72. Alexander Mikaberidze, *The Russian Officer Corps in the Revolutionary and Napoleonic Wars, 1792–1815* (Staplehurst: Spellmount, 2005), pp. 7–11 (General Introduction).

73. Catriona Kennedy, *Narratives of the French Revolutionary and Napoleonic Wars: Military and Civilian Experience in Britain and Ireland* (Basingstoke: Palgrave Macmillan, 2013), p. 46; David Bell, *The First Total War: Napoleon's Europe and the Birth of Modern Warfare As We Know It* (Boston: Houghton Mifflin, 2007), pp. 36–7.

74. Paddy Griffith, *The Art of War of Revolutionary France 1789–1802* (London: Greenhill, 1998), pp. 126–8.

75. Griffith, *The Art of War of Revolutionary France*, pp. 126–8.

76. Griffith, *The Art of War of Revolutionary France*, p. 128.

77. Griffith, *The Art of War of Revolutionary France*, p. 127.

78. Griffith, *The Art of War of Revolutionary France*, p. 127.

79. David G. Chandler (ed.), *Napoleon's Marshals* (London: Weidenfeld & Nicolson, 1987), p. 7 (General Introduction).

80. Jeremy Black, *European Warfare 1660–1815* (London and New Haven: Yale University Press, 1994), p. 237.

81. F.B. Sullivan, 'The Origin and Development of Education in the Royal Navy from 1702 to 1802' (Ph.D. thesis, University of Reading, May 1975), pp. 8–9.

82. F.D. Artz, *The Development of Technical Education in France 1500–1850* (Cambridge: MIT Press, 1966), pp. 54–5.

83. Lewis Maidwell, *An essay upon the necessity and excellency of education. With an account of erecting the Royal Mathematical School* (London: J. Nutt, 1705).

84. Sullivan, 'The Origin and Development of Education in the Royal Navy', pp. 140–2.

85. Sullivan, 'The Origin and Development of Education in the Royal Navy', pp. 145–7.

86. Stanley Hoffmann, 'Rousseau on War and Peace', *The American Political Science Review*, Vol. 57 No. 2 (Jun. 1963), pp. 317–33.

87. Azar Gat, *The Origins of Military Thought, From the Enlightenment to Clausewitz* (Oxford: Clarendon, 1989), pp. 25–53; Peter Paret, *The Cognitive Challenge of War, Prussia 1806* (Princeton: Princeton University Press, 2009), pp. 79–81; R.R. Palmer, 'Frederick the Great, Guibert, Bulow: From Dynastic to National War', pp. 91–119; Spenser Wilkinson, *The French Army before Napoleon* (Oxford: Clarendon, 1915), pp. 33–67; Milan N. Vego, *Joint Operational Warfare, Theory and Practice* (London: The Government Printing Office, 2009), p. v–13.

88. Sandra L. Powers, 'Studying the Art of War: Military Books known to American Officers and their French counterparts during the Second half of the Eighteenth-Century', *JMHS*, Vol. 70 No. 3 (Jul. 2006), pp. 781–814. Two studies worthy of note regarding the British Officer Corps during this earlier period are: M.Odintz, 'The British Officer Corps 1754–1783' (Ph.D. thesis, University of Michigan, 1988) and A. Guy, *Economy and Discipline: officership and administration in the British Army 1714–1783* (Dover: Manchester University Press, 1985); J.L. Pimlott, 'The Administration of the British Army, 1783–1793' (Ph.D. thesis, Leicester University, 1975).

89. Edward J. Jowell, *The Hessians and the other German auxiliaries of Great Britain in the Revolutionary War* (New York: Harper & Brothers, 1884), pp. 226–7; Powers, 'Studying the Art of War', p. 791.

90. Gary Sheffield, 'Review of Anthony Clayton, *The British Officer, Leading the Army from 1660 to the Present, AHR*, Vol. 111 No. 5 (Dec. 2006), pp. 1593–4 at p. 1593; John P. Kiszely, 'The Relevance of History to the Military Profession: a British view' in Murray and Sinnreich (eds), *The Past as Prologue*, pp. 23–33 at p. 24.

91. Houlding, *Fit for Service*, pp. 220–1. Two writers to place an emphasis on the need for military education in Britain were Lewis Locheé, *An Essay on Military Education* (1773) and Major Robert Donkin, *Military Collections and Remarks* (New York: 1777). Examples of the general type of British military writings available to serving officers during the late eighteenth and early nineteenth centuries are as follows: Thomas Simes, *Military Medley* (1768); An Old Officer,

Cautions and Advices to officers of the Army (Edinburgh: Aeneas Mackay, 1777); Major William Young, *Manoeuvres, or Practical Observations on the Art of War* (1771). See also: Ira Gruber, *Books and the British Army in the Age of the American Revolution* (Chapel Hill: University of North Carolina Press, 2010).

92. Corelli Barnet, 'The Education of Military Elites', *Journal of Contemporary History*, Vol. 2 No. 3 (Jul. 1967), pp. 15–35 at p. 18.

93. Gat, *The Origins of Military Thought*, pp. 67–8; James Jay Carafano, 'Lloyd, Henry Humphrey Evans (*c*.1718–1783)', *Oxford Dictionary of National Biography* (Oxford: Oxford University Press, 2004), http://www.oxforddnb.com/view/article/16836; Patrick J. Speelman, *Henry Lloyd and the Military Enlightenment of Eighteenth-Century Europe* (London: Praeger, 2002).

94. Paret, *The Cognitive Challenge of War*, pp. 79–83; Peter Paret, 'Education, Politics, and War in the Life of Clausewitz', *Journal of the History of Ideas*, Vol. 29 No. 3 (Jul.–Sep., 1968), pp. 394–408 at p. 399.

95. For a detailed study of the Berlin Military Society see: Charles Edward White, *The enlightened soldier: Scharnhorst and the Militärische Gesellschaft in Berlin, 1801–1805* (New York: Praeger, 1989); further information at: http://www.scholarly-societies.org/history/White.html.

96. Jānis Langins, *Conserving the Enlightenment: French Military Engineering from Vauban to the Revolution* (Cambridge: MIT Press, 2004), p. 200; David G. Chandler, *The Campaigns of Napoleon* (London: Weidenfeld & Nicolson, 1967), p. 136.

97. Strachan, *The Politics of the Army*, p. 126.

98. Huw Strachan, *The Reform of the British army, 1830–54* (Manchester: Manchester University Press, 1984), p. 126.

99. Ward, *Wellington's Headquarters*, p. 159.

100. Strachan, *The Politics of the Army*, p. 31–3.

101. Walter H. James, Captain, Late Royal Engineers, 'Military Education and Training', *RUSI*, 26 (1883), p. 369 quoted in Andrew Limm, 'The British Army 1795 to 1815: An Army Transformed?' in Ross Mahoney, Stuart Mitchell and Michael LoCicero (eds), *Transformation and Innovation in the British Military 1792–1945* (Solihull: Helion, 2014).

Chapter 3

1. David Hollins, *The Battle of Marengo 1800* (Oxford: Osprey, 2000), pp. 40–85.

2. Piers Mackesy, *Statesmen at War, The Strategy of Overthrow 1798–1799* (London: Longman, 1974), pp. 4–9. Michael Duffy, 'Pitt, Grenville and the Control of British Foreign Policy in the 1790s' in Jeremy Black (ed.), *Knights Errant and True Englishmen: British Foreign Policy, 1660–1800* (Edinburgh: John Donald, 1989), pp. 168–9; John M. Sherwig, 'Lord Grenville's plan for a concert of Europe, 1797–99', *JMH*, Vol. 34 No. 3 (Sep., 1962), pp. 284–93 at p. 292.

3. Cyril Matheson, *The Life of Sir Henry Dundas, First Viscount Melville 1742–1811* (London: Constable, 1933), pp. 223–4.

4. Mackesy, *Statesmen at War*, pp. 11–12. Sherwig, 'Lord Grenville's plan for a concert of Europe, p. 285; Ehrman, *The Younger Pitt*, p. 520.

5. Paul Schroeder, 'The Collapse of the Second Coalition', *JMH*, Vol. 59 No. 2 (Jun. 1987), pp. 244–90 at p. 260.

6. Ehrman, *The Younger Pitt*, p. 644. For a traditional view of Tsar Paul I see: A.B. Rodger, *The War of the Second Coalition 1798 to 1801, A Strategic Commentary* (Oxford: Clarendon, 1964), p. 1 and for a revisionist perspective see Muriel Atkin, 'The Pragmatic Diplomacy of Paul I: Russia's Relations with Asia 1796–1801', *Slavic Review*, Vol. 38 No. 1 (Mar. 1979), pp. 60–74.

7. Hugh Ragsdale, 'Russia, Prussia, and Europe in the Policy of Paul I', *Jahrbücher für Geschichte Osteuropas, Neue Folge*, Bd. 31 H. 1 (1983), pp. 81–118 at p. 82; Ole Feldbæk, 'The Foreign Policy of Tsar Paul I, 1800–1801: An Interpretation', *Jahrbücher für Geschichte Osteuropas, Neue Folge*, Bd. 30 H. 1 (1982), pp. 16–36, p. 18.

8. Dennis Castillo, *The Maltese Cross: A Strategic History of Malta* (Westport: Praeger, 2006) p. 110.

9. Mackesy, *Statesmen at War*, p. 74.
10. 1 April 1798, 'Minute of a conference with Count Starhemburg, Inclusive of a despatch received from his court on 18 March', *Dropmore, VI,* pp. 153–4.
11. Mackesy, *Statesmen at War*, pp. 74–5.
12. 30 April 1798, Lord Spencer to Lord Grenville, *Dropmore, VI*, p. 181.
13. Colonel K.W. Maurice-Jones, *History of Coast Artillery in the British Army* (Uckfield: Naval & Military Press, 2009), pp. 86–90; John A. Murphy, *The French are in the Bay: The Expedition to Bantry Bay* (Cork: Mercier Press, 1997).
14. Mackesy, *Statesmen at War*, p. 3; G.E Mainwaring, 'The Expedition to Ostend in 1798. Blowing up the Gates of the Bruges Canal', *RUSI*, No. 63 (1 Feb. 1918), p. 624.
15. Anon., *British Minor Expeditions*, pp. 28–30; Sir Eyre Coote to H. Dundas, on a ridge of Sand Hills, three miles to the East of Ostend, May 19, 1798, *London Gazette*, Saturday, 21 July 1798. For a recent study of the Zeebrugge Raid see: Paul Kendall, *The Zeebrugge Raid 1918 'The Finest Feat of Arms'* (Brimscombe Port: Spellmount, 2008).
16. Pitt to Grenville, 16 August 1798, *Dropmore, IV*, pp. 283–4.
17. A.B. Piechowiak, 'The Anglo-Russian Expedition to Holland in 1799', *The Slavonic and East European Review,* Vol. 41 No. 96 (Dec. 1962), pp. 183–4.
18. D.C. Elliot, 'The Grenville Mission to Berlin, 1799', *HLQ,* Vol. 18 No. 2 (Feb. 1955), pp. 129–30.
19. W. Pitt, W. W. Grenville, Wm. Eden, J. Holland Rose, 'The Missions of William Grenville to the Hague and Versailles in 1787', *EHR*, Vol. 24 No. 94 (Apr. 1909), pp. 278–95.
20. Mackesy, *Statesmen at War*, pp. 74–5.
21. Mackesy, *Statesmen at War*, pp. 76–85.
22. Rothenberg, *Napoleons Great Adversaries*, p. 59.
23. For a detailed analysis of Allied planning in 1798 and Anglo-Russian negotiations see Mackesy, *Statesmen at War*, pp. 76–92.
24. Lord Grenville to Rufus King, November 1798, *Dropmore, IV*, p. 366.
25. Lord Grenville to Sir Charles Whitworth, 16 November 1798, *Dropmore, IV*, p. 379.
26. Mackesy, *Statesmen at War*, pp. 36–7.
27. Grenville to King, *Dropmore, IV,* p. 365.
28. John M. Sherwig, *Guineas and Gunpowder, British Foreign Aid in the Wars with France 1793–1815* (Cambridge: Harvard University Press, 1969), p. 120; Anon., *British Minor Expeditions, 1746 to 1814, Compiled in the Intelligence Branch of the Quartermaster-General's Department* (London: 1884), p. 32; John A. Lukas, 'Russian Armies in Western Europe: 1799, 1814, 1917', *American Slavic and East European Review,* Vol. 13 No. 3 (Oct. 1954), p. 332; Piechowiak, 'The Anglo-Russian Expedition to Holland in 1799', p. 184.
29. J. Holland Rose review of M.H. Weil, 'Le Général de Stamford, d'après sa Correspondance Inédite, 1793–1806', *EHR*, Vol. 39 No. 154 (Apr. 1924), pp. 297–8.
30. Mackesy, *Statesmen at War*, p. 106.
31. Mackesy, *Statesmen at War*, p. 109; Hugh Popham, *A Damned Cunning Fellow – The Eventful Life of Rear-Admiral Sir Home Popham, K.C.B., K.C.H., K.M., F.R.S., 1762–1820* (Tywardreath: The Old Ferry, 1991), p. 256.
32. Michael Duffy, *Soldiers, Sugar and Seapower, the British expeditions to the West Indies and the war against revolutionary France* (Oxford: Clarendon Press, 1987), p. 185.
33. Mackesy, *Statesmen at War*, p. 111.
34. Mackesy, *Statesmen at War*, pp. 111–14.
35. Hall, *British Strategy in the Napoleonic War*, p. 43; Rodger, *The Command of the Ocean*, p. 475. For a wider study of the problems encountered by the British in the procurement of maritime transportation see: David Syrett, *Shipping and Military Power in the Seven Year War, 1756–1763, The Sails of Victory* (Liverpool: Liverpool University Press, 2008); David Syrett, *Shipping and the American War 1775–1783: A Study of British Transport Organization* (London: Athlone Press, 1970).

36. Paul Patrick Reese, '"The Ablest Man in the British Army" The Life and Career of General Sir John Hope' (Ph.D thesis, Electronic Theses, Treatise and Dissertations, Florida State University, 2007), p. 38; Coleman O. Williams, 'The Role of the British Navy in the Helder Campaign, 1799' (Ph.D. dissertation, Auburn University, 1995), pp. 76–9.

37. Rothenberg, *Napoleon's Great Adversaries*, p. 54; Elting, *Swords Around a Throne*, p. 53.

38. Steven T. Ross, 'The Military Strategy of the Directory: The Campaigns of 1799', *French Historical Studies*, Vol. 5 No. 2 (Autumn, 1967), pp. 170–87 at pp. 175–6; Fortescue, *A History of the British Army, Vol. IV*, pp. 628–31; Rodger, *The War of the Second Coalition*, pp. 158–64.

39. Howard G. Brown, 'Review of Alan Forrest: The Revolution in Provincial France: Aquitaine, 1789–1799', *JMH*, Vol. 71 No. 3 (Sept. 1999), pp. 708–9.

40. Ross, 'The Military Strategy of the Directory: The Campaigns of 1799', pp. 174–6.

41. *Introduction to Dropmore, V*, p. 7.

42. Fortescue, *A History of the British Army, Vol. IV*, p. 630.

43. Blanning, *The French Revolutionary Wars*, pp. 230–8.

44. Duffy, *Soldiers, Sugar and Seapower*, pp. 328–33.

45. H. Dundas to Grenville, 21 July 1798, *Dropmore, IV*, p. 264.

46. BL Add 43770: H. Dundas, 'Effective army in Great Britain', 1st October 1798, Melville Papers, Vol. IV, 1794–1804.

47. Mackesy, *Statesmen at War*, p. 166.

48. TNA WO 1/180: 'Projected arrangement of the troops ordered for service under the command of Lieutenant-General Sir Ralph Abercromby, June 1799', Commanders Dispatches, Helder Expedition, p. 5; TNA WO 1/179: Deputy Adjutant-General Sir J. Hope, 'State of the troops under the command of Lieut-General Sir Ralph Abercromby 31 July 1799'; TNA WO 1/179: Hope to Dundas, 'Return of the Troops under the command of Sir Ralph Abercromby, 4 Aug 1799'. BL Add MSS 38735: 'Formation of the brigades assembled at Barham Downs', The Huskisson Papers Vol. II Correspondence 1798–1799.

49. David Armitage and Sanjay Subrahmanyam (eds), *The Age of Revolutions in Global Context c. 1760–1840* (Basingstoke: Palgrave Macmillan, 2010), p. 48.

50. For a detailed analysis of the recruitment system in the British army see: Kevin Linch, *Britain and Wellington's Army, Recruitment, Society and Tradition, 1807–15* (Basingstoke: Palgrave Macmillan, 2011), pp. 31–44, 83–98.

51. Cookson, *The British Armed Nation*, p. 32.

52. Kennedy, *Narratives of the Revolutionary and Napoleonic Wars*, p. 35.

53. Fortescue, *History of the British Army, Vol. IV*, pp. 639–42.

54. Conway, 'The Politics of British Military and Naval Mobilization', p. 1182.

55. Lois G. Schwoerer, 'The Grenville Militia List for Buckinghamshire, 1798–1799', *HLQ*, Vol. 68 No. 4 (Dec. 2005), pp. 667–76 at p. 673.

56. Fortescue, *A History of the British Army, Vol. IV*, pp. 641–2.

57. Glover, *Peninsular Preparation*, pp. 25, 227; Phillip. J Haythornthwaite, *The Armies of Wellington* (London: Brockhampton, 1998), p. 51.

58. Ian. F.W. Beckett, *The Amateur Military Tradition, 1558–1945* (Manchester: Manchester University Press, 1991), p. 79.

59. Linch, 'The Recruitment of the British Army 1807–1815', p. 140.

60. The chosen units were the 4th; 5th; 9th; 17th; 20th; 35th; 40th; 56th; 63rd; 31st Regiments of Foot.

61. Mackesy, *Statesmen at War*, p. 155.

62. BL Add MSS 38735: 'General return of the effective numbers of the regiments as they are encamped upon Barham Downs – the 14th August 1799 with observations', The Huskisson Papers, Vol. II Correspondence 1798–1799.

63. BL Add MSS 3873: General Morning state of the troops encamped upon Barham Downs – 18 August 1799', The Huskisson Papers, Vol. II Correspondence 1798–1799; BL Add MSS 38735:

'Formation of Brigades assembled at Barham Downs', The Huskisson Papers, Vol. II Correspondence 1798–1799; BL Add MSS 38735: General Morning state of the troops encamped upon Barham Downs – 18 August 1799', The Huskisson Papers, Vol. II Correspondence 1798–1799. The Brigades were organised as follows: 1st Brigade Major-General The Earl of Chatham – comprising three battalions (Bn) of the 4th Regiment (Regt) of foot and one Bn 31st Regt of foot (2800 rank and file(r & f)); 2nd Brigade Major General H.R.H Prince William – 2 Bn 5th Regt of Foot, 2 Bn 35th Regt of Foot (2715 r & f); 3rd Brigade Major General Manners – 2 Bn 9th Regt Foot, 1 Bn 56th Regt Foot (2767 r & f); 4th Brigade-Major General Don 2 Bn 17th Regt Foot, 2 Bn 40th Regt Foot (2366 r & f); 5th Brigade Major-General Earl of Cavan – 2 Bn 20th Regt Foot, 1 Bn 63rd Regt Foot (2086 r & f) Total r & f: 12, 734.

64. James Lord Dunfermline, *Lieutenant-General Sir Ralph Abercromby 1793–1801, A Memoir by his son* (Uckfield: Naval & Military Press), pp. 19–20.

65. T.A. Heathcote, *Wellington's Peninsular War Generals & Their Battles, A Biographical and Historical Dictionary* (Barnsley: Pen & Sword, 2010), p. 140.

66. TNA WO 1/179: 'Instructions' sited by Abercromby to Grenville, 6 July 1799, p. 6.

67. BL Add MSS 38735: 'Formation of the brigades assembled at Barham Downs', The Huskisson Papers, Vol. II Correspondence 1798–1799.

68. Piechowiak, 'The Anglo-Russian Expedition to Holland in 1799', pp. 185–6.

69. Mackesy, *Statesmen at War*, p. 136.

70. TNA WO 1/ 179: Sir Ralph Abercromby to Lord Grenville, 6 July 1799; Reese, 'The Ablest Man in the British Army', pp. 39–41.

71. TNA WO 1/ 179: Abercromby to Grenville, 6 July 1799; BL Add MSS 40101: Melville Papers Vol. II, Lord Grenville to Dundas, 30 July 1799, pp. 25–9.

72. BL Add MSS 72703L: Grenville to Pitt, 1 August 1799.

73. BL Add MSS 72703L: 'Letter from Grenville to Pitt arguing in favour of the planned Allied expedition to the Netherlands', Cleveland Row, 1 August 1799.

74. Mackesy, *Statesmen at War*, p. 191.

75. Mackesy, *Statesmen at War*, p. 190.

76. Mackesy, *Statesmen at War*, p. 164.

77. Fortescue, *A History of the British Army, Vol. IV*, pp. 648–9.

78. Mackesy, *Statesmen at War*, p. 173.

79. J. David Davies, 'Adam Viscount Duncan, 1731–1804' in Peter Le Fevre and Richard Harding (eds), *British Admirals of the Napoleonic Wars, The Contemporaries of Nelson* (London: Chatham Publishing, 2005), p. 63.

80. Rodger, *The War of the Second Coalition*, p. 176.

81. TNA WO 1/179: Abercromby to H. Dundas, HMS Isis, 14 August 1799 Commanders Dispatches, Helder Expedition.

82. TNA WO 1/179: Abercromby to H. Dundas, HMS Isis 23 August and 24 August 1799, Commanders, Dispatches, Helder Expedition.

83. BL Add MSS 40102: Melville Papers, Vol. III: Admiral Duncan to H. Dundas, HMS Kent off the Texel 24 August 1799, Melville Papers, Vol. III: Drafts and Manuscripts 1794–1805.

84. The list of Dutch forces is taken from an amalgam of those noted in Mackesy, *Statesmen at War*, p. 194; J.W. Fortescue, *A History of the British Army, Vol. IV, Part II, 1789–1801* (London: Macmillan, 1906), p. 653. For a more detailed analysis of the Batavian defences see Lieutenant General H.W. Daendels, *Rapport des opérations de la division du lieutenant-general Daendels, depuis le 22 août, jusqu'à la capitulation de l'Armeé Anglais et Russe, le 18 octobre 1799* (The Hague, n.d.).

85. TNA, WO 1/179: Abercromby to H. Dundas, The Helder, 28 August 1799, Commanders' Dispatches, Helder Expedition.

86. Fortescue, *A History of the British Army, Vol. IV, Part II*, pp. 654–5.

87. E.Walsh, *A Narrative of the Expedition to Holland in the autumn of the year 1799 Illustrated with a map of north Holland and Seven Views* (London: G.G and J. Robinson, Pater-Noster, S. Hanson, 1800), pp. 27–8.

88. Mackesy, *British Victory in Egypt*, p. 38.

89. This was the officer who had formerly been known as Sir James Murray and had been York's ADC during the Dunkirk campaign in 1793; he became Murray-Pulteney in 1794.

90. J.F. Maurice, *The Diary of Sir John Moore, Vol. 1* (London: Arnold, 1904), p. 342.

91. TNA WO 1/179: Sir Ralph Abercromby to Sir Henry Dundas, The Helder, 28 August 1799, Commanders' Dispatches, Helder Expedition.

92. Major Francis Maule, *Late of the 2nd or Queens Regiment and on the Staff on the Severn District, Memoirs of the Principal Events in the Campaigns of North Holland and Egypt Together with a Brief Description of the Islands of Crete, Rhodes, Syracuse, Minorca and the Voyage to the Mediterranean* (Uckfield: Naval & Military Press), p. 7.

93. Maurice, *The Diary of Sir John Moore, Vol. 1*, p. 343.

94. Anon., *The New Annual Register, or General Repository of History, Politics and Literature, For the Year 1799* (London: 1805), pp. 107–8.

95. TNA WO 1/182: 'A list of the Dutch ships and vessels taken and destroyed in the late expedition against Holland by His Majesty's squadron under the command of Admiral Mitchell', p. 17.

96. TNA, WO 1/179: Abercromby to H. Dundas, The Helder, 4 September 1799, Dispatches, Helder Expedition.

97. TNA, WO 1/179: Abercromby to H. Dundas, The Helder, 4 September 1799, Dispatches, Helder Expedition.

98. TNA, WO 1/179: Abercromby to H. Dundas, The Helder, 4 September 1799, Dispatches, Helder Expedition.

99. BL Add MSS 38735: Huskisson Papers: Captain W. Young, Ramsgate 18 August 1799.

100. Piechowiak, 'The Anglo-Russian Expedition to Holland in 1799', p. 188: The first Russian force consisted of 6,000 men and had been transported to the Helder in seven warships converted to act as troop ships; plus one troop transport. The largest Russian vessel in the first convoy was the *Alex Neskoi*, a 74-gun ship-of-the-line. The remaining six warships ranged in size from 66-gunners, which could carry 850 soldiers, to the 38-gun *Nicolai*, which had space for 250 officers and men. The British transport *Neptune* transported 200 men.

101. Mackesy, *Statesmen at War*, p. 216.

102. Maurice, *The Diary of Sir John Moore, Vol. 1*, p. 346.

103. Maurice, *The Diary of Sir John Moore, Vol. 1*, p. 347.

104. TNA WO 1/179: Abercromby to H. Dundas, Headquarters Schafen Bas, 11 September 1799.

105. TNA WO 1/179: Abercromby to H. Dundas, Headquarters Schafen Bas, 11 September 1799; Lieutenant Colonel Nathaniel Steevens (ed.), *Lt. Colonel Charles Steevens, Reminisces of my Military Life, from 1795 to 1818* (Winchester: Warren & Sons, n.d.): Steevens commanded the 20th following the Battle of the Zype.

106. TNA WO 1/180: York to H. Dundas, Commanders Dispatches, Helder Expedition, the Helder, 14 September 1799, p. 71.

107. TNA WO 1/180: H. Dundas to York, 5 September 1799, pp. 3–4.

108. Lieutenant General Sir Henry Bunbury, *Narratives of some passages in the Great War with France. From 1799 to 1810* (London: Richard Bentley, 1854), pp. 6, 43.

109. Piechowiak, 'The Anglo-Russian Expedition to Holland in 1799', pp. 189–90.

110. TNA WO 1/180: York to H. Dundas, 19 September 1799, p. 125.

111. For a detailed breakdown of the Allied Order of Battle on 19 September and for York's instructions see TNA WO 1/180: York to H. Dundas, 19 September 1799, pp. 125–30.

112. Bunbury, *Narratives*, p. 50.

113. William Surtees, *Twenty-Five Years in the Rifle Brigade* (London: T. Cadall, 1833), pp. 10–13.

114. Maurice, *The Diary of Sir John Moore, Vol. 1*, p. 348.

115. Bunbury, *Narratives*, p. 22.
116. TNA WO 1/180: Taylor to York, 'Report of the proceedings of the Right column of Russians under the command of Lieut-General Hermann in the attack of the 19 Sept 1799', Head Quarters Schaagen Brug, 20 September 1799, pp. 169–83. The author of this source was York's trusted ADC, Taylor, who as a French and German speaker was tasked with acting as a means of liaison between the Russian high command and the British. Taylor was well suited to this role, having been ADC to Murray-Pulteney in Flanders in 1793 and had been made assistant secretary to York in 1795. For more on Taylor and family see R.H. Vetch, 'Taylor, Sir Herbert (1775–1839)', rev. K.D. Reynolds, *Oxford Dictionary of National Biography* (Oxford: Oxford University Press, 2004); online edn, Jan. 2008, http://www.oxforddnb.com/view/article/27031, accessed 17 May 2012.
117. TNA WO 1/180: Taylor, 'Report of the proceedings', 20 September 1799, p. 171.
118. TNA WO 1/180: Taylor, 'Report of the proceedings', 20 September 1799, pp. 173–4.
119. Mackesy, *Statesmen at War* , p. 266.
120. TNA WO 1/180: Taylor, 'Report of the proceedings', 20 September 1799, p. 176.
121. Mackesy, *Statesmen at War*, p. 263.
122. Bunbury, *Narratives*, p. 16.
123. TNA WO 1/ 180: Copy of a letter from Murray-Pulteney to York dated by AG Colonel Sir John Hope, 20 September 1799, p. 159.
124. Bunbury, *Narratives*, p. 16.
125. TNA WO 1/ 180: Copy of a letter from Coote to Murray-Pulteney, 20 September 1799, p. 156.
126. TNAWO 1/ 180: Murray-Pulteney to York, 20 September 1799, p. 159.
127. TNA WO 1/ 180: Murray-Pulteney to York, 20 September 1799, p. 161.
128. TNA WO 1/ 180: Murray-Pulteney to York, 20 September 1799, p. 162.
129. TNA WO 1/180: Taylor, 'Report of the proceedings', 20 September 1799, pp. 179–80.
130. TNA WO 1/180: Taylor, 'Report of the proceedings', 20 September 1799, pp. 181–2.
131. TNA WO 1/180: Taylor, 'Report of the proceedings', 20 September 1799, pp. 182–3.
132. TNA WO 1/180: Taylor, 'Report of the proceedings', 20 September 1799, p. 183.
133. Bunbury, *Narratives* pp. 18–20.
134. Bunbury, *Narratives*, p. 19.
135. Mackesy, *Statesmen at War*, p. 274.
136. TNA WO 1/180: York to H. Dundas, 20 September 1799, p. 131.
137. York to H. Dundas, 20 September 1799, *Dropmore, V*, pp. 416–17; Piechowiak, 'The Anglo-Russian Expedition to Holland in 1799', p. 190.
138. Bunbury, *Narratives*, p. 23.
139. Ferdinand Brock Tupper (ed.), *The Life and Correspondence of Major-General Sir Isaac Brock* (London: Simpkin, Marshal, 1847), pp. 10–11.
140. Surtees, *Twenty-Five Years in the Rifle Brigade*, pp. 8–9, 13.
141. Bunbury, *Narratives*, p. 23.
142. Tupper, *The Life and Correspondence of Major-General Sir Isaac Brock*, pp. 11–12.
143. Jonathan Keep, *Soldiers of the Tsar, Army and Society in Russia 1462–1874* (Oxford: Clarendon, 1984), pp. 155–6.
144. Duffy, *Russia's Military Way to the West*, p. 125.
145. Mackesy, *Statesmen at War*, p. 225; Vincent J. Esposito and John R. Elting, *A Military History and Atlas of the Napoleonic Wars* (London: Greenhill, 1999, orig. publ. Praeger: 1964), map 35.
146. Mark Melenovsky, 'The Influence of the French Revolution and Napoleon on the Imperial Russian Army, 1789–1814', Consortium on Revolutionary Europe, 1750–1850 (1994), pp. 501–9 at p. 501. Tensions within the officer corps continued throughout the Napoleonic Wars and came to a head in 1812, with the mutiny of several senior Russian commanders in response to the perceived incompetence of the rest of their colleagues. For a detailed analysis of the mutiny see Alexander Mikaberidze, 'The Conflict of Command in the Russian army in 1812: Peter Bagration and Barclay de Tolly in the "Mutiny of Generals", in Frederick C. Schneid, *Warfare in Europe 1792–1795* (Aldershot: Ashgate, 2007), pp. 365–76; Alexander Mikaberidze,

The Russian Officer Corps in the Revolutionary and Napoleonic Wars, 1792–1815 (Staplehurst: Spellmount, 2005). See also John P. LeDonne, 'Outlines of Russian Military Administration 1762–1796 Part II: The High Command', *Jahrbücher für Geschichte Osteuropas, Neue Folge*, Bd. 33 H. 2 (1985), pp. 175–204.

147. Melenovsky, 'The Influence of the French Revolution and Napoleon on the Imperial Russian Army', p. 501.

148. For an analysis of the long-term influence of Suvorov's military writings see: Bruce W. Menning, 'Train Hard, Fight Easy: The Legacy of A. V. Suvorov and his "Art of Victory"', *Air University Review* (Nov.–Dec. 1986), pp. 79–88; Gunther E. Rothenberg, *The Art of Warfare in the Age of Napoleon* (Staplehurst: Spellmount, 1997, orig. pub. 1978), pp. 21–2.

149. Bruce W. Menning, 'Russian Military Innovation in the Second Half of the Eighteenth Century' in Jeremy Black (ed.), *Warfare in Europe 1650–1792, The International Library of Essays on Military History* (Aldershot: Ashgate, 2005), pp. 275–93 at p. 289.

150. John L.H. Keep, 'The Russian Army's Response to the French Revolution', *Jahrbücher für Geschichte Osteuropas, Neue Folge*, Bd. 28 H. 4 (1980), pp. 500–23 at pp. 506–7.

151. Keep, 'The Russian Army's Response to the French Revolution', p. 510.

152. Christopher Duffy, *Eagles over the Alps, Suvorov in Italy and Switzerland, 1799* (Chicago: The Emperors Press, 1999), p. 28.

153. For a detailed analysis of the Russian army's supply problems in the period before 1799 see John Keep, 'Feeding the Troops: Russian Army Supply Policies during the Seven Years War' in Jeremy Black (ed.), *Warfare in Europe 1650–1792, The International Library of Essays on Military History* (Aldershot: Ashgate, 2005), pp. 253–73.

154. TNA WO 1/180: York to H. Dundas, 20 September 1799, p. 132.

155. Walsh, *A Narrative of the Expedition to Holland in the autumn of the year 1799*, p. 63.

156. Mackesy, *Statesmen at War*, p. 281.

157. Walsh, *A Narrative of the Expedition to Holland*, p. 63.

158. Maurice, *The Diary of Sir John Moore, Vol. 1*, p. 353.

159. TNA WO 1/180: York to H. Dundas, 'Dispositions for the attack to be made upon the left of the enemy's position', September 1799, pp. 249–53. The total strength of the Allied army deployed at the Battle of Alkmaar on 2 October was 29,870 officers and men.

160. Walsh, *A Narrative of the Expedition to Holland*, p. 65.

161. Surtees, *Twenty-Five Years in the Rifle Brigade*, p. 15.

162. TNA WO 1/180: York to H. Dundas, 6 October 1799, Headquarters, Alkmaar, p. 358.

163. Lieutenant Colonel C. Greenhill Gardyne, *The Life of a Regiment or, the Origin and History of the Gordon Highlanders from its formation in 1794 to 1816* (Edinburgh: David & Douglas, 1901), p. 67.

164. TNA WO 1/180: York to H. Dundas, 6 October 1799, Headquarters, Alkmaar, pp. 358–9.

165. Bunbury, *Narratives*, pp. 25–6.

166. Maurice, *The Diary of Sir John Moore, Vol. 1*, p. 355.

167. Tupper, *The Life and Correspondence of Major-General Sir Isaac Brock*, pp. 12–13.

168. Maurice, *The Diary of Sir John Moore, Vol. 1*, pp. 355–6.

169. TNA WO 1/180: York to H. Dundas, 6 October 1799, Headquarters, Alkmaar, p. 359.

170. TNA WO 1/180: York to H. Dundas, 6 October 1799, Headquarters, Alkmaar, pp. 360–1.

171. TNA WO 1/180: York to H. Dundas, 6 October 1799, Headquarters, Alkmaar, p. 361.

172. Mackesy, *Statesmen at War*, p. 292. Moore was not the only British officer to be hit and several regimental commanders were killed and wounded, including Lieutenant Colonel Erskine of the 15th Light Dragoons, the Anglo-Dutch liaison officer Lieutenant Colonel Sontag and Captain Nickoll of the Royal Artillery. Colonel A. Campbell of the 79th Foot also suffered a mortal wound, whilst commanding a body of grenadiers in the sand hills, alongside Moore's brigade. The list also included tens of junior officers. For a detailed list of British officer casualties see TNA WO 1/180: 'Return of the Killed, Wounded and Missing of His Majesty's Forces under

the Command of His Royal Highness the Duke of York in the Battle of Bergen fought on 2nd October 1799, Headquarters Alkmaar 6th October 1799'.

173. Tupper, *The Life and Correspondence of Major-General Sir Isaac Brock*, p. 14.

174. Bunbury, *Narratives*, p. 24.

175. Hermann had been captured in the sand hills on 19 September in trying to rally his men.

176. Hunt, *Journal kept by Lieut. and Adjutant Hunt, of the 7th (or Queen's Own) Light Dragoons, during the Regiment's absence on the Expedition to North Holland, in the year 1799 RUSI*, 59 (1914: Jul./Nov.), pp. 169–70.

177. Maurice, *Diary of Sir John Moore, Vol. 1*, p. 358; Mackesy, *Statesmen at War*, p. 296.

178. Mackesy, *Statesmen at War*, pp. 294–6.

179. Walsh, *A Narrative of the Expedition to Holland*, pp. 80–1.

180. TNA WO 1/182: 'Statement of Supplies demanded from England, and the quantities arrived and purchased in Holland, for the use of the Army, as also number of persons victualed there from the 30th August to 18th November 1799', p. 305.

181. TNA WO 1/180: 'Opinions of Generals Sir Ralph Abercromby, Lieutenant-General Dundas, Hulse and Pulteney', Alkmaar, 6 October 1799, pp. 379–85.

182. TNA WO 1/180: 'Report of Lieut-Colonel Sontag, Military Commissary to the Dutch troops', 11 October 1799, pp. 481–2.

183. TNA WO 1/180: 'Report of Lieut-Colonel Sontag, Military Commissary to the Dutch troops', 11 October 1799, p. 483.

184. Schroeder, 'The Collapse of the Second Coalition', p. 245.

185. Mackesy, *Statesmen at War*, p. 307.

Chapter 4

1. Robert Harvard, *Wellington's Welsh General, A Life of Sir Thomas Picton* (London: Aurum Press, 1996), p. 106.

2. Hall, *British Strategy in the Napoleonic War*, p. 1.

3. Clive Emsley, 'Review of Cookson', *EHR*, Vol. 114 No. 455 (Feb. 1999), pp. 216–17; J.E. Cookson, 'The British Volunteer Movement of the French Wars 1793–1815: Some Contexts', *HJ*, Vol. 32 No. 4 (Dec. 1989), pp. 867–91; Clive Emsley, 'Wooden Walls and Volunteers: 1803–5' in C. Emsley (ed.), *British Society and the French Wars 1793–1815* (London and Basingstoke: Macmillan, 1979), pp. 99–123.

4. Linch, 'The Recruitment of the British Army', pp. 22–3.

5. Linch, 'The Recruitment of the British Army', p. 23.

6. Hall, *British Strategy in the Napoleonic War*, pp. 147–8.

7. *Minutes of a Court Martial holden on Board his Majesty's ship Gladiator, in Portsmouth Harbour, on Friday, the 6th day of March, 1807 And continued by Adjournment till Wednesday, March 11 following For the Trial of Capt. Sir Home Popham including a complete copy of his defence, taken from the original* (London: 1807), p. 43.

8. Fletcher, *The Waters of Oblivion*, pp. 25–40.

9. *Minutes of a Court Martial holden on Board his Majesty's ship Gladiator* (London: 1807), p. 180.

10. Hughes, *The British Invasion of the River Plate*, pp. 183–206; Jeremy Black, *Britain as a military power, 1688–1815* (London: UCL Press, 1999), pp. 250–1; Fletcher, *The Waters of Oblivion*, p. 93–122.

11. Vincent Robert Ham, 'Strategies of Coalition and Isolation: British War Policy and North-West Europe, 1803–1810' (D.Phil. thesis, University of Oxford, 1977), p. 292.

12. Brent Nosworthy, *Battle Tactics of Napoleon and his Enemies* (London: Constable, 1995), pp. 146–9; Richard Hopton, *The Battle of Maida 1806, Fifteen Minutes of Glory* (London: Leo Cooper, 2002).

13. Black, *Britain as a military power*, p. 204.

14. Hall, *British Strategy in the Napoleonic War*, pp. 118–19, 160; Ham, *Strategies of Coalition and Isolation*, p. 241.
15. Blanning, *The Pursuit of Glory*, p. 658.
16. Knight, *Britain against Napoleon*, pp. 400–1.
17. Richard Glover, *Britain at Bay, Defence against Bonaparte 1803–14* (London: George Allen & Unwin, 1973), p. 17, Rodger, *The Command of the Ocean*, p. 552.
18. Owen Connelly, *Napoleon's Satellite Kingdoms, Managing Conquered People* (Malabar: R.E. Krieger, 1965), pp. 132–4.
19. A.N. Ryan, 'The Causes of the British Attack upon Copenhagen in 1807', *EHR*, Vol. 68 No. 266 (Jan. 1953), pp. 37–55; A.N. Ryan, 'The Defence of British Trade with the Baltic, 1808–1813', *EHR*, Vol. 74 No. 292 (Jul. 1959), pp. 443–66.
20. C. Northcote Parkinson, *Britannia Rules, The Classic Age of Naval History 1793–1815* (Stroud: Sutton Publishing, 1997), p. 120.
21. Hilton, *A Mad, Bad & Dangerous People?*, p. 211.
22. Esdaile, *The Peninsular War*, p. 27.
23. Esdaile, *The Peninsular War*, pp. 62–86.
24. Muir, *Wellington*, pp. 234–57.
25. Muir, *Britain and the Defeat of Napoleon*, p. 68.
26. Phillip Haythornthwaite, *Corunna 1809, Sir John Moore's Fighting Retreat, Osprey Campaign Series No. 83* (Oxford: Osprey, 2001), pp. 22–66.
27. Esdaile, *History of the Peninsular War*, p. 140.
28. Christopher Hibbert, *Corunna,* (Moreton-in-Marsh: Windrush Press, repr., 1996), p. 149.
29. James Allen Vann, 'Habsburg Policy and the Austrian War of 1809', *Central European History,* Vol. 7 No. 4 (4 Dec. 1974), pp. 291–310 at p. 291; Rothenberg, *Napoleon's Great Adversaries*, p. 121.
30. Gordon C. Bond, *The Grand Expedition, The British invasion of Holland in 1809* (Athens: The University of Georgia Press, 1979), p. 6.
31. David G. Chandler, *The Campaigns of Napoleon* (London: Weidenfeld & Nicolson, 1966), p. 664.
32. Adam Zamoyski, *1812, Napoleon's Fatal March on Moscow* (London: Harper Collins, 2004), pp. 36–7.
33. Charles Esdaile, *Napoleon's War's, An International History* (London: Penguin, 2006), pp. 390–1.
34. Shering, *Guineas and Gunpowder*, p. 208.
35. Piers Mackesy, *War without Victory, The Downfall of Pitt 1799–1802* (Oxford: Oxford University Press, 1984), pp. 69–72.
36. J.W. Fortescue, *A History of the British Army, Vol. VII 1809–1810* (London: Macmillan, 1912), p. 37.
37. Anthony Brett-James, 'The Walcheren failure', Part One, *History Today*, Vol. 13 No. 12 (Dec. 1963), pp. 811.
38. For a comprehensive history of the 1809 campaign between Napoleon and the Austrians see: John H. Gill, *1809 Thunder on the Danube, Napoleon's defeat of the Habsburgs,* 3 vols (Barnsley: Frontline, 2008–10).
39. Brett-James, 'The Walcheren failure', Part One, p. 811.
40. Richard Glover, 'The French Fleet, 1807–1814: Britain's Problem: and Madison's Opportunity', *JMH*, Vol. 39 No. 3 (Sep. 1967), p. 233.
41. Glover, 'The French Fleet', *JMH*, Vol. 39, No. 3, p. 235.
42. Hall, *British Strategy in the Napoleonic War,* pp. 10–11.
43. BL Add Ms 38735: Lord Spencer to Sir William Huskisson, 25 April 1798, Huskisson Papers Vol. II Correspondence 1798–1799; Abercromby to Grenville, July 20 1799 in Fortescue, *Dropmore, V–VII* (His Majesty's Stationery Office, 1906), p. 165.

44. *Substance of General Craufurd's speech in the House of Commons on Tuesday March 27th 1810 upon the Inquiry into the Policy and conduct of the Expedition to the Scheldt.* (London: John Stockdale, 1810), pp. 27–32.

45. Vice Admiral Thomas Russell had extensive experience in blockade duties. Russell, for example, had spent much of 1801 stationed off the Flanders coast and also in close proximity to the ports of Dunkirk, Calais and Gravelines. For further detail see: NMM Artificial collections previously assembled, Phillipps-Croker CRK/10/150 Russel to Nelson, HMS GIER, off Gravelines, 17 August 1801; Phillipps-Croker CRK/10/151, Russel to Nelson, HMS GIER off Calais, 18 August 1801; Phillips-Croker, CRK/10/153, Russel to Nelson, HMS GIER, off Calais, 24 August 1801.

46. TNA ADM 1/ 3987: Captain John Campbell to Lord Mulgrave, 27th September 1807. 'A Précis of all the papers in the Admiralty office which have any relation to the Expedition to the Scheldt from the first intelligence to the enemy's forces collecting at Antwerp, down to the final evacuation of Flushing', p. 6.

47. TNA ADM 1/ 3987: 'A paper without signature 7 March 1808', p. 7.

48. TNA ADM 1/ 3987: Minutes of a speech by Mulgrave to the Cabinet 25 March 1809, p. 12.

49. C.A. Christie, 'The Royal Navy and the Walcheren Expedition of 1809' in Crag L. Symonds (ed.), *New Aspects of Naval History, Selected Papers presented at the Fourth Naval History Symposium*, United States Naval Academy 25–6 October 1979 (Annapolis: Naval Institute Press, 1981), pp. 190–200 at p. 190.

50. Fortescue, *History of the British Army, Vol. VII*, pp. 47–8.

51. C.K. Webster, *The Foreign Policy of Castlereagh 1812–1815, Britain and the Reconstruction of Europe* (London: Bell & Sons, 1931), pp. 12–13.

52. Charles William Vane, Marquess of Londonderry (ed.), *Correspondence, Despatches And Other Papers of Viscount Castlereagh Second Series. Military and Miscellaneous. Vol. VI* (London: William Shorberl, 1851), pp. 270–1.

53. Haythornthwaite, *The Armies of Wellington*, p. 16.

54. The officers chosen by Dundas were all former subordinates of York at the Horse Guards: Lieutenant Colonel Willoughby Gordon, the Adjutant General Sir William Calvert, the Quartermaster General Sir Robert Brownrigg and General Alexander Hope.

55. Major General Calvert, 'Memorandum relative to the projected Expedition to the Scheldt', Horse Guards, 3 June 1809 in Vane (ed.), *Correspondence, Despatches And Other Papers*, pp. 269–70.

56. Christie, 'The Royal Navy and the Walcheren Expedition of 1809', p. 192.

57. PP Scheldt Inquiry: Sir Home Popham to the Right Hon, Sir John Anstruther, Bart., 8 February 1810, p. 58.

58. The River Scheldt's course has since been altered hence the use of the past tense.

59. Bindoff, *The Scheldt Question*, p. 1; Bond, *The Grand Expedition*, p. 39.

60. Ham, 'Strategies of Coalition and Isolation', pp. 254, 272.

61. Rodger, *The Command of the Ocean*, p. 470.

62. Rodger, *The Command of the Ocean*, pp. 550–1.

63. Vane (ed.), *Correspondence, Despatches, And Other Papers*, p. 274.

64. Vane (ed.), *Correspondence, Despatches, And Other Papers*, p. 274.

65. Hall, *British Strategy in the Napoleonic War*, p. 73.

66. Vane (ed.), *Correspondence, Despatches, And Other Papers*, p. 274.

67. PP Scheldt Inquiry: Dundas to Anstruther, 5 February 1810, p. 5.

68. Christie, 'The Royal Navy and the Walcheren Expedition of 1809', p. 192.

69. Christie, 'The Royal Navy and the Walcheren Expedition of 1809', pp. 191–2.

70. Bond, *The Grand Expedition*, p. 17.

71. Haythornthwaite, *The Armies of Wellington*, p. 17.

72. Haythornthwaite, *The Armies of Wellington*, p. 234.
73. Christie, 'The Royal Navy and the Walcheren Expedition of 1809', pp. 196–7.
74. Muir, *Wellington, The Path to Victory*, pp. 259–82.
75. PP: Scheldt Inquiry: Rear Admiral Sir Richard Strachan to Sir John Anstruther, 15 February 1810, p. 98.
76. Bond, *The Grand Expedition*, pp. 19–20.
77. Wendy Hinde, *Castlereagh* (n.p.: University of California Press, 1981), p. 161.
78. Christopher Hibbert (ed.), *The Recollections of Rifleman Harris, As Told to Henry Curling* (Moreton-in-Marsh: Windrush Press, 2000), p. 113.
79. Anon., *Letters from Flushing, An Account of the Expedition to Walcheren, Beveland, and the Mouth of the Scheldt, Under the command of the Earl of Chatham, To which is added A Topographical and Statistical Account of the Islands of Walcheren and Beveland, By an Officer of the Eighty-First Regiment* (London: Naval & Military Press, in Association with the National Army Museum, n.d.), p. 2.
80. Reginald W. Jeffrey (ed.), *Dyott's Diary, A selection from the Journal of William Dyott, sometime General in the British Army and aide-de-camp to his Majesty King George III, Vol. 1* (London: Archibald Constable and Company, 1907), p. 275.
81. Esdaile, *Napoleon's Wars, An International History*, p. 393.
82. Chandler, *The Campaigns of Napoleon*, p. 730. Fortescue noted that news arrived of Wagram 'about the 22nd'– *A History of the British Army, Vol. VII*, p. 55; G. Bond states that the news of Wagram arrived in London on 18 July; Bond, *The Grand Expedition*, p. 26.
83. PP Scheldt Inquiry: Chatham to Anstruther, 22 February 1810, p. 183.
84. PP Scheldt Inquiry: Chatham to Anstruther, 22 February 1810, p. 183.
85. Vane (ed.), *Correspondence, Despatches, And Other Papers*, p. 282.
86. TNA WO 133/16: Journal of the Proceedings of the Army under the command of Lieutenant General the Earl of Chatham, 28 July 1809, p. 1. Sir Thomas Graham's Division, for instance, embarked on 16 July only for the troops to endure a further two weeks of frustration and seasickness aboard ship before the expedition finally sailed; NLS Ms 16079: Military Notebook and Papers of General Sir Thomas Graham, Lord Lynedoch, Diary entry 16 July 1809.
87. Bond, *The Grand Expedition*, p. 40.
88. Bond, *The Grand Expedition*, p. 42.
89. Bond, *The Grand Expedition*, p. 42.
90. NMM COO/ 2/ B.1: Strachan to Owen, *HMS Clyde*, 26 July 1809.
91. TNA WO 133/16: Journal of the Proceedings of the Army, 29 July 1809, p. 2.
92. Bond, *The Grand Expedition*, p. 43.
93. B.H. Liddell Hart, *The Letters of Private Wheeler, 1809–1828* (Moreton-in-Marsh: Windrush Press, 1999), pp. 23–4.
94. Ian Fletcher (ed.), *In the Service of the King, The Letters of William Thornton Keep, at Home, Walcheren, and in the Peninsula, 1808–1814* (Staplehurst: Spellmount, 1997), p. 37.
95. Liddell Hart, *The Letters of Private Wheeler*, p. 24.
96. Liddell Hart, *The Letters of Private Wheeler*, p. 25.
97. Anon., *Letters from Flushing*, p. 20.
98. NAM 2002-02-729-1: Typescript manuscript of the memoir of Capt. Peter Bowlby, 4th [or King's Own] Regiment of Foot, Entry for July 1809 (National Army Museum: London), p. 7.
99. For more on inter-service friction during the period see: Richard Harding, 'Sailors and Gentlemen of Parade: Some Professional and Technical Problems Concerning the Conduct of Combined Operations in the Eighteenth-Century', *HJ*, Vol. 32 No. 1 (Mar. 1989), pp. 35–55 at p. 52; Charles John Fedorak, 'The Royal Navy and British Amphibious Operations during the Revolutionary and Napoleonic Wars', *Military Affairs*, Vol. 52 No. 3 (Jul. 1988), pp. 141–6.

100. Bond, *The Grand Expedition*, p. 40.
101. TNA WO 133/ 16: Journal of the Proceedings of the Army, 29 July 1809, pp. 2–3.
102. Bond, *The Grand Expedition*, p. 41.
103. Harding, 'Sailors and Gentlemen of Parade', p. 53.
104. PP Scheldt Inquiry: Chatham to the Committee, 27 February 1810, p. 200.
105. Fortescue, *A History of the British Army, VII*, p. 73.
106. Sam Willis, *The Glorious First of June, Fleet Battle in the Reign of Terror* (London: Querces, 2011), p. 46.
107. Ham, 'Strategies of Coalition and Isolation', pp. 276–7.
108. When summoned to sit in the House of Lords in 1807 Huntly temporarily assumed the title of Baron Gordon of Huntley, a minor peerage in the county of Gloucestershire, which had formerly been held by his late father the 4th Duke of Gordon. Although Huntly continued to hold his original title, and eventually abandoned the name 'Huntley', he was wrongly referred to as the 'Marquis of Huntley' in the minutes of the Scheldt Inquiry. In order to avoid any further confusion, I have chosen to ignore Huntly's temporary title and have referred to the General throughout by his more prestigious title: the Marquis of Huntly.
109. Ron McGuigan, 'British Generals of the Napoleonic Wars, 1793–1815'. The Napoleon Series: Research. http://www.napoleonseries.org/research/biographies/BritishGenerals/c_Britishgenerals219.html. Placed on database: Jan. 2011.
110. PP Scheldt Inquiry: Lieutenant General the Right Hon. The Marquis of Huntly to the Committee, 20 February 1810, p. 145.
111. PP Scheldt Inquiry: Huntly to the Committee inc. 'Details of Instructions to the Lieutenant-General the Marquis of Huntly from Lieutenant-General Sir Robert Brownrigg Q.M.G to the Forces, 25 July 1809', p. 145.
112. PP Scheldt Inquiry: Huntly to the Committee, 20 February 1810, p. 145.
113. Bond, *The Grand Expedition*, pp. 46–7.
114. PP Scheldt Inquiry: Owen to the Committee, 9 February 1810, p. 74.
115. PP Scheldt Inquiry: Brigadier-General Montresor to the Committee, 9 February 1810, p. 82.
116. PP Scheldt Inquiry: Owen to the Committee, 9 February 1810 p. 74; Bond, *The Grand Expedition*, p. 47.
117. PP Scheldt Inquiry: Owen to Strachan, 29th July 1809 in Appendix to the 7th Day's Minutes, 15th February 1810, p. 116.
118. PP Scheldt Inquiry: Owen to the Committee. 9 February 1810, pp. 74–5.
119. Bond, *The Grand Expedition*, p. 46.
120. Jeffrey (ed.), *Dyott's Diary*, p. 279.
121. PP Scheldt Inquiry: Owen to the Committee. 9 February 1810, p. 75.
122. Fortescue, *A History of the British Army, Vol. VII*, p. 74.
123. NMM. COO/ 2/ B.1: Strachan to Gardiner, 3 August 1809.
124. Jeffrey (ed.), *Dyott's Diary*, p. 279.
125. Bond, *The Grand Expedition*, p. 52.
126. Fortescue, *A History of the British Army, Vol.VII*, p. 75.
127. Anon., *Letters from Flushing*, p. 23.
128. Liddell Hart, *The Letters of Private Wheeler*, pp. 27–8.
129. NAM 1992-04-148-1: Memoirs of Sergeant Solomon Rich, 28th Regiment of foot 1803–1809, pp. 83–4; John Wardell (ed.), *Major-Ross-Lewin, With the Thirty-Second in the Peninsular and other Campaigns* (Dublin: Hodges & Figges, 1904), p. 126.
130. Fortescue, *A History of the British Army, Vol. VII*, p. 68.
131. Christopher Hibbert (ed.), *A Soldier of the Seventy-First, The Journal of a Soldier the Highland Light Infantry 1806–1815* (London: Leo Cooper, 1976), pp. 46–7. Pack would go on to command a brigade under Beresford in the Portuguese army, serving with distinction at a number

of battles, notably Salamanca in 1812. His career reached its peak when he commanded a division at Waterloo.

132. Frederick Myatt, *Peninsular General, Sir Thomas Picton 1758–1815* (London: David & Charles, 1980), pp. 67–8.

133. Martin Howard, *Walcheren 1809, The Scandalous Destruction of a British Army* (Barnsley: Pen & Sword, 2012), pp. 74–5.

134. TNA WO 133/16: Journal of the Proceedings of the Army, 28 July 1809, p. 9.

135. Fletcher (ed.), *In the Service of the King*, p. 46.

136. TNA WO 133/16: Journal of the Proceedings of the Army, 28 July 1809, p. 9.

137. Wardell, *Major-Ross-Lewin, With the Thirty-Second in the Peninsular*, pp. 126–7.

138. Liddell Hart, *The Letters of Private Wheeler*, p. 30.

139. Liddell Hart, *The Letters of Private Wheeler*, p. 30.

140. TNA WO 133/16: Journal of the Proceedings of the Army, 31 July 1809, p. 11.

141. TNA WO 133/16: Journal of the Proceedings of the Army, 2 August 1809, p. 14.

142. Bond, *The Grand Expedition*, p. 62.

143. Major General Sir John Jones, Bart., R.E., *Journal of Sieges carried on by The Army under the Duke of Wellington in Spain during the years 1811 to 1814, with notes and additions, also Memoranda Relative to the lines thrown up to cover Lisbon in 1810 Vol. II* (London: John Weale, M.DCCC.XLVI), p. 249.

144. Jones, *Journal of Sieges*, pp. 249–50.

145. TNA WO 133/ 16: Journal of the Proceedings of the Army, 1 August 1809, p. 13.

146. See map, p. 000: The siege of Flushing.

147. Bindoff, *The Scheldt Question*, p. 82.

148. Bond, *The Grand Expedition*, pp. 28–9.

149. Jones, *Journal of Sieges*, pp. 247–8.

150. A.D. Harvey, 'Captain Paisley at Walcheren, August 1809', *JSAHR*, Vol. LXIX, No. 277 (Spring, 1991), p. 17.

151. Liddell Hart, *The Letters of Private Wheeler*, p. 33.

152. Michael Duffy, '"Science and Labour". The Naval Contribution to Operations Ashore in the Great Wars with France, 1793–1815' in Captain Peter Horne (ed.), *Seapower Ashore, 200 Years of Royal Navy Operations On Land* (London: Chatham Publishing in Association with the National Maritime Museum, 2001), pp. 50–1.

153. Wardell, *Major-Ross-Lewin, With the Thirty-Second in the Peninsular*, p. 128.

154. Fortescue, *A History of the British Army, Vol. VII*, p. 76.

155. TNA WO 133/16: *Journal of the Proceedings of the Army*, 28 July, p. 13.

156. TNA WO 133/16: *Journal of the Proceedings of the Army*, 28 July, p. 23.

157. Howard, *Walcheren 1809*, p. 114.

158. Hibbert (ed.), *A Soldier of the Seventy-First*, p. 43.

159. Colonel William Fyers, R.E., 'Journal of the Siege of Flushing in the year 1809 by a detachment of the Army commanded by the Earl of Chatham. Under the Immediate orders of Lieutenant-General Sir Eyre Coote, K.B', ed. by Major Evan W.H. Fyers, *JSAHR*, Vol. 13 (1934), p. 157.

160. Fortescue, *A History of the British Army, Vol. VII*, pp. 75–6.

161. Fyers, 'Journal of the Siege of Flushing', p. 150.

162. Bond, *The Grand Expedition*, p. 84.

163. Fyers, 'Journal of the Siege of Flushing', p. 151.

164. Harvey, 'Captain Paisley at Walcheren', pp. 17–18; Paisley's account of the conduct of the engineer officers provides an important insight into the conduct of the expedition at a lower level.

165. Harvey, 'Captain Paisley at Walcheren', p. 19.

166. Harvey, 'Captain Paisley at Walcheren', p. 19.

167. Paisley was wounded during the expedition to the Scheldt, rendering him unfit for further operations. He was an intelligent officer who wrote an important study of military engineering titled *Essay on the Military Policy and Institutions of the British Empire* (1810). Although he did not return to active duty he established (1812) and later commanded a college for sappers and miners at Chatham. He was made a Major General in 1841 and KCB in 1850.

168. Bond, *The Grand Expedition*, p. 94.

169. Wardell, *Major-Ross-Lewin, With the Thirty-Second in the Peninsular*, p. 130.

170. David Yarrow (ed.), 'A Journal of the Proceedings of His Majesty's Sloop of War the GALQO during the Siege of Flushing in the Year 1809 under the Command of John Gardene McBride McKillop Esq. and Especially Genl. Sir Wm. Congreve, Bart', by Joseph Palmer Wrangle, *The Mariners Mirror*, Vol. 61 No. 2 (May 1975), pp. 183–9 at pp. 188–9.

171. TNA ADM 1/3987: Strachan, 12 August 1809, p. 40.

172. NAM 1992-04-148-1: Memoirs of Sgt. Salomon Rich, p. 93.

173. Jones, *Journal of Sieges*, pp. 268–9.

174. Fletcher (ed.), *In the Service of the King*, p. 49.

175. T.W. Cooper and M. Medhurst, *The Military Career of Colonel Francis Tidy, C.B.* (London: National Army Museum, March 1997), p. 10. Reports of this action were quickly fed back to Britain, with the *Morning Chronicle* detailing what occurred outside Flushing in an article titled 'Private Correspondence', published on 14 August 1809, *Journal of the Morning Chronicle*, Issue 12561.

176. Jones, *Journal of Sieges*, p. 270; NAM 1978-12-55-2: Diary of Lieutenant-General Jasper Nicholls.

177. TNA WO 133/16: Coote to 'The General Commanding in Chief Flushing', *Journal of the Proceedings of the Army*, 14 August 1809, p. 59.

178. TNA WO 133/16: 'Intelligence Transmitted to Lt. General Sir J. Hope', *Journal of the Proceedings of the Army*, 6 August 1809, p. 25; TNAWO 133/16: *Journal of the Proceedings of the Army*, 7 August 1809, p. 30; TNA WO 133/16: *Journal of the Proceedings of the Army*, 8 August 1809, p. 36; TNA WO 133/16: *Journal of the Proceedings of the Army*, 9 August 1809, p. 40; TNA WO 133/16: *Journal of the Proceedings of the Army*, 11 August 1809, p. 49; TNA WO 133/16: *Journal of the Proceedings of the Army*, 12 August 1809, p. 52.

179. Harvey, 'Captain Paisley at Walcheren', pp. 19–20.

180. Jones, *Journal of Sieges*, p. 272.

181. TNA WO 133/16: *Journal of the Proceedings of the Army*, 28 July 1809, p. 58.

182. Bond, *The Grand Expedition*, p. 107.

183. TNA WO 133/16: *Journal of the Proceedings of the Army*, 22 August 1809, p. 73.

184. Howard, *Walcheren 1809*, p. 142; TNA WO 133/16: 'Intelligence Transmitted to Lt. General Sir J. Hope', *Journal of the Proceedings of the Army*, 22 August 1809, p. 73.

185. TNA WO 133/16: *Journal of the Proceedings of the Army*, 28 August 1809, p. 79.

186. This will be analysed in detail later in this chapter.

187. TNA WO 133/16: *Journal of the Proceedings of the Army*, 27 August 1809, p. 78.

188. *The London Times*, Tuesday 29 August 1809, Issue 7761; col. D, p. 2.

189. Martin Howard, 'Walcheren 1809: A Medical Catastrophe', *BMJ*, Vol. 319 No. 7225 (18–25 Dec. 1999), pp. 1642–5 at p. 1643; Howard, *Walcheren 1809*, pp. 156–86.

190. Howard, 'Walcheren 1809: A Medical Catastrophe', p. 1643.

191. PP Scheldt Inquiry: Deputy-Inspector General of Army Hospitals Dr John Webb to the Committee, 6 March 1810, p. 254.

192. T.H. McGuffie, 'The Walcheren expedition and the Walcheren Fever', *EHR*, Vol. 62 No. 243 (Apr. 1947), pp. 191–202 at p. 194; NAM 1968-07-261-1: Diagram showing 'Distribution of the Medical Staff' taken from a book containing misc. notes and Journals of General Sir Frederick William Trench, 'Diary of the Walcheren Expedition, 1809', General Orders-Landing-Reserve-

John Hope. Orders for Officers of Q.M.G Department. Reserve to which I was attached as A.Q.M. General, Aug. 1–Sept. 1, p. 5.

193. Dr Martin Howard, *Wellington's Doctors, The British Army Medical Services in the Napoleonic Wars* (Stroud: The History Press, 2008), pp. 85–6.
194. Howard, *Wellington's Doctors*, p. 199.
195. Elizabeth Crowe, 'The Walcheren Expedition and the New Army Medical Board: A Reconsideration', *EHR*, Vol. 88 No. 349 (Oct. 1973), pp. 770–85 at p. 771.
196. Abercromby to Lord Grenville, 20 July 1799, *Dropmore, V–VII*, p. 165.
197. Anthony Brett-James, 'The Walcheren failure', Part Two, *History Today*, Vol. 14 No. 1 (Jan. 1964), pp. 60–8 at p. 62.
198. Webb quoted in Richard L. Blanco, 'The Development of British Military Medicine, 1793–1814', *Military Affairs*, Vol. 38 No. 1 (Feb. 1974), pp. 4–10 at pp. 7–8.
199. Harvard, *Wellington's Welsh General*, p. 108.
200. Howard, 'Walcheren 1809: A Medical Catastrophe', pp. 1643–4.
201. Yarrow, 'A Journal of the Proceedings of His Majesty's Sloop of War the GALQO', p. 186.
202. Hibbert (ed.), *A Soldier of the Seventy-First*, p. 45; hospital mates also made a habit of stealing belongings from the sick patients.
203. 'ART. IV. An Account of the Islands of Walcheren and South Beveland, against which the British Expedition proceeded in 1809, describing the different Operations of his Majesty's Army during the Siege of Flushing, and containing Observations on the Character, Custom, Religion, and Commerce of the Inhabitants', *Monthly Review* Issue, 70 (1813: Mar.), p. 263.
204. Bond, *The Grand Expedition*, p. 132; Vane (ed.), *Correspondence, Despatches And Other Papers*, Castlereagh to Coote, 24 September 1809, p. 327.
205. Howard, 'Walcheren 1809: A Medical Catastrophe', p. 1645.
206. Crowe, 'The Walcheren Expedition and the New Army Medical Board', pp. 776, 780.
207. Hibbert (ed.), *The Recollections of Rifleman Harris*, p. 115.
208. NAM 1974-12-154-1: Lt. Col. Charles Stevenson, Late of the XXth Regt. *Reminiscences of my military life from 1795–1818*, p. 45.
209. NAM 1979-12-21-1: Diary of an unidentified Soldier of 38th (1st Staffordshire) Regiment of Foot, p. 10.
210. Harvard, *Wellington's Welsh General*, pp. 106–7.
211. Fletcher (ed.), *In the Service of the King*, p. 65.
212. NAM 1979-12-21-1: Diary of an unidentified Soldier, p. 11; Hibbert (ed.), *A Soldier of the Seventy-First*, p. 45.
213. Robert Burnham and Ron McGuigan, *The British Army against Napoleon, Facts, Lists and Trivia 1805–1815* (Barnsley: Frontline Books, 2010), p. 229.
214. NAM 1979-12-21-1: Diary of an unidentified Soldier of 38th (1st Staffordshire) Regiment of Foot, p. 11.
215. 'Copy of a dispatch from Chatham to Castlereagh, dated 7th September 1809 – Received 10th September' in Anon., *A Collection of Papers relating to the expedition to the Scheldt, presented to Parliament in 1810* (London: A. Strahan, 1810), p. 123; 'Copy of a dispatch from Chatham to Castlereagh, dated 9th September 1809' in Anon., *A Collection of Papers relating to the expedition to the Scheldt*, p. 126.
216. NAM 1970-8-11-1: Letters of William Dent, Dent to his mother, Colchester Barracks, letter dated Sept. 12th 1809.
217. NAM 2002-02-729-1: Memoirs of Captain Peter Bowlby, 4th (or Kings Own) regiment of Foot, p. 8.
218. Fletcher (ed.), *In the Service of the King*, p. 67.
219. Hall, *British Strategy in the Napoleonic War*, p. 178,
220. Leigh Hunt, 'Walcheren Expedition; or the Englishman's Lament for the loss of his countrymen', *Potential Register*, Vol. 7 (Jan. 1812), p. 250. N.B. the rhythm of this poem is the basis of a number of others, written before and after Hunt's rendition. With different words, it is better known in the form of the 1970s track 'Shelter from the Storm' by Bob Dylan!

221. Howard, *Walcheren 1809*, pp. 201–2.

222. John Bew, *Castlereagh, from Enlightment to Tyranny* (London: Quercus, 2011), pp. 260–1.

223. For a detailed examination of the feud and subsequent duel see: Giles Hunt, *The Duel, Castlereagh, Canning and the Deadly Cabinet Rivalry* (London: Tauris, 2008). Following the duel, both Canning and Castlereagh vacated their government posts.

224. Muir, *Britain and the Defeat of Napoleon*, pp. 105–7.

225. Howard, *Walcheren 1809*, p. 203; Bew, *Castlereagh*, p. 272; David R. Fisher, 'The Scheldt divisions, 1810', http://www.historyofparliamentonline.org/periods/hanoverians/scheldt-divisions-1810.

226. His full title was: Sir John Anstruther, 4th Baronet of Nova Scotia. Anstruther was Member of Parliament for the Anstruther Burghs and had also been part of the judicial team in the attempt to impeach a former Governor General of India, Sir Warren Hastings, between 1788 and 1795.

227. David Dundas was chiefly examined on 2 and 5 February 1810. For details of what passed between Dundas and Anstruther see PP Scheldt Inquiry, pp. 3–16.

228. Howard, *Walcheren 1809*, p. 204.

229. 'Monthly Retrospect of Politics', *Belfast Monthly Magazine*, Vol. 4 No. 19 (28 February 1810), pp. 138–42 at p. 139.

230. PP Scheldt Inquiry: Chatham to the Committee, 27 February 1810, p. 209.

231. PP Scheldt Inquiry: Chatham to the Committee, 27 February 1810, p. 213.

232. *The Annual Register, Vol. 52, Chapter IV: 1810*, p. 51.

233. PP Scheldt Inquiry: Strachan to the Committee, 13 March 1810, p. 299.

234. Howard, *Walcheren 1809*, pp. 206–7.

235. Howard, *Walcheren 1809*, p. 204; Bond, *The Grand Expedition*, p. 144.

236. The conduct of the Scheldt Inquiry contrasts unfavourably with the efficient and learned manner in which the Prussians reviewed their defeat in 1806–7. For more on the Prussian response during this period see Conclusion.

Chapter 5

1. Brigadier General H.H. Austin (ed.), *Old Stick Leg: Extracts from the Diaries of Major Thomas Austin* (London: Geoffrey Bles, 1926), p. 186.

2. Adam Zamoyski, *1812, Napoleon's Fatal March on Moscow* (London: Harper Collins, 2004), p. 544; Muir, *Britain and the Defeat of Napoleon*, pp. 229–31. Created by Napoleon in 1806, after his defeat of the Austrians and Russians at Austerlitz, the Confederation of the Rhine fused together the former member states of the Holy Roman Empire into a military/political alliance system which was run by Napoleonic laws and customs. As its 'protector', Napoleon routinely called upon its member states to provide financial and military assistance, particularly during the Invasion of Russia in 1812.

3. Sherwig, 'Lord Grenville's Plan for a Concert of Europe', pp. 284–93; Renier, *Great Britain and the Establishment of the Kingdom of the Netherlands*, p. 34.

4. Bew, *Castlereagh*, p. 315.

5. Bew, *Castlereagh*, p. 315.

6. Jonathan Riley, *1813: Empire at Bay, The Sixth Coalition & the Downfall of Napoleon* (Barnsley: Praetorian Press, 2013), p. 16.

7. Knight, *Britain against Napoleon*, p. 375; Muir, *Britain and the Defeat of Napoleon*, p. 292.

8. Michael V. Leggiere, *Napoleon and Berlin: The Franco-Prussian War in North Germany, 1813* (Norman: University of Oklahoma Press, 2002), pp. 121–2.

9. Munro Price, *Napoleon, The End of Glory* (Oxford: Oxford University Press, 2014), pp. 103–4.

10. Price, *Napoleon, The End of Glory*, p. 111.

11. Riley, *1813: Empire at Bay*, pp. 165–85; Muir, *Britain and the Defeat of Napoleon*, p. 299; C.K. Webster, *The Foreign Policy of Castlreagh 1812–1815* (London: Bell and Sons, 1931), p. 179. The Allied war effort had already received a boost when Wellington and his Anglo-Portuguese

Army crossed into Southern France on 7 October. For more on Wellington's invasion of France see: F.C. Beatson, *Wellington and the Invasion of France: The Bidassoa to the Battle of the Nivelle, 1813* (London: Leonaur, 2007).

12. Price, *Napoleon: The End of Glory*, p. 153.

13. Michael V. Leggiere, *The Fall of Napoleon, Vol. 1: The Allied Invasion of France, 1813–1814* (Cambridge: Cambridge University Press, 2007), p. 20.

14. H.A. Schmitt, '1812: Stein, Alexander I and the Crusade against Napoleon', *JMH*, 31 (1959), pp. 325–8.

15. Philip G. Dwyer, 'Self-Interest versus the Common Cause: Austria, Prussia and Russia against Napoleon', *JSS*, 31:4 (2008), pp. 605–32 at p. 624; Leggiere, *The Fall of Napoleon*, pp. 28–9.

16. Riley, *1813: Empire at Bay*, p. 203.

17. For more on the negotiations and the concept of 'Natural Frontiers' see: Price, *Napoleon: The End of Glory*, pp. 153–69; Paul W. Schroeder, 'An Unnatural "Natural Alliance": Castlereagh, Metternich, and Aberdeen in 1813', *IHR*, Vol. 10 No. 4 (Nov. 1988), pp. 522–40 at pp. 533–4; Leggiere, *The Fall of Napoleon Vol. 1*, pp. 42–62; Chandler, *Campaigns of Napoleon*, pp. 947–8.

18. Price, *Napoleon: The End of Glory*, p. 167.

19. Renier, *Great Britain and the Establishment of the Kingdom of the Netherlands*, p. 36; Bew, *Castlereagh*, p. 333; Leggiere, *The Fall of Napoleon Vol. 1*, p. 55. For details of Castlereagh's views regarding the importance of Antwerp see: Public Records Office of Northern Ireland: (PRONI) D3030/G/11, Castlereagh Papers, Castlreagh to Lord Liverpool, 8 January 1814.

20. Chandler, *The Campaigns of Napoleon*, p. 948.

21. Connelly, *Napoleon's Satellite Kingdoms*, pp. 132–4.

22. Rothenberg, *Napoleon's Great Adversaries*, p. 186.

23. 'The Frankfurt Declaration' in Leggiere, *The Fall of Napoleon, Vol. 1*, p. 563.

24. Chandler, *The Campaigns of Napoleon*, pp. 948–9.

25. Leggiere, *The Fall of Napoleon, Vol. 1*, pp. 131–2.

26. Leggiere, *The Fall of Napoleon, Vol. 1*, pp. 68–9; Ralph Ashby, *Napoleon Against Great Odds, The Emperor and the defenders of France, 1814* (Santa Barbara: 2010), pp. 3, 9.

27. Troop numbers and other details in this section are taken from: Chandler, *The Campaigns of Napoleon*, pp. 949–50; Leggiere, *The Fall of Napoleon, Vol. 1*, pp. 65–9.

28. Bamford, *A Bold and Ambitious Enterprise*, p. 31; J.W. Fortescue, A *History of the British Army, Vol. X, 1814–1815* (London: Macmillan, 1920), p. 1; Leggiere, *The Fall of Napoleon*, Vol. 1, p. 100.

29. Renier, *Great Britain and the Establishment of the Kingdom of the Netherlands*, pp. 121–3.

30. Bamford, *A Bold and Ambitious Enterprise*, p. 81.

31. TNA WO 1/414: 'Major General Taylor's Mission to Holland, 1813–1814', Sir Herbert Taylor to Bathurst, 23 November, Harwich, 1813, pp. 1–2; TNA WO 1/414: 'Taylor's Mission to Holland', Instructions received by Major General Taylor and Colonel Fagel, HMS *Jason* at Sea, 28 November 1813, pp. 39–48; Renier, *Great Britain and the Establishment of the Kingdom of the Netherlands*, p. 124; Bamford, *A Bold and Ambitious Enterprise*, p. 42.

32. A Hessian by birth, Winzegorode (as he was known in Russia) served in the Russian army during the 1813–14 campaigns and as such I have chosen to use his Russian name. Benkendorff, meanwhile, had served under Winzegorode during the campaign of 1812 and had also been commandant of Moscow: Mikaberidze, *The Russian Officer Corps in the French Revolutionary and Napoleonic Wars*, pp. 32–3, 444–5.

33. Bamford, *A Bold and Ambitious Enterprise*, pp. 47–8. Both Bülow and Winzegorode were under the overall commander of the Crown Prince of Sweden: Bernadotte.

34. Cooke's small force comprised a detachment of 300 men from the 1st Foot Guards, 400 men from the 2nd Battalion of the 3rd Foot Guards and the 400 officers and men of the 3rd Battalion of the Coldstream Guards. Guards' strength taken from: TNA WO 6/16: 'Memorandum': details of the force ordered to proceed on a particular service under the command of Lieutenant General Sir Thomas Graham, Horse Guards, 21 December 1813, p. 18.

35. Gibbs and his brigade had been despatched to Stralsund in July 1813 to support the Swedes. For details about this mission and Gibbs's new orders see: Bamford, *A Bold and Ambitious Enterprise*, pp. 13–20, 33, 39.

36. E.I. Carlyle, 'Cooke, Sir George (1768–1837)', rev. Roger T. Stearn, *Oxford Dictionary of National Biography* (Oxford: Oxford University Press, 2004).

37. TNA WO 1/199: Copy No. 1 Bathurst to Cooke, Downing Street, 27 November 1813, p. 1; TNA WO 6/16: Bathurst to Cooke, Letter No. 1, Downing Street, 27 November 1813, p. 1.

38. TNA WO 6/16: Bathurst to Cooke, Letter No. 1, Downing Street, 27 November 1813, pp. 1–3; Gibbs had received instructions to sail for the Roompot on the same day as Cooke received his twin instructions: TNA WO 6/16: Bathurst to Gibbs, Downing Street, 27 November 1813, pp. 5–6.

39. TNA WO 6/16: Bathurst to Cooke, Letter No. 2, Downing Street, 27 November 1813, p. 4.

40. E.J. Rapson, 'Gibbs, Sir Samuel (1770–1815)', rev. Alan Harfield, *Oxford Dictionary of National Biography*, (Oxford: Oxford University Press, 2004); online edn, Jan. 2008.

41. Bamford, *A Bold and Ambitious Enterprise*, p. 53.

42. Ian Fletcher, *Vittoria 1813, Osprey Campaign Series No. 59* (Oxford: Osprey, 1998), pp. 38–9; 45; 48; 62; Heathcote, *Wellington's Peninsular War Generals*, p. 59.

43. For more on this lesser known engagement see: John Grehan and Martin Mace, *The Battle of Barrosa, 1811: Forgotten Battle of the Peninsular War* (Barnsley: Pen & Sword, 2012).

44. TNA WO 1/199: Bathurst to Graham, Copy, No. 1, Downing Street, 4 December 1813, pp. 29–34.

45. TNA WO 1/198: Col. Henry Torrens to Col. Henry Bunbury, The Horse Guards, 19 December 1813, p. 39; Bamford, *Sickness, Suffering and the Sword*, p. 164; TNA WO 6/16: Bathurst to Graham, Memorandum, 21 November 1813, pp. 18–19; Bamford, *A Bold and Ambitious Enterprise*, p. 267; TNA WO 6/16 Bathurst to Graham, Memorandum, Horse Guards, 21 December 1813, p. 18.

46. Bamford, *Sickness, Suffering and the Sword*, p. 165; http://www.napoleonseries.org/military/organization/Britain/Strength/Bamford/c_BritishArmyStrengthStudyNorthernEurope.html.

47. Linch, *The Recruitment of the British Army*, p. 23.

48. Linch, *The Recruitment of the British Army*, pp. 21–3.

49. Linch, *The Recruitment of the British Army*, p. 22.

50. For more on the creation of new battalions and Wellington's measures see Bamford, *Sickness, Suffering and the Sword*, pp. 144–58.

51. See Chapter 3.

52. Cookson, *The British Armed Nation*, pp. 118–19.

53. Biographical information taken from: David Gates, 'Mackenzie, Kenneth (later Sir Kenneth Douglas, first baronet) (1754–1833)', *Oxford Dictionary of National Biography* (Oxford: Oxford University Press, 2004); Gates, *British Light Infantry Arm*, p. 93.

54. For details see: http://www.napoleon-series.org/cgi-bin/forum/archive2012_config.pl?md=read;id=137565.

55. Bamford, *A Bold and Ambitious Enterprise*, p. 49.

56. TNA WO 6/16: Bathurst to Cooke, Letter No. 4, Downing Street, 4 December 1813, pp. 10–11.

57. TNA WO 1/199: Cooke to Bathurst, The Hague, 8 December 1813, p. 69; TNA WO 1/199: Cooke to Bathurst, Willemstadt, 16 December 1813, pp. 77–9. The British would retain a garrison on Tholen until early March 1814 when a force of Russians was sent to hold the island: TNA WO 1/200: British Army in Holland and Flanders 1813–14 March–April–May, Vol. 2 General Lord Lynedoch, Sir Thomas Graham to Lord Bathurst, Head-Quarters Calmhout, 4 March 1814, pp. 67–8.

58. Thomas Morris, *Recollections of Military Service in 1813, 1814, & 1815 through Germany, Holland, and France including some details of the battles of Quatre Bras and Waterloo* (London: James Madden and Co, 1845), p. 72.

59. For more on the Dutch see: Johan Joor, '"A Very Rebellious Disposition": Dutch Experience and Popular Protest under the Napoleonic Regime (1806–1813)' in Alan Forrest, Karen Hagemann and Jane Rendall (eds), *Soldiers, Citizens and Civilians, Experiences and Perceptions of the Revolutionary and Napoleonic Wars, 1790–1820* (Basingstoke: Palgrave Macmillan, 2009), pp. 181–204 at p. 197.

60. Hall, *British Strategy in the Napoleonic War*, p. 202.

61. Glover, 'The French Fleet, 1807–1814', pp. 233–52 at pp. 244–5.

62. TNA WO 6/16: Bathurst to Graham, No. 2, Downing Street, 4 December 1813, p. 20.

63. TNA WO 6/16: Bathurst to Graham, No. 8, Downing Street 13 December 1813, pp. 33–5; Bathurst to Graham, No. 10, Downing Street 17 December 1813, pp. 38–9; Bathurst to Graham, No. 12, Downing Street 21 December 1813, pp. 42–3; Bathurst to Graham, No. 13, Downing Street 21 December 1813, p. 45; Bathurst to Graham, No. 17, Downing Street, 31 December 1813, pp. 48–9; Bathurst to Graham, No. 20, Downing Street, 11 January 1814, pp. 55–3.

64. Bamford, *A Bold and Ambitious Enterprise*, p. 56.

65. TNA PRO 35/30/6: Carmichael Smyth Papers, Netherlands and France. Dispatches to Lieutenant-General (Gother) Mann (Inspector General of Fortifications) Entry Books. 1 Vol. Dec. 1813–Dec. 1818, Smyth to Mann, No. 2, Klundert, 31 December 1813, p. 3. Smyth had been appointed to command Graham's engineers at on 2 December 1813; see TNA PRO 35/30/6: Smyth to Mann, No. 1, Ramsgate, 2 December 1813, pp. 1–2; Bamford, *A Bold and Ambitious Enterprise*, p. 53; TNA WO 1/198: Expedition to Holland, Miscellaneous – 1813, Vol. 3, Commander-in-Chief, Treasury, Ordnance, Foreign Office and Commssisionary General in Chief: Treasury, Mr Harrison Esq, Storekeeper Generals Office, 'A supply of blankets and shoes for Helvoetsluys' No. 18031, 16 December 1813, pp. 65–6; TNA WO 1/198: Mr Harrison Esq, Storekeeper Generals Office, 24 December 1813, p. 73; TNA WO 1/198: Copy, Return of clothing with Orange facings and equipment shipped by the Storekeeper General the 18 and 20 December 1813 on board the undermentioned transports consigned to the charge of the Adjutant-Storekeeper General Van Zulicom, in part of a supply for 20,000 men, ordered by Lord Commissioners of His Majesty's Treasury, the 19th, p. 81.

66. Bamford, *A Bold and Ambitious Enterprise*, pp. 268–9.

67. Gareth Glover (ed.), *Eyewitness to the Peninsular War and the Battle of Waterloo, The Letters and Journals of Lieutenant-Colonel the Honourable James Stanhope 1803–1825* (Barnsley: Pen & Sword, in association with Chevening Trust, 2010), pp. ix–x.

68. Glover, *Eyewitness to the Peninsular War*, p. 129. The brigade sent to hold Breda by Graham was commanded by Gibbs: TNA WO 1/199: Graham to Bathurst, Tholen, 15 December 1813, p. 188.

69. TNA WO 1/199: Graham to Bathurst, No. 7, Tholen, 21 December 1813, p. 171; TNA WO 1/199: 'Report of Allied Intelligence 15 Dec 1813' mentioned by Graham to Bathurst, Tholen, pp. 187–8.

70. Glover, *Eyewitness to the Peninsular War*, p. 131.

71. Oppen had led Bülow's advance guard into the Dutch Provinces in November: Leggiere, *The Fall of Napoleon, Vol. 1*, pp. 148–9.

72. Bamford, *A Bold and Ambitious Enterprise*, pp. 84–7.

73. TNA WO 1/199: Graham to Bathurst, No. 13, Calmhout, 14 January 1814, pp. 389–92. The fighting at Merxem has been analysed in detail by Bamford in his study of the campaign in the Low Countries and as this chapter is focused on the attack upon Bergen-Op-Zoom there is little need to repeat what has already been said by Bamford about the engagement at Merxem. For details of the attack see Bamford, *A Bold and Ambitious Enterprise*, pp. 90–100; TNA WO 1/199 'Return of killed, wounded, and missing of the Army under his Excellency General Sir Thomas Graham K.B in the affair at the village of Merxem connected with the reconnaissance upon Antwerp on the 13th of January 1814', p. 393.

74. Glover, *Eyewitness to the Peninsular War*, pp. 131–3.
75. Bamford, *A Bold and Ambitious Enterprise*, p. 118.
76. Bülow informed Graham of his intention to attack again on 21 January 1814: TNA WO 1/199: Graham to Bathurst, Private, 21 January 1814, p. 481; Graham's 'Memorandum', undated, pp. 533–7.
77. Bamford, *A Bold and Ambitious Enterprise*, pp. 144–5; Glover, *Eyewitness to the Peninsular War*, p. 135.
78. Glover, *Eyewitness to the Peninsular War*, pp. 135–6.
79. Taylor to York, 4 February 1814, *Taylor Papers*, pp. 138–9.
80. Ashby, *Napoleon Against Great Odds*, p. 40.
81. Anon., *British Minor Expeditions*, p. 83.
82. Taylor to the Duke of York, 4 February 1814, *Taylor Papers*, p. 140.
83. TNA PRO 35/30/6: No. 4, Smyth to Mann, Calmhout in Brabant, 14 January 1814, p. 13.
84. TNA WO 1/199: No. 20, Graham to Bathurst, Groot Zundert, 10 February 1814, p. 597.
85. TNA WO 1/199: Private, Graham to Bathurst, Groot Zundert, 10 February 1814, pp. 617–20. 'We might get hold of Bergen-Op-Zoom': underlined by Graham.
86. TNA WO 1/ 199: Extract, Graham to Clancarty, 11 February 1814, p. 637.
87. TNA WO 1/199: Extract, Clancarty to Graham, The Hague, 12 February 1814, p. 639.
88. Bamford, *A Bold and Ambitious Enterprise*, p. 160. Although Perponcher-Sedlnitsky would only play a minor role in this campaign, he would go on to provide a vital support role for the British at the Battle of Quatre Bras in 1815. See Mike Robinson, *The Battle of Quatre Bras 1815* (Stroud: Spellmount, 2009).
89. For strength of Graham's army at this point in time see Bamford, 'The British Army in the Low Countries, 1813–1814', http://www.napoleon-series.org/military/battles/c_lowcountries1814.html#Notes.
90. TNA WO 1/ 199: Graham to John Mordaunt Johnson esq, Groot-Zundert, 19 February 1814, pp. 673–5; TNA WO 1/199: Intelligence Report Flanders Coast, Copy, 21 February 1814, pp. 739–41. As Graham became increasingly interested with Bergen-Op-Zoom, the British also sought to devise how to organise the Belgians if they, like the Dutch, rebelled against the French after the fall of the fortresses in Brabant. A scheme for arming the Belgians had already been circulated by Saxe-Weimar and on 2 March a copy of a 'Plan for the military organisation of the Belgian Provinces' was presented to Graham. For finer details see: TNA WO 1/200: Copy, Brussels, 2 March 1814, pp. 97–102. By 4 March, Graham could report to Bathurst that, 'The demand for arms' from the Prussians to arm the Belgians 'becomes very great', taken from TNA WO 1/200: Graham to Bathurst, Calmhout, 4 March 1814, p. 68.
91. Bamford, *A Bold and Ambitious Enterprise*, p. 107; M.H. Port, 'Trench, Sir Frederick William (c.1777–1859)', *Oxford Dictionary of National Biography* (Oxford: Oxford University Press, 2004); http://www.oxforddnb.com/view/article/27699; George Spiller, *Observations on certain branches of the Commissariat System, particularly connected with the present Military State of the Country* (London: 1806).
92. TNA WO 1/199: Copy of a latter from the Duke of Wellington to Sir Thomas Graham, St Jean de Luz, 17 January 1814, pp. 625–7; Bamford, *A Bold and Ambitious Enterprise*, p. 107.
93. TNA WO 1/199: Graham to Bathurst, Groot Zundert, 15 February 1814, pp. 643–9.
94. Rothenberg, *Napoleon's Great Adversaries*, p. 189.
95. Ashby, *Napoleon against Great Odds*, pp. 93–102; Bamford, *A Bold and Ambitious Enterprise*, pp. 164–5; Chandler, *The Campaigns of Napoleon*, pp. 959–64.
96. Price, *Napoleon, The End of Glory*, p. 199.
97. Bamford, *A Bold and Ambitious Enterprise*, p. 164; Alex M. Delavoye, *Life of Sir Thomas Graham, Lord Lynedoch* (London: Richardson, 1880), p. 714.
98. Delavoye, *Life of Sir Thomas Graham*, pp. 714–15.
99. Graham had despatched Major. Hon. James Stanhope to meet with the Crown Prince in mid-February and Stanhope's report of his meeting with Bernadotte had reached Graham on

26 February 1814; TNA WO 1/200: Stanhope to Graham, pp. 31–42 and p. 47; TNA WO 1/200: Graham to Bunbury, Groot-Zundert, 1 March 1814, pp. 17–21.

100. Glover, *Eyewitness to the Peninsular War*, p. 139.
101. Glover, *Eyewitness to the Peninsular War*, p. 142.
102. Jan Egbertus van Gorkum, 'De bestorming der vesting Bergen op Zoom op den 8sten Maart 1814' (Leiden: 1862), p. 12.
103. TNA WO 1/200: Graham to Bathurst, No. 26, Head-Quarters Calmhout, 4 March 1814, pp. 67–8.
104. TNA WO 1/200: Graham to Bathurst, No. 26, Head-Quarters Calmhout, 4 March 1814, p. 68.
105. TNA PRO 30/35/6: Smyth to Mann, No. 6, Calmhout in Brabant, 10 March 1814, pp. 19–30.
106. See: www.brabantsewal.nl/.
107. Bamford, *A Bold and Ambitious Enterprise*, p. 178.
108. Geoffrey Parker, 'The Military Revolution – A Myth?' in Clifford Rogers (ed.), *The Military Revolution Debate, Readings on the Military Transformation of Early Modern Europe* (Oxford: Westview, 1995), p. 43.
109. Christopher Duffy, *Siege Warfare, The Fortress in the Early Modern World 1494–1660* (London: Routledge & Kegan, 1979), p. 90.
110. Revetted walls were built out of masonry.
111. This sunken area of ground had been formed by a major flood in 1530 and may possibly have been used for the excavation of clay for the Antwerp pottery trade.
112. The Antwerp Gate was located to the south of the main square, whilst the Breda Gate was positioned to the right of the town.
113. Jones, *Journal of Sieges*, p. 288.
114. Fortescue, *A History of the British Army, Vol. X*, p. 36.
115. Taylor to the Duke of York, 22 January 1814, *Taylor Papers*, p. 126.
116. http://andriessen.pl/verrassende-familieverbanden/jan-egbertus-van-gorkum.html.
117. Smyth to Taylor, Wouw, 21 January 1814, *Taylor Papers*, p. 125.
118. Van Gorkum, *De bestorming der vesting Bergen op Zoom*, pp. 14–15.
119. Van Gorkum, *De bestorming der vesting Bergen op Zoom*, pp. 18–19; Bamford, *A Bold and Ambitious Enterprise*, p. 181.
120. TNA WO 1/200: 'Right Attack', Memorandum No. 4 Headquarters, 8 March 1814, p. 159.
121. TNA WO 1/200: 'Left Attack', Memorandum No. 1 Headquarters, 8 March 1814, p. 147.
122. TNA WO 1/200: 'False Attack', Memorandum No. 3 Headquarters, 8 March 1814, p. 155 (Fortescue wrongly named the commander of this attack as Colonel Henry).
123. The Kijk in dem Pot was a large fortified camp which had originally been constructed during the French siege of Bergen Op Zoom in 1747.
124. TNA WO 1/200: 'Left Attack', Memorandum No. 1 Headquarters, 8 March 1814, p. 148.
125. TNA WO 1/ 200: 'Centre Attack', Memorandum No. 2 Headquarters, 8 March 1814, pp. 151–2.
126. The only official map of the fortress to have survived the siege belonged to Smyth and even this is not particularly detailed. TNA WO 78/ 2726: 'Plan of the Attack upon Bergen-Op-Zoom'.
127. Bamford, *A Bold and Ambitious Enterprise*, p. 189.
128. John Sperling, *Letters of an officer of the Corps of Royal Engineers to his Father from the British Army in Holland, Belgium and France, from the latter end of 1813 to 1816* (London: James Nisbet, 1872), p. 40.
129. Bamford, *A Bold and Ambitious Enterprise*, pp. 64–5, 195; Davies, *Wellington's Wars*, p. 191.
130. Bamford, *A Bold and Ambitious Enterprise*, p. 195.
131. Bamford, *A Bold and Ambitious Enterprise*, pp. 194–5.
132. *Narrative of the campaign of 1814 in Holland, by Lieut T.W.D Moodie, 21ˢᵗ Fusiliers in the Memoirs of the late War: The Personal Narrative of Captain Cooke, of the 43ʳᵈ Regiment Light Infantry, Vol. 2* (London: Henry Colburn, 1831), p. 286.
133. TNA WO 1/200: Copy, General Cooke to Graham, Bergen-Op-Zoom, 10 March 1814, p. 129.
134. TNA WO 1/200: No. 28, Graham to Bathurst, Calmhout, 10 March 1814, p. 118.

135. TNA PRO 30/35/6: Smyth to Mann, Calmhout, 10 March 1814, p. 21.
136. TNA WO 1/200: No. 28, Graham to Bathurst, Calmhout, 10 March 1814, p. 120, TNA PRO 30/ 35/6: Smyth to Mann, Calmhout, 10 March 1814, p. 22.
137. Bamford, *A Bold and Ambitious Enterprise*, pp. 199–200.
138. TNA WO 1/200: Copy, General Cooke to Graham, Bergen-Op-Zoom, 10 March 1814, p. 129; Sperling, *Letters of an officer of the Corps of Royal Engineers*, p. 41.
139. Bamford, *A Bold and Ambitious Enterprise*, p. 203.
140. Jones, *Journals of the Sieges*, p. 297.
141. Jones, *Journals of the Sieges*, p. 298.
142. Sperling, *Letters of an officer of the Corps of Royal Engineers*, p. 44. As Bamford has noted, Smyth took his leave at about 4am: Bamford, *A Bold and Ambitious Enterprise*, p. 209.
143. Sperling, *Letters of an officer of the Corps of Royal Engineers*, p. 45.
144. For more on Proby and his contemporaries see Ron McGuigan biographies of British generals online at: www.napoleonseries.org.
145. See Chapter 3.
146. Van Gorkum, *De bestorming der vesting Bergen op Zoom*, p. 84.
147. *Narrative of the campaign of 1814 in Holland, by Lieut T.W.D Moodie*, pp. 292–3.
148. TNA WO 1/200: No. 28, Graham to Bathurst, Calmhout, 10 March 1814, p. 122.
149. TNA WO 1/200: Copy, General Cooke to Graham, Bergen-Op-Zoom, 10 March 1814, p. 131.
150. TNA WO 1/200: Copy, General Cooke to Graham, Bergen-Op-Zoom, 10 March 1814, p. 132, TNA WO 1/200: No. 28, Graham to Bathurst, Calmhout, 10 March 1814, p. 122; Fortescue, *History of the British Army, Vol. X*, p. 50.
151. Totals calculated from: TNA WO 1/200: 'Return of Killed, Wounded and Missing of the Army under the Command of His Excellency General Sir Thomas Graham KB in the attack upon Bergen Op Zoom by storm on the Night of the 8th and Morning of the 9th March 1814', p. 211; TNA WO 1/200: 'State of English Prisoners included in the Capitulations', p. 223.
152. For a comparison see Burnham and McGuigan, *The British Army against Napoleon*, pp. 217–18.
153. TNA WO 1/200: Private, Graham to Bathurst, Calmhout, 10 March 1814, p. 141; TNA WO 1/200: Graham to Bathurst, Calmhout, 11 March 1814 enclosed in private letter of 10 March.
154. *Taylor Papers*, p. 152; Glover, *Eyewitness to the Peninsular War*, pp. 151–2.
155. *Taylor Papers*, pp. 152–3.
156. Glover, *Eyewitness to the Peninsular War*, p. 152.
157. *Taylor Papers*, p. 153; Bamford, *A Bold and Ambitious Enterprise*, p. 233.
158. Bamford, *A Bold and Ambitious Enterprise*, p. 234.
159. Chandler, *The Campaigns of Napoleon*, pp. 988–91.
160. The historian of Wellington's sieges, John.T Jones, observed that it would have been prudent to provide flares for the various columns. Jones, *Journal of Sieges*, p. 296.
161. Delavoye, *Life of Sir Thomas Graham*, p. 736.

Conclusion

1. Huw J. Davies, '"Nothing Except a Battle Lost Can be Half so Melancholy as a Battle Won" Explaining the Mixed Success of the British Army, 1815–1857', paper presented to the Society of Military History Annual Meeting Kansas City, Missouri, Apr. 2014, p. 7. Some of the points made by Davies in this paper can be found in his book: *Wellington's Wars, The Making of a Military Genius* and in a research article entitled: 'Wellington's First Command: The Political and Military Campaign Against Dhoondiah Vagh, February–September 1800', *Modern Asian Studies*, Vol. 44 (2010), pp. 1081–1113. David Pinder, Mark Urban and E.J. Evelyn have made similar arguments: David Pinder, 'Leather Stocks and Wooden Heads? British Military Thought during and as a consequence of the Seven Years' War, 1756–6', *BCMH Newsletter* (Apr. 2009),

pp. 1–38 at pp. 7–17; Urban, *Fusiliers;* Evelyn, '"I learned what one ought not to do": The British Army in Flanders and Holland 1793–95' in Guy (ed.), *The Road to Waterloo*, pp. 16–22.

2. John P. Kiszely, 'The relevance of history to the military profession: a British view' in Murray & Richard Sinnereich (eds), *The Past as Prologue*, p. 23; Hew Strachan (ed.), *Big Wars and Small Wars: The British Army and the Lessons of War in the 20ᵗʰ Century* (Abingdon: Routledge, 2006), p. 3; Sheffield, 'Review of Anthony Clayton', pp. 1593–4 at p. 1593; Griffith, *The Art of War of Revolutionary France*, p. 111.
3. Clayton, *The British Officer*, p. 9.
4. PP: index to the Reports of the Commissioners of Military Enquiry: 1806–1812 (Printed by order of the House of Commons 23 February 1816), pp. 1–31.
5. Richard Middleton, 'The Clinton–Cornwallis Controversy and Responsibility for the British Surrender at Yorktown', *History,* Vol. 98 Issue 331 (Jul. 2013), pp. 370–89.
6. http://www.royalnavy.mod.uk/The-Fleet/The-Royal-Marines/About-the-Royal-Marines/History.
7. Britt Zerbe, '"That most useful body of men": The Operational Doctrine and Identity of the British Marine Corps, 1755–1802' (Ph.D. thesis, University of Exeter, Sept. 2010), pp. 153–67.
8. Examples of the works available included: Thomas Molyneaux, *Conjunct Operations: or expeditions that have been carried on jointly by the fleet and army* (London: 1759); J. Robson, *The British Mars, Containing several schemes and inventions, to be practised by land or sea against the enemies of Great Britain* (London: 1763); Lieutenant John MacIntire, *A Military Treatise on the Discipline of Marine Forces when at Sea* (1763); Zerbe, '"That most useful body of men"', pp. 154–5, 163–5.
9. Mackesy, *British Victory in Egypt*, pp. 38–44. For more on learning and amphibious operations in the age of sail see Richard Harding, *Amphibious Warfare in the Eighteenth Century: British Expedition to the West Indies, 1740–42* (London: The Royal Historical Society, 1991).
10. Davies, *Wellington's Wars*, p. 97.
11. Paret, *The Cognitive Challenge of War*, p. 84; Geoffrey L. Herrera and Thomas G. Mahnken, 'Military Diffusion in Nineteenth-Century Europe: The Napoleonic and Prussian Military Systems' in Emily O. Goldman and Leslie C. Eliason, *The Diffusion of Military Technology and Ideas* (Stanford: Stanford University Press, 2003), pp. 205–42 at p. 213. For further on the Prussian response to defeat in 1806 see Gunther E. Rothenberg, *The Art of Warfare in the Age of Napoleon* (Bloomington: Indiana University Press, 1978), pp. 191–2; Denis E. Showalter, 'The Prussian Landwehr and Its Critics, 1813–1819' *Central European History,* Vol. 4 No. 1 (Mar. 1971), pp. 3–33 at p. 4.
12. Paret, *The Cognitive Challenge of War*, pp. 84–5.
13. Historians have debated the role played by the Prussians at Waterloo since the events of 18 June with traditional British histories fostering the view that the Prussians played only a minor role. The German response, led by Peter Hofschroer, attests that Blucher's role was far more significant and that his forces actually played a crucial role in defeating the French both at Plancenoit and in holding off the attentions of Marshals Grouchy and Gerard at Wavre. Although Wellington sought to downplay Blücher's role in later years, he was more generous in his official despatch immediately after the battle.
14. For a detailed study of the Dutch and Belgians at Waterloo see Veronica Baker-Smith, *Wellington's Hidden Heroes: The Dutch and the Belgians at Waterloo* (Oxford: Casemate, 2015).
15. Muir, *Wellington*, p. 81.
16. This much-neglected topic has been given a study worthy of its subject in the form of Veronica Baker-Smith's *Wellington's Hidden Heroes*.
17. Ward, *Wellington's Headquarters*, pp. 163–4.
18. Davies, *Wellington's Wars*, pp. 50–7, 73–5; Elizabeth Longford, *Wellington, The Years of the Sword* (London: World Books, 1971), pp. 91–121; Jac Weller, *Wellington in India* (London: Longman, 1972); Randolph G.S. Cooper, 'Wellington and the Marathas in 1803', *IHR,* Vol. II

No. 1 (Feb. 1989), pp. 31–8; David G. Chandler, 'Introduction: Regular and Irregular Warfare', *IHR*, Vol. II No. 1 (Feb. 1989), pp. 2–13 at p. 4.

19. Muir, *Wellington*, pp. 228–9.
20. Muir, *Wellington*, p. 165.
21. C. Esdaile (ed.), *The Duke of Wellington, Military Dispatches* (London: Penguin, 2014), pp. 14–17, 23, 148–51; Muir, *Wellington*, pp. 238–9; Mackesy, 'Wellington : The General', pp. 28–9. For a detailed study of Wellington's logistical system in the Iberian Peninsula see: Toby Michael Ormsby Redgrave, 'Wellington's Logistical Arrangements in the Peninsular War 1809–14' (doctoral thesis, Kings College, University of London, 1979); Ian Robertson, *A commanding presence, Wellington in the Peninsula, 1808–1814 : logistics, strategy, survival* (Stroud: Spellmount, 2008); Christopher D. Hall, *Wellington's Navy: Sea Power and the Peninsular War 1807–1814* (London: Chatham Publishing, 2004).
22. Bamford, *Sickness, Suffering and the Sword*, pp. 187–216.
23. Haythornthwaite, *The Armies of Wellington*, pp. 169–70.
24. Phillp Henry, 5th Earl of Stanhope, *Notes of Conversations with the Duke of Wellington 1831–1851* (New York: Longmans Green & Co., 1888), p. 182.
25. Esdaile, *The Duke of Wellington, Military Dispatches*, p. 145.
26. Edward Costello, *The Adventures of a Soldier or the Memoirs of Edward Costello* (London: Henry Coulburn, 1841), pp. 339, 343.
27. Heathcote, *Wellington's Peninsular Generals*, pp. 9–12; 24–7; 63–8; 101–8.
28. Gordon L Teffeteller, 'Wellington and Sir Rowland Hill', *IHR*, Vol. 11 No. 1 (Feb. 1989), pp. 68–75 at p. 69.
29. This line is most often associated with Wellington's former ADC, Fitzroy-Somerset, whom as Lord Raglan later commanded a British army during the Crimean War, 1854–6. Quoted in Allan Mallinson, *The Making of the British Army, From the English Civil War to the War on Terror* (London: Transworld, 2009), pp. 204–5. For a study of the career of Lord Raglan see: Christopher Hibbert, *The Destruction of Lord Raglan* (London: Longmans, 1961); John Sweetman, *Raglan, From the Peninsula to the Crimea* (London: Armour Press, 1993).
30. Tim Clayton, *Waterloo: Four Days that Changed Europe's Destiny* (London: Abacus, 2015), pp. 88–94.
31. Bruce Collins has suggested that British success in 1815 is evidence of lessons having been learnt when in reality it was chiefly due to Wellington's generalship. For Collins's argument see: Collins, *War and Empire: The Expansion of Britain*, pp. 347–61.

Bibliography

Archival Sources

The National Archives, Kew

TNA ADM 1/3987: 'A Prècis of all the papers in the Admiralty office which have any relation to the Expedition to the Scheldt from the first intelligence to the enemy's forces collecting at Antwerp, down to the final evacuation of Flushing'.

TNA F0 37/44: 'Holland, Letters and Papers from Lord Auckland at The Hague, the Secretary of State: with drafts'.

TNA FO 37/46: 'Holland, Letters and Papers from Lord Auckland at The Hague, the Secretary of State: with drafts. From March 12th: 1793 to March 31st: 1793 Volume the Fourth.'

TNA PRO 35/30/6: Carmichael Smyth Papers, Netherlands and France. Dispatches to Lieutenant-General Gother Mann, Inspector General of Fortifications, Entry Books. 1 Vol. Dec. 1813–Dec. 1818.

TNA WO 1/166: War Department – French Wars – Flanders campaign Feb.–Aug. 1793.

TNA WO 1/167: War Department – French Wars – Flanders campaign Sept.–Dec. 1793.

TNA WO 1/168: War Department – French Wars – Flanders campaign Jan.–Apr. 1794.

TNA WO 1/169: War Department – French Wars – Flanders campaign May.–Jul. 1794.

TNA WO 1/170: War Department – French Wars – Flanders campaign Jul.–Oct. 1794.

TNA WO 1/171: War Department – French Wars – Flanders campaign Nov.–Dec. 1794.

TNA WO 1/172: War Department – French Wars – Flanders campaign Jan.–Apr. 1795.

TNA WO 1/173: War Department – French Wars – Flanders campaign Apr.–Dec. 1795.

TNA WO 1/179: War Department – French Wars – Helder Expedition – Misc. correspondence. Commanders Dispatches (Jul.–Oct.).

TNA WO 1/180: War Department in letters and papers: i. of the French wars period. Helder Expedition: Commanders dispatches (Oct.–Nov. 1799).

TNA WO 1/181: War Department in letters and papers – French Wars – Helder expedition: Other government departments.

TNA WO 1/182: War Department in letters and papers – French Wars – Helder expedition. Miscellaneous.

TNA WO 1/198: Expedition to Holland, Miscellaneous – 1813, Vol. 3 Commander-in-Chief, Treasury, Ordnance, Foreign Office and Commssisionary General in Chief.

TNA WO 1/199: British Army in Holland 1813–14 December–January–February Vol. 1, M. Generals Cooke & Gibbs and General Sir Thomas Graham.

TNA WO 1/200: British Army in Holland and Flanders 1813–14 March–April–May, Vol. 2, General Lord Lynedoch.

TNA WO 1/414: Major General Taylor's Mission to Holland, 1813–1814.

TNA WO 3/11: William Fawcett to the Duke of York, 27 March 1793, Horse Guards, Commander in Chief General Letters, Nov. 1792–Dec. 1793.

TNA WO 3/ 28: 'Army Circular of 12 March 1795'.

TNA WO 6/7: Sir Henry Dundas to Lieutenant-Colonel Sir James Murray, 16 April 1793, Whitehall War Department and Successors: Secretary of State for War and Secretary for War and the Colonies Out-Letters. 01 February 1793–31 August 1793.

TNA WO 6/16: War Department and successors: Secretary of State for War and the Colonies, Out-Letters. Continent. Holland, Flanders and France I January 1813–31 December 1818.

TNA WO 78/2726: 'Plan of the Attack upon Bergen-Op-Zoom' 1814.

TNA WO 78/5822: 'Plan of Encampments of Windsor Forest' 23 July 1798.

TNA WO 78/5823: 'Plan of Encampments of Windsor Forest' 24 June 1799.

TNA WO 78/5824: 'Plan of Encampments of Bagshot Heath' – 1–Jan. 1799.

TNA WO 78/5825: – 'Plan of Encampments of Swindley Camp' – (under Duke of York and David Dundas) – 29 June 1800'.

WO 124/8: Entry Book of Correspondence of Ensign Andrew Durnford of the Corps of Engineers at Dunkirk 1 vol. 1772 Apr.–1773 Mar.

TNA WO 124/13: Copy of a Report of the British Engineers concerning the work of demolition at Dunkirk, and two copies of an extract from it prepared specially for the French Ambassador (1766).

TNA WO 124/18 Two copies of Papers proposing, in the event of war with France, (a) an invasion of Dieppe, and (b) the closure of Dunkirk harbour (1773).

TNA WO 133/16: *Journal of the Proceedings of the Army* under the command of Lieutenant General the Earl of Chatham, 28 July 1809.

TNA FO 37/44: Letter No. 25, Auckland to Grenville, 8 February 1793 The Hague.

TNA HO 50/ 369: Colonel William Congreve to Sir James Murray, 2 July 1793.

The National Army Museum, London

NAM 1968-07-261-1: Diagram showing 'Distribution of the Medical Staff' taken from Book containing misc. notes and Journals of General Sir Frederick William Trench, 'Diary of the Walcheren Expedition, 1809' General Orders-Landing-Reserve-John Hope. Orders for Officers of Q.M.G. Department, Aug. 1–Sept. 1.

NAM 1974-12-154-1: Lt. Col. Charles Stevenson, Late of the XXth Regt. *Reminiscences of my military life from 1795–1818.*

NAM 1978-12-55-2: Diary of Lieutenant-General Jasper Nicholls.

NAM 1979-12-21-1: Diary of an unidentified Soldier of 38th (1st Staffordshire) Regiment of Foot.

NAM 1992-04-148-1: Memoirs of Sergeant Solomon Rich, 28th Regiment of foot 1803–1809.

NAM 2002-02-729-1: Typescript manuscript of the memoir of Capt. Peter Bowlby, 4th (or King's Own) Regiment of Foot.

The National Maritime Museum, London

NMM Artificial collections previously assembled by Phillipps-Croker: Vice-Admiral Lord Horatio Nelson in letters: CRK/10/150: Russel to Nelson, HMS GIER, off Gravelines, 17 August 1801; CRK/10/151: Russel to Nelson, HMS GIER off Calais, 18 August 1801; CRK/10/153: Russel to Nelson, HMS GIER, off Calais, 24 August 1801.

NMM COO/ 2/ B.1: Admiral Sir Richard Strachan to Captain Owen of His Majesty's Ship Clyde, 26 July 1809.

British Library Manuscript Collections, London

BL Add MSS 38733–38735: The Huskisson Papers, Vol. II Correspondence 1798–1799.

BL Add MSS 40101: The Papers and Correspondence of Henry Dundas, 1st Viscount Melville (1742–1811) Vol. II (ff. 95); Letters of William Wyndham Grenville, Baron Grenville, Secretary of State for Foreign Affairs, to Henry Dundas, 1798–1801.

BL Add MSS 40102: Melville Papers Vol. III: Drafts and Manuscripts 1794–1805.

BL Add MSS 43770: The Melville Papers Vol. IV.

BL Add MSS 72703L: Letter from Lord Grenville as Foreign Secretary to Pitt The Younger, Cleveland Row 1 August 1799.

House of Commons Parliamentary Papers Online (Proquest)

PP: 'Return of the number of effective men in the British army, from the 1st January 1775 to the 1st January 1783; distinguishing each year:--as far as can be made up from the documents in the War-Office' by Richard Fitzpatrick, 22nd May 1806: Table 172, p. 393.

PP: Scheldt Inquiry, *Minutes of evidence taken before the Committee of the whole house, appointed to consider the policy and conduct of the late expedition to the Scheldt* (1810).

PP: 'An account of the effective numbers and established strength of regiments of cavalry, guards, and infantry, borne on the British establishment; and the general distribution of the said forces; in the years 1791 and 1792' by Lord Palmerston, 22 February 1816: House of Commons, Parliamentary Papers Online (Proquest, 2006), Table. 40, p. 391.

The National Library of Scotland, Edinburgh

NLS Ms 16079: Military Notebook and Papers of General Sir Thomas Graham, Lord Lynedoch.

Published Primary Sources

Anon. 'An Old Officer'. *Cautions and Advices to officers of the Army* (Edinburgh: Aeneas Mackay, 1777).

Anon. *The Present State of the British Army in Flanders, with an authentic account of the British retreat from before Dunkirk by a British officer in that Army who was living on the 24th of September* (London: H.D. Symonds, 1793).

Anon. *The New Annual Register, or General Repository of History, Politics and Literature, For the Year 1799* (London: 1805).

Anon. *Minutes of a Court Martial holden on Board his Majesty's ship Gladiator, in Portsmouth Harbour, on Friday, the 6th day of March, 1807 And continued by Adjournment till Wednesday, March 11 following For the Trial of Capt. Sir Home Popham including a complete copy of his defence, taken from the original* (London: 1807).

Anon. *A Collection of Papers relating to the expedition to the Scheldt, presented to Parliament in 1810* (London: A. Strahan, 1810).

Anon. *Letters from Flushing, An Account of the Expedition to Walcheren, Beveland, and the Mouth of the Scheldt, Under the command of the Earl of Chatham, To which is added A Topographical and Statistical Account of the Islands of Walcheren and Beveland, By an Officer of the Eighty-First Regiment* (London: Naval & Military Press, in Association with the National Army Museum, n.d.).

Anon. *Memorandum of a collection of bulletins: 1793 to 1823, Foreign and Commonwealth Office Collection* (1823).

Anon. *The Campaign in Holland, 1799 by a Subaltern* (London: W. Mitchell, 1861).

Anon. *Her Majesty's Stationery Office, British Minor Expeditions 1746 to 1814, Compiled in the Intelligence Branch of the Quartermaster-General's Department* (London: 1884).

The Marquis of Anglesey (ed.). 'Two brothers in the Netherlands, 1794–1795', Part of the Duke of York's campaign as seen through the eyes of two young commanding officers based upon hitherto unpublished letters in the "Plas Newydd papers"', *JSAHR*, Volume 32, (1954), 74–82.

Austin, Brigadier General H.H. (ed.). *Old Stick Leg: Extracts from the Diaries of Major Thomas Austin* (London: Geoffrey Bles, 1926).

Bourcet, General P. *Principes de la guerre des montages* (Paris: 1775).

Brown, Robert. *Corporal Brown's Campaigns in the Low Countries: Recollections of a Coldstream Guard in the Early Campaigns Against Revolutionary France, 1793–1795* (London: Leonaur, 2008).

Bunbury, Lieutenant General Sir Henry. *Narratives of the some passages in the great war with France, from 1799 to 1810* (London: Richard Bentley, 1854).

Cook, Colonel H.C.B. (ed.). 'The St George Diary A junior regimental officer in the Low Countries, 1794–95', *JSAHR*, V. 47 (1969), 233–250.

Cooper, T.W. & Medhurst, M. *The Military Career of Colonel Francis Tidy, C.B* (London: National Army Museum, Mar. 1997).

Croker, John Wilson. *The Croker Papers: The Correspondence and Diaries of John Wilson Croker, Secretary to the Admiralty from 1809 to 1830 Vol. I* (London: 1885).

Daendels, H.W. *Rapport des opérations de la division du lieutenant-general Daendels, depuis le 22 août, jusqu'à la capitulation de l'Armeé Anglais et Russe, le 18 octobre 1799* (The Hague).

Donkin, Major Robert. *Military Collections and Remarks* (New York: 1777).

Dundas, Colonel Sir David. *Principles of Military Movements Chiefly applied to the infantry, illustrated by the manoeuvres of the Prussian troops, and by an outline of the British campaigns in Germany during the War of 1757* (London: T. Cadell, N.DCC.LXXXVIII).

Lord Dunfermline, James. *Lieutenant-General Sir Ralph Abercromby 1793–1801, A Memoir by his Son* (Uckfield: Naval & Military Press, 1861).

The Dropmore Papers: *The Manuscripts of J.B. Fortescue preserved at Dropmore Vol. II (Being the Correspondence and Papers of Lord Grenville 1698–1820)* (London: His Majesty's Stationery Office, 1894).

The Dropmore Papers: *The Manuscripts of J.B. Fortescue preserved at Dropmore Vol. IV (Being the correspondence and papers of Lord Grenville 1698–1820)* (London: His Majesty's Stationery Office, 1905).

Emmerich, Lieutenant Colonel A. *The Partisan in War: Or The Use of a Corps of Light Troops to an Army* (1789).

Ewald, Oberst-Leutnant von. *Abhandlung von dem Dienst der liechten Truppen* (Flensburg, Schleswig and Leipzig: 1790).

Fletcher, Ian (ed.). *In the Service of the King, The Letters of William Thornton Keep, at Home, Walcheren, and in the Peninsula, 1808–1814* (Staplehurst: Spellmount, 1997).

Fyers, Colonel William. 'Journal of the Siege of Flushing in the year 1809 by a detachment of the Army commanded by the Earl of Chatham. Under the Immediate orders of Lieutenant-General Sir Eyre Coote, K.B.', ed. by Major Evan W.H. Fyers, *JSAHR*, Vol. 13 (1934), 145–58.

Glover, Gareth (ed.). *Eyewitness to the Peninsular War and the Battle of Waterloo, The Letters and Journals of Lieutenant-Colonel the Honourable James Stanhope 1803–1825* (Barnsley: Pen & Sword, in association with Chevening Trust, 2010).

Gorkum, Jan Egbertus van. 'De bestorming der vesting Bergen op Zoom op den 8sten Maart 1814' (Leiden: 1862).

Grazebrook, Lieutenant Colonel R.M. (ed.). '"The Campaign in Flanders of 1793–1795" Journal of Lieutenant-Colonel Charles Stewart, 28th Foot', *JSAHR*, Vol. 28 (1951), 3–16.

Grehan, John and Mace, Martin. *Despatches from the Front, British Battles of the Napoleonic Wars 1793–1806* (Barnsley: Pen & Sword, 2013).

Harvey, A.D. 'Captain Paisley at Walcheren, August 1809', *JSAHR*, Vol. LXIX, No. 277 (Spring, 1991), 16–21.

Henry, Phillip 5th Earl of Stanhope. *Notes of Conversations with the Duke of Wellington 1831–1851* (New York: Longmans Green & Co., 1888).

Hibbert, Christopher (ed.). *The Recollections of Rifleman Harris, As Told to Henry Curling* (Moreton-in-Marsh: Windrush Press, 2000).

Hibbert, Christopher (ed.). *A Soldier of the Seventy-First, The Journal of a Soldier the Highland Light Infantry 1806–1815* (London: Leo Cooper, 1976).

Hunt, Leigh. 'Walcheren Expedition; or the Englishman's Lament for the loss of his countrymen', *Potential Register*, Vol. 7 (Jan. 1812).

Hunt, 'Journal kept by Lieut. and Adjutant Hunt, of the 7th (or Queen's Own) Light Dragoons, during the Regiment's absence on the Expedition to North Holland, in the year 1799', *RUSI* 59 (1914, Jul./Nov.), 169–170.

James, Charles. *The Regimental Companion: containing the relative duties of every soldier in the British Army* (London: 1800).

James, Walter H. Captain, Late Royal Engineers. 'Military Education and Training', *Royal United Service Institutional Journal* 26 (1883), 369.

Jarry, General Francis. *Instruction Concerning the Duties of Light Infantry in the Field* (1803).

Jeffrey, Reginald W. (ed.). *Dyott's Diary, A selection from the Journal of William Dyott, sometime General in the British Army and aide-de-camp to his Majesty King George III, Vol. 1* (London: Archibald Constable and Company, 1907).

Jeney, M.de. *The Partisan: Or the Art of Making War in Detachments* (1760).

Jones, Major General Sir John T. *Journals of the Sieges carried on by the Army under the Duke of Wellington in Spain during the years 1811 to 1814; with some notes and additions; also memoranda relative to the lines thrown up to cover Lisbon in 1810, Vol. II* (London: John Weale, 1846).

Jones, Captain L.T. *An Historical Journal of the British Campaign on the Continent in the Year 1794* (London: 1797).

Kelly, Paul. 'Strategy and Counter-Revolution: The Journal of Sir Gilbert Elliot, 1–22 September 1793', *EHR*, Vol. 98 No. 387 (Apr. 1983), 328–48.

Lecointe, M. *The Science of Military Posts, for the use of Regimental Officers who frequently Command Detached Parties* (1761).

Liddell Hart, B.H. *The Letters of Private Wheeler, 1809–1828* (Moreton-in-Marsh: Windrush Press, 1999).

Locheé, Lewis. *An Essay on Military Education* (1773).

MacIntire, Lieutenant John. *A Military Treatise on the Discipline of Marine Forces when at Sea* (1763).

Maidwell, Lewis. *An essay upon the necessity and excellency of education. With an account of erecting the Royal Mathematical School* (London: J. Nutt, 1705).

Maule, Major Francis. *Late of the 2nd or Queens Regiment and on the Staff on the Severn District, Memoirs of the Principal Events in the Campaigns of North Holland and Egypt Together with a Brief Description of the Islands of Crete, Rhodes, Syracuse, Minorca and the Voyage to the Mediterranean* (Uckfield: Naval & Military Press, 1861).

Maurice, J.F. *The Diary of Sir John Moore, Vol. 1* (London: Arnold, 1904).

Molyneaux, Thomas. *Conjunct Operations: or expeditions that have been carried on jointly by the fleet and army* (London: 1759).

Moodie, Lieutenant T.W.D. *Narrative of the campaign of 1814 in Holland, by Lieut T.W.D. Moodie, 21st Fusiliers in the Memoirs of the late War: The Personal Narrative of Captain Cooke, of the 43rd Regiment Light Infantry, Vol. 2* (London: Henry Colburn, 1831).

Morris, Thomas. *Recollections of Military Service in 1813, 1814, & 1815 through Germany, Holland, and France including some details of the battles of Quatre Bras and Waterloo* (London: James Madden and Co., 1845).

Ross, Charles (ed.). *Correspondence of Charles, First Marquis Cornwallis, Vol. II* (London: 1859).

Rothenberg, Baron de. *Regulations for the Exercise of Riflemen and Light Infantry, and Instructions for their conduct in the field* (1799).

Simcoe, J.G. *Military Journal: a history of the operations of a partisan corps, called the Queen's Rangers, commanded by Lieut. Col. J.G. Simcoe, during the war of the American Revolution; now first published, with a memoir of the author and other additions* (1844).

Simes, Thomas. *Military Medley* (1768).

Spiller, George. *Observations on certain branches of the Commissariat System, particularly connected with the present Military State of the Country* (London: 1806).

Steevens, Lieutenant Colonel Charles. *Reminisces of my Military Life, from 1795 to 1818* (Winchester: Warren & Sons, n.d.).

Stewart, Brigadier General. *Outlines of a Plan for the general Reform of the British Land Forces* (second edn, 1806).

Surtees, William. *Twenty-Five Years in the Rifle Brigade* (London: T. Cadall, 1833).

Tarleton, Lieutenant Colonel Banastre. *A History of the campaigns of 1780 and 1781, in the southern provinces of North America* (Dublin: Colles, 1787).

Taylor, Sir Herbert. *The Taylor Papers being a Record of certain Reminisces, Letters, and Journals in the life of Lieutenant-General Sir Herbert Taylor G.C.B., G.C.H.* (London: Longmans, 1913).

Tupper, Ferdinand Brock (ed.). *The Life and Correspondence of Major-General Sir Isaac Brock* (London: Simpkin, Marshal, 1847).

Vane, Charles William, Marquess of Londonderry (ed.). *Correspondence, Despatches, And Other Papers of Viscount Castlereagh Second Series. Military and Miscellaneous. Vol. VI* (London: William Shorberl, 1851).

Verney, Sir Harry (ed.). *The Journals and Correspondence of General Sir Harry Calvert, comprising the campaigns in Flanders and Holland in 1793-4* (London: Hurst and Blackett, 1823).

Walsh, E. *A Narrative of the Expedition to Holland in the autumn of the year 1799 Illustrated with a map of north Holland and Seven Views* (London: G.G. and J. Robinson, Pater-Noster, S. Hanson, 1800).

Wardell, John (ed.). *Major-Ross-Lewin, With the Thirty-Second in the Peninsular and other Campaigns* (Dublin: Hodges & Figges, n.d.).

Yarrow, David (ed.). 'A Journal of the Proceedings of His Majesty's Sloop of War the GALQO during the Siege of Flushing in the Year 1809 under the Command of John Gardene McBride McKillop. Esq. and Especially Genl. Sir Wm. Congreve, Bart', by Joseph Palmer Wrangle in the *Mariners Mirror*, Vol. 61 No. 2 (May 1975), 183–9.

Young, Major William. *Manoeuvres, or Practical Observations on the Art of War* (1771).

Newspapers
Annual Register.
Belfast Monthly Magazine.
London Gazette.
The London Times.

Secondary Sources
Andress, David. *The Savage Storm: Britain on the brink in the age of Napoleon* (London: Little Brown, 2012).

Armitage, David and Subrahmanyam, Sanjay (eds). *The Age of Revolutions in Global Context c. 1760–1840* (Basingstoke: Palgrave Macmillan, 2010).

Artz, F.D. *The Development of Technical Education in France 1500–1850* (Cambridge: MIT Press, 1966).

Ashby, Ralph. *Napoleon Against Great Odds, The Emperor and the Defenders of France, 1814* (Santa Barbara: Praeger, 2010).

Aspinall, A. (ed.). *The Later Correspondence of George III, Published by Authority of Her majesty Queen Elizabeth II, Volume II February 1793 to December 1797* (Cambridge: Cambridge University Press, 1963).

Atkin, Muriel. 'The Pragmatic Diplomacy of Paul I: Russia's Relations with Asia 1796–1801', *Slavic Review*, Vol. 38 No. 1 (Mar. 1979), 60–74.

Atkinson, C.T. 'Gleanings from the Cathcart MSS: Part IV: The Netherlands, 1794–1795', *JSAHR*, XXIX (120) (1951), 97–157.

Bamford, Andrew. *A Bold and Ambitious Enterprise, The British Army in the Low Countries 1813–1814* (Barnsley: Frontline, 2013).

Bamford, Andrew. *Sickness, Suffering and the Sword, The British Regiment on Campaign, 1808–1815* (Norman: University of Oklahoma Press, 2013).

Barnet, Corelli. *Britain and Her Army 1509–1970, A Military, Political and Social Survey* (London: Allen Lane, 1970, repr. Penguin, 1974).

Barnet, Corelli. 'The Education of Military Elites', *Journal of Contemporary History*, Vol. 2 No. 3, Education and Social Structure (Jul. 1967), 15–35.

Beatson, F.C. *Wellington and the Invasion of France: The Bidassoa to the Battle of the Nivelle, 1813* (London: Leonaur, 2007).

Beckett, Ian F.W. *The Amateur Military Tradition, 1558–1945* (Manchester: Manchester University Press, 1991).

Bell, David A. *The First Total War, Napoleon's Europe and the Birth of Modern War* (London: Bloomsbury, 2007).

Belloc, Hilaire. *British Battles: Tourcoing* (London: Steven Swift, 1912).

Bew, John. *Castlereagh, from Enlightment to Tyranny* (London: Quercus, 2011).

Bindoff, S.T. *The Scheldt Question to 1839* (London: George Allen & Unwin, 1945).

Black, Jeremy. 'British Strategy and the Struggle with France 1793–1815', *JSS*, Vol. 31 No. 4 (Aug. 2008), 553–69.

Black, Jeremy. *George III, America's Last King* (New Haven and London: Yale University Press, 2006, repr. 2008).

Black, Jeremy. *Rethinking Military History* (Abingdon: Routledge, 2004).

Black, Jeremy. 'Historiographical Essay: Britain as a Military Power, 1688–1815', *The Journal of Military History*, Vol. 64 No. 1 (Jan. 2000), 159–77.

Black, Jeremy. *Britain as a military power, 1688–1815* (London: UCL Press, 1999).

Black, Jeremy. *British Foreign Policy in the Age of Revolutions, 1783–1793* (Cambridge: Cambridge University Press, 1994).

Black, Jeremy. *European Warfare 1660–1815* (London and New Haven: Yale University Press, 1994).

Black, Jeremy. 'Eighteenth-Century English Politics: Recent Work and Current Problems', *Albion: A Quarterly Journal Concerned with British Studies*, Vol. 25 No. 3 (Autumn, 1993), 419–41.

Blanco, Richard L. 'The Development of British Military Medicine, 1793–1814', *Military Affairs*, Vol. 38 No. 1 (Feb. 1974), 4–10.

Blanning, T.C.W. *The Pursuit of Glory, Europe 1648–1815* (Cambridge: Allen Lane, 2007).

Blanning, T.C.W. *The French Revolutionary Wars 1787–1802* (London: Arnold, 1996).

Bond, Gordon C. *The Grand Expedition, The British invasion of Holland in 1809* (Athens: The University of Georgia Press, 1979).

Bourke, Joanna. 'New Military History' in Mathew Hughes and William J. Philpott, *Palgrave advances in modern military history* (Basingstoke: Palgrave, 2006).

Bossche, Geert, van den. 'Political propaganda in the Brabant Revolution: Habsburg "negligence" versus Belgian nation-building', *History of European Ideas*, 28:3, 119–44.

Boxer, C.R. *The Anglo-Dutch Wars of the 17ᵗʰ Century* (London: HMSO, 1974).

Brake, Wayne P. Te. 'Popular Politics and the Dutch Patriot Revolution', *Theory and Society*, Vol. 14, No. 2 (Mar. 1985), 199–222.

Brett-James, Anthony. 'The Walcheren failure' Part One, *History Today*, Vol. 13 No. 12 (Dec. 1963), 811–20.

Brett-James, Anthony. 'The Walcheren failure' Part Two, *History Today*, Vol. 14 No. 1 (Jan. 1964), 60–8.

Brewer, John. *The Sinews of Power: War, Money and the English State 1688–1783* (London: Unwin Hyman, 1989).

Brown, Gerald S. 'The Anglo-French Naval Crisis, 1778: A Study of Conflict in the North Cabinet', *WMQ*, Third Series, Vol. 13 No. 1 (Jan. 1956), 3–25.

Brown, Howard G. 'Review of Forrest, Alan. *The Revolution in Provincial France: Aquitaine, 1789–1799*', *JMH*, Vol. 71 No. 3 (Sept. 1999), 708–9.

Bruce, Anthony P. C. *The Purchase System in the British Army, 1660–1871* (London: Royal Historical Society, 1980).

Bull, Stephen. *The Furie of the Ordnance, Artillery in the English Civil Wars* (Woodbridge: Boydell, 2008).

Burne, Alfred H. *The Noble Duke of York, The Military Life of Frederick Duke of York and Albany* (London: Staples, 1949).

Burnham, Robert and McGuigan, Ron. *The British Army against Napoleon, Facts, Lists and Trivia 1805–1815* (Barnsley: Frontline Books, 2010).

Burroughs, Peter. 'An Unreformed Army? 1815–1868' in G. Chandler and I. Beckett (eds), *The Oxford History of the British Army* (Oxford: Oxford University Press, 2003).

Buttery, David. *Wellington against Junot, The First Invasion of Portugal 1807–1808* (Barnsley: Pen & Sword, 2011).

Brewer, John. *The Sinews of Power: War, Money and the English State, 1688–1783* (New York: Alfred A. Knopf, 1989).

Carlyle, E.I. 'Cooke, Sir George (1768–1837)', rev. Roger T. Stearn, *Oxford Dictionary of National Biography* (Oxford: Oxford University Press, 2004).

Castillo, Dennis. *The Maltese Cross: A Strategic History of Malta* (Westport: Praeger, 2006).

Chandler, David G. 'Introduction: Regular and Irregular Warfare', *IHR*, Vol. II No. 1 (Feb. 1989), 2–13.

Chandler, David G. (ed.), *Napoleon's Marshals* (London: Weidenfeld & Nicolson, 1987).

Chandler, David G. *The Campaigns of Napoleon* (London: Weidenfeld & Nicolson, 1967).

Chandler, G. and Beckett, I. (eds), *The Oxford History of the British Army* (Oxford: Oxford University Press, 2003).

Childs, John. *Armies and Warfare in Europe, 1648–1789* (New York: Holmes & Meier, 1982).

Christie, C.A. 'The Royal Navy and the Walcheren Expedition of 1809' in Crag L. Symonds (ed.), *New Aspects of Naval History, Selected Papers presented at the Fourth Naval History Symposium*, United States Naval Academy, 25–6 October 1979 (Annapolis: Naval Institute Press, 1981).

Clausewitz, Carl von. *On War*, eds and trans Howard, Michael and Paret, Peter (Princeton: Princeton University Press, 1976).

Clayton, Anthony. *The British Officer, Leading the Army from 1660 to the Present* (Harlow: Pearson Longman, 2007).

Clayton, Tim. *Waterloo: Four Days that Changed Europe's Destiny* (London: Abacus, 2015).

Cobb, Richard and Jones, Colin (eds). *The French Revolution, Voices from a momentous epoch 1789–1795* (London: Guild Publishing, 1988).

Cohen, Eliot A. 'Change and Transformation in Military Affairs', *JSS*, 27:3 (2004), 395–407.

Collins, Bruce. *War and Empire: The Expansion of Britain 1790–1830* (Harlow: Pearson Longman, 2010).

Connelly, Owen. *Napoleon's Satellite Kingdoms, Managing Conquered Peoples* (Malabar: R.E. Krieger, 1965).

Conway, Stephen. 'Britain and the Revolutionary Crisis' in P.J. Marshall (ed.), *The Eighteenth-Century, Volume II, The Oxford History of the British Empire* (Oxford: Oxford University Press, 1998, repr. 2006).

Conway, Stephen. 'The Politics of British Military and Naval Mobilization, 1775–83', *EHR*, Vol. 112 No. 449 (Nov. 1997), 1179–1201.

Conway, Stephen. 'Bentham versus Pitt: Jeremy Bentham and British Foreign Policy 1789', *HJ*, 30 (1987), 791–809.

Conway, Stephen. 'To Subdue America: British Army Officers and the Conduct of the Revolutionary War', *WMQ*, Third Series, Vol. 43 No. 3 (Jul. 1986), 381–407.

Conway, Stephen. 'British Army Officers and the American War for Independence', *WMQ*, Third Series, Vol. 41 No. 2 (Apr. 1984), 265–76.

Cook, B.A. and Germani, I. 'The Face of Battle: Hondschoote 1793', *Selected Papers: Consortium on Revolutionary Europe 1750–1850* (Baton Rouge: 2002), (Florida State: 2002).

Cookson, J.E. *The British Armed Nation 1793–1815* (Oxford: Clarendon Press, 1997).

Cookson, J.E. 'The English Volunteer Movement of the French Wars, 1793–1815: Some Contexts', *HJ*, Vol. 32 No. 4 (Dec. 1989), 867–91.

Cooper, Randolph G.S. 'Wellington and the Marathas in 1803', *IHR*, Vol. II No. 1 (Feb., 1989), 31–8.

Crowe, Elizabeth. 'The Walcheren Expedition and the New Army Medical Board: A Reconsideration', *EHR*, Vol. 88 No. 349 (Oct. 1973), 770–85.

Cusick, Raymond P. *Wellington's Rifles, The Origins, Development and Battles of the Rifle Regiments in the Peninsular War and at Waterloo 1758 to 1815* (Barnsley: Pen & Sword, 2013).

Daly, Gavin. 'English Smugglers, the Channel, and the Napoleonic Wars, 1800–1814', *Journal of British Studies*, Vol. 46 No. 1 (Jan. 2007), 30–46.

David, Paul K. 'Military Transformation? Which Transformation, and what lies ahead?' in Stephen J. Cimbala (ed.), *The George W. Bush Defence Program: Policy, Strategy, and War* (Dulles: Potomac Books, 2010).

Davies, Huw J. '"Nothing Except a Battle Lost Can be Half so Melancholy as a Battle Won" Explaining the Mixed Success of the British Army, 1815–1857', paper presented to the Society of Military History Annual Meeting Kansas City (Missouri: Apr. 2014).

Davies, Huw J. *Wellington's Wars, The Making of a Military Genius* (New Haven and London: Yale University Press, 2012).

Davies, Huw J. 'Wellington's First Command: The Political and Military Campaign Against Dhoondiah Vagh, February–September 1800', *Modern Asian Studies*, Vol. 44 (2010), 1081–1113.

Delavoye, Alex M. *Life of Sir Thomas Graham, Lord Lynedoch* (London: Richardson, 1880).

Divall, Carole. *Burgos 1812: Wellington's Worst Scrape* (Barnsley: Pen & Sword, 2012).

Divall, Carole. *Napoleonic Lives, Researching the British Soldiers of the Napoleonic Wars* (Barnsley: Pen & Sword, 2012).

Divall, Carole. *Redcoats against Napoleon, The 30th Regiment During the Revolutionary and Napoleonic Wars* (Barnsley: Pen & Sword, 2009).

Duffy, Christopher. *Eagles over the Alp's, Suvorov in Italy and Switzerland, 1799* (Chicago: The Emperors Press, 1999).

Duffy, Christopher. *Russia's Military Way to the West, Origins and Nature of Russian Military Power 1700–1800* (London: Routledge & Kegan Paul, 1981).

Duffy, Christopher. *Siege Warfare, The Fortress in the Early Modern World 1494–1660* (London: Routledge & Kegan, 1979).

Duffy, Christopher. *The Army of Maria Theresa, The Armed Forces of Imperial Austria, 1740–1780* (London: David & Charles, 1977).

Duffy, Michael. 'Pitt, Grenville and the Control of British Foreign Policy in the 1790s' in Jeremy Black (ed.), *Knights Errant and True Englishmen: British Foreign Policy, 1660–1800* (Edinburgh: John Donald, 1989).

Duffy, Michael. *Soldiers, Sugar and Seapower, The British Expeditions to the West Indies and the War against Revolutionary France* (Oxford: Clarendon Press, 1987).

Duffy, Michael. 'A Particular Service': The British Government and the Dunkirk Expedition of 1793', *EHR*, Vol. 91 No. 360 (Jul. 1976), 529–54.

Dwyer, Philip G. 'Self-Interest versus the Common Cause: Austria, Prussia and Russia against Napoleon', *JSS*, 31:4 (2008), 605–32.

Edmonds, Bill. '"Federalism" and Urban Revolt in France in 1793', *JMH* Vol. 55 No. 1 (Mar. 1983), 22–53.

Elliot, D.C. 'The Grenville Mission to Berlin, 1799', *HLQ*, Vol. 18 No. 2 (Feb. 1955), 129–30.

Elting, John R. *Swords Around a Throne, Napoleon's Grande Armée* (New York: DeCapo Press, 1997).

Emsley, Clive. 'Review of John Cookson, *The British Armed Nation*', *EHR*, Vol. 114 No. 455 (Feb. 1999), 216–17.

Emsley, Clive (ed.). *British Society and the French Wars 1793–1815* (London and Basingstoke: Macmillan, 1979).

Emsley, Clive. 'Wooden Walls and Volunteers: 1803–5' in Clive Emsley (ed.), *British Society and the French Wars 1793–1815* (London and Basingstoke: Macmillan, 1979).

Erhman, John. *The Younger Pitt, The Reluctant Transition* (London: Constable, 1983).

Esdaile, Charles (ed.). *The Duke of Wellington, Military Dispatches* (London: Penguin, 2014).

Esdaile, Charles. *Napoleon's War's, An International History* (London: Penguin, 2006).

Esdaile, Charles. *The Peninsular War, A New History* (London: Penguin, 2003).

Esposito, Vincent J. & Elting, John R. *A Military History and Atlas of the Napoleonic Wars* (London: Greenhill, 1999).

Evelyn, E.J. '"I learned what one ought not to do": The British Army in Flanders and Holland 1793–95' in A.J. Guy (ed.), *The Road to Waterloo: The British Army and the Struggle Against Revolutionary and Napoleonic France, 1793–1815* (London: National Army Publications, 1990).

Farrell, Theo. 'The dynamics of British military transformation', *International Affairs* 84: 4 (2008), 777–807.

Fedorak, Charles John. 'The Royal Navy and British Amphibious Operations during the Revolutionary and Napoleonic Wars', *Military Affairs*, Vol. 52 No. 3 (Jul. 1988), 141–6.

Feldbæk, Ole. 'The Foreign Policy of Tsar Paul I, 1800–1801: An Interpretation', *Jahrbücher für Geschichte Osteuropas, Neue Folge*, Bd. 30, H. 1 (1982), 16–36.

Fletcher, Ian. *The Waters of Oblivion, The British Invasion of the Rio De La Plata 1806–1807* (Stroud: Spellmount, 2006).

Fletcher, Ian. *Vittoria 1813, Osprey Campaign Series No. 59* (Oxford: Osprey, 1998).

Foley, Robert T., Griffin, Stuart and McCartney, Helen. '"Transformation in contact": learning the lessons of modern war', *International Affairs*, 87:2 (2011), 253–70.

Forrest, Alan. *The Revolution in Provincial France: Aquitaine, 1789–1799*, review by Howard G. Brown, *JMH*, Vol. 71 No. 3 (Sept. 1999).

Forrest, Alan. *Soldiers of the French Revolution* (Durham and London: Duke University Press, 1990).

Fortescue, J.W. *A History of the British Army, Vol. III 1763–1793* (London: Macmillan, 1911).

Fortescue, J.W. *A History of the British Army Vol. IV 1789–1801 Part 1*(London: Macmillan, 1906).

Fortescue, J.W. *A History of the British Army Vol. IV 1789–1801 Part 2* (London: Macmillan, 1915).

Fortescue, J.W. *A History of the British Army, Vol. VII 1809–1810* (London: Macmillan & Co. Limited, 1912).

Fortescue, J.W. *A History of the British Army, Vol. X 1814–1815* (London: Macmillan, 1920).

Fortescue, J.W. *British Campaigns in Flanders 1690–1794: being extracts from 'A History of the British Army'* (London: Macmillan, 1918).

Fortescue, J.W. *The British Army 1783–1802, Four Lectures Delivered at the Staff College and Cavalry School* (London: Macmillan, 1905).

Fraser, Ronald. *Napoleon's Cursed War, Popular Resistance in the Spanish Peninsular War 1808–1814* (London: Verso, 2008).

Fuber, Holden. *Henry Dundas, First Viscount Melville, 1742–1811, Political Manager of Scotland, Statesmen, Administrator of India* (Oxford: Oxford University Press, 1931).

Gardyne, Lieutenant Colonel C. Greenhill. *The Life of a Regiment or, the Origin and History of the Gordon Highlanders from its formation in 1794 to 1816* (Edinburgh: David & Douglas, 1901).

Gat, Azar. *The Origins of Military Thought, From the Enlightenment to Clausewitz* (Oxford: Clarendon, 1989).

Gates, David. 'Graham, Thomas, Baron Lynedoch (1748–1843)', *Oxford Dictionary of National Biography* (Oxford: Oxford University Press, 2004).

Gates, David. 'Mackenzie, Kenneth [*later* Sir Kenneth Douglas, first baronet] (1754–1833)', *Oxford Dictionary of National Biography* (Oxford: Oxford University Press, 2004).

Gates, David. 'The Transformation of the British Army 1783–1815' in David Chandler and Ian Beckett (eds), *The Oxford History of the British Army* (Oxford: Oxford University Press, 1994).

Germani, Ian. 'Terror in the Army: Representatives on Mission and Military Discipline in the Armies of the French Revolution', *Journal of Military History*, Vol. 75 Issue 3 (Jul. 2011), 733.

Gill, John H. *1809 Thunder on the Danube, Napoleon's defeat of the Habsburgs*, 3 vols (Barnsley: Frontline, 2008–10).

Glover, Michael. *Wellington's Army in the Peninsula 1808–1814* (London: David & Charles, 1977).

Glover, Richard. 'The French Fleet, 1807–1814: Britain's Problem: and Madison's Opportunity', *JMH*, Vol. 39 No. 3 (Sept. 1967), 233–52.

Glover, Richard. *Peninsular Preparation, The Reform of the British Army 1795 to 1809* (Cambridge: Cambridge University Press, 1963).

Gray, Colin S. *Strategy and History, Essays on Theory and Practice* (Abingdon: Routledge, 2006).

Gray, Colin S. *The Leverage of Sea Power, The Strategic Advantage of Navies in War* (New York: The Free Press, 1992).

Greene, Jack P. 'Empire and Identity from the Glorious Revolution to the American Revolution' in Louis, William Roger, Low, Alaine M. and Marshall, Peter James (eds), *The Eighteenth-Century, Volume II* (Oxford: Oxford University Press, 1998).

Greene, Jerome A. *The Guns of Independence, The Siege of Yorktown, 1781* (New York: Savas Beatie, 2005).

Grehan John and Mace, Mace. *The Battle of Barrosa, 1811: Forgotten Battle of the Peninsular War* (Barnsley: Pen & Sword, 2012).

Grehan, John. *Britain's German allies of the Napoleonic Wars: The armies of Hanover, Brunswick & the Kings German Legion 1793–1815* (Newthorpe: Partizan, Cavalier Books, 1999).

Griffith, Paddy. *The Art of War of Revolutionary France, 1789–1802* (London: Greenhill, 1998).

Gruber, Ira. *Books and the British Army in the Age of the American Revolution* (Chapel Hill: University of North Carolina Press, 2010).

Guy, A.J. (ed.). *The Road to Waterloo, The British Army and the Struggle Against Revolutionary and Napoleonic France 1793–1815* (London: National Army Museum Publications, 1990).

Guy, A. *Economy and Discipline: officership and administration in the British Army 1714–1783* (Dover: Manchester University Press, 1985).

Hainsworth, Roger and Churches, Christine. *The Anglo-Dutch Naval Wars, 1652–1674* (Stroud: Sutton, 1998).

Hall, Christopher D. *Wellington's Navy: Sea Power and the Peninsular War 1807–1814* (London: Chatham Publishing, 2004).

Hall, Christopher D. *British Strategy in the Napoleonic War 1803–1815* (Manchester: Manchester University Press, 1992).

Harding, Richard. 'Sailors and Gentlemen of Parade: Some Professional and Technical Problems Concerning the Conduct of Combined Operations in the Eighteenth-Century', *HJ*, Vol. 32 No. 1 (Mar. 1989), 35–55.

Harris, Tim. *Revolution, The Great Crisis in the British Monarchy, 1685–1720* (London: Penguin, 2007).

Harvard, Robert. Wellington's *Welsh General, A Life of Sir Thomas Picton* (London: Aurum Press, 1996).

Harvey, Robert. *A Few Bloody Noses, The American War of Independence* (London: John Murray, 2001).

Haythornthwaite, Phillip. *Corunna 1809, Sir John Moore's Fighting Retreat, Osprey Campaign Series No. 83* (Oxford: Osprey, 2001).

Haythornthwaite, Phillip J. *The Armies of Wellington* (London: Brockhampton Press, 1997).

Haythornthwaite, Phillip J. *Die Hard!, Dramatic Actions from the Napoleonic Wars* (London: Arms & Armour Press, 1996).

Heathcote, T.A. *Wellington's Peninsular War Generals & Their Battles, A Biographical and Historical Dictionary* (Barnsley: Pen & Sword, 2010).

Hebbert, F.J. 'The Belle Isle expedition of 1761', *JSAHR*, 64 (1986), 81–93.

Herrera, Geoffrey L. and Mahnken, Thomas G. 'Military Diffusion in Nineteenth-Century Europe: The Napoleonic and Prussian Military Systems' in Emily O. Goldman and Leslie C. Eliason, *The Diffusion of Military Technology and Ideas* (Stanford: Stanford University Press, 2003).

Hibbert, Christopher. *Corunna,* (Moreton-in-March: Windrush Press repr., 1996).

Hibbert, Christopher, *The Destruction of Lord Raglan* (London: Longmans, 1961).

Hilton, Boyd. *A Mad, Bad and Dangerous People? England 1783–1846, New Oxford History of England* (Oxford: Oxford University Press, 2006).

Hoffmann, Stanley. 'Rousseau on War and Peace', *The American Political Science Review*, Vol. 57 No. 2 (Jun. 1963), 317–33.

Hofschröer, Peter. *The Hanoverian Army of the Napoleonic Wars Osprey Men at Arms Series No. 206* (London: Osprey, 1989).

Holland Rose, J. 'Review of Weil, M.H *Le Général de Stamford, d'après sa Correspondance Inédite, 1793–1806*', *EHR*, Vol. 39 No. 154 (Apr. 1924), 297–8.

Holland Rose, J. 'The Duke of Richmond on the Conduct of the War in 1793', *EHR*, Vol. 25 No. 99 (Jul. 1910), 554–5.

Holland Rose, J. 'Pitt and the Campaign of 1793', *EHR*, Vol. 24 No. 96 (Oct. 1909), 744–9.

Holland Rose, J. 'The Missions of William Grenville to the Hague and Versailles in 1787', *EHR*, Vol. 24 No. 94 (Apr. 1909), 278–95.

Hollins, David. *The Battle of Marengo 1800* (Oxford: Osprey, 2000).

Holmes, Richard. *Marlborough, England's Fragile Genius* (London: Harper Press, 2008).

Holmes, Richard. *Wellington, The Iron Duke* (London: Harper Collins, 2002).

Hopton, Richard. *The Battle of Maida 1806, Fifteen Minutes of Glory* (London: Leo Cooper, 2002).

Horne, Captain Peter (ed.). *Seapower Ashore, 200 Years of Royal Navy Operations On Land* (London: Chatham Publishing in Association with the National Maritime Museum, 2001).

Houlding, John. *Fit for Service, The Training of the British Army 1715–1795* (Oxford: Oxford University Press, 1981).

Houtte, Jan A. van. and Buyten, Leon van. 'The Low Countries' in Charles Wilson and Geoffrey Parker (eds), *An Introduction to the Sources of European Economic History 1500–1800 Volume 1: Western Europe* (London: Methuen, 1980), p. 82.

Howard, Martin. *Walcheren 1809, The Scandalous Destruction of a British Army* (Barnsley: Pen & Sword, 2012).

Howard, Dr Martin. *Wellington's Doctors, The British Army Medical Services in the Napoleonic Wars* (Stroud: The History Press, 2008).

Howard, Martin. 'Walcheren 1809: A Medical Catastrophe', *BMJ*, Vol. 319 No. 7225 (18–25 Dec. 1999), 1642–5.

Howard, Michael. 'Military history and the history of war' in Williamson Murray and Richard Hart Sinnreich (eds), *The Past as prologue: The importance of history to the military profession* (Cambridge: Cambridge University Press, 2006).

Howard Michael (ed.). *Wellingtonian Studies, Essays on the first Duke of Wellington by five Old Wellingtonian historians, written to celebrate the Centenary of the College, 1859–1959* (Aldershot: Gale & Polden, 1959).

Hughes, Ben. *The British Invasion of the River Plate 1806–1807, How the Redcoats were humbled and a nation was born* (Barnsley: Pen & Sword, 2013).

Hughes, Matthew and Philpott, William J. *Palgrave advances in modern military history* (Basingstoke: Palgrave, 2006).

Hunt, Giles. *The Duel, Castlereagh, Canning and the Deadly Cabinet Rivalry* (London: Tauris, 2008).

Ireland, Bernard. *The Fall of Toulon: The Royal Navy and the Royalist Last Stand against the French Revolution* (London: Weidenfeld & Nicolson, 2005).

Israel, Jonathan I. *The Dutch Republic, Its Rise, Greatness, and Fall 1477–1806, The Oxford History of Early Modern Europe* (Oxford: Clarendon Press, 1998).

Janco, Andrew P. 'Training in the Amusements of Mars: Peter the Great, War Games and the Science of War, 1673–1699', *Russian History/ Histoire Russe*, 30, Nos 1–2 (Spring–Summer) 2003, 35–112.

Jones, J.R. *The Anglo-Dutch Wars of the Seventeenth Century* (London: Longman, 1996).

Jones, Colin. 'The Military Revolution and the Professionalization of the French Army under the Ancien Regime' in Clifford J. Rogers (ed.), *The Military Revolution Debate, Readings on the Military Transformation of Early Modern Europe* (Oxford: Westview, 1995).

Joor, Johan. '"A Very Rebellious Disposition": Dutch Experience and Popular Protest under the Napoleonic Regime (1806–1813)' in Alan Forrest, Karen Hagemann and Jane Rendall (eds),

Soldiers, Citizens and Civilians, Experiences and Perceptions of the Revolutionary and Napoleonic Wars, 1790–1820 (Basingstoke: Palgrave Macmillan, 2009).

Jowell, Edward J. *The Hessians and the other German auxiliaries of Great Britain in the Revolutionary War* (New York: Harper & Brothers, 1884). Jupp, Peter. *The Governing of Britain 1688–1848, The Executive, Parliament and the People* (London: Routledge, 2006).

Jupp, Peter. *Lord Grenville 1759–1834* (Oxford: Clarendon Press, 1985).

Keep, John. 'Feeding the Troops: Russian Army Supply Policies during the Seven Years War' in Jeremy Black (ed.), *Warfare in Europe 1650–1792, The International Library of Essays on Military History* (Aldershot: Ashgate, 2005).

Keep, John L.H. *Soldiers of the Tsar, Army and Society in Prussia 1462–1874* (Oxford: Clarendon Press, 1985).

Keep, John L.H. 'The Russian Army's Response to the French Revolution', *Jahrbücher für Geschichte Osteuropas, Neue Folge*, Bd. 28 H. 4 (1980), 500–23.

Kennedy, Catriona. *Narratives of the Revolutionary and Napoleonic Wars: Military and Civilian Experience in Britain and Ireland* (Basingstoke: Palgrave Macmillan, 2013).

Kennedy, Catriona and McCormack, Matthew (eds), *Soldiering in Britain and Ireland, 1750–1850: Men of Arms* (Basingstoke: Palgrave Macmillan, 2012).

Kidd, Colin. *British Identities before Nationalism, Ethnicity and Nationhood in the Atlantic World 1600–1800* (Cambridge: Cambridge University Press, 1999, repr. 2004).

Kiszely, John P. 'The Relevance of History to the Military Profession: a British view' in W. Murray and R. Sinnreich (eds), *The Past as Prologue, The Importance of Military History to the Military Profession* (Cambridge: Cambridge University Press, 2006).

Knight, Roger. *Britain against Napoleon: The Organisation of Victory 1793–1815* (London: Allen Lane, 2013).

Knight, Roger and Wilcox, Martin. *Sustaining the Fleet, 1793–1815: War, the British Navy and the Contractor State* (Woodbridge: Boydell, 2010).

Kubben, Raymond. *Regeneration and Hegemony, Franco-Batavian Relations in the Revolutionary Era, 1795–1803*, Studies in the History of International Law 1 (The Hague: Martinus Hijhoff, 2011).

Langins, Jānis. *Conserving the Enlightenment: French Military Engineering from Vauban to the Revolution* (Cambridge: MIT Press, 2004).

Latham, Andrew. 'Warfare Transformed: A Braudelian Perspectve on the "Revolution in Military Affairs"', *European Journal of International Relations*, 8:2 (2002), 231–66.

Lee, Sidney (ed.). *Dictionary of National Biography Vol. XXXIX Morehead-Myles* (New York: Macmillan, 1894).

Le Fevre, Peter and Harding, Richard (eds). *British Admirals of the Napoleonic Wars, The Contemporaries of Nelson* (London: Chatham Publishing, 2005).

Leggiere, Michael V. *The Fall of Napoleon, Vol. 1: The Allied Invasion of France, 1813–1814* (Cambridge: Cambridge University Press, 2007).

Leggiere, Michael V. *Napoleon and Berlin: The Franco-Prussian War in North Germany, 1813* (Norman: University of Oklahoma Press, 2002).

Liaropoulos, Andrew N. 'Revolutions in Warfare: Theoretical Paradigms and Historical Evidence: The Napoleonic and First World War Revolutions in Military Affairs', *JMHS*, Vol. 70 No. 2 (Apr. 2006), 363–84.

Lieven, Dominic. *Russia against Napoleon, The Battle for Europe, 1807 to 1814* (London: Penguin, 2010, orig. pub. 2009).

Limm, Andrew. 'The British Army 1795 to 1815: An Army Transformed?' in Ross Mahoney, Stuart Mitchell, and Michael LoCicero (eds), *Transformation and Innovation in the British Military 1792–1945* (Solihull: Helion, 2014).

Linch, Kevin and McCormack, Matthew (eds). *Britain's Soldiers: Rethinking War and Society, 1715–1815* (Basingstoke: Palgrave Macmillan, 2014).

Lipscombe, Nick. *Wellington's Guns, The Untold Story of Wellington and his Guns in the Peninsula and at Waterloo* (Oxford: Osprey, 2013).

Longford, Elizabeth. *Wellington, The Years of the Sword* (London: World Books, 1969).

Lonsdale, David. 'Clausewitz and Information Warfare' in Hew Strachan and Andreas Herberg-Rothe (eds), *Clausewitz in the Twenty-First Century* (Oxford: Oxford University Press, 2007).

Lowe, Rodney. *The Official History of the British Civil Service, Reforming the Civil Service, Volume 1: The Fulton Years, 1966–81* (London: Routledge, 2011).

Lukas, John A. 'Russian Armies in Western Europe: 1799, 1814, 1917', *American Slavic and East European Review*, Vol. 13 No. 3 (Oct. 1954), 319–37.

Lynn, John A. *Giant of the Grand Siècle, The French Army, 1610–1715* (Cambridge: Cambridge University Press, 1997).

Lynn, John A. *Bayonets of the Republic, Motivations and Tactics in the Army of Revolutionary France 1791–94* (Urbana and Chicago: University of Illinois Press, 1984).

McGuffie, T.H. 'The Walcheren expedition and the Walcheren Fever', *EHR*, Vol. 62 No. 243 (Apr. 1947), 191–202.

McGuigan, Ron, Muir, Howie and Muir, Rory. *Inside Wellington's Peninsular Army* (Barnsley: Pen & Sword, 2006).

Mackesy, Piers. *The British Victory in Egypt, The End of Napoleon's Conquest* (London: Routledge 1995).

Mackesy, Piers. *War without Victory, The Downfall of Pitt 1799–1802* (Oxford: Oxford University Press, 1984).

Mackesy, Piers. 'What the British Army Learned' in Ronald Hoffmann and Peter J. Albert (eds), *Arms and Independence, The Military Character of the American Revolution* (Charlottesville: University of Virginia, 1984).

Mackesy, Piers. *Statesmen at War, The Strategy of Overthrow 1798–1799* (London: Longman, 1974).

Macleod, Julia H. 'The Duke of York's Plans for the Army', *HLQ*, Vol. 9 No. 1 (Nov. 1945), 95–100.

Mainwaring, G.E. 'The Expedition to Ostend in 1798. Blowing up the Gates of the Bruges Canal', *RUSI*, No. 63 (1 Feb. 1918), 624–7.

Mallinson, Allan. *The Making of the British Army, From the English Civil War to the War on Terror* (London: Transworld, 2009).

Marshall, Douglas W. 'Military Maps of the Eighteenth Century and the Tower of London Drawing Room', *Imago Mundi*, Vol. 32 (1980), 21–44.

Marquis, Hughes. 'Le Général François Jarry au service de L'Angleterre (1793–1806)', *Annales historiques de la Révolution française*, No. 356 (Avril/Juin 2009), 93–118.

Marston, Daniel. *The American Revolution 1774–1783, Osprey Essential Histories No. 45* (Osprey: Oxford, 2002).

Matheson, Cyril. *The Life of Sir Henry Dundas, First Viscount Melville 1742–1811* (London: Constable, 1933).

Maude, F.N. *The Ulm Campaign 1805: Napoleon and the Defeat of the Austrian Army During the 'War of the Third Coalition'* (London: Leonaur, 2008).

Maurice-Jones, Colonel K.W. *History of Coast Artillery in the British Army* (Uckfield: Naval & Military Press, 2009).

May, Robin and Embleton, Gerry. *The British Army in North America 1775–1783, Osprey Men at Arms Series No. 39* (London: Osprey, 1997).

Meeüs, Adrien de. *History of the Belgians* (New York: Praeger, 1962).

Melenovsky, Mark. 'The Influence of the French Revolution and Napoleon on the Imperial Russian Army, 1789–1814', Consortium on Revolutionary Europe, 1750–1850 (1994).

Menning, Bruce W. 'Russian Military Innovation in the Second Half of the Eighteenth Century' in Jeremy Black (ed.), *Warfare in Europe 1650–1792*, The International Library of Essays on Military History (Aldershot: Ashgate, 2005).

Menning, Bruce W. '"Train Hard, Fight Easy": The Legacy of A. V. Suvorov and his "Art of Victory"', *Air University Review* (Nov.–Dec. 1986), 79–88.

Middleton, Richard. 'The Clinton–Cornwallis Controversy and Responsibility for the British Surrender at Yorktown, *History*, Vol. 98 Issue 331 (Jul. 2013), 370–89.

Mikaberidze, Alexander. 'The Conflict of Command in the Russian army in 1812: Peter Bagration and Barclay de Tolly in the "Mutiny of Generals"' in Frederick C. Schneid, *Warfare in Europe 1792–1795* (Aldershot: Ashgate, 2007).

Mikaberidze, Alexander. *The Russian Officer Corps in the Revolutionary and Napoleonic Wars, 1792–1815* (Staplehurst: Spellmount, 2005).

Mori, Jennifer. *William Pitt and the French Revolution 1785–1795* (Edinburgh: Keele University Press, 1997).

Mori, Jennifer. 'The British Government and the Bourbon Restoration: The Occupation of Toulon, 1793', *HJ*, 40 No. 3 (1997), 699–719.

Morillo, Stephen, with Pavkovic, Michael F. *What is Military History?* (Cambridge: Polity, 2006).

Morrissey, Brendan. *Yorktown 1781, The World Turned Upside Down, Osprey Campaign Series No. 47* (Oxford: Osprey Publishing, 1997).

Muir, Rory. *Wellington, The Path to Victory, 1769–1814* (New Haven and London: Yale University Press, 2013).

Muir, Rory. *Britain and the defeat of Napoleon 1807–1815* (Yale: Yale University Press, 1996).

Muir, Rory and Esdaile, Charles. 'Strategic Planning in a Time of Small Government: the Wars against Revolutionary and Napoleonic France, 1793–1815' in C.M. Woolgar (ed.), *Wellington Studies I* (Hartley Institute: University of Southampton, 1996).

Murphy, John A. *The French are in the Bay: The Expedition to Bantry Bay* (Cork: Mercier Press, 1997).

Murray, Williamson and Knox, MacGregor. 'Thinking about revolutions in warfare' in W. Murray and M. Knox (eds), *The Dynamics of Military Revolution 1300–2050* (Cambridge: Cambridge University Press, 2001).

Myatt, Frederick. *Peninsular General, Sir Thomas Picton 1758–1815* (London: David & Charles, 1980).

Nelson, Paul David. *Francis Rawdon-Hastings, Marquess of Hastings: Soldier, Peer of the Realm, Governor-General of India* (Cranbury: Associated University Press, 2005).

Nosworthy, Brent. *Battle Tactics of Napoleon and his enemies,* (London: Constable, 1995).

Oman, Sir Charles. 'The 15th Light Dragoons at Villers-en-Cauchies, 24th March 1794', *JSAHR*, XVII (1938).

Palmer, M.A.J. 'The "Military Revolution" Afloat: The Ear of the Anglo-Dutch Wars and the transition to Modern Warfare at Sea', *War in History*, 1997, Vol. 4 (2), 123–49.

Palmer, R.R. 'Frederick the Great, Guibert, Bulow: From Dynastic to National War' in Peter Paret (ed.), *Makers of Modern Strategy, From Machiavelli to the Nuclear Age* (Oxford: Clarendon, 1986).

Palmer, Robert R. *Twelve Who Ruled* (Princeton: Princeton University Press, 1941).

Paret, Peter. *The Cognitive Challenge of War, Prussia 1806* (Princeton and Oxford: Princeton University Press, 2009).

Paret, Peter. 'The New Military History', *Parameters: The Journal of the Army War College*, 31/3 (autumn, 1991), 13–36.

Paret, Peter. 'Education, Politics, and War in the Life of Clausewitz', *Journal of the History of Ideas*, Vol. 29 No. 3 (Jul.–Sept. 1968), 394–408.

Parker, Geoffrey. '"The Military Revolution" – A Myth?' in Clifford Rogers (ed.), *The Military Revolution Debate, Readings on the Military Transformation of Early Modern Europe* (Oxford: Westview, 1995).

Parker, Geoffrey. *The Military Revolution, Military innovation and the rise of the West, 1500–1800* (Cambridge: Cambridge University Press, 1988).

Parkinson, C. Northcote. *Britannia Rules, The Classic Age of Naval History 1793–1815* (Stroud: Sutton Publishing, 1997).

Pearce, Edward. *Pitt the Elder, Man of War* (London: Bodley Head, 2010).

Peaty, Dr John. 'Architect of Victory: The Reforms of the Duke of York', paper presented at the International Commission for Military History Annual Congress, Madrid, 26 August 2005, British

Commission for Military History Newsletter: 'Land & Sea Warfare in the Age of Nelson and Wellington' (Autumn Conference, 2005), 31–9.

Philip, Mark (ed.). *Resisting Napoleon, the British Response to the Threat of Invasion, 1797–1815* (Aldershot: Ashgate, 2006).

Phipps, Ramsey Weston. *The Armies of the First French Republic and the rise of the Marshals of Napoleon I: The Armée du Nord* (London: Oxford University Press, 1926).

Piechowiak, A.B. 'The Anglo-Russian Expedition to Holland in 1799', *The Slavonic and East European Review*, Vol. 41, No. 96 (Dec. 1962), 182–95.

Piecuch, Jim (ed.). *Cavalry of the American Revolution* (Yardley: Westholme, 2012).

Pincus, Steve. *1688, The First Modern Revolution* (New Haven and London: Yale University Press, 2009).

Pinder, David. 'Leather Stocks and Wooden Heads? British Military Thought during and as a consequence of the Seven Years' War, 1756–6', *BCMH Newsletter* (Apr. 2009), 1–38.

Polasky, Janet L. 'Democrats, and Jacobins in Revolutionary Brussels', *JMH*, Vol. 56 No. 2 (Jun. 1984), 227–62.

Popham, Hugh. *A Damned Cunning Fellow – The Eventful Life of Rear-Admiral Sir Home Popham, K.C.B., K.C.H., K.M., F.R.S., 1762–1820* (Tywardreath: The Old Ferry, 1991).

Powers, Sandra L. 'Studying the Art of War: Military Books known to American Officers and their French counterparts during the Second half of the Eighteenth-Century', *The Journal of Military History*, Vol. 70 No. 3 (Jul. 2006), 781–814.

Prak, Maarten. 'Citizen Radicalism and Democracy in the Dutch Republic: The Patriot Movement of the 1780s', *Theory and Society*, Vol. 20 No. 1 (Feb. 1991), 73–102.

Price, Munro. *Napoleon, The End of Glory* (Oxford: Oxford University Press, 2014).

Ragsdale, Hugh. 'Russia, Prussia, and Europe in the Policy of Paul I', *Jahrbücher für Geschichte Osteuropas, Neue Folge*, Bd. 31, H. 1 (1983), 81–118.

Renier, G.J. *The Dutch Nation, An Historical Study* (London: George Allen & Unwin, 1944).

Renier, G.J. *Great Britain and the Establishment of the Kingdom of the Netherlands 1813–1815, A Study in British Foreign Policy* (London: Allen & Unwin, 1930).

Riley, Jonathan. *1813: Empire at Bay, The Sixth Coalition & the Downfall of Napoleon* (Barnsley: Praetorian Press, 2013).

Roberts, Michael. 'The Military Revolution, 1560–1660' in Clifford J. Rogers (ed.), *The Military Revolution, Debate, Readings on the Transformation of Early Modern Europe* (Oxford: Westview, 1995).

Robertson, Ian. *A commanding presence, Wellington in the Peninsula, 1808–1814: logistics, strategy, survival* (Stroud: Spellmount, 2008).

Robinson, Mike. *The Battle of Quatre Bras 1815* (Stroud: Spellmount, 2009).

Robson, J. *The British Mars, Containing several schemes and inventions, to be practised by land or sea against the enemies of Great Britain* (London: 1763).

Rodger, A.B. *The War of the Second Coalition 1798 to 1801, A Strategic Commentary* (Oxford: Clarendon, 1964).

Rodger, N.A.M. 'Review of Roger Knight and Martin Wilcox, *Sustaining the Fleet, 1793–1815: War, the British Navy and the Contractor State* & Janet MacDonald, *The British Navy's Victualling Board, 1793–1815: Management Competence and Incompetence*', *EHR*, cxxvi. 519 (Apr. 2011), 465–6.

Rodger, N.A.M. *The Command of the Ocean, A Naval History of Britain, 1649–1815* (London: Penguin, 2006).

Rogers, Clifford J. (ed.). *The Military Revolution Debate, Readings on the Transformation of Early Modern Europe* (Oxford: Westview, 1995).

Rommelse, Gijs. *The Second Anglo-Dutch War (1665–1667): International Raison d'État, Mercantilism and Maritime Strife* (Hilversum, The Netherlands: Uitgeverif Verloren, 2006).

Ross, Steven T. 'The Military Strategy of the Directory: The Campaigns of 1799', *French Historical Studies*, Vol. 5, No. 2 (Autumn, 1967), 170–87.

Ross, Steven T. 'The Development of the Combat Division in Eighteenth-Century French Armies', *French Historical Studies*, Vol. 4, No. 1 (Spring, 1965), 84–94.

Rothenberg, Gunther E. *Napoleon's Great Adversaries, The Archduke Charles and the Austrian Army 1792-1814* (London: Batsford, 1982).

Rothenberg, Gunther E. *The Art of Warfare in the Age of Napoleon* (Bloomington: Indiana University Press, 1978).

Russell, David Lee. *The American Revolution in the Southern Colonies* (Jefferson: McFarland, 2000).

Ryan, A.N. 'The Defence of British Trade with the Baltic, 1808-1813', *EHR,* Vol. 74 No. 292 (Jul. 1959), 443-66.

Ryan, A.N. 'The Causes of the British Attack upon Copenhagen in 1807', *EHR,* Vol. 68 No. 266 (Jan. 1953), 37-55.

Schama, Simon. *Citizens, A Chronicle of the French Revolution* (London: Penguin, 1989).

Schama, Simon. *Patriots and Liberators, Revolution in the Netherlands 1780-1813* (Collins: London, 1977).

Schechter, Barnet. *The Battle for New York, The City at the Heart of the American Revolution* (London: Jonathan Cape, 2003).

Schmitt, H.A. '1812: Stein, Alexander I and the Crusade against Napoleon', *JMH,* 31 (1959), 325-8.

Schroeder, Paul W. 'An Unnatural "Natural Alliance": Castlereagh, Metternich, and Aberdeen in 1813', *IHR,* Vol. 10 No. 4 (Nov. 1988), 522-40.

Schroeder, Paul. 'The Collapse of the Second Coalition', *JMH,* Vol. 59 No. 2 (Jun. 1987), 244-90.

Schwoerer, Lois G. 'The Grenville Militia List for Buckinghamshire, 1798-1799', *HLQ,* Vol. 68 No. 4 (Dec. 2005), 667-76.

Scott, H.M. 'Sir Joseph Yorke, Dutch Politics and the Origins of the Fourth Anglo-Dutch War', *HJ,* Vol. 31 No. 3 (Sept. 1988), 571-89.

Scott, Samuel F. 'The Regeneration of the Line Army during the French Revolution', *JMH,* Vol. 42 No. 3 (Sept. 1970), 307-30.

Shanahan, William O. *Prussian Military Reforms 1786-1813* (New York: AMS Press, 1966).

Sheffield, Gary. 'Review of Clayton, Anthony *The British Officer, Leading the Army from 1660 to the Present'* in *The American Historical Review,* Vol. 111 No. 5 (Dec. 2006),1593-4.

Sherwig, John M. *Guineas and Gunpowder, British Foreign Aid in the Wars with France 1793-1815* (Cambridge: Harvard University Press, 1969).

Sherwig, John M. 'Lord Grenville's plan for a concert of Europe, 1797-99', *JMH,* Vol. 34 No. 3 (Sept. 1962), 284-93.

Showalter, Denis E. 'The Prussian Landwehr and Its Critics, 1813-1819', *Central European History,* Vol. 4 No. 1 (Mar. 1971), 3-33.

Simms, Brendan. *Three Victories and a Defeat, The Rise and Fall of the First British Empire, 1714-1783* (London: Penguin, repr. 2008).

Smith, Hannah. 'Politics, Patriotism, and Gender: The Standing Army Debate on the English Stage, circa 1689-1720', *Journal of British Studies,* Vol. 50 No. 1 (Jan. 2011), 48-75.

Snow, Peter. *To War with Wellington, From the Peninsula to Waterloo* (London: John Murray, 2010).

Sorel, Albert. *L'Europe et la Revolution Francaise* (1885).

Speelman, Patrick J. *Henry Lloyd and the Military Enlightenment of Eighteenth-Century Europe* (London: Praeger, 2002).

Steppler, G.A. 'The British Army on the Eve of War' in A.J. Guy (ed.), *The Road to Waterloo, The British Army and the struggle against Revolutionary and Napoleonic France 1793-1815* (London: National Army Museum Publications, 1990).

Strachan, Hew. 'The Idea of War' in Catherine Mary McLoughlin (ed.), *The Cambridge Companion to War Writing* (Cambridge: Cambridge University Press, 2009).

Strachan, Hew (ed.). *Big Wars and Small Wars: The British Army and the Lessons of War in the 20th Century* (Abingdon: Routledge, 2006).

Strachan, Hew. 'Review of Richard Glover, *Peninsula Preparation: The Reform of the British Army 1795-1809,* John Houlding, *Fit for Service, The Training of the British Army 1715-1795* & Piers

Mackesy, *British Victory in Egypt, The End of Napoleon's Conquest'*, EHR, Vol. 112 No. 446 (Apr. 1997), 497.

Strachan, Hew. *The Politics of the Army* (Oxford: Clarendon, 1997).

Strachan, Hew. *From Waterloo to Balaclava: Tactics, Technology, and the British Army, 1815–1854* (Cambridge: Press Syndicate of the University of Cambridge, 1985).

Strachan, Hew. *Wellington's Legacy, The Reform of the British Army 1830–54* (Manchester: Manchester University Press, 1984).

Syrett, David. *Shipping and Military Power in the Seven Year War, 1756–1763, The Sails of Victory* (Liverpool: Liverpool University Press, 2008).

Syrett, David. *Shipping and the American War 1775–1783: A Study of British Transport Organization* (University of London: Athlone Press, 1970).

Tatum III, William P. 'Challenging the New Military History: the case of Eighteenth-Century British Army Studies', *History Compass*, 4 (2006), 1–13.

Teffeteller, Gordon L. 'Wellington and Sir Rowland Hill', *IHR*, Vol. 11 No. 1 (Feb. 1989), 68–75.

Telp, Claus. *The Evolution of Operational Art, 1740–1813 From Frederick the Great to Napoleon* (London: Frank Cass, 2005).

Thomas, Hugh. *The Story of Sandhurst* (London: Hutchinson, 1961).

Thomas, R.N.W. 'Reponses to War: The Military Reaction of the British Government to the French Declaration of War in February 1793', *The Consortium on Revolutionary Europe 1750–1850 Proceedings 1993* (Tallahassee: University of Florida Press, 1993).

Thomas, R.N.W. 'Command and Control in the First Coalition: the Duke of York in the Low Countries, 1793–1794' in K.A Roider and John C. Horgan (eds), *The Consortium on Revolutionary Europe, 1750–1850: Proceedings 1991* (Tallahassee: University of Florida Press, 1992).

Thomas, R.N.W. 'Wellington in the Low Countries, 1794–1795', *IHR*, Vol. 11 No. 1 (Feb. 1989), 14–30.

Tracy, Nicholas. *The Battle of Quiberon Bay 1759, Hawke and the Defeat of the French Invasion* (Barnsley: Pen & Sword, 2010).

Turner, Michael J. *Pitt the Younger: A life* (London: Hambledon Continuum, 2003).

Unwin, Peter. *The Narrow Sea, Barrier, Bridge and Gateway to the World, The History of the English Channel* (London: Headline, 2003).

Urban, Mark. *Fusiliers, How the British Army lost America but learned to fight* (London: Faber & Faber, 2007).

Urban, Mark. *Generals, Ten British Commanders who shaped the World* (London: Faber & Faber, 2005).

Vann, James Allen. 'Habsburg Policy and the Austrian War of 1809', *Central European History*, Vol. 7 No. 4 (4 Dec. 1974), 291–310.

Vego, Milan N. *Joint Operational Warfare, Theory and Practice* (The Government Printing Office, 2009).

Ward, A.W. and Gooch, G.P. *The Cambridge History of British Foreign Policy, 1783–1919 Volume I: 1783–1815* (London: Cambridge University Press, 1922).

Ward, S.P.G. *Wellington's Headquarters, A Study of the Administrative problems in the Peninsula 1809–1814* (Oxford: Oxford University Press, 1957).

Webster, C.K. *The Foreign Policy of Castlereagh 1812–1815, Britain and the Reconstruction of Europe* (London: Bell & Sons, 1931).

Weller, Jac. *Wellington in India* (London: Longman, 1972).

White, Charles Edward. *The enlightened soldier: Scharnhorst and the Militärische Gesellschaft in Berlin, 1801–1805* (New York: Praeger, 1989).

Whitridge, Arnold. 'Baron von Steuben, Washington's Drillmaster', *History Today*, v. 26 issue 7 (Jul. 1976), 429–36.

Wiggins, Mark H. and Dabeck, Chaplain (Major) Larry (eds), *Symposium Report, Fort Leavenworth Ethics Symposium, Exploring the Professional Military Ethic* (Fort Leavenworth: CGSC Foundation Press, 2011).

Wilkinson, Spenser. *The French Army before Napoleon* (Oxford: Clarendon, 1915).

Willcox, William B. 'Too Many Cooks: British Planning before Saratoga', *Journal of British Studies*, Vol. 2, No. 1 (Nov. 1962), 56–90.

Willcox, William B. 'The British Road to Yorktown: A Study in Divided Command', *The American AHR*, Vol. 52 No. 1 (Oct. 1946), 1–35.
Willis, Sam. *The Glorious First of June, Fleet Battle in the Reign of Terror* (London: Querces, 2011).
Wishon, Mark. *German Forces and the British Army: Interactions and Perceptions, 1742–1815* (Basingstoke: Palgrave Macmillan, 2013).
Zamoyski, Adam. *1812, Napoleon's Fatal March on Moscow* (London: Harper Collins, 2004).

Online Resources
http://andriessen.pl/verrassende-familieverbanden/jan-egbertus-van-gorkum.html.
Bamford, Andrew 'The British Army in the Low Countries, 1813–1814': http://www.napoleonseries.org/military/battles/c_lowcountries1814.html#Notes; http://www.napoleonseries.org/military/organization/Britain/Strength/Bamford/c_BritishArmyStrengthStudyNorthernEurope.html.
www.brabantsewal.nl/.
Fisher, David R. 'The Scheldt divisions, 1810', http://www.historyofparliamentonline.org/periods/hanoverians/scheldt-divisions-1810.
Lira, Leonard L. 'Transformation and the Evolution of the Professional Military Ethic: A current assessment', a paper presented for the United States Army Command and General Staff College, Combined Arms Centre at Fort Leavenworth, Kansas and the CGSC Foundation, Inc. Conference on Exploring the Professional Military Ethic (15–18 Nov. 2010): 1–34. www.leavenworthethicssymposium.org/resource/resmgr/2010.../Lira.pdf.
McGuigan Ron. 'British Generals of the Napoleonic Wars, 1793–1815', the Napoleon Series: Research: http://www.napoleonseries.org/research/biographies/BritishGenerals/c_Britishgenerals219.html. Placed on database: Jan. 2011.
Port, M.H. 'Trench, Sir Frederick William (c.1777–1859)', *Oxford Dictionary of National Biography* (Oxford: Oxford University Press, 2004): http://www.oxforddnb.com/view/article/27699.
Rapson, E.J. 'Gibbs, Sir Samuel (1770–1815)', rev. Alan Harfield, *Oxford Dictionary of National Biography* (Oxford: Oxford University Press, 2004; online edn, Jan. 2008): http://oxfordindex.oup.com/view/10.1903/ref:odnb/10607.
Vetch, R.H. 'Taylor, Sir Herbert (1775–1839)', rev. K.D. Reynolds, *Oxford Dictionary of National Biography* (Oxford: Oxford University Press, 2004; online edn, Jan. 2008): http://www.oxforddnb.com/view/article/27031.
United States Department of Defence: 'Transformation Planning Guidance, Apr. 2003: http://www.defense.gov/brac/docs/transformationplanningapr03.pdf.

Theses
Bartlett, Keith John. 'The Development of the British Army during the wars with France, 1793–1815', (doctoral thesis, Durham University, 1998), Durham E-Theses Online (Proquest, 2006).
Hackman, W.K. 'English military expeditions to the coast of France 1757–1761' (unpublished Ph.D. thesis, Ann Arbor: 1968).
Ham, Vincent Robert. 'Strategies of Coalition and Isolation: British War Policy and North-West Europe, 1803–1810' (D.Phil. thesis, University of Oxford, 1977).
Linch, Kevin Barry. 'The Recruitment of the British Army 1807–1815' (Ph.D. thesis, University of Leeds, Oct. 2001).
Murley, J.T. *The Origin and Outbreak of the Anglo-French War of 1793* (D.Phil. thesis, University of Oxford, 1959).
Odintz, M. 'The British Officer Corps 1754–1783' (Ph.D. thesis, University of Michigan, 1988).
Pimlott, J.L. 'The Administration of the British Army, 1783–1793' (Ph.D. thesis, Leicester University, 1975).
Redgrave, Toby Michael Ormsby. 'Wellington's Logistical Arrangements in the Peninsular War 1809–14' (doctoral thesis, Kings College, University of London 1979).

Reese, Paul Patrick. '"The Ablest Man in the British Army" The Life and Career of General Sir John Hope' (Ph.D. thesis, Electronic Theses, Treatise and Dissertations, Florida State University, 2007).

Sullivan, F.B. 'The Origin and development of Education in the Royal Navy from 1702 to 1802' (Ph.D. thesis, University of Reading, May 1975).

Watson, Martha. 'The Duke of York and the Campaigns of the British Army in the Low Countries 1793–1795' (M.A. thesis, University of Warwick, 2006).

Williams, Coleman O. 'The Role of the British Navy in the Helder Campaign, 1799' (Ph.D. dissertation, Auburn University, 1995).

Zerbe, Britt. '"That most useful body of men": The Operational Doctrine and Identity of the British Marine Corps, 1755–1802' (Ph.D. thesis, University of Exeter, Sept. 2010).

Index